Exploring the Cognitive, Social, Cultural, and Psychological Aspects of Gaming and Simulations

Brock R. Dubbels
University of Minnesota, USA

A volume in the Advances in Game-
Based Learning (AGBL) Book Series

Published in the United States of America by
    IGI Global
    Information Science Reference (an imprint of IGI Global)
    701 E. Chocolate Avenue
    Hershey PA, USA 17033
    Tel: 717-533-8845
    Fax: 717-533-8661
    E-mail: cust@igi-global.com
    Web site: http://www.igi-global.com

Library of Congress Cataloging-in-Publication Data

Names: Dubbels, Brock Randall, editor.
Title: Exploring the cognitive, social, cultural, and psychological aspects
  of gaming and simulations / Brock R. Dubbels, editor.
Description: Hershey, PA : Information Science Reference, [2019] | Includes
  bibliographical references.
Identifiers: LCCN 2018028318| ISBN 9781522574613 (h/c) | ISBN 9781522574620
  (eISBN)
Subjects: LCSH: Video games--Psychological aspects. | Computer
  games--Psychological aspects. | Simulation games--Psychological aspects.
Classification: LCC GV1469.34.P79 E97 2019 | DDC 306.4/87--dc23 LC record available at
https://lccn.loc.gov/2018028318

This book is published in the IGI Global book series Advances in Game-Based Learning (AGBL) (ISSN: 2327-1825; eISSN: 2327-1833)

British Cataloguing in Publication Data
A Cataloguing in Publication record for this book is available from the British Library.

All work contributed to this book is new, previously-unpublished material.
The views expressed in this book are those of the authors, but not necessarily of the publisher.

For electronic access to this publication, please contact: eresources@igi-global.com.

Advances in Game-Based Learning (AGBL) Book Series

ISSN:2327-1825
EISSN:2327-1833

Editor-in-Chief: Robert D. Tennyson, University of Minnesota, USA

MISSION

The **Advances in Game-Based Learning (AGBL) Book Series** aims to cover all aspects of serious games applied to any area of education. The definition and concept of education has begun to morph significantly in the past decades and game-based learning has become a popular way to encourage more active learning in a creative and alternative manner for students in K-12 classrooms, higher education, and adult education. **AGBL** presents titles that address many applications, theories, and principles surrounding this growing area of educational theory and practice.

COVERAGE

- Curriculum Development Using Educational Games
- Digital Game-Based Learning
- Edutainment
- Electronic Educational Games
- Game Design and Development of Educational Games
- MMOs in Education
- Pedagogical Theory of Game-Based Learning
- Psychological Study of Students Involved in Game-Based Learning
- Role of instructors
- Virtual worlds and game-based learning

IGI Global is currently accepting manuscripts for publication within this series. To submit a proposal for a volume in this series, please contact our Acquisition Editors at Acquisitions@igi-global.com or visit: http://www.igi-global.com/publish/.

The Advances in Game-Based Learning (AGBL) Book Series (ISSN 2327-1825) is published by IGI Global, 701 E. Chocolate Avenue, Hershey, PA 17033-1240, USA, www.igi-global.com. This series is composed of titles available for purchase individually; each title is edited to be contextually exclusive from any other title within the series. For pricing and ordering information please visit http://www.igi-global.com/book-series/advances-game-based-learning/73680. Postmaster: Send all address changes to above address. ©© 2019 IGI Global. All rights, including translation in other languages reserved by the publisher. No part of this series may be reproduced or used in any form or by any means – graphics, electronic, or mechanical, including photocopying, recording, taping, or information and retrieval systems – without written permission from the publisher, except for non commercial, educational use, including classroom teaching purposes. The views expressed in this series are those of the authors, but not necessarily of IGI Global.

Titles in this Series

For a list of additional titles in this series, please visit:
https://www.igi-global.com/book-series/advances-game-based-learning/73680

Design, Motivation, and Frameworks in Game-Based Learning
Wee Hoe Tan (Sultan Idris Education University, alaysia)
Information Science Reference • ©2019 • 306pp • H/C (ISBN: 9781522560265) • US $175.00

Handbook of Research on Collaborative Teaching Practice in Virtual Learning Environments
Gianni Panconesi (Esplica, Italy) and Maria Guida (National Institute for Documentation, Innovation, and Educational Researc, Italy)
Information Science Reference • ©2017 • 637pp • H/C (ISBN: 9781522524267) • US $240.00

Gamification-Based E-Learning Strategies for Computer Programming Education
Ricardo Alexandre Peixoto de Queirós (Polytechnic Institute of Porto, Portugal) and Mário Teixeira Pinto (Polytechnic Institute of Porto, Portugal)
Information Science Reference • ©2017 • 350pp • H/C (ISBN: 9781522510345) • US $200.00

Handbook of Research on Serious Games for Educational Applications
Robert Zheng (The University of Utah, USA) and Michael K. Gardner (The University of Utah, USA)
Information Science Reference • ©2017 • 496pp • H/C (ISBN: 9781522505136) • US $285.00

Handbook of Research on 3-D Virtual Environments and Hypermedia for Ubiquitous Learning
Francisco Milton Mendes Neto (Federal Rural University of the Semiarid Region, Brazil)
Rafael de Souza (Federal Rural University of the Semiarid Region, Brazil) and Alex Sandro Gomes (Federal University of Pernambuco, Brazil)
Information Science Reference • ©2016 • 673pp • H/C (ISBN: 9781522501251) • US $235.00

Handbook of Research on Gaming Trends in P-12 Education
Donna Russell (Walden University, USA) and James M. Laffey (University of Missouri at Columbia, USA)
Information Science Reference • ©2016 • 663pp • H/C (ISBN: 9781466696297) • US $325.00

For an entire list of titles in this series, please visit:
https://www.igi-global.com/book-series/advances-game-based-learning/73680

701 East Chocolate Avenue, Hershey, PA 17033, USA
Tel: 717-533-8845 x100 • Fax: 717-533-8661
E-Mail: cust@igi-global.com • www.igi-global.com

As in everything I do,
this is dedicated to my wife Lisa,
and our children Liam and Rowan.

Table of Contents

Detailed Table of Contents

Chapter 1

A serious game can be entertaining and enjoyable, but it is designed to facilitate the acquisition of skills and knowledge performance in the workplace, classroom, or therapeutic context. Claims of improvement can be validated through assessments successful, measurable practice beyond the game experience, the targeted context of the workplace, classroom, or clinical using the same tools as multiple traits and multiple measure (MTMM) models. This chapter provides a post-mortem describing the development of the initial design and development of a measurable model to inform the design requirements for validation for a serious game. In this chapter, the reader will gain insight into the implementation of lean process, design thinking, and field observations for generative research. This data informs the assessments and measurement of performance, validated through the MTMM model criteria for requirements. The emphasis examines the role of research insights for onboarding and professional development of newly hired certified nursing assistants in a long-term care facility.

Chapter 2

Decision making for professionals in crisis situations can be highly stressful and mission critical. It is a kind of naturalistic decision making (NDM), characterized by highly fluid situations under great stress and uncertainty and involving interprofessional teams. A major challenge to the effective handling of crisis situations is the tendency for the personnel involved to ignore alternatives and make irrational decisions, a phenomenon referred to as Groupthink. This chapter reports on a case study of the application of a set of design principles for an online role play simulation (RPS) in addressing Groupthink in crisis management professional training. The training effectiveness on participants' Groupthink tendency was investigated using Bale's interaction process analysis (IPA). The design principles underpinning the RPS training system is discussed in light of the findings.

Thomas B. Talbot, University of Southern California, USA
Albert Skip Rizzo, University of Southern California, USA

The USC Standard Patient is a virtual human-based conversational agent serving in the role of a simulated medical patient, also known as a virtual standardized patient (VSP). This research identified deficiencies of extant VSP systems, defined a robust set of requirements, and successfully achieved nearly all of them. Markedly impressive advancements were made in virtual human technology, techniques to apply natural language processing, automated assessment artificial intelligence, and pedagogical design. The effort succeeded with performance parameters of high conversational performance, accurate assessment, and strongly demonstrated user training effect. Although working well within its confined are of expertise, the ability for computers to create authentic mixed initiative conversations remains elusive. This effort leaves behind many lessons for interactive serious games, clinical virtual humans, and conversational virtual human training applications.

Mario Martinez-Garza, Independent Researcher, USA
Douglas B. Clark, University of Calgary, Canada

The authors apply techniques of statistical computing to data logs to investigate the patterns in students' play of The Fuzzy Chronicles and how these patterns relate to learning outcomes related to Newtonian kinematics. This chapter has two goals. The first goal is to investigate the basic claims of the proposed two-system framework for game-based learning (or 2SM) that may serve as part of a general-use explanatory framework for educational gaming. The second goal is to explore and demonstrate the use of automated log files of student play as evidence of learning through educational data mining techniques. These goals were pursued via two research questions. The first research question examines whether students playing the game showed evidence of dichotomous fast/slow modes of solution. A second research question investigates the connection between conceptual understanding and student performance in conceptually-laden challenges. Implications in terms of game design, learning analytics, and refinement of the 2SM are discussed.

Chapter 5

Mina C. Johnson, Arizona State University, USA & Embodied Games, USA

David Birchfield, SmalLab Learning, USA

Colleen Megowan-Romanowicz, American Modeling Teachers Association, USA

To understand how students learn while engaged in active and embodied science games, two gears games were created. Would students' gear switching skills during the game be correlated with pre- and post-knowledge tests? Twenty-three seventh graders, playing as dyads, used gestures to manipulate virtual gears in the games. The Microsoft Kinect sensor tracked arm-spinning movements. Paper and pencil gear knowledge tests were administered before and after. In Game 1 (the easier one), the in-game switching data was significantly negatively correlated with only pretest gear knowledge. In Game 2 (the harder one), switching was negatively associated with both pre- and posttests. Negative correlations mean that fewer switches were used and that demonstrated better knowledge of mechanical advantage. In-game process data can provide a window onto learner's knowledge. However, the games need to have appropriate sensitivity and map to the learner's ZPD. In ludo (or in-process) data from videogames with high sensitivity may attenuate the need for repetitive traditional knowledge tests.

Chapter 6

Karrie E. Godwin, Kent State University, USA

Derek Lomas, IO Delft University of Technology, The Netherlands

Ken R. Koedinger, Carnegie Mellon University, USA

Anna V. Fisher, Carnegie Mellon University, USA

Selective sustained attention, or the ability to allocate perceptual and mental resources to a single object or event, is an important cognitive ability widely assumed to be required for learning. Assessing young children's selective sustained attention is challenging due to the limited number of sensitive and developmentally appropriate performance-based measures. Furthermore, administration of existing assessments is difficult, as children's engagement with such tasks wanes quickly. One potential solution is to provide assessments within an engaging environment, such as a video game. This chapter reports the design and psychometric validation of a video game

(Monster Mischief) designed to assess selective sustained attention in preschool children. In a randomized controlled trial, the authors demonstrate that Monster Mischief is significantly correlated with an existing measure of selective sustained attention (rs ≥ 0.52), and more motivating for young children as almost three times more children preferred Monster Mischief to the existing measure.

Yu-Hao Lee, University of Florida, USA
Norah E. Dunbar, University of California – Santa Barbara, USA
Keri Kornelson, University of Oklahoma, USA
Scott N. Wilson, University of Oklahoma, USA
Ryan Ralston, University of Oklahoma, USA
Milos Savic, University of Oklahoma, USA
Sepideh Stewart, University of Oklahoma, USA
Emily Ann Lennox, University of Oklahoma, USA
William Thompson, University of Oklahoma, USA
Javier Elizondo, University of Oklahoma, USA

This study has two goals: first, to investigate the effectiveness of using a digital game to teach undergraduate-level calculus in improving task immersion, sense of control, calculation skills, and conceptual understanding, and second, to investigate how feedback and visual manipulation can facilitate conceptual understanding of calculus materials. One hundred thirty-two undergraduate students participated in a controlled lab experiment and were randomly assigned to either a game-playing condition, a practice quiz condition, or a no-treatment control condition. The authors collected survey data and behavioral-tracking data recorded by the server during gameplay. The results showed that students who played the digital game reported highest task immersion but not in sense of control. Students in the game condition also performed significantly better in conceptual understanding compared to students who solved a practice quiz and the control group. Gameplay behavioral-tracking data was used to examine the effects of visual manipulation and feedback on conceptual understanding.

Liz Owens Boltz, Michigan State University, USA

Historical empathy has increasingly been recognized as a multidimensional construct that involves both cognitive and affective dimensions. Research suggests that engaging learners with diverse historical perspectives in activities like debate, writing, and role play can be more effective for historical empathy than traditional instruction. Although several studies have investigated the effectiveness of these strategies, little is known about the effectiveness of games in promoting historical empathy. Through observation, recorded game play, and semi-structured interviews, this chapter examined how historical empathy manifested as eighth graders played a videogame about World War I (Valiant Hearts). The findings indicate that specific elements of game play may foster particular dimensions of historical empathy better than others, and that some dimensions tend to arise spontaneously while others require (or even resist) prompting.

Chapter 9

Julie A. Brown, Ohio University, USA
Bob De Schutter, Miami University, USA

Play is a lifelong construct that is individually defined and is influenced by multiple variables that affect how play is interpreted and experienced in old age. This chapter highlights the significance of using a life course perspective to explore how play is shaped and reflected through digital gameplay and preferences as a game player ages. Using grounded theory methodology, 51 participants (age 43–77) were interviewed individually. The resulting transcripts were coded to identify emergent themes. The findings demonstrate 1) how play changes throughout the lifespan, 2) how play preferences established in childhood influence digital gameplay for aging adults, and 3) how aging adult gamers aspire to continue gaming as they grow older. Collectively, these themes provide insight into the aspects that need to be taken into account when designing games for aging gamer populations.

Chapter 10

Tuomas Kari, University of Jyvaskyla, Finland
Miia Siutila, University of Turku, Finland
Veli-Matti Karhulahti, University of Turku, Finland

This chapter is an extended revision of the authors' earlier study (2016) on the training routines of professional and high-level esport players, with added focus on their physical exercise. The study is methodologically mixed with a quantitative survey sample (n=115) and a qualitative interview sample (n=7). Based on this data, high-level esport players train approximately 5.28 hours every day around the year, and professional esport players at least the same amount. Approximately 1.08 hours of that training is physical exercise. More than half (55.6%) of the professional and high-level esport players believe that integrating physical exercise into their training programs has a positive effect on esport performance; however, no less than 47.0% do the physical exercise chiefly to maintain their overall state of health. Accordingly, the study indicates that professional and high-level esport players are physically active as well: those of age 18 and older exercising more than three times the daily 21-minute physical activity recommendation given by the World Health Organization.

Preface

INTRODUCTION

With the rise of video game play as sport, education and training, entertainment, marketing brand experience, as well as for therapeutic value and clinical intervention, game experiences permeate our lives. In the past, gamification was a big idea, however expectations. Although games have many of the behavioral techniques proven effective as behavioural hooks, many companies are no longer willing to risk their brand value on techniques used in laboratories and mental hospitals to create the form of motivation better known as compliance. we are experiencing Games have been adapted for enhancing productivity tools, customer experiences, marketing, communication, teaching and learning, data collection, and even medical interventions. Games are still games, and thanks to computers and communications infrastructure, we can now experience a wide variety of gaming experiences with a great variety of content, purpose, and participation. Articles in these sections present insight and exploration, extending what we know about games, gamification, and simulations. This collection is drawn from articles selected as enhanced, top-articles published in a leading, peer-reviewed journal.

This preface begins with a brief background about the journal, and then provides an overview and summary of the 10 chapters in this book. The book is organized in three sections by theme: User Research, Learning Applications, and Health Enhancement. Each section is briefly defined, and each chapter is given an overview related to that section theme. This preface concludes with some recommendations and goals for future research, policy, and practice.

IJGCMS

The *International Journal of Games and Computer-Mediated Simulations* (IJGCMS) was launched in 2009 (http://www.igi-global.com/ijgcms). The journal is devoted to the theoretical and empirical understanding of electronic games and computer-mediated simulations. The journal is interdisciplinary in nature; it publishes research from fields and disciplines that share the goal of improving the foundational knowledge base of games and simulations. The journal publishes critical theoretical manuscripts, qualitative and quantitative research studies, meta-analyses, worked examples, industry post mortems on product research and implementation for development, and methodologically sound case studies.

The journal also includes book reviews to keep readers on the forefront of this continuously evolving field. Occasional special issues from the journal provide deeper investigation into areas of interest within either gaming or simulations.

The main goal of this peer-reviewed, international journal is to promote a deep conceptual and empirical understanding of the roles of electronic games and computer-mediated simulations across multiple disciplines. A second goal is to help build a significant bridge between research and practice on electronic gaming and simulations, supporting the work of researchers, practitioners, and policymakers.

In the following paragraphs, the editorial policy of IJGCMS, and five guiding principles are presented.

Principle 1: Quality and Rigor in Content and Review

IJGCMS follows a double-blind review process to ensure anonymity and a fair review. The review process is intended to be critical, but helpful and instructive. We want the journal to provide high-value function, positive emotional experience, and potentially, transformation, and social impact.

Research articles that are published may contain either quantitative or qualitative data collection & analyses. However, articles using either method must present data to support and justify claims made within the article. Articles that simply summarize data without presenting it or the analytical techniques used, are not considered.

Theoretical manuscripts are also published. However, these theoretical reviews must create new knowledge by synthesizing and critiquing past research. Simple summaries of existing literature without thoughtful and considerate analyses are not considered.

Principle 2: Interdisciplinary Focus

IJGCMS seeks to publish about games and simulations within and across the numerous fields and disciplines that undertake research related to games and simulations. Psychology, Education, History, Journalism, Literature, Computer Science, Engineering, Fine Arts, and Medicine are just a few of the areas where one could find gaming and simulation research. Unfortunately in academia, the notion of standing on the shoulders of giants has implied an historical perspective, but often only within the well-defined academic fiends. There are often well-defined boundaries, useful for maintaining traditions, and content-domain-specific concepts and methods. The journal seeks to celebrate history and progress. This is an important part of moving the field forward. But the journal is intended to cross traditional boundaries, and include parallel work in other fields to address and explore the complex natures of games and simulations.

IJGCMS publishes articles from any discipline as long as the content of the work is related to games and simulations. Including multiple fields helps researchers recognize their similarities as well as introducing them to colleagues from distinctly different backgrounds.

Principle 3: International Contributions

A third principal of this journal is its international focus. The journal editorial board seeks and recruits scholars to represent different international perspectives on the Editorial Board of IJGCMS. Having diverse, international perspectives provides two interesting opportunities. First, readers are able to see how researchers from various countries conduct and report scientific inquiry, and their interests on games and simulations. For example, what are the current inquiries and interests on games in various countries around the world?

Principle 4: Innovation

Gaming and simulation researchers often create new concepts, new methods, new implementation, and new technologies in their work. IJGCMS is a journal where authors who create new approaches can publish their findings. IJGCMS is also a resource for readers who want to keep up with the latest and most cutting-edge technologies. Special, focused issues with guest editors promote new insights; connect readers with new ideas, new researchers, and new topics for in-depth analyses of conceptual or technological innovations. As part of the journal mission, proposals for special issues are welcomed at any time.

Principle 5: Implication for Practice and Theory

Research should inform theory and application. We seek the betterment of humanity. Our intent to provide some improvement in whatever means possible: entertainment, research methods, our interactions with contributors and readers; we seek to examine and share cultural issues ranging from gender bias and misogyny, cultural diversity, and representation (or the lack thereof) as race, age, and gender. Games and entertainment have much to teach us about our society, and provide a mirror report on our culture. How we play and what we seek for entertainment can be indicative of our cultural values.

Developing a strong research foundation for games and simulations is important, but only to the extent that the research provides a positive impact. We ask our reviewers directly:

- "What are the implications of this work on other research, policy, and practice?"

Recommended topics for the journal include (but are not limited to) the following:

- User research: Psychological aspects of gamers
- Cognitive, social, and emotional impact of games and simulations
- Critical reviews and meta-analyses of existing game and simulation literature
- Current and future trends, technologies, and strategies related to game, simulation development, and implementation
- Electronic games and simulations in government, business, and the workforce
- Electronic games and simulations in teaching and learning
- Frameworks to understand the societal and cultural impacts of games and simulations
- Impact of game and simulation development use on race and gender game and simulation design
- Innovative and current research methods and methodologies to study electronic games and simulations
- Teaching of games and simulations at multiple age and grade levels
- Medical usage of games for clinical assessment and intervention
- Postmortems on game development.

Additionally, IJGMCS partners with academic and professional conferences. A tremendous amount of cutting-edge research in games and simulations is first presented at conferences. In an attempt to capture these findings, IJGCMS often partners with conferences and organizations to create special issues focused on the leading research from conferences including the Meaningful Play Conference, Serious Games Conference, Ludica Medica, and the American Education Research Association (AERA) Games Special Interest Group.

The IJGCMS' editorial board consists of four separate groups (http://www.igi-global.com/ijgcms).

1. The international advisory board consists of a panel of leading experts from around the world. The advisory board provides insight and helpful recommendations to the editor; they are also available for suggestions and recommendations of future journal goals and special issues.
2. IJGCMS has a panel of associate editors. Each submission goes to one associate editor. Having a smaller number of associate editors has provided a way to maintain consistency in reviews.
3. Each submission receives three double blind, peer reviews. The associate editor and the editorial review board members are matched as closely as possible based on the topic of the submission and the expertise of the reviewer. However, the reviews are double blind. In other words, the authors do not know the identity of the reviewers assigned to their paper, nor do the reviewers know the author.
4. The fourth group is a panel of co-book review editors who help select books, solicit reviewers, and edit reviews. IJGCMS publishes a book review with almost every issue.

Journal special issues are also peer-reviewed. This can be done in a number of different ways. Often, for conference special issues, submissions are reviewed once at the submission stage, where they are accepted or rejected for presentation. Accepted papers are then offered the chance to submit for journal submission, where they are again reviewed either by the conference review panel or IJGCMS' own review board.

The four issues for 2012 and 2013 produced a total of 46 peer-reviewed papers. The editorial board selected fifteen articles as the top articles. Upon selection the authors were given the opportunity to update their paper with new data, new findings, or related articles since the original publication of their paper. The purpose and goal of this book is to highlight the work of those authors, presenting findings that will impact the field of gaming and simulations in multiple ways.

It should be noted that the purpose of this summary is to highlight the main ideas. It is not intended to take away from the rich insights or deep conversations included in each chapter. For instance, one of the goals of IJGCMS is to publish articles that directly impact policy, research, and practice. Each chapter in this book contains a rich description of the 'so what?' for those working in various fields. A thorough reading of each chapter will provide such detailed information.

1. Requirements-Based Design of Serious Games and Learning Software: An Introduction to the Vegas Effect (Dubbels)

In our first chapter, Dr. Dubbels describes a requirements-based game design technique. A serious game can be entertaining and enjoyable, but it is designed to facilitate the acquisition of skills and knowledge performance in the workplace, classroom, or therapeutic context. Claims of improvement can be validated through assessments successful, measurable practice beyond the game experience, the targeted context of the workplace, classroom, or clinical using the same tools as Multiple Traits and Multiple Measure (MTMM) models. A process is presented as Lean Design Thinking, drawing upon generative techniques drawing upon the traditional methodologies of psychological and ethnographic methods.

2.   Design Principles for Online Role Play Simulations to Address Groupthink Tendency in Professional Training: An Exploration

In the second chapter, Drs. Leung and Law present a new perspective on crisis management in the context of law enforcement. gamification. The article proposes that a major challenge to the effective handling of crisis situations is the tendency for the personnel involved to ignore alternatives and make irrational decisions as Groupthink. This chapter describes the design of an online Role Play Simulation RPS for crisis management training and its implementation in in-service police training. The interactions of participants recorded during the RPS training were categorized using Bales' Interaction Process Analysis IPA. The results show that participation in the RPS has positive effect on the reduction of Groupthink tendency.

3.   Virtual Standardized Patients for Interactive Conversational Training: A Grand Experiment and New Approach

In Chapter 3, Dr. Talbot explores Virtual Standardized Patients (VSPs) as a conversational training tool. Conversational agents have improved with Natural Language Processing technologies, and the chapter provides an overview of VSPs VSPs along with the important technical, practical and pedagogical lessons that resulted from their experience. The implications from this work can inform virtual human / avatar conversational training of all types and applications, p[ushing the boundaries beyond medical education.

4.   Investigating Epistemic Stances in Game Play Through Learning Analytics

In Chapter 4, Drs. Garza and Clark applied techniques of statistical computing to data logs to investigate the patterns in students' play of The Fuzzy Chronicles. Analysis explored how game play patterns relate to learning outcomes in Newtonian kinematics. The chapter examines whether students playing the game showed evidence of dichotomous fast/slow modes of solution and the connection between conceptual understanding and performance in conceptual challenges.

5.   If the Gear Fits, Spin It Again! Embodied Education, Design Components, and In-Play Assessments

In Chapter 5, Drs. Johnson, Birchfield, and Megan-Romanowicz explored the influence of embodied cognition and learning in video game play. Their research examined two games called Tour de Force and the Winching Game, which were designed to instruct middle schoolers in the concepts associated with gear trains. Learners used the body to map the relatively abstract concept of mechanics in science to physical, kinesthetic sensations. Analysis indicated that significant gains in learning were made. However, the valence and magnitude of the correlations between gear switches varied between the two games. This may be due to the relative perceived and experiential difficulty conveyed by the learners, suggesting that the learner may be understanding the concept and gesturing adroitly in the game, but still not be able to demonstrate that comprehension on a symbolically-oriented assessment measure.

6.   *Monster Mischief*: A Game-Based Assessment of Selective Sustained Attention in Young Children

In Chapter 6, Drs. Godwin, Lomas, Koedinger, and Fisher describe an exploration of a design model that calls for extraneous cognitive load to be added to the intrinsic cognitive load of the core task. In the design of the game mechanics, extraneous cognitive load was germane in the assessment of selective sustained attention. Through this model, distracting design elements were a desirable part of the game's design intent. "Extraneous" game elements contributed to game play to provide a richer spectrum of difficulty. This approach to designing games through inclusion of distracting elements as optional and flexible parameters, can be used as a measure of player performance. The model suggests that assessment cognitive skills, such as those associated with inhibiting distraction, may be particularly well-suited for game-based assessment using this model.

7. A Digital Game for Undergraduate Calculus: Immersion, Calculation, and Conceptual Understanding

In Chapter 7, the team of Lee, Dunbar, Kornelson, Wilson, Ralston, Savic, Stewart, Thompson, and Elizondo compare the use of a digital game to a traditional methods for teaching university-level calculus for solving practice questions. Additionally, they investigate and describe differences in goal affordances to promote student conceptual understanding.

8. "Nervousness and Maybe Even Some Regret": Videogames and the Cognitive-Affective Model of Historical Empathy

In Chapter 8, researcher Owens Boltz examines whether games can be used to raise awareness in players that diverse and contradictory viewpoints existed within past societies just as they do today. This approach explores Russell's (2011) assertion that historical empathy can encourage students to examine how their own values have been shaped by societal and historical context. The researcher observed children playing a videogame that allows game play from multiple perspectives to examine whether particular types of game play tend to elicit historical empathy more often than others.

9. Using Notions of "Play" Over the Life Course to Inform Game Design for Older Populations

In Chapter 9, Drs. Brown and De Schutter provides insight into the characteristics and distinctions among older age cohorts of gamers. Current recommendations for the design of games for older adults do not fully capture the nuances that are unique to older generations and have often been built on the analysis of contemporary context and the issues that older adults face when trying to play games.

10. An Extended Study on Training and Physical Exercise in E-Sports

In Chapter 10, the authors Kari, Karhlahti, and Siutila explore the training routines of professional and high-level eSport players with added focus on their physical exercise. explore the training routines of professional and high-level e-sport players with added focus on their physical exercise. This paper extends their earlier work, with supplementary data and insights via qualitative interviews of five professional e-sport players.

CONCLUSION

The work that has been published on games and simulations in IJGCMS is continuing to advance research, policy, practice, and improve people's lives. In conclusion, one could ask, what can we learn about the current state of the field from these 16 publications? Listed below are some of the key findings from each of these studies:

1. User experience research is essential in game development. Developers need research data to understanding the user for the design, development, and implementation of software as games and simulations.
2. Digital games and simulations exist in many forms, but those that provide high-value experiences to the user are more likely to lead to optimal experience. These experiences are built upon delivering intuitive functionality, positive emotional tone, and personal transformation, resulting in trust and loyalty in customers, leading to social impact.
3. There is a difference between making a difficult game, and a challenging game. Challenging games have activities that can be overcome in the flow of game play, difficult activities must be over powered – to do this the player leaves the focus and flow of the game.
4. Software, products, and services should look beyond enhancing tedious activities with parts of games, and consider how to deliver the best experiences that games offer.
5. Avatar creation and play creates self-exploration and provides the potential for life-changing experience.
6. Gamification require an abundance of context-sensitive and descriptive empirical research that identifies the boundaries of their use and replicates findings.
7. Small differences in game presentation can alter the beliefs and approach to a game experience. Platform and presentation provide a demonstrable difference in response in basic cognitive processes between digital and non-digital game play experience and impact.
8. Games can increase contact and accessibility for sharing important information, and learning about life transitions.
9. Games for medical education and training should be planned based upon how much fidelity is necessary.
10. Game and simulation designers can improve learning outcomes by considering the interaction and representation– not just the content. In well-designed games and gamification, the interaction is the content.

11. Consistency, feedback, and the appropriate use of representations through game interfaces can positively impact user learning and cognitive development.
12. Games and game-play can be used as hooks to help students then help students understand and explore real-world rites of passage.
13. Play is an important part of learning content in simulations and gaming. The ability to practice and explore can be signaled through design and provide a playful approach. Play can increase motivation in academic learning.
14. Games have the potential to provide complex experiences to present a new frontier in cognitive aging and quality of life.
15. Physical behavior aligned with digital game play can be motivating, and potentially lead to cognitive enhancement, improved academic learning, and improved well-being.

Brock Dubbels
University of Minnesota, USA

Chapter 1

Requirements–Based Design of Serious Games and Learning Software:
An Introduction to the Vegas Effect

Brock Randall Dubbels
McMaster University, USA

ABSTRACT

A serious game can be entertaining and enjoyable, but it is designed to facilitate the acquisition of skills and knowledge performance in the workplace, classroom, or therapeutic context. Claims of improvement can be validated through assessments successful, measurable practice beyond the game experience, the targeted context of the workplace, classroom, or clinical using the same tools as multiple traits and multiple measure (MTMM) models. This chapter provides a post-mortem describing the development of the initial design and development of a measurable model to inform the design requirements for validation for a serious game. In this chapter, the reader will gain insight into the implementation of lean process, design thinking, and field observations for generative research. This data informs the assessments and measurement of performance, validated through the MTMM model criteria for requirements. The emphasis examines the role of research insights for onboarding and professional development of newly hired certified nursing assistants in a long-term care facility.

DOI: 10.4018/978-1-5225-7461-3.ch001

INTRODUCTION

This article provides a post mortem for developing serious games to answer the question:

How do you know your serious game had the intended impact?

This chapter builds upon this theme to emphasize the importance of a Lean Process approach, when integrated with Design Thinking, User Experience Research, traditional psychology and psychometrics, and Agile Development. These approaches to product design potentially provide a synthesis to reduce uncertainty, facilitate action, increase transparency, flexibility, velocity, and learning.

BACKGROUND

In the case study presented here as a post-mortem, the five different fields are presented and synthesized to present an approach to developing a video game to train inexperienced care-givers to become effective certified nursing assistants.

One of the foundations of serious games is that they deliver on a claim. If a claim is made that performance, training, or a health outcome is improved, it must be observable inside the game—the activity is the assessment in a serious game (Dubbels, 2016; 2017)—and that the improvement from playing in the game transfers to improvement in the wild of the non-digital world, and measurable with the same models from the game. This makes a case for having evidence-supported requirements. Although this is not always possible initially, research techniques can be used to generate and test insights as part of an iterative process, culminating incremental improvement of requirements, models, and testing as part of a build, measure, learn process(Ries, 2011, 2013) If we do not have a clear understanding of the activities and how to model and measure the behavior we want out users to learn, we are essentially throwing the dice, hoping we guessed correctly. This does not have to be the case, as there is a history of user research to reduce risk and uncertainty in developing and designing games.

History of Game User Research

What is odd is that game user research is not new. In his keynote address at the Games User Research Summit, Michael Medlock (Medlock, 2014) provided a history of games research, going back to 1972, when Atari hired Carol Kanter. She shared that:

It all started on a bet. I met Gene Lipkin VP of Atari. I asked him how he could tell if his games were good or not. I bet him that in 6 months I could tell which game will do better in the market than the others, and if I could then he needed to hire me full time. I did, and then he did.

Although Kanter is listed as the first in a tradition of game user research, the early games user researchers focused on marketing—showing which games would be successful and why. This approach focused on generative research techniques such as focus group work and field methods. These techniques culminated in the creation of teams at Nintendo, and the creation of guides for usability (Al-Awar, Chapanis, & Ford, 1981).

Recently, more companies are creating new positions in user experience research, user experience design, and even behavioral economics. The intent is to generate insights that guide game development to improve the game experience, and to examine new ways to generate income. However, few game development companies have begun to integrate the field of psychometrics from psychology, and examine whether games can provide services like training, diagnosis, performance enhancement, and skill and knowledge acquisition. This chapter provides a synthesis of traditional psychology and psychometrics with current practices in project management, development, and design.

However, the recent emergence of brain fitness games had led to research psychologists looking at ways that games can be used as cognitive, affective, behavioral, and physiological interventions. Research using video games identified that playing these games can lead to physiological, behavioral, affective, and cognitive changes (Anguera et al., 2013; Bavelier et al., 2011; Dubbels, 2012; Green & Bavelier, 2008; Green, Benson, Kersten, & Schrater, 2010; Green & Bavelier, 2003; Jaeggi, Buschkuehl, Jonides, & Perrig, 2008; Loftus & Loftus, 1983; Merzenich et al., 1996; Smith et al., 2009). This approach had drawn heavily from the research perspective developed by research psychologists, with great emphasis on the ability to objectively measure and differentiate psychological states as categories and constructs for diagnosis, identification of casual origin, and potential treatment.

The ability to identify, describe, diagnose, and treat with psychological tools is the history of psychology. Psychology was once a subfield of philosophy until the 1870s, when people interested in psychological processes began to formalize their methods of study with the adoption of objective scientific method. According to historical studies of psychology ("Timeline of psychology," 2015), studies of reaction time by Franciscus Donders, the creation of psychophysics as a field of study in 1860, and the publication of the first textbook of experimental psychology by William Wundt in 1874, which led to academic studies of psychology. William Wundt created a laboratory dedicated to psychological research on the nature of religious beliefs, identification of mental disorders and abnormal behavior, and to study brain structure and function through identification of damaged parts of the brain. In doing so, he was able to establish psychology as a separate science from other topics, but still faced criticism about the methods that relied upon introspection and questioned whether psychology could be called a legitimate science.

With the evolution and growth of psychology as an objective science, new methods have been created to answer the question: *How do you know?*

Serious Games as Informative Assessment

Serious games are already very much like the tools used in psychological assessments and evaluations. Games, by their very nature assess, measure, and evaluate as informative assessments (Black & Wiliam, 2009; Forster, 2009; Wiliam & Thompson, 2007). This makes sense. Informative assessments provide measurement and feedback in the flow of the activity. This is in contrast to formative and summative assessments, which are measures that occur outside the flow of an activity.

In games, assessment is part of the game play. Informative assessment provides an activity where the player learns the scoring criteria through feedback from interaction in the game environment. If a game is to act as an informative assessment, it will stress meaningful, timely, and continuous feedback about learning concepts, and provide adaptive situations through introduction of ambiguity and least/worst situations in game play to expose weaknesses in knowledge and performance, and scaffold learning.

Evidence supports that informative assessments are powerful learning tools. Research findings from over 4,000 studies indicate that informative assessment has the most significant impact on achievement (Wiliam, 2007). When serious games are built as an informative assessment, the scoring criteria becomes the roadmap for learning (Dubbels, 2016). The criteria can also provide a framework for construct validity for learning in the game, as well as a tool for measuring activities outside the game. This approach can increase the likelihood that learning and performance recorded inside the game, can be measured as a training effect outside of the game—avoiding the Vegas Effect.

Currently, most games are not designed as informative assessments. This means that learning in a serious game might suffer from the Vegas Effect—learning that happens in games, stays in games. For a game to act as informative assessment, the learning must transfer. This is accomplished when the learning concepts are accurately defined, measured, and depicted as game play; and the in------game assessment tools can be used in an actual work or clinical environment.

Why Go to All of This Trouble?

When games are used as tools for assessment, diagnosis and performance evaluation, they can have a serious impact on a person's life—whether the game is used for a clinical diagnosis or for a work performance review. If serious games are to be taken seriously, they need to account for two concerns:

1. People are being judged: if serious games are to be used to measure and evaluate the performance and abilities of an individual, the process should be done with great care.
2. Serious games are significant investments: a serious game should provide clear evidence of learning for return on investment (ROI).

The adoption of methods and techniques from psychometrics can reduce the gamble associated with serious game development. Increasing certainty about learning outcomes should be at the top of the list. This can be addressed through adoption of existing models from the research literature, and implementing methods from the field of psychometrics. The integration of validated research models and psychometric methodology can the reduce risk associated with poor assessment, measurement evaluation. This can easily be accomplished through a review of the research letter in the content area being modeled and using the criteria of the construct being described, and building game mechanics based upon valid, reliable, and replicated metrics and outcomes described in the research.

The review of psychometric models, assessments, and data should be modeled prior to the construction of the prototype. This saves time, money, and the sanity of the programmers, artists, and subject matter experts. There will always be learning in development, but when psychometric methods are used to build models from established criteria, analysis can be conducted prior to, during, and after development, rather than waiting until after the game has been finished. This approach is often called an agile approach (Kane, 2003). In academic research, building these models is required prior to experimentation – why should it be different for serious games?

As an analogy, the author worked in construction one summer, and often heard experienced builders laugh when talking about the impatience of customers, and their fear of planning expenses. The veteran builders would say:

Sure, why bother planning—we can always build it twice.

There are many companies that realize that upfront planning and modeling from user experience research can actually reduce expense. Companies like Boeing Co. Fidelity Investments reported that poor user experience can add as much as 50%

to the total cost of software. Additionally, the Gardner Group reported that 25% of software development efforts fail outright due to poor planning, and another 65% of efforts result in sub-standard performance (Kwong, Healton, & Lancaster, 1998). User experience research requires a bit of planning up front, but it saves time and resources. Avoiding the Vegas Effect may lead to serious economic opportunities as saving money and measurable improvements in performance outside of the game.

It is in our nature to make predictions based upon assumption. Can we assume that a serious game delivers on its' promises? When the outcome is high-stakes, such as learning to deliver medical treatment, or operating heavy equipment? We need to know quickly that the games as intervention is effective before we introduce real-world risk. We often draw on assumptions and educated guessing to create requirements and learning criteria. This approach seems not only risky and potentially wasteful, but also a common theme for constructing requirements. It is not enough to start with a business case. Best practice suggests that we can reduce risk and uncertainty by adopting a Lean Process (Ries, 2011), which offers a method for increasing certainty.

The Lean Process seeks to:

- identify how people currently solve a problem (current behavior),
- propose a better process (proposed behavior)
- conduct a gap analysis
- identify the value provided in the proposed behavior (value hypothesis)
- identify a measurement of efficacy to support the business case (growth metric)

These steps provide a powerful approach for the development of software requirements. Better requirements make for better design, development, and customer experience. When requirements for building any type of software are validated with the user needs as a focus, and this focus is informed from research and evidence, we can feel more confident that our software will deliver the experience we claim it delivers.

Using a Lean process (Eisenmann, Ries, & Dillard, 2012; Frederiksen & Brem, 2017; Ries, 2011, 2012, 2013; Womack & Jones, 1997) one can use empirical scientific methods to have greater confidence and certainty in the design and development requirements, as well as greater certainty that what happened in the game experience, leads to improved performance as potential training and therapy.

To start with a Lean Process, we need to take a close look at the business case development of criteria to design models for game mechanics. We need to ask, "what do we know about how people are currently solving this problem?" If the development team thinks of the software as a jigsaw puzzle, the business case should provide framing as corners and edges. If there are gaps in the business case, these gaps can be identified as assumptions. The riskier the assumption, the greater the business risk. This can be achieved through what Jeff Patton describes as user story mapping (Patton, 2002; Patton & Economy, 2014).

The process starts with proposed ideas and goals from the business case, which leads to steps in the process supporting the customer experience:

I want to build X for these reasons, and for these people to experience.

This can be drawn from designing a GIST model. A Gist model (Gilad, 2018) is for the creation of "lightweight plans that are built for change, lower management overhead, improved team velocity and autonomy, better cross-company alignment and ultimately better products and solutions." The GIST model was created to quickly develop, and right-size project planning into simple steps, as compared to waterfall approaches ("Waterfall model," 2018).

This form of planning is a ton of work—just getting all stakeholders to agree is a massive undertaking, yet ROI is very low. The plans quickly go out of sync with reality—the longer they are the more they are wrong. It took me awhile to realize that my fancy roadmaps and project gantts were already outdated the day I published them. Also, it's a waterfall (different from the famous project waterfall), meaning that there is almost no room for agility—changes at the top cause huge ripple effects of replanning and project cancellations at the bottom. Agile development addressed project waterfall, but didn't change planning waterfall. And then there's the impact on innovation and culture. As roadmaps allow only for a few big projects to be funded you have to prioritize and kill many potentially good ideas upfront. In top-down orgs the winner ideas come from management. In bottom-up orgs getting your idea to win became a very big deal, hence pitching, salesmanship and hype are now mandatory product management skills. To me it all felt very mid-20th century. (Gilad, 2018).

Gilad developed the GIST model in alignment with Lean Process and Agile Development. The benefits include:

- No split of ideation, planning and execution—they all happen concurrently all the time
- Goals rather than solutions or vague strategy statements.
- Idea banks rather than product backlogs.
- Short sub-quarter step-projects rather than long multi-quarter/multi-year projects.

- No betting on just a few big ideas that take forever to implement—we test many ideas quickly and pursue the ones that work.
- Iterations—we revisit every part of the plan regularly and systematically and stay agile at all levels.

The intention is to create light-weight plans that are *"built for change, lower management overhead, improved team velocity and autonomy, better cross-company alignment and ultimately better products and solutions"(Ibid)*. The main building blocks of the GIST model are depicted below in figure 1 as: Goals, Ideas, Step-Projects, and Tasks.

According to Gilad each level of this model embody a principle.

- **Goals:** The principle is to focus on strategy informed by desired outcomes. Whenever there is a question about the rationale behind an activity in design and development, a goal should give an answer. This approach comes from Gilad's experience at Google, where each quarter employees are asked to state and define measurable goals in the form of Objectives and Key Results (OKRs)—(for more on OKRs, read: Doerr, 2018).
- **Ideas:** Ideas and approaches to achieving goals. (author note, I prefer the term *approach* to the term *solution*, as it promotes that this is a testable hypothesis rather than the end of the inquiry and testing).
- **Step-Projects:** These are defined and identified based upon goals and ideas prioritized at the beginning of the quarter.
- **Tasks:** This category i intended to identify tasks as activities necessary to complete step-projects. This category can also be used for identification of tasks within the steps of a customer journey as a finer-grain depiction of the user journey well as identification of customer activities within a journey map for planning.

Figure 1. GIST Model
(Gilad, 2018)

To formulate steps from an idea, your team can implement a story map methodology as depicted below in figure 2.

In story mapping, the team can propose Step Plans from Ideas (Patton, 2002; Patton & Economy, 2014). In Figure 2, the team can replace the term "epic" with idea and propose steps as part of the project backbone. The proposed experience is expressed as steps in a user/customer journey. Each step in the journey can be described below the step as a vertical column as details supporting the narrative flow of the story with outcomes, behavior, and features. As the steps on the backbone of the process are identified horizontally, details of each step are built as sublevels below each step. As the story map is refined, the designers and developers can prioritize activity by identifying release for aspects of each step.

As the story map is generated, gaps can be identified for assumptions, opportunity, elimination, and automation. As these decisions are made, prioritization can be made, and research questions can be identified as part of right-sizing. This may include

According to Patton, there are five powerful reasons for using story mapping as a generative methodology:

- User stories let you focus on building small things, it's easy to lose sight of the big picture, resulting in an experience cobbled together from mismatched parts—aka, a "Franken-product".

Figure 2. User story map

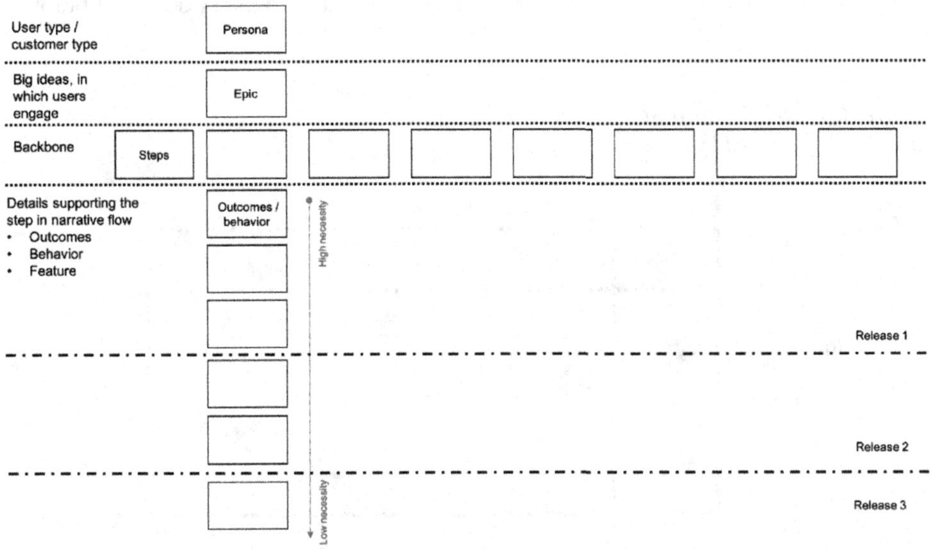

9

- User stories provide scope, which provides estimates for timelines, resources, on what is delivered, when, how, and by whom. This improves velocity and morale.
- Story maps serve as documentation techniques. Stories are about conversations, and in the midst of the experience of story, we may forget what they talked about and agreed to in the conversations.
- User stories provide acceptance criteria, common understanding of what needs to be built, and when – helping teams finish the work they plan on in the projected timeframe.
- Even in instances where product features does not seem to have direct users, we may build without any consideration of the potential user. The story map accounts for the parts users may not see or use.

Generative work like GIST models and Story Mapping can help to organize and identify features as a continuous experience, gaps in the experience, and opportunities to provide value, and planning roadmaps for design and development sprints. As the ideas and step-process are defined, riskiest assumptions can be identified and the step processes can be scored for effort and impact. Confidence

As the story map is developed as a step-by-step experience, the team can identify gaps in in steps for activities lacking support, gain new insights, focus on what should be removed from the experience, as well as look for opportunities and actions that can be automated to create value and delight. As the proposed story map is reviewed and discussed, changes can be proposed for prioritization in redesign and development. The gaps identified can be charted as in the Prioritization Matrix depicted below.

Figure 3. Prioritization matrix as an ICE score
(Ellis, 2010 – modified by Dubbels)

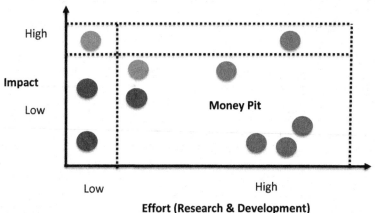

Prioritization of gaps as steps typically identifies cost and effort, as shown above. It is important that the category on the x-axis "Effort" is informed by design, development, and research resources. In the category of effort, the assumptions identified in the gap analysis of the story map should identify areas requiring research. The larger and riskier the assumption, the greater the research need.

The identification of gaps should include riskiest assumptions in the redesign and development. When research cannot be conducted due to limited time and resources, the time can create a risk mitigation document, identifying risks and assumptions that were identified, but not addressed. This allows the project to move forward while documenting shortcomings, concerns, and limitations. The goal of Agile, Lean Process, and User Experience Research is to be flexible and willing to pivot as new information becomes available. The risk mitigation plan documents awareness of the riskiest assumptions and provides transparency.

Applied Case With CNA Game

In the context of the certified nursing assistant game, a number of data points were gathered in resource review. The company had great interest in building a serious game and provided a business case that showed the potential value in using a video game as a training system for on-boarding and on-going training. The big idea was that the video game would take the pressure off of experienced care givers by directing new hires to practice in a controlled environment where failure to perform would not result in consequences for the vulnerable populations for whom the provide medical support.

As the team worked to gather requirements, the team did not initially use a story map to elicit and document the experience of the newly-hired certified nursing assistant. This may have led to tension in communications expectations. Upon delivery of the MVP, the stakeholders expressed confusion. The MVP provided a very limited functional training experience, lacking ideas and expectations from the subject matter experts and stakeholders. What resulted from the initial design and development as an MVP (minimum viable product) were very simple case-based experiences, which provided only task-based knowledge as a procedural rhetoric (Bogost, 2007). This provided distress between the design and development team and the customer stakeholders.

In order bridge the gap in the expected product and MVP, the author was brought in to revisit discovery, mend fences, and build trust as product owner and researcher. To do this, stakeholder interviews were conducted, and a story map was created. This story map suggested that the experience of the new certified nursing assistant (CNA) is task-based: following a schedule, doing certain tasks, in specific places, at specific times, for specific people. Although this task-based procedure is important, it was not what the stakeholders or subject matter experts (SMEs) wanted in the game. The stakeholders and SMEs required that game focus on building soft-skills such as relationships, trust, and having the ability to empower the residents of the care facility to become autonomous, thus relying less upon the CNAs for task-based assistance.

With the new information, the requirements were evaluated and scored for a confidence level Figure 4 (below) (Gilad, 2018). The team used the confidence wheel to identify the types of evidence we needed to move forward. For each category below, the assumptions and gaps from the story map, and our confidence level of what was currently known led to a research plan for incremental development, to gather evidence for requirements and insight as iterative development.

Reducing Assumption and Risk Early

It is a is has always been having substantive data early in the development cycle, especially when a product does not yet exist:

How do I generate data to support dev and design before there is something to test?

Figure 4. Confidence Wheel
(Gilad, 2018 – modified by Dubbels 2018)

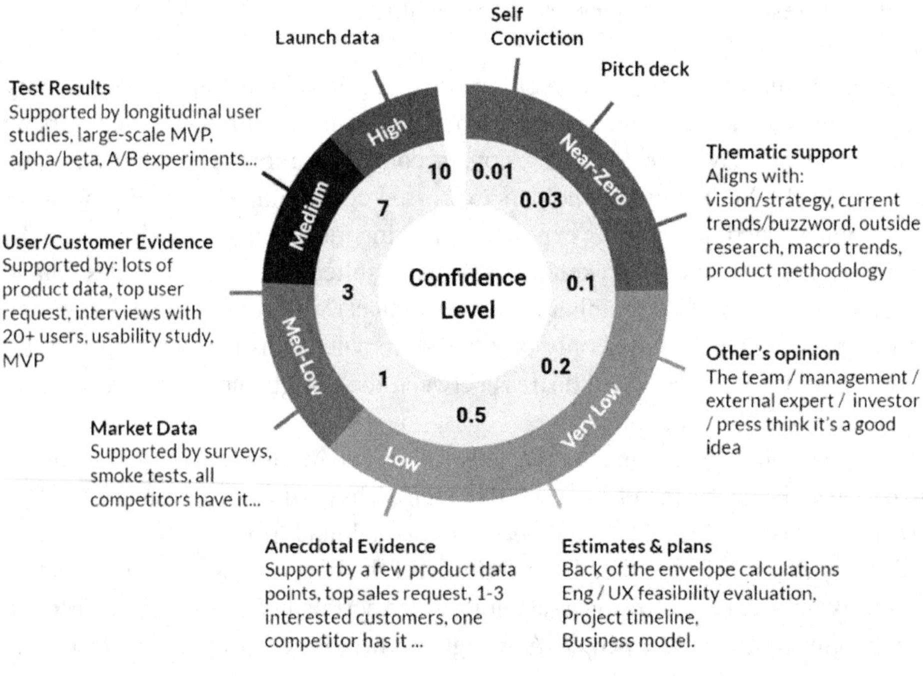

There are many techniques for generative research that align with Agile and Lean Process. One popular school of thought is Design Thinking. In Design Thinking, it is important to test early and often as part of a co-design process, connecting with customers, and potential customers early and often. The core expression in Design Thinking is that *"you are not the user."*

Design Thinking is about understanding users and/or customers in the pre-production phase. With Design Thinking methods, generative research can be conducted as means of co-design, between the researcher and the potential user/customer. More than just generative methods, it is also a mindset (Buchanan, 1992). Design thinking is intended to identify and explore assumptions in early design and development. Design Thinking makes use of extensive user research, feedback loops and iteration cycles to develop models of behavior and assessment, which can be observed and tested as concepts early on, saving the developer effort and expense. Innovation Focus: Both concepts have the same goal, which is to foster innovations.

Lean Design Thinking

The Lean, and Design Thinking processes can potentially complement each other by converging the strategies as iterative design and development. By getting a clear sense of the voice of the customer/ user, and planning implementation of feedback testing and iteration loops earlier in the process, even before there is a prototype, the designer/ developer can have a better understanding of the customers actual needs, observe key characteristics of an activity for modeling and validation criteria, as well as process, required content, and motivational factors. Having stronger models informed by user data early in the process can save effort, time, and resources. Especially when compared to starting with the proposed needs outlined in a business case.

This allows the designer/ developer to pivot when they find differences between assumption and evidence. This is especially important in planning digital training tasks and activities in the contexts of serious games. Building a game on assumptions without early testing of concepts and expectations can result in incredible waste of effort and resources.

Early research could be implemented after the Point of View (the creation of the problem statement) and/or after Ideation (learning from prototypes and mock-ups). The testing of early problem hypotheses, that can be falsified or validated saves time and resources, and results in the probability of successful project results. Although the level of confidence may be low initially, introducing a generative approach from Design Thinking will address assumptions, mitigate risk, and quickly increase confidence, thus increasing viability and confidence in the project.

Although testing in Design Thinking is commonly performed as a qualitative method, the use of quantitative methods and measures are also essential for increasing scope and reducing uncertainty. The transition does not need to be difficult. Observable qualities can be quantified – quantities are qualities, e.g. frequency, quality, etc.

Unlike design thinking, Lean Process does not prescribe how to collect customer input. To increase confidence level, qualitative research methods—e.g. ethnographic methods—can be used to provide context to quantitative data in Lean Process. Additionally, structured frameworks and the generation of a qualitative persona might help designers to better understand and develop their customers and their respective needs and problems. Both Lean Process and Design Thinking should be scheduled at the beginning of the process with emphasis on ideation techniques, as they are applied in design thinking, to develop concept variations.

Although Lean Process usually starts with a concrete business idea, it might be helpful to use structured ideation methods to iterate that idea within the process, specifically before the problem-solution fit is achieved. Consequently, pivoting should be applied earlier (already on the initial concept). And finally, qualitative feedback evaluation, such as qualitative user interviews, could be implemented in the pivoting steps, in addition to the metric-based evaluation techniques.

Serious Games and Generative Research

To make a serious game, scores in the game should be associated should simulate and create improvements in performance that can be measured outside of the game. To do this, progress in the game should represent progress in the real world. A first step must include guided observations of professional CNAs working in situ. A technique for generative research and validation of a story map is field observation.

Field Reporting as Methodological Fit

Field reporting can be used to help validate theoretical models such as empathy maps and personas; provide context and behavior for analytical data; they can also be used as an initial pilot to understand user context, purpose, and need. Designing systems on assumption is risky behavior. It is important to test assumptions with observed behavior in the wild. One should understand that the future behavior can best be predicted from past behavior, and that any type of service design, instructional design, product design, and/or system design should be tested with actual user where they would actually be using it. It is essential to see if the projected behavior of the personas is the way people (which they approximate) actually behave. Conversely, field observation and cognitive ethnography are method-specific for defining personas, and mapping out process for how people solve problems.

Cognitive Ethnography as a Form of Field Reporting

As a methodological approach, cognitive ethnography assumes that cognition is distributed through rules, roles, language, relationships and coordinated activities, and can be embodied in artifacts and objects (Dubbels, 2008). For this reason, cognitive ethnography is an effective way to study activity systems like games, models, and simulations –whether mediated digitally or not.

In its traditional form, ethnography often involves the researcher living in the community of study, learning the language, doing what members of the community do—learning to see the world as it is seen by the natives in their cultural context, Fetterman (1998). Cognitive ethnography follows the same protocol, but its purpose is to understand cognitive process and context—examining them together, thus, eliminating the false dichotomy between psychology and anthropology.

Observational techniques such as ethnography and cognitive ethnography attempt to describe and look at relations and interaction situated in the spaces where they are native, including virtual and natural environments. Cognitive ethnography is methodologically tuned for mapping and describing how cognition and cognitive activities like decision making and problem solving, Specifically, cognitive ethnography assumes that cognition is distributed across systems that may be composed of combinations of tools, roles, and off-loading complexity onto the environment.

Theory of Distributed Cognition

Cognitive ethnography assumes that cognition is distributed. Specifically, cognitive ethnography is used to map the systems created solve complex tasks. When people face a difficult task, they may attempt to recruit others and create a system with tools, cooperation, and language to distribute the complexity. For example, people often coordinate their activities in teams. Members of teams are given roles, they use language to create rules and process, and they use tools. Groups, roles, rules, language, and tools off-load complexity to achieve a purpose. A complex problem is simplified by off-loading the complexity onto a system.

It is important to consider whether cognitive ethnography provides methodological fit with the research problem and questions. The focus of observation in cognitive ethnography is the description of how an activity is distributed across a system. There are three main systems: physical (virtual), social, and conceptual. These observations should inform the design of objects, systems, services, and understanding.

Cognitive ethnography emphasizes inductive field observation, but also uses theory in a deductive process to analyze behavior (. This approach is useful to increase external validity, operationalize terms, and develop content validity through expanding a study across new designs, across different time frames, in different programs, from different observational contexts, and with different groups (Cook and Campbell, 1979; Campbell & Stanley, 1966). Study of these features can help the researcher determine the organization, transfer, and representation of information (Hutchins, 2010; 1995).

Ontology/Purpose of Cognitive Ethnography Methodology

As stated, cognitive ethnography assumes that human cognition adapts to its natural surroundings. Therefore, the role of cognitive ethnographer is to transform observational data and interpretation into meaningful representations so that cognitive properties of the system become visible (Hutchins, 2010; 1995). According to Hutchins (2010), the study of the space where an activity takes place is a primary feature of observation in cognitive ethnography. He lists three kinds of important spaces for consideration:

1. **Physical/Virtual Space:** What is near to what, seen from each position, how bodies fit in space.
2. **Social Space:** Social organization, groups, identities, status roles, rules and how they affect the flow of information.
3. **Conceptual Space:** The conceptual structures of activities determine the content and organization.

Cognitive ethnography offers both an inductive and deductive methodology. It works for contextual inquiry and task analysis, and as a prerequisite for task analysis to model and understand user cognition, engagement, and physical interaction.

Methods

There are many general approaches and techniques that can be used for data collection in cognitive ethnography. What is important is the systematic observation and accurate recording of the varying aspects of a situation. Researchers should always approach their field study with a detailed plan for cognitive ethnography, including what will be observed, where to conduct observations, and the method by which they will collect and record their data. Although there is no rule about data gathering techniques, there are generally accepted and implemented techniques:

- Note Taking
- Video and Audio Recordings
- Illustrations and Drawings

- Artifact collection

Real-Time Observation and Running Records

In data collection, it is essential to continuously analyze observations as a running record. As observations are recorded, look for the meaning underlying the observed actions, coding patterns, themes, and insights in real time. Ask yourself: "What's going on here? What does this observed activity mean? What else does this relate to?" Note that observation and recording is an on-going process of reflection and analysis.

A running record can lead to scope creep in observation. Although one may find the unexpected, it is essential to keep the scope of research questions and purpose in mind during observing. Recording is not a random process, and should not be conducted haphazardly. Field observation requires focus, and emphasis on attending to details. Enter the observation site [i.e., "field"] with a clear plan about what the goals and purpose of the observation, but the researcher should be prepared to adapt to changing circumstances as they may arise.

Conscientious observations, recordings, and analysis will provide focus and what is heard and seen in the context of a theoretical framework. This will simplify the coding, analysis, interpretation, and reporting.

This theoretical focus is also what separates data collection and observation from simple reporting. The theoretical framework should guide observations to help determine what, when, and how observations are reported, and act as the foundation for interpretation for findings. Generally, the following can serve as a framework for things to document:

- **Physical Setting**: The characteristics of an occupied space and the human use of the place where the observation(s) are being conducted.
- **Objects and Material Culture:** The presence, placement, and arrangement of objects that impact the behavior or actions of those being observed. If applicable, describe the cultural artifacts representing the beliefs--values, ideas, attitudes, and assumptions--used by the individuals you are observing.
- **Use of Language:** Don't just observe but listen to what is being said, how is it being said, and, the tone of conversation among participants.
- **Behavior Cycles:** This refers to documenting when and who performs what behavior or task and how often they occur. Record at which stage is this behavior occurring within the setting.
- **The Order in Which Events Unfold:** Note sequential patterns of behavior or the moment when actions or events take place and their significance.

- **Physical Characteristics of Subjects:** If relevant, note age, gender, clothing, etc. of individuals being observed.
- **Expressive Body Movements**: This would include things like body posture or facial expressions. Note that it may be relevant to also assess whether expressive body movements support or contradict the language used in conversation

Along with these suggested items, what should drive your observations and analysis are he research problem, the theoretical perspective that is driving your analysis, and the observations that you make, which determine how to format the field report. Field reports should be written in the past tense. Your reader's only knowledge and understanding of what happened will come from the description section of the report because the reader was unlikely to have been a witness to the situation, people, or events being writing about. Given this, it is crucial that sufficient details are provided as thick description, to place the analysis into proper context; don't make the mistake of providing a description without context. As a general activity flow, figure %% (below) provides a general process once the research problem and purpose have been identified.

Figure 5. Contextual Inquiry as Ethnographic Method

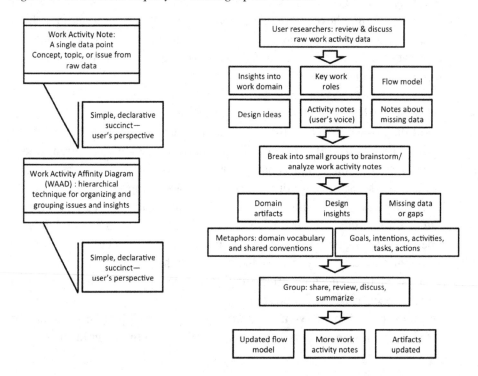

Design and Validity for Methodological Choice

Although cognitive ethnography starts with a clear purpose and research problem, and one or more research questions, the sequence of steps through the process can vary in order (i.e., they are not necessarily linear or unidirectional), and even the question and/or purpose can be revised when needed.

To briefly summarize, cognitive ethnography as a research process model comprises eight distinct steps: (1) determine the research question; (2) determine whether the research design is appropriate; (3) define the methods for sampling and data collection; (4) collect the data; (5) analyze the data; (6) interpret the data; (7) legitimate the data; and (8) draw conclusions (if warranted) and write the final report.

Once these steps are completed, the construction of the final report can be presented in a variety of formats, depending upon the purpose, audience, and methodological/ theoretical orientation. The description section of a cognitive ethnography should align with the format of a field report, which is often similar to a well-written piece of journalism. A helpful approach to systematically describing the varying aspects of an observed situation is to answer the "Five W's of Investigative Reporting."

- **Description:** The "Five W's"
- **What:** Describe what you observed. Note the temporal, physical, and social boundaries you imposed to limit the observations you made. e.g., what is your impression of the application of iPads as a learning device?
- **Where:** Information about the setting, and, if necessary, note important material objects that are present that help contextualize the observation [e.g., arrangement of computers in relation to student engagement with the teacher].
- **When:** Record factual data about the day and the beginning and ending time of each observation. Note that it may also be necessary to include background information or key events, which impact upon the situation you, were observing.
- **Who:** Note background and demographic information about the individuals being observed e.g., age, gender, ethnicity, and/or any other variables relevant to your study]. Record who is doing what and saying what, as well as, who is not doing or saying what. If relevant, be sure to record who was missing from the observation.
- **Why:** Why were you doing this? Describe the reasons for selecting particular situations to observe. Note why something happened. Also note why you may have included or excluded certain information.

What We Learned

In *A Better Life©*, the player faces a dynamic tension. The CNA does not have enough time to meet obligations in the scheduled tasks but must still build relationships. If the CNA does not build relations, the residents become resistant and take more time. Conversely, if the CNA spends too much time in building relations, she may fall behind in completing her scheduled tasks with other residents. An example of this is shown in Figure 1 (below).

The CNA has a number of things to do in a 15-minute increment. The CNA must prioritize and compromise, as there are no correct answers. A close look at the care recipients shows that both have special needs (figures 2 and 3).

Al Jorgenson has dementia, and if he is not checked on every 15 minutes, he will wonder off. If this happens, he could get hurt, or hurt someone else Figure 2. By knowing Al's needs, what he can and cannot do, the CNA can identify how Al can be independent and what makes him cooperative, such as turning on the radio.

Eunice, figure 3, also needs special care. Although she wants to be independent and autonomous, there are certain things she cannot do such as walking, and she can be argumentative and disagreeable. Because the CNA is new to the care facility, the CNA must navigate the relationship through effective communication and time management. By spending more time with Eunice, she builds rapport and trust, and Eunice becomes more autonomous.

However, if the CNA does not return to check on Al every 15 minutes, he wanders, and this throws the CNA, and other staff off their scheduled tasks, reducing trust, rapport, and autonomy with other residents. All the while the clock is running and tasks must be completed. There is no correct answer. The player must adapt and compromise.

Figure 6. Scheduled Tasks for a CNA

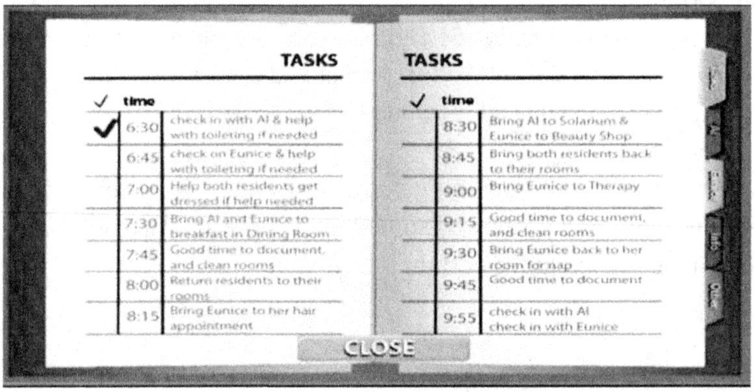

Figure 7. Al Jorgenson Profile

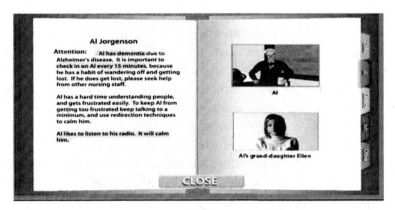

Figure 8. Eunice Howard Profile

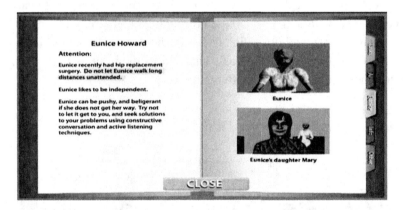

Throughout the day, the CNAs are asked to help their charges participate in the care facility, and this may include dressing, medications, activities, and transportation.

When the CNA spends time building trust, the CNA is rewarded with cooperation and independent behavior, i.e., Eunice will dress herself while the CNA goes to check on Al. The key is managing time and relations. When the residents cooperate, the CNA's job is easier, but the CNA must be careful to know when and where to spend time, otherwise Al may wander, or the CNA will not get time to perform the functional requirements of their job, such as tidying rooms or documenting resident behaviors for the care plan.

Documentation is also an important part of the CNAs job description. It is one of the ways that the business partner is capable of making data driven decisions. The accuracy of observation and interactions is of great importance, and a central part of their workday. According to the SME, the CNAs are trained to enter their observations into data collection programs in the care facility. This game emphasizes that practice (see figure 4 below).

Because observation and documentation are an important part of the CNAs functional role, they were emphasized as a game feature. When the CNA reports their observed ADL, the reports are scored for accuracy based upon their interactions with the residents. The ADL are modeled in game scenarios and scored for accuracy.

What we find through story mapping are opportunities for creating a flow model that can be validated through automation and augmentation through machine learning from learning reinforcement models. In the case of the game, the flow of the game play experience started with a simple set of challenges, where the player cared for two residents of the facility. For each resident there was a flow model for personalization in figure 10 (below).

As the player is onboarded into the game they are presented with choices as the game learns about their functional requirements. As the player moves to their first decision point, the algorithm uses the scoring criteria to assess and evaluate the level of challenge. Challenge is increased through greater ambiguity in resolving a situation (least/worst), and observing to see of the player takes short term actions which undermine their long-term goal. This is how the brief and debrief train the player, and then provide feedback after game play.

Figure 9. Documentation Screen at Kiosk

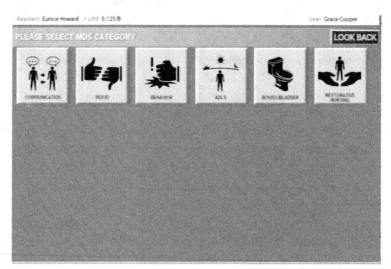

Figure 10. Flow model for challenges in game

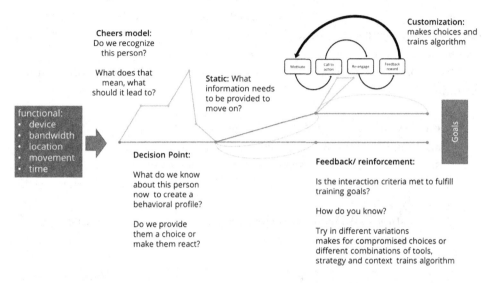

Cognitive Ethnography

The in game artifacts from cognitive ethnography (Dubbels, 2011, 2014; Hutchins, 2011) in care facilities operated by the business partner informed the story map and the flow model. Cognitive ethnography is efficacious for these activities, as it assumes that human cognition adapts to its natural surroundings (Hutchins, 1995, 2010) with emphasis on analysis of activities as they happen in context; how they are represented; and how they are distributed and experienced in space.

More specifically, cognitive ethnography emphasizes observation and key feature analysis of space, objects, concepts, actions, tools, rules, roles, and language. Study of these features can help the researcher determine the organization, transfer, and representation of information (Hutchins, 1995, 2010) and affords an initial qualitative approach which can inform game design, and methodologies leading up to the formation of construct validity (Cook & Campbell, 1979; Campbell & Stanley, 1966) through the creation of a nomological network (Cronbach & Meehl, 1955). Through gathering models of the space, social relations, and the conceptual space (what must be known), the game storyboard is informed, and the game criteria are defined and weighted for coding from the collected theories and tools.

The cognitive ethnography involved taking hundreds of pictures, analysis of artifacts such as schedules, task descriptions, documents, process, and protocol, and chains of interaction. In order to model a long term care facility, it was important to have a strong sense of a facility, and to analyze the gathered data using themes generated from the interviews (discovery process) with SMEs.

The SMEs had proposed a number of factors that could easily inform a construct. The work of the CNA shares some theoretical approaches and tools associated with nursing. These approaches and tools were examined for application, and resulted in a construct proposed here as the *Perceived Quality of Life* (PQoL) construct.

The PQoL construct is conceptualized as having four different skills that are operationalized and modeled in the game play:

- **Complex Relationship Building**: How the CNA interacts with residents.
- **Functional Performance**: Whether the CNA is able to complete scheduled tasks such as transport, assistance in ADL, and housekeeping.
- **Schedule Adherence**: Whether the CNA meets scheduled functional tasks in timely manner.
- **Observation and Documentation:** Of the Activities of Daily Living in the facility documentation software.

The *Perceived Quality of Life* (PQoL) construct is used here to inform the game play as well as performance in the care environment. PQoL is composed of a number of skills, theories, and assessment, just as the construct called Intelligence is mapped to specific skills, theories, and assessments. The value of developing a construct such as PQoL is that the developer can operationalize these skills, assessments to be modeled and tracked in the game as quantified scoring criteria. The relationships informing the PQoL construct are presented below in figure 5.

- The central cog in Figure 5, Psychological Needs, draws from Self------ Determination Theory (Deci & Ryan, 2000).

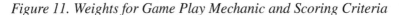

Figure 11. Weights for Game Play Mechanic and Scoring Criteria

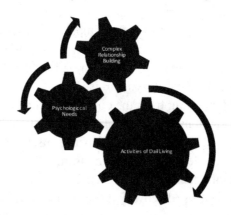

- The base measure, or bottom cog, draws from the Activities of Daily Living (Roper, Logan, & Tierney, 1980; 2000) and is hypothesized to be influenced through interpersonal relations.
- The interpersonal relations were modeled from operationalization of Complex Relationship Building (Bulechek, Butcher, & Dochterman, 2008)

This leads to two testable propositions:

1. When there is a high level of PQoL, the CNAs will enjoy their jobs more, have a longer tenure, and provide a higher quality of care.
2. When there is a high PQoL, the care recipients will improve in their general health and this should reduce training and care costs, with reduced dependence on medication for pain management, catastrophic care, and the need to replace and train CNAs.

Although it is useful to model hypothetical relationships in a game as in figure 5, it should not be enough. A next step to test the model can be taken, before it is modeled as a game mechanic. A conceptual model is a proposition that can be tested. Through testing these propositions, the relationships can be quantified to determine how they work proportionally. This can be done with paper and pencil models for what is called discount usability (Kane, 2003; Nielsen, 1994, 2009; Pagulayan, Steury, Fulton, & Romero, 2005).

Ultimately, the developer must decide if the theories and assessments guiding the interactions being modeled in the game actually inform the training (Medlock, Wixon, Terrano, Romero, & Fulton, 2002). Thus, when the developer conducts analysis and attempts to use the outcomes of that analysis for developing game mechanics, such as weighting relationships between the Activities of Daily Living and Complex Relationship building and examine influence them as mediated by Self-Determination Theory, they are building theory. In the case of this game, the analysis of the initial concepts such as SDT and ADLS, they may find through observation and factorial regression, that they are actually theory building. They are building assessments, interventions, and theory contiguously. In this way, game design becomes a form of research methodology.

Assessment and Validity

Surface level validity is a useful beginning for serious game development, but it should only be considered a step towards having a valid assessment and a validated serious game. It should be considered a gamble to build a serious game on surface validity. A step towards certainty might include attempts at criterion validity. For example, criterion validity can be attempted through measuring learning outcomes with a game and correlating those outcomes with external tools such as formative and summative assessments. Playing the game may lead to improved outcomes with existing assessment tools.

Thus, the success of the game may be evaluated through external measures with criterion validity and reduce the likelihood of a Vegas Effect. However, there may not be assessment tools designed to evaluate, and research design is essential in using criterion validity. In this case, there are four different assessments that could be used to model and measure the PQoL construct. Since these assessment tools were developed to measure specific constructs:

Self-Determination Theory, Complex Relationship Building, and Activities of Daily Living, the use of these assessments may not provide the degree of validity and certainty necessary to avoid the Vegas Effect.

Correlation Does Not Imply Causation

There may be a number of factors that could influence the outcome of an assessment, and it is important to have some certainty that the game actually led to an improvement in outcomes that matter to the business partner. If the game was built to provide an experience, but not based upon the criteria of the external assessment, there is only correlation to support the efficacy of the game. When they play the game, there is an improvement on this assessment.

To really avoid the Vegas Effect, the serious game developer could develop for construct validity. A construct is a concept like intelligence, relationship building, or happiness. In the case of this game, the construct is called Perceived Quality of Life (PQoL). Validating a construct can require significant investment in time and money, however, some methods from psychometrics in the development process can be adopted to reduce time and cost, and reduce the probability of the Vegas Effect.

To do this, it may be in the interest of the developer and business partner to conduct some research and build construct validity. To do this, they can draw from existing assessment tools, and identify important traits for measurement, that lead to an improved Perceived Quality of Life (PQoL).

To ascertain validity in the PQoL constrict, two things need to be examined:

- The validity of the measuring tools (e.g. psychometric test, observational rubric, the scoring criteria in a game)
- The validity of the procedure of the study.

When we claim construct validity, we are essentially claiming that our observed pattern—how things operate in reality—corresponds with our theoretical pattern—how we think the world works. This is an important consideration for modeling activities in a game. To do this, we create a workflow pattern that fit a deductive/inductive framework:

- **Deductive:** Theory, hypothesis, observation, and confirmation.
- **Inductive:** Observation, pattern, and tentative hypothesis.

Most social research involves both inductive and deductive reasoning processes at some time in the project. It may be reasonable to look at deductive/inductive approaches as part of the development cycle.

To do this, the researcher should provide a theoretical framework for what is being measured, an empirical framework for how it is to be measured, and specification of the linkage between these two frameworks. This is called a nomological network.

The idea of creating nomological network in research came from Cronbach and Meehl (1955) in attempt to provide better assurance of construct validity. Although this was a theoretically sound position, Cronbach and Meehl did not provide a method for operationalizing a nomological network, and it was not until later that Campbell and Fiske (1959) provided the *Multi Trait Multimethod Matrix* (MTMM) for doing so.

Figure 12. Multi Trait Multi Method

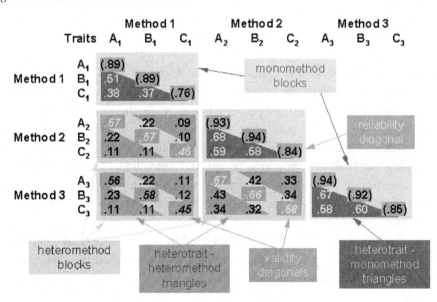

Through the use of this methodology, the researcher creates a matrix or table of correlations arranged to facilitate the interpretation of construct validity. The MTMM assumes that you measure each of several concepts by each of several methods (e.g., a paper and pencil test, a direct observation, a performance measure). The MTMM is a very restrictive methodology—ideally you should measure each concept by each method. The reasoning behind this is to know that you are measuring what you say you are measuring.

In the case of PQoL, the traits thought to be essential from the Activities of Daily Living (ADL) and Self-Determination Theory (SDT) are aggregated into three assessments. The central traits are then tabulated and compared for reliability and analysis is conducted for convergent and discriminant validity. These traits may be drawn from assessments from the ADL and SDT and the traits used in the matrix.

The new assessments can then be used investigate the influence of Complex Relationship Building on measures of ADLs and SDT. This provides an ability to compare multiple traits through multiple methods. The emphasis in using the MTMM is multiple replication of the same trait across method. In the case of our serious game, we provide in------game measures, observations from the workplace, and surveys of the caregivers and care recipients.

The idea is to provide three measures for construct validity. To construct an MTMM, you need to arrange the correlation matrix by concepts within methods. The figure shows an MTMM for three concepts (traits A, B and C) each of which is measured with three different methods (1, 2 and 3) Note that you lay the matrix out in blocks by method. Essentially, the MTMM is just a correlation matrix between your measures, with one exception—instead of 1's along the diagonal (as in the typical correlation matrix), substitute an estimate of the reliability of each measure as the diagonal.

As these relationships are validated, the game developer and the key stakeholders can depend upon a greater degree of certainty when modeling a game on the quantified relationships attained through this process. For example, the Nursing Interventions Classification suggests that more than one hour of CRB is necessary to promote insight and behavioral change (Bulechek, Butcher, & Dochtman, 2008, p.831). It may be useful to observe this relation to SDT and ADLs to validate the PQoL construct. When this step is taken, in game criteria presented though game mechanics can be modeled on ratios taken from the analysis of the observed behaviors and outcomes from the analysis tools.

Once the initial data collection is conducted in the observational setting, and the outcomes of the analysis used to create the game mechanics, the observational process can be turned inside out.

Figure 13. Design Flow of Serious Game

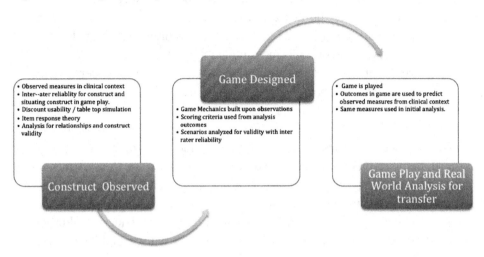

The developer begins with validation of the measures of their construct, in this case PQoL, and then uses the assessment and observation tools to account for quantitative relationships in the form of ratios and probabilities. Thus, if a CNA provides so many minutes in CRB, this may effect improvement in PQoL.

These relationships, qualitative and quantitative are then used to model the behavior in the game. A video game is a serious of calculations that serve as if------then statements, i.e., if this, then that. What is important is whether these relationships modeled in the game, have any external validity to the work environment. Do they extend to other populations and contexts? What we model in the game can be built from what we observe in the world. The effectiveness of what we model in the game depends upon the fidelity and veracity of what we model from.

New Perspectives in Serious Game Development

In this modified model of software development, the developer works with SMEs to define the testable hypothesis and learn how to turn them into tools and an intervention. In the case of the A Better Life© game, a prediction was made that specific communicative and autonomy--supporting behaviors would improve health outcomes and reduce employment attrition. The subject matter experts had asserted that many functionally capable CNAs are hired, but very few have the communication and relational skills. It was the belief of the SMEs that if the caregivers, certified nursing assistants (CNAs) were able to build caring relationships with the residents in the long term care facilities where they worked, several things would happen:

- The CNAs would enjoy their work more and be less likely to quit.
- The residents would build trust with the CNAs and would improve their response to care giving. Trust and improved communication could result in improved health outcomes as measured by the activities of daily living.
- Improved health outcomes could yield greater autonomy, less dependence on pain medication, and reduced catastrophic care.

These were testable statements and were turned into propositions for hypothesis testing. When we bring these worlds together in game development, we move back and forth between theory and observation—between what we think is happening in the world of caregiving and health, and what is actually going on in it— we are investigating a cause and effect relationship, we have a theory of what causes performance to change. For example, if we are testing a new educational program, we must have an idea of what it would look like and what we are ideally trying to affect and measure.

As an example, if we are interested in a behavioral act like active caregiving, or aspects of caregiving like listening, information gathering, or presence, each of these concepts, must be *operationalized*. This done through defining the construct and translate it into tools for criteria for success as assessment, operations, and procedures. It is no longer an idea or figment of our minds, it becomes an object or tool that others can observe and interact with for themselves. Thus, when we describe caregiving, we have an operationalized definition in the form of an assessment tool.

In simpler terms, we must question whether we are implementing the program we intend to implement, and whether we can measure the outcome we want to measure. Additionally, we need to question whether we operationalized the ideas of the cause and the effect operates with fidelity in the activities in the game. We will find ourselves in hot water if we ask those questions after the game is finished, and the answer to those questions is *no*. Quite simply, if we attempt to answer our guiding questions after the game is finished, it will have been too late. We may have to start again, and this can be expensive!

The utilization of the techniques from Lean Process, Design Thinking, and Psychometrics and Cognitive Ethnography provide the generative insights to develop a serious game that is capable of delivering training and providing data for ROI analysis. This is essential when considering the development of training, health, and medical software and evangelizing the value these process, and your team bring to your organization. Although many development teams will jump right into creating a prototype right away, your approach to user experience research can reduce costs and development time, and increase the quality of software.

REFERENCES

Al-Awar, J., Chapanis, A., & Ford, W. R. (1981). Tutorials for the first-time computer user. *IEEE Trans. Profess. Commun, 24*(1), 30–37.

Amazon.com. (n.d.). *The Lean Startup: How Today's Entrepreneurs Use Continuous Innovation to Create Radically Successful Businesses.* Retrieved June 17, 2018, from https://www.amazon.com/Lean-Startup-Entrepreneurs-Continuous-Innovation/dp/0307887898

Anguera, J. A., Boccanfuso, J., Rintoul, J. L., Al-Hashimi, O., Faraji, F., Janowich, J., ... Gazzaley, A. (2013). Video game training enhances cognitive control in older adults. *Nature, 501*(7465), 97–101. doi:10.1038/nature12486 PMID:24005416

Basak, C., Boot, W. R., Voss, M. W., & Kramer, A. F. (2008). Can training in a real-time strategy video game attenuate cognitive decline in older adults? *Psychology and Aging, 23*(4), 765–777. doi:10.1037/a0013494 PMID:19140648

Bavelier, D., Green, C. S., Han, D. H., Renshaw, P. F., Merzenich, M. M., & Gentile, D. A. (2011). Brains on video games. *Nature Reviews. Neuroscience, 12*(12), 763–768. doi:10.1038/nrn3135 PMID:22095065

Black, P., & Wiliam, D. (2009). Developing the theory of formative assessment. *Educational Assessment, Evaluation and Accountability, 21*(1), 5–31. doi:10.100711092-008-9068-5

Bogost, I. (2007). *Persuasive games: The expressive power of videogames.* MIT Press. Retrieved from https://books.google.ca/books?hl=en&lr=&id=vjbOnZw1wfUC&oi=fnd&pg=PP6&dq=ian+bo gost&ots=xkkxhHzOC2&sig=kFr1ICwyE-moUXdfqsN5uywhsM8

Buchanan, R. (1992). Wicked problems in design thinking. *Design Issues, 8*(2), 5–21. doi:10.2307/1511637

Doerr, J. (2018). *Measure what Matters: How Google, Bono, and the Gates Foundation Rock the World with OKRs.* Penguin.

Dubbels, B. (2011). Cognitive Ethnography. *International Journal of Gaming and Computer-Mediated Simulations, 3*(1), 68–78. doi:10.4018/jgcms.2011010105

Dubbels, B. (2014). Cognitive Ethnography as a Mixed-Method for Game User Research. *CHI 2014.*

Dubbels, B. (2016). Pedagogy & Play: Creating Playful Curriculum for Academic Achievement and Engaged Learning. In Learning, Education, and Games. (Vol. 2). Etc. Press.

Dubbels, B. R. (2012). *The Brain Is For Action: Embodiment, Causality, and Conceptual Learning with Video Games to Improve Reading Comprehension and Scientific Problem Solving*. University of Minnesota.

Dubbels, B. R. (2017). Gamification Transformed: Gamification Should Deliver the Best Parts of Game Experiences, Not Just Experiences of Game Parts. *Transforming Gaming and Computer Simulation Technologies across Industries*, 17–47. doi:10.4018/978-1-5225-1817-4.ch002

Eisenmann, T. R., Ries, E., & Dillard, S. (2012). *Hypothesis-driven entrepreneurship: The lean startup*. Academic Press.

Forster, M. (2009). *Informative Assessment—understanding and guiding learning*. Retrieved from http://research.acer.edu.au/research_conference/ RC2009/17august/11/

Frederiksen, D. L., & Brem, A. (2017). How do entrepreneurs think they create value? A scientific reflection of Eric Ries' Lean Startup approach. *The International Entrepreneurship and Management Journal*, *13*(1), 169–189. doi:10.100711365-016-0411-x

Gilad, I. (2018, February 1). *Why you should stop using product roadmaps and try GIST Planning*. Retrieved July 1, 2018, from https://hackernoon.com/why-i-stopped-using- product-roadmaps-and-switched-to-gist-planning-3b7f54e271d1?ref=http% 3A%2F%2Fproduct-frameworks.com

Green, C., & Bavelier, D. (2003). Action video game modifies visual selective attention. *Nature*, *423*(6939), 534–537. doi:10.1038/nature01647 PMID:12774121

Green, C. S., & Bavelier, D. (2008). Exercising Your Brain: A Review of Human Brain Plasticity and Training-Induced Learning. *Psychology and Aging*, *23*(4), 692–701. doi:10.1037/a0014345 PMID:19140641

Green, C. S., Benson, C., Kersten, D., & Schrater, P. (2010). Alterations in choice behavior by manipulations of world model. *Proceedings of the National Academy of Sciences of the United States of America*, *107*(37), 16401–16406. doi:10.1073/ pnas.1001709107 PMID:20805507

Hays, R. T. (2006). *The Science of Learning: A Systems Theory Perspective*. Universal-Publishers.

Hutchins, E. L. (2011, December 15). *Cognitive Ethnography*. Retrieved from http://hci.ucsd.edu/102b/

Jaeggi, S. M., Buschkuehl, M., Jonides, J., & Perrig, W. J. (2008). Improving fluid intelligence with training on working memory. *Proceedings of the National Academy of Sciences of the United States of America, 105*(19), 6829–6833. doi:10.1073/pnas.0801268105 PMID:18443283

Kane, D. (2003). Finding a place for discount usability engineering in agile development: throwing down the gauntlet. In *Agile Development Conference, 2003. ADC 2003. Proceedings of the* (pp. 40–46). IEEE. Retrieved from http://ieeexplore.ieee.org/xpls/abs_all.jsp?arnumber=1231451

Kwong, A. W., Healton, B., & Lancaster, R. (1998). *State of siege: new thinking for the next decade of design. IEEE Aerospace Conference, 4*, pp. 85–93. doi:10.1109/AERO.1998.682158

Loftus, G., & Loftus, E. R. (1983). *Mind at Play: The Psychology of Video Games*. Basic Books.

Medlock, M. (2014, March). *History of Video Games User Research*. Keynote presented at the Games User Research Summit, San Francisco, CA. Retrieved from http://www.gamesuserresearchsig.org/gur-sig---library.html

Medlock, M. C., Wixon, D., Terrano, M., Romero, R., & Fulton, B. (2002). Using the RITE method to improve products: A definition and a case study. *Usability Professionals Association, 51*. Retrieved from http://www.computingscience.nl/docs/vakken/musy/RITE.pdf

Merzenich, M. M., Jenkins, W. M., Johnston, P., Schreiner, C., Miller, S. L., & Tallal, P. (1996). Temporal processing deficits of language-learning impaired children ameliorated by training. *Science, 271*(5245), 77–81. doi:10.1126cience.271.5245.77 PMID:8539603

Nielsen, J. (1994). Guerrilla HCI: Using discount usability engineering to penetrate the intimidation barrier. *Cost-Justifying Usability*, 245–272.

Nielsen, J. (2009). Discount usability: 20 years. *Jakob Nielsen's Alertbox*. Available at http://www. useit. com/alertbox/discount-usability. html

Pagulayan, R. J., Steury, K. R., Fulton, B., & Romero, R. L. (2005). Designing for fun: User-testing case studies. In *Funology* (pp. 137–150). Springer. Retrieved from http://link.springer.com/content/pdf/10.1007/1-4020-2967-5_14.pdf

Patton, J. (2002). Designing requirements: incorporating usage-centered design into an agile SW development process. In *Conference on Extreme Programming and Agile Methods* (pp. 1–12). Springer. 10.1007/3-540-45672-4_1

Patton, J., & Economy, P. (2014). *User story mapping: discover the whole story, build the right product.* O'Reilly Media, Inc.

Ries, E. (2011). *The lean startup: How today's entrepreneurs use continuous innovation to create radically successful businesses.* Crown Books.

Ries, E. (2012). *The lean startup methodology.* The Lean Startup.

Ries, E. (2013, May 22). *The Lean Start Up Methodology.* Retrieved May 22, 2013, from http://theleanstartup.com/principles

Smith, G. E., Housen, P., Yaffe, K., Ruff, R., Kennison, R. F., Mahncke, H. W., & Zelinski, E. M. (2009). A Cognitive Training Program Based on Principles of Brain Plasticity: Results from the Improvement in Memory with Plasticity-based Adaptive Cognitive Training (IMPACT) Study. *Journal of the American Geriatrics Society, 57*(4), 594–603. doi:10.1111/j.1532-5415.2008.02167.x PMID:19220558

Squire, K. (2005). *Game-based learning: Present and future state of the field.* Masie Center e-Learning Consortium. Retrieved from https://pantherfile.uwm.edu/tjoosten/ LTC/Gaming/Game-Based_Learning.pdf

Timeline of psychology. (2015, February 17). In *Wikipedia, the free encyclopedia.* Retrieved from http://en.wikipedia.org/w/index.php?title=Timeline_of_ psychology&oldid=647514853

Waterfall model. (2018, June 3). In *Wikipedia.* Retrieved from https://en.wikipedia. org/w/index.php?title=Waterfall_model&oldid=844245639

Wiliam, D. (2007). Changing classroom practice. *Educational Leadership, 65*(4), 36.

Wiliam, D., & Thompson, M. (2007). *Integrating assessment with learning: what will it take to make it work?* Retrieved July 4, 2012, from http://eprints.ioe.ac.uk/1162/

Womack, J. P., & Jones, D. T. (1997). Lean thinking—banish waste and create wealth in your corporation. *The Journal of the Operational Research Society, 48*(11), 1148–1148. doi:10.1057/palgrave.jors.2600967

Chapter 2

Design Principles for Online Role Play Simulations to Address Groupthink Tendency in Professional Training:
An Exploration

Lawrence Leung
Hong Kong Police College, Hong Kong

Nancy Law
University of Hong Kong, Hong Kong

ABSTRACT

Decision making for professionals in crisis situations can be highly stressful and mission critical. It is a kind of naturalistic decision making (NDM), characterized by highly fluid situations under great stress and uncertainty and involving interprofessional teams. A major challenge to the effective handling of crisis situations is the tendency for the personnel involved to ignore alternatives and make irrational decisions, a phenomenon referred to as Groupthink. This chapter reports on a case study of the application of a set of design principles for an online role play simulation (RPS) in addressing Groupthink in crisis management professional training. The training effectiveness on participants' Groupthink tendency was investigated using Bale's interaction process analysis (IPA). The design principles underpinning the RPS training system is discussed in light of the findings.

DOI: 10.4018/978-1-5225-7461-3.ch002

INTRODUCTION

In general, a crisis is a major event, which can bring damaging effects to individuals, groups, organisations and even society. Crisis management is a process for an organisation to deal with such critical events. However, there is no official or agreed definition for crisis among researchers. According to Oxford English Dictionary, crisis is a state of change, uncertainty, which can either become better or worse. Hermann (1963) states that there are three conditions for the occurrence of crisis: there exists a severe danger to the organisation's survival, there is a very short period of time to act, and the situation will become worse if the further development of the situation is not correctly anticipated. A fundamental characteristic of crisis is its ill-structuredness. Billings, Milburn, and Schaalman (1980) also point out that crisis can be disruptive, and no one can be fully prepared for a crisis because of its unpredictability. Coombs (2007) summarises four key characteristics of crisis from previous research. First, crises are low-probability events and are thus hard for decision-makers to even have the motivation to plan for them. Therefore, management will normally start planning only when the organisation has been hit by a severe crisis. Second, crises can induce severe damage or loss. The extent of the damage may go far beyond an organisation or even a country, such as in case of natural disasters like earthquakes and tsunamis. Third, the cause-effect relationships of crises are generally not easily identifiable. Because of this ambiguity, it is not easy to pinpoint even if the cause of the crisis is due to negligence. Fourth, crisis management requires quick and effective decision-making. If the organisation cannot respond with a quick and effective decision-making process, the crisis may rapidly intensify, resulting in significant damage and loss.

Crisis management poses great challenges for professionals who have to handle crisis situations due to their inherent uncertainty, as both problems and consequences are not well understood, at least at the time of occurrence. If crisis decision-makers are not well prepared both mentally and organisationally, the consequences could be chaos management rather than crisis management (Boin, 't Hart, Stern and Sundelius, 2005). Since each crisis has its own specific context and conditions, there is no single or predefined solution even for the same kind of problem. Therefore, decision-makers have to be mentally prepared through previous experience or training. Under such circumstance, previous crisis experience can offer lessons for learning, but not as solutions to be modelled (Flin, 1996). In other words, crisis personnel should learn something from previous crisis experience, but observations alone have little value in handling crisis. There is a difference between procedural operations in crisis management training and strategic level crisis decision-making. For example, it is essential for a fire-fighter to practise and learn how to extinguish a fire through step-by-step instructions, which are usually well-defined and relatively routine. This kind of skills can be acquired through practicing the procedures. On the other hand, crisis management at a more strategic level cannot simply follow a routine process or predefined schema, such as in following the crisis management process adopted during the fatal fire at the London King's Cross underground railway station in 1987. That operation involved multiple government units such as police, fire and paramedic personnel, and the aspects to be handled in the crisis was complex and dynamic (Boin, 't Hart, Stern and Sundelius, 2005). This kind of crisis requires strategic level management for effective handling.

Due to the complexity and time constraints, as well as the non-routine nature of the problems, strategic level crisis management requires thinking out of the box and flexible decision-making (Borodzicz, 2005). Unlike procedural instructions, strategic level crisis management training should help learners to understand that there is more than one solution to resolving a crisis, and to encourage creative thinking in the decision-making process. The objective of crisis management training is to develop learners' ability to solve problems that require different adaptations to rapidly changing situations.

Sniezek, Wilkins, and Wadlington (2001) summarise the following challenges in crisis management training. First, crises do not occur frequently or regularly such that learning from direct experience in a specific crisis situation is not possible. Second, it is impossible for learners to test the causal relationships in crisis processes, as these are non-deterministic and complex. Third, the conditions in real crises are not favourable for training or observation. Fourth, as each crisis has its own unique features, the skills of crisis management cannot be generalised to all kinds of crises. Fifth, there is a need for crisis management personnel to continuously update their knowledge and skills continuously due to the dynamic nature of crisis environments, changes in regulations and technologies for managing crises.

GROUPTHINK

Groupthink is a term coined by Janis in 1972 from his book *Victim of Groupthink*. Groupthink is what happens when a group fails to make effective decisions due to group pressures that lead to a deterioration of "mental efficiency, reality testing, and moral judgment" (p. 9). Under the influence of groupthink, constructive ideas and alternatives offered by one group may be ignored by members of another group, and irrational actions may be taken because of stereotypic perceptions of each other across groups. Group cohesiveness refers to the attractiveness a group has for its members. A group could be any collection of people, friends or even a government. In summary, groupthink occurs when there is pressure for conformity towards consensus. Cohesiveness and conformity affect a group's ability to analyse and make judgments, resulting in poor decision-making. Victims of groupthink hence lose their ability to engage in creative and independent thinking. Janis's groupthink model (illustrated in Figure 1) is adopted to guide this study.

Janis's groupthink model is based on his analyses of historical decision-making activities in government policy-making committees or groups and supported by the associated content analysis of several political-military fiascos. The latter includes: Nazi Germany's decision to invade the Soviet Union (1941), US's failure to be prepared for the Japanese attack on Pearl Harbour (1941), the immature decision to launch the Bay of Pigs invasion in Cuba (1961), the stalemate in the North Korean War (1950), the escalation of the Vietnam War (1975) and the Watergate Cover-up scandal (1972). In general, the term groupthink describes a problematic decision that occurs when a group makes faulty decisions due to group pressure, without going through discussion, testing and exercising discrete judgment. Janis further explains that victims of groupthink neglect the seeking of alternatives, taking irrational actions to attack people of other groups. In addition, the hierarchical nature, rank cautiousness of law enforcement agencies and the existence of social cohesiveness in

Figure 1.

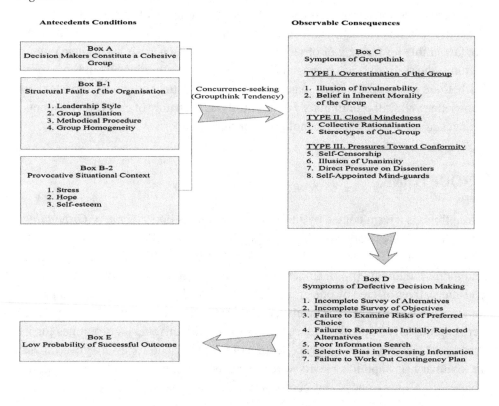

crisis management teams can also increase the possibility of groupthink (Rosander, Stiwne and ranstorm, 1998). In addition, the high stress levels due to uncertainty, ill-defined goals and high stakes of the decisions can increase the rigidity of decision-making, and reduce the motivation to find alternatives, leading to poor decision-making. Other factors that can induce groupthink include over-evaluation, isolation, and homogeneity among members.

Training through role play simulations (RPS) is a possible method to foster critical decision-making skills and reduce decision error or groupthink (Boin et. al., 2005). In order to make the training more realistic, the simulations should induce psychological processes to be similar to those that are experienced during an actual crisis (Salas, Bowers and Rhodenizer, 1998). Acute stress is a state that happens in situations of potential harm, time pressure, and arousal. Therefore, it is especially important that crisis management training can provide learners with a high degree of psychological fidelity in experiencing stress in decision-making. In RPS, learners can practise crisis management in a realistic environment that is safe to make mistakes, and to learn from those mistakes.

ROLE PLAY SIMULATIONS

The conventional way of transferring crisis management knowledge is through lectures that provide general knowledge of the necessary skills. Knowledge, either implicit or explicit, is emphasised as the skills learned can be applied to real crises. However, traditional crisis management training in the form of classroom lectures and presentations mainly focuses on individual tasks such as getting a situation update report from site officers using an agreed protocol. The communication mode is mostly one-way and top-down from trainer to trainees. Moreover, the conventional training is more focused on the responsibilities of the team members, rather than on the team aspects in the process. Role Play Simulation (RPS) is a useful technique for fostering virtual learning processes. It takes inspiration from "situated constructivism" approaches, which state that an educational experience has to be realistic for learners to observe and reflect critically (Winn, 1997).

Effective decision-making is essential for crisis decision-makers handling critical incidents, as serious consequences, including high casualty may be involved. In addition, crisis incidents are always dynamic and scenario-based. As such, the effectiveness of crisis management training through lecturing alone is very limited. Instead of individually focused, role plays offer experiential learning opportunities that are team- and scenario-based, allowing participants to evaluate their own competencies based on explicit behaviour in authentic contexts. Hence, RPS has become an integral component in assessment and training of crisis management in many law enforcement agencies, particularly for the resolution of high-risk problems without using violence (Schneid and Collins, 2001).

Online Role Play Simulations

Online role play simulation, a special form of Computer Supported Collaborative Learning (CSCL) facilitated by a set of technologies in an online environment designed to support and structure group interactions for the purpose of information exchange, problem solving and decision-making. Through the development of various scenarios, the crisis decision process can be realised and monitored. Online RPS supports activities such as idea creation, message exchange, project planning, document preparation, joint planning and decision-making, which are usually provided by Group Support Systems (Poole and DeSanctis, 1989).

Various forms of Online RPS have become increasingly popular in education and training. Online RPS is different from earlier forms of computer-based RPS in that the former mediate interactions among learners via computers rather than offerings interactions between an individual learner and a computer simulation model (Wills and McDougall, 2008). The support provided by online RPS platforms range from simple text discussions to video games, e-simulations, social media and multi-user virtual environments such as Second Life, and the possibilities are widening all the time (Wills, Leigh and Ip, 2011). McLaughlan and Kirkpatrick (2005) also observe that the scope of online RPS can be widened to include inter-location and international interactions, as well as augmentation with web-based information, multimedia and computer-based information management.

Although physical embodiment and immediacy are lost in the translation of face-to-face RPS to online formats, Wills, Leigh and Ip (2011) claim that online RPS retains the pedagogical power of face-to-face RPS. In addition, the possibilities of online interactions for asynchronicity and anonymity offer distinct advantages for learning (Freeman and Capper, 1999). Face-to-face RPS cannot be sustained for long periods and demands spontaneous action, with little time for planning or analysis before action, and less opportunity for reflection. In contrast, online RPS can stretch over several weeks, providing more opportunity for research, data gathering, reflections on the implications and consequences of actions taken, consolidation and internalisation.

Anonymity can break down hierarchies that dominate typical meetings and equalise the participation of all group members. Freeman and Capper (1999) argue that online RPS, because of the anonymity of the interactions, is particularly well-suited to those with learning disadvantages in face-to-face role plays, such as shyness, timidity and lack of self-confidence. Anonymity can also be helpful to learners whose mother language is not the language used in the role play as it can reduce self-consciousness of the language problem, thereby promoting creativity and imagination.

Based on the Project EnROLE, an Australian project on adoption of role-based e-Learning in university education, Wills et al. (2009) identified the following as key features to be attended to in the design of online RPS:

1. **Learning Objective:** To increase the understanding of human interactions and dynamics in real world situations;
2. **Role Assignment:** Learners play the role of some else, so that he or she can learn in a situated environment from others' perspectives;
3. **Task Authenticity:** Learners undertake authentic tasks as in real life contexts during role play;
4. **Task Design Requirement:** To focus learners' attention on role interactions, so as to foster collaboration, debate or negotiation;
5. **Interactions Among Roles:** Mainly carried out an online in the RPS environment;
6. **Learning Outcomes Targeted:** Are assessable and can encourage reflection from learners.

Conventional face-to-face role play approaches have serious limitations in crisis management training, such as maintaining realism and involvement of large amounts of resources in the form of manpower and props for scenario setting. Moreover, only a small number of officers can be trained in such settings. Advanced online technologies can reduce these limitations. There are three major technology components in an online RPS:

1. An immersive multimedia interface,
2. A crisis simulator, and
3. A critiquing system (Sniezek, Wilkins, Wadlington and Baumann, 2001).

In online RPS, the term "simulation" often refers to a number of technical implementations used to mimic social, political, economic, and/or psychological processes. Here, learners participate in the simulation rather than directing it (Portney and Cohen, 2006).

In contrast to other simulations such as stock market simulations or role play games, which allow participants or learners to set parameters, start a simulation, and see what happens as events unfold over time, participants of online RPS have no parameters to set and only the facilitator can start a simulation. Although online role-play decisions may be flexible, the flexibility is not in the hands of learners. Learners participate in the simulation and make one or more decisions that influence an outcome (Borodzicz, 2005). Online RPS may allow simulation administrators the flexibility to modify the simulations systematically and analyse how different interactions might influence decisions and their learning outcomes (Portney and Cohen, 2006).

In crisis management training, online RPS allows trainers or teachers to create synthetic or artificial crisis situations to teach participants about the appropriate decisions they should make and their underlying processes without any pre-set consequences. It requires participants to play roles in order to deliver simulation materials and to facilitate decision-making skills under stress through computer-mediated interactions.

GROUPTHINK FOCUSED DESIGN PRINCIPLES FOR ONLINE RPS SYSTEMS

The Naturalistic Decision-making (NDM) approach examines how people make decisions in natural settings, which can be difficult to reproduce in experimental laboratory studies. It supports explorations of collaboration and cooperation between people, between people and systems, as well as situations involving diagnosis, planning, supervision and control processes (Klein et al. 1993). Four principles have been formulated based on the literature review in our design of the online Role Play Simulation platform to address the problems of Groupthink. These principles also ensure that the online Role Play Simulation platform can support holistic observations of the participants' interactions according to the Groupthink model and analyse the Groupthink tendency of participants during training. The following is a description of the design principles we have adopted in this study.

The first principle requires that the platform setting must be able to simulate real-world situations in terms of the working environment and communication protocols for the training context. According to Klein (1993), the importance of naturalistic settings is frequently ignored in decision-making research. Real world settings are particularly important and essential for studying Groupthink, given the typically stressful and high stakes situations and the uncertain dynamic environments involved (Janis 1982).

The second principle stipulates that participants must be assigned specific roles and that the assignment must be made anonymously. Anonymity ensures that all participants can enact the roles assigned and practise the corresponding communication protocols in decision-making without interference from pre-existing roles and relationships among participants in their actual workplace. It is essential that participants can play the role of someone else and think from others' perspectives (Wills et al. 2009).

The third principle concerns the design of the communication platform in the RPS online system. There should be no rules or platform limitations that restrict communication. Further, all communications need to be recorded for the Groupthink tendency analysis using IPA (to be described in a later section). According to Dickens (2003), when groups become too close, the quality of decision-making may suffer from the lack of intense discussion. Cornelius, Gordon, and Harris (2011) suggest that the anonymity of online RPS can also encourage open discussion and argument. In fact, open discussion and argument can reduce the tendency of Groupthink (Janis 1982). Hence, this unrestricted environment can promote creative thinking, encourage collaboration, argument and information exchange during decision-making. The recorded transactions are very useful during debriefing to provide elaborations of the Groupthink tendency, and allow discussions on the remedies for problematic issues of Groupthink.

The fourth principle requires the platform to allow facilitators to change or adjust scenario settings according to the development of the episode. This would allow the training the flexibility to engage participants in more or less challenging tasks in a situated environment. Participants may thus be able to experience during training evolving and increasingly treacherous scenarios as in real world situations.

THE DESIGN FEATURES OF THE ONLINE RPS USED IN THE STUDY

Crisis management simulation should also produce the same emotional experiences and responses as in a real crisis scenario, such as frustration, stress, time pressure and uncertainty (Borodzicz, 2005). In order to set up a realistic crisis scene, the design of the online RPS and crisis scenario should be treated as high-threat, high-surprise event and has to be solved within a limited time frame. In addition, Gredler (1992) suggests that there are four essential elements in building a RPS: role assignment, background information, stimulus to learner's responses and reaction to learner's actions. Gredler further suggests that simulations should also facilitate both learner's reflective reaction and the generation of new thinking.

Janis's (1982) suggestion for the avoidance of groupthink provides the basic concepts for the design of the online RPS platform to be developed in this study. Janis suggests that acceptance of criticism can reduce the tendency of groupthink, as this provides a social climate within which learners are able to discuss and express their opinions freely without any penalty or restriction. In order to achieve this, the platform should be able to eliminate the physical organisational hierarchy during the training. The environment should also allow learners to enact their assigned roles using all available channels of communication provided on the platform. In addition, learners should be able to access external information or references. The key design concepts and features of the online RPS to implement Janis's suggestion in the avoidance of groupthink is summarised in Table 1.

In the design of the online RPS system, the appropriate selection and design of technology is critical to ensure that the learning environment and tasks provide the necessary learning experience. Otherwise the training effectivness would be jeopardized. From the previous work by Miranda (1994), Bostrom and Anson (1992), groupthink tendency may be reduced by applying appropriate technologies. The reduction of groupthink is achieved by decreasing the occurrence of certain antecedent conditions (such as cohesiveness among team members and group homogeneity) and procedural conditions of groupthink (such as few alternatives examined and discouragement of dissent). The design features adopted in the online RPS used in this study to tackle groupthink tendency (summarized in Table 2) has taken the above into consideration.

Table 1. RPS design concepts and skill development objectives to tackle groupthink

Skills to Avoid Groupthink (Janis, 1982)	Behavioral Indicators	Supportive RPS Design Features
Acceptance of criticism	• No restriction on discussions • No rules or restrictions for decision-making / discussion • No penalty for criticism	• Physical organisational hierarchy should not exist, but learners have to act according to the roles assigned • Communication tool/channel is available to all learners
Impartial leadership	• Each member should have the same right of speech • Leaders should not have any stating preferences, expectation or specific solutions that he or she would like to see accepted	• Anonymity • Access to external information is available
Seek peer feedback on plans/ decisions	• Double checking of plans or decisions by other team members • Welcome devil's advocate	• Peer review and argumentation • Group decision
Seek expert input	• Willing to seek external sources of information • Awareness of expertise relevant to the situation	• Access to external information is available • Upon request, expert is available to give advice anonymously.
Prepare for contingency	• Prepare for the worst case scenario	• Preparation of a contingency plan as a required written group assignment
Openness before consensus	• Hold review meetings for any critical consensus • Encourage argument/expression of conflicting views on critical issues	• No restriction on topics for discussion • Equal communication right for all • Facilitator gives credit for open sharing of ideas

Table 2. Design features of the online RPS mapped to conditions for groupthink reduction

Design Feature of the Online RPS	Conditions for Reduction of Groupthink Tendency (Miranda, 1994; Bostrom and Anson, 1992; Nunamaker et al., 1991)
Anonymity on the computer network	*Antecedent conditions* Directive leadership Group homogeneity *Procedural conditions* Discouragement of dissent Few alternatives examined
Simultaneous input / Group communication and Synchronous communication	*Antecedent conditions* Directive leadership Group homogeneity Nature of task *Procedural conditions* Discouragement of dissent Few alternatives examined
Process structuring / Scenario builder (role play platform design)	*Antecedent conditions* High cohesiveness Group homogeneity Nature of task *Procedural conditions* Discouragement of dissent Few alternatives examined
Extended information processing capacity / Web hosted resources	*Antecedent conditions* Nature of task *Procedural conditions* Few alternatives examined
Access to external information / Internet search and Anonymous expert connection (Intranet)	*Procedural conditions* Perception of invulnerability Lack of expert advice
Written input / Asynchronous or synchronous communication	*Antecedent conditions* High cohesiveness Directive leadership *Procedural conditions* Few alternatives examined
Electronic recording	*Antecedent conditions* Nature of task
Public screen	*Antecedent conditions* High cohesiveness Group homogeneity Nature of task Directive leadership

RESEARCH DESIGN AND DATA COLLECTION

In this study, 16 trainees from the Hong Kong Police College participated in an online RPS exercise as part of a 4-week crisis management training programme. In this exercise, trainees were randomly assigned to 4 different teams named Alpha (α), Beta (β), Gamma (γ) and Delta (δ) with specific functional roles in a crisis scenario. The teams were assigned to different rooms within the exercise vicinity without face-to-face contact. The facilitator (i.e. the exercise controller) located at the control room could communicate with the trainees in all the groups through a computer networked RPS platform called SIMS (Scenario-based Interactive RPS System). Participants did not know the scenario of the role play before the start of the exercise. SIMS provides all the simulated communication tools for professional training in decision-making, including chat-box, e-mail, beat radio, telephone and video conferencing. Trainees can use the tools provided to carry out all communications, decision-making and Command and Control operations during the role play simulation. In addition, the Controller can also send out instant multimedia information (such as TV news, video clips) according to scenario development and to enhance realism of the crisis situation. All role play interactions and communications are logged by the system for data analysis and debriefing.

The whole exercise was divided into two phases with two debriefings as illustrated in Figure 2. Trainees took part in two role plays in Phases I and II respectively. Each phase had the same duration of 2 hours. Before the commencement of Phase I, the participants had to complete a 40-question Groupthink Index (Glaser, 1993) questionnaire before the exercise commenced. Debriefing I was conducted after the completion of Phase I. In this 30-minutes session, the facilitator gave a short introduction on groupthink to participants. The participants then took a break before commencing Phase II. Debriefing II was the post-exercise discussion. The facilitator discussed with participants their experience throughout the entire exercise. At the end of the exercise, participants completed the Groupthink Index questionnaire again to find out if there have been any changes in participants' groupthink tendency.

Figure 2.

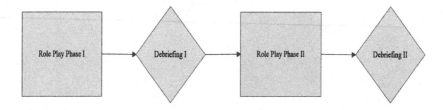

ANALYSIS OF RESULTS

Two instruments were used in this study to measure groupthink: Glaser's Groupthink Index (GTI) and Bales' Interaction Process Analysis (IPA).

Glaser's Groupthink Index

Groupthink Index (GTI) (Glaser, 1993) is a commercial instrument often used in management training to measure the groupthink tendency of an individual or a team. The 40-item questionnaire comprises eight sets of five items, each designed to measure one of the eight groupthink symptoms. Each item uses a 5-point Likert-scale with responses ranging from "almost never" to "almost always". Each groupthink symptom sub-category consisted of 5 questions, giving a maximum score of 25 for each groupthink symptom. According to the GTI scale, a score for "very insignificant" groupthink is less than 93, a score for "insignificant" groupthink is 94-111, a score for "moderate" groupthink is 112-129, a score for "significant" groupthink is 130-147, and a score equal to or over 148 indicates "very significant" groupthink. Glaser further suggests that for each symptom subcategory, a score for "very insignificant" groupthink is less than 8, a score for "insignificant" is 9-13, a score for "moderate" is 14-15, a score for "significant" is 16-17, and a score for "very significant" is 18-25. Hence GTI yields an overall groupthink index and sub-scale scores for each of the 8 groupthink symptoms. Table 3 presents the overall GTI scores of each team before and after the online RPS exercise, and the percentage improvement achieved.

The Groupthink Indices of the four teams were found to have been reduced from Significant to Moderate level after the exercise, but to different extents. The reduction in groupthink tendency indicates that online RPS may have contributed to the change. However, this can not be substantiated unless one can establish the link between online RPS behavior and change in groupthink tendency. The IPA analysis reported in the next section is to investigate this relationship.

Table 3. Pre- and post- GTI scores and percentage improvement achieved of the four teams

Team	Team Average (Glaser's Groupthink Index)		% of Improvement
	Pre-Role Play Simulation	Post-Role Play Simulation	
Alpha (α)	147	125	15.0
Beta (β)	139	127	8.6
Gamma (γ)	141	116	17.7
Delta (δ)	142	113	20.4

Bales' Interaction Process Analysis (IPA)

Interaction Process Analysis (IPA) is a generic method developed in 1950 by Robert F. Bales to analyse interactions in small groups. Bales' IPA is the first and most frequently used tool to study small group dynamics through analyzing interactions. It is a structured coding system to identify and examine task and socio-emotional communication activities in groups, based on the social psychological belief that group interactions are driven either by social or task needs (Bales, 1950). Bales' IPA consists of 12 specific behavioural categories nested within 4 overarching process categories as shown in Table 4. Three categories describe positive socio-emotional activities (Codes 1-3), three categories describe negative socio-emotional activities (Codes 10-12). Three describe active task activities (Codes 4-6), and three describe passive task activities (Codes 7-9). A total of 871 transactions recorded by the system. About 0.8% of the total transactions had input error or were incomplete statements with no logical meaning and was not transcribed. A total of 864 transactions (307 in Phase I and 557 in Phase II) were transcribed and analysed.

In Phase I, the percentages of task-based and social-emotional interactions were 78% and 22% respectively. The corresponding percentages for Phase II were 86% and 14%. From Table 5 and Table 6, the IPA category (code) with the highest mean is "Asks for information" in Phase I and "Gives information" in Phase II. On the other hand, the lowest mean is "Shows antagonism" for both phases. Moreover, the most frequent interaction categories were task-based. This indicates that exchange of information, suggestions and opinions were the predominant activities and not social-emotional interactions. In fact, this implies that the groups' crisis decision-making had gone through the processes of information gathering, discussion and teamwork, as expected from the literature (McGrath 1984). This distribution of IPA codes is significantly different from the study by Bales (1950), which was a face-to-face free form role play, but is similar to the studies by Hiltz (1978) on problem solving via computer conferencing.

The interactions among the four teams observed during the two phases (I & II) of the online RPS exercises are illustrated in Figure 3a-d. It should be noted that the percentages in these figures are computed with the total number of interactions during the corresponding phase as the denominator.

FINDINGS

Analyses of the group interactions using the IPA framework show indications of a reduction in Groupthink tendency of the participants after the online RPS exercise,

Table 4. Bales' 12 interaction categories (Adapted from Bales, 1950, p.9)

Code	Behavior Category	Type of Interaction
1	Shows solidarity – Raises other's status, gives help, encourages others, reinforces (rewards) contribution, greets others in a friendly manner, and uses positive social gesture.	Social Emotional: Positive Emotions
2	Shows tension release – Jokes, laughs, shows satisfaction, relives or attempts to remove tension, express enthusiasm, enjoyment, satisfaction.	
3	Agrees – Shows passive acceptance, acknowledges understanding, compiles, co-operates with others, and expresses interest and comprehension.	
4	Gives suggestion – Makes firm suggestion, provides direction or resolution, implying autonomy for others, attempts to control direction or decision.	Task: Giving (Neutral emotions)
5	Gives opinion: Offers opinion, evaluation, analysis. Expresses a feeling or wish. Seeks to analyse, explore, and enquire. Provides insight and reasoning.	
6	Gives information: Provides background or further information, repeats, clarifies, confirms. Brings relevant matters into the forum, acts and assists group focus.	
7	Asks for information: Asks for further information, repetition or confirmation. Acts used to request relevant information and understand the topic.	Task: Asking (Neutral emotions)
8	Asks for opinion: Asks for opinion, evaluation, analysis, or expression of feeling on the matter.	
9	Asks for suggestion: Asks for suggestion, direction, and possible ways of action. Requests for firm contribution, solution or closure to problem.	
10	Disagree: Shows passive rejection, formality, withhold help, does not support view or opinion, fails to concur with view, and rejects a point, issue or suggestion.	Social Emotional: Negative Emotions
11	Shows tension: Shows concern, apprehension, dissatisfaction or frustration. Persons interacting are tense, on edge. Acts that express sarcasm or are condemning.	
12	Shows antagonism: Acts used to deflate other status, defends or asserts self, purposely blocks another or makes a verbal attack.	

triangulating the same finding based on the pre- and post- exercise GTI survey. The findings from the analyses of group interactions are presented in this section.

Reduction of Cohesiveness

Due to the group homogeneity (all participants are police officers with similar years of service and training background), there is a high risk of intuitive social cohesiveness, which is an important antecedent condition for groupthink, a major challenge in crisis management decision-making. Effective communications in such context should

Table 5. Bales' IPA categories – sorted by mean (Phase I)

IPA Category (Code)	Mean	Std. Dev.
Asks for information (7)	15.5	3.9
Gives information (6)	11.8	3.9
Gives suggestion (4)	8.8	2.6
Asks for suggestion (9)	8.8	2.2
Agrees (3)	8.3	3.3
Gives opinion (5)	7.5	3.9
Asks for opinion (8)	7.3	1.5
Disagree (10)	3.3	1.9
Shows tension release (2)	2.5	1.7
Shows solidarity (1)	2.3	1.5
Shows tension (11)	1.0	0.8
Shows antagonism (12)	0.0	0.0

Table 6. Bales' IPA categories – sorted by mean (Phase II)

IPA Category (Code)	Mean	Std. Dev.
Gives information (6)	33.3	16.0
Asks for information (7)	21.8	4.5
Gives opinion (5)	17.3	6.6
Asks for opinion (8)	17.0	4.8
Gives suggestion (4)	16.3	8.1
Asks for suggestion (9)	13.8	2.2
Agrees (3)	9.8	3.3
Disagree (10)	5.3	5.0
Shows solidarity (1)	2.3	1.3
Shows tension release (2)	1.3	0.5
Shows tension (11)	1.3	1.3
Shows antagonism (12)	0.3	0.5

be basically task-based (Emmitt & Gorse, 2006). The results presented in Table 5 and 6 show that the amount of task-based communications (IPA 4-9) is higher than social-emotional communications (IPA 1-3 and IPA 10-12), which is reasonable for such situations. In fact, a high level of social-emotional communications is indicative of groupthink, as high social cohesion due to friendship or social ties may lead to

Figure 3. A-D

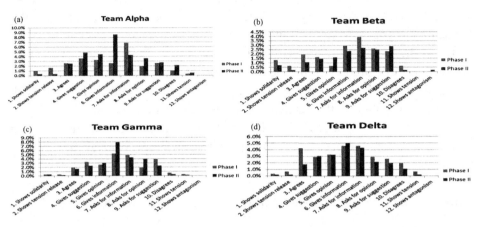

immature decisions, a phenomenon known as the "illusion of unanimity" (Cline, 1994). Table 7 summarizes the number and percentages of social-emotional and task-based communications across the four teams.

It can be seen that all teams have shown a decrease in social-emotional communication in Phase II, with the reduction varying from the smallest difference of 0.6% for Team Alpha, to a maximum of 4.4% for Team Delta. Team Beta, which showed the lowest gain in GTI between Phases I and II also contributed the lowest percentage (14.0% and 13.5% respectively) of task-based communication, when all the other teams contributed about 20% or more.

Reduction in the Risk of Directive Leadership

Anonymity in an online RPS allows for openness in communication, which can foster equal participation and hence reduce the danger of directive leadership and groupthink tendency (Miranda, 1994). From the interactions recorded by the system,

Table 7. Percentages* of social-emotional and Task-based communications among teams

		Team Alpha	Team Beta	Team Gamma	Team Delta
Phase I	Social-emotional	6.5%	4.6%	3.6%	7.8%
	Task-based	20.8%	14.0%	21.8%	20.8%
Phase II	Social-emotional	5.9%	2.3%	2.7%	3.4%
	Task-based	28.5%	13.5%	23.9%	19.7%

*N.B. All communications contributed by the four teams within one phase adds up to 100%.

it can be shown that all learners have actively involved in the exercise. Information seeking behavior (asking and giving information) constitute the most popular interaction categories. Asking and giving opinions and suggestions constitute behavior related to the seeking of alternatives (Emmitt & Gorse, 2006). The results show that both the total amount of interactions as well as the proportion constituted by task-based interactions have increased from 78% in Phase I to 86% in Phase II, with a corresponding drop in the percentage of interactions that were socio-emotional in nature. Janis (1972) suggests that information and alternative solution seeking interactions during the decision-making process contribute positively towards the avoidance of groupthink.

Facilitation of Procedural Process in Decision-Making

From the analysis IPA (4-6) – giving suggestions, opinion and information and IPA (7-9) – asking for information, opinion and suggestion, all teams have positive differences (comparison between phase I and Phase II of the exercise), which indicates that all teams engaged in all necessary processes for decision-making: fact finding, information gathering and decision-making (Emmitt & Gorse, 2006). Hence, it can be concluded that the teams were able to communicate through the SIMS platform to establish a structured process for crisis decision-making, which is considered to be a remedy for groupthink arising from lack of methodical procedures (Miranda, 1994).

In crisis communications, the "asking for" categories (IPA 7-9) are considered more constructive than "giving" categories (4-6), as more new ideas may be generated, giving more chances for the seeking of alternative solutions, which are essential in the reduction of groupthink tendency. As a whole, all teams have shown positive contributions in those categories as shown in Figure 3 (a-d). However, it is interesting that Team Beta has shown a high level of 6% increase in "Gives opinion" (IPA 5) but a relatively low score in GTI reduction. Subsequently, a review of the transactions was conducted, which found that the quality of the opinions given was not high and some opinions were not useful. This shows that while GTI and IPA analyses are helpful indicators, qualitative semantic analysis of the communication protocol is necessary to understand the actual quality of the interactions in relation to groupthink.

Promotion of Constructive Conflict in Crisis Communications

A high level of social cohesiveness is considered harmful for crisis decision-making as some good alternatives may be neglected. In fact, constructive or task-based conflict is necessary to ensure that the group will not jump to conclusions directly by simple "agreement" (Cline, 1994). By avoiding disagreements, group members may also overlook the vulnerability of a proposal. The Watergate cover-up scandal is considered a classic case of groupthink in the crisis management literature. Cline (1994) reports on a study using the IPA framework to analyze instances of agreement and disagreement in three transcripts presented by the prosecutors in the Watergate Scandal. The study found that interactions in the Watergate Scandal exhibited a much higher ratio of "agreement to disagreement" than those reported from similar analyses of non-groupthink cases, showing evidence that those involved in this case were trapped by groupthink.

Figure 4 presents the agreement-disagreement ratios for the Watergate case and the role plays in Phases I and II. Cline (1994) suggests that ratios higher than 2:1 are prone to groupthink. In the Watergate Scandal, the ratio is 5.2: 1, which is considered too high and risky. In the present study, the percentage of agreements in both Phases I and II were higher than the percentage of disagreements. Further, it can be seen that there is a sizeable decrease in "Agreement" from 10.7% in Phase I to 7.0% in Phase II, and also a slight decrease in "Disagreement" from 4.2% to 3.8%. As a result, the "agreement:disagreement" ratios for the two Phases were 2.8:1 and 2.2:1 respectively. As both ratios are higher than 2:1, this indicates inadequate constructive conflicts during the online RPS interactions. On the other hand, the decrease in this ratio also shows a reduction in groupthink tendency in Phase II, triangulating with the reduction in overall GTI reported earlier.

Table 8 presents the "agreement to disagreement" ratios for each of the four teams. It can be seen that the ratios are lower than that of the Watergate Scandal for all teams except Team Beta. In fact, the groupthink tendency for both teams Beta and Gamma are high. On the other hand, Team Alpha has the lowest "agreement to disagreement" ratio among teams. In addition, the relatively high level of antagonism interactions shown by Team Beta members is indicative of barriers to constructive discussions.

Figure 4.

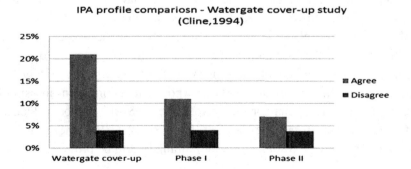

Table 8. Agreement:Disagreement Ratios for the teams during Phases I and II

	Team Alpha	Team Beta	Team Gamma	Team Delta
Phase I	2.7:1	3:1	3:1	2.2:1
Phase II	1.2:1	6.2:1	4.4:1	1.7:1
Difference (%)	-55.6	+106.7	+46.7	-22.7

Findings from this study show that online RPS can contribute positively to the reduction of groupthink tendency in crisis management training. SIMS provides a simulated environment to foster constructive discussions and provides a safe and authentic situation for crisis management training. However, it does also reveal wide variations in behavior and improvement across the different teams, which warrants further investigation.

LIMITATIONS OF THIS STUDY

The present study has shown the usability of the SIMS online RPS system for crisis management training and some indications of success in reducing participants' groupthink tendency. However, there are some important limitations in this study that needs to be addressed in future studies. First of all, although the number of interactions collected and analysed is relatively large, the number of teams and trainees participating in the exercise is small – only four teams and 16 trainees. Hence the findings from this study are only exploratory in nature, and may not be generalizable to a wider population.

The second limitation relates to participants' background. While the participants in this study are heterogeneous in terms of gender, age, culture, academic background and learning style, they were all law enforcement officers. This is different from actual crisis situations in which some of the teams would be from other agencies such as the fire department or medical emergency services. The interactions and results in this study may be influenced by the culture of the law enforcement profession, and may not be generalizable to real life crisis situations.

A third limitation relates to the ICT competence of the participants. Unlike conventional face-to-face role play, online RPS requires participants to have basic ICT skills to function effectively. In other words, online RPS can be a hurdle for participants (both facilitators and learners) who are less competent in using ICT. As a result, participants' behavior and performance in SIMS may be influenced by their ICT competence. In fact, a few learners have expressed this concern in the post-exercise questionnaire, and suggested that training should be provided beforehand to help them overcome such problems in order not to affect their participation in the RPS.

A fourth limitation relates to the fact that this study involves only one crisis management scenario. There could be differences in participant behavior and challenges to avoiding groupthink tendency due to the nature of the crisis.

While there are limitations to the generalizability of the findings from the present study, the fact that all task design, facilitation and interactions are recorded automatically in an online RPS system allows for much more systematic investigations on the pedagogical design and assessment of crisis management than would be possible in face-to-face RPS training. It is hoped that this study will stimulate further work in this area.

ENHANCING THE DESIGN OF ONLINE RPS

Both the data analysis and the facilitator's feedback indicate that the use of the SIMS online RPS system has been effective in providing an authentic simulated environment for crisis management training. There are distinctive advantages in using online instead of face-to-face RPS in crisis management training through the anonymity that online communications offer. On the other hand, the present SIMS system is designed to basically support synchronous interactions mimicking those in traditional face-to-face RPSs that have been used in past training situations. In reflecting on the observations and findings from the present study, we have seen further possibilities for enhancement of SIMS by incorporating asynchronous communications into the platform to foster deeper reflection between role plays and to support more effective debriefing.

Introducing Asynchronous Communication to Foster Reflection

In the current design, participants only have half an hour for the debriefing, which takes place immediately after the role play ends. Hence, much of what takes place during this time is for the instructor to explain what Groupthink is and to give comments on the students' performance. There is really no time for students to engage in deep reflection and learn from their experience in Phase I before launching into Phase II. With the addition of asynchronous communications, learners will have more opportunities to engage in reflection. In particular, they would be able to read their logged discourse during the RPS. They can also be asked to analyze and identify instances of groupthink, give justifications on their evaluation, and to give suggestions on how to avoid similar occurrences in the future.

Debriefing as a Blended Learning Process

The availability of automatic recording of interactions in online RPS is a valuable resource for conducting debriefing after each role play session. In contrast to face-to-face RPS, due to the lack of automated recording facilities, all interactions have to be recorded manually. In online RPS, facilitators can retrieve any interaction from the computer and display on a screen for discussion instantly. The facilitator can also select and compile recorded interactions into a knowledge database to support learning.

If the two phases of the online RPS can be conducted on different days, the debriefing process can also be conducted in two phases to allow for deeper reflection taking place between the two parts of the exercise. The first part can be conducted through asynchronous online discussions before the face-to-face debriefing. There are a number of advantages in adopting such an arrangement:

- The facilitator will have more time to prepare for the debriefing by reviewing the logged communication transactions to identify good sample excerpts for participants' exploration and discussion.
- Leaners may be able to seek expert advice or accessing external information and share with others during the online debriefing discussion.
- Some learners who are reluctant to speak up spontaneously in face-to-face discussions may be able to find their voice in asynchronous online media such as email or discussion forum.
- The online debriefing discussion can be further refined and summarized to form a useful knowledge database to be further developed through face-to-face debriefing that follows.

FINAL DISCUSSIONS

In this paper, a case study of using an online RPS platform designed according to the four theoretically grounded design principles for addressing groupthink in crisis management training is presented. The results show that participants have achieved a reduction of groupthink tendency after the Online RPS training. Moreover, the IPA analyses of the group interactions in the two phases of the RPS show evidence of reductions in cohesiveness, directive leadership, and increases in task interactions for decision-making and constructive conflict, which are all indicative of reduction in groupthink tendency.

Existing groupthink research mainly uses content analysis of retrospective information/ data or empirical experience in laboratory settings as their basis for understanding the interaction processes. Very often, only a partial model is examined. This study shows that the online RPS developed on the basis of the four design principles offers an alternative approach to groupthink research. Online RPS can support the design of holistic scenarios for crisis management training such that the different stages in the exercise can be visualised by researchers and facilitators. Furthermore, the interactions can be automatically recorded and analyzed later to reveal groupthink tendency. In fact, due to the complexity of the groupthink model, researchers using traditional methods generally only focus on a partial selection of behavior during the whole process to record and study. Online RPS can serve both as a training platform as well as a research tool for holistic groupthink research. Researchers can explore the effect of different settings and scenario designs on groupthink behavior and how to reduce groupthink using online RPS. In addition, the same set of recorded data can be used by different researchers to explore different aspects of the interactions and research questions. In this final section, we review the four design principles for online RPS systems we formulated and adopted in the light of the research findings and latest technology developments.

Virtual reality (VR) technology has become much more sophisticated and accessible, providing an alternative technology platform for the development of online RPS that can provide more authentic simulations of real world situations. In fact, the first author has piloted the deployment of VR in online RPS in late 2017 with the objective to improve the realism of the scenario. Using this pilot system, participants can observe the key training scenes in 360 degrees with the VR headsets provided. It is not within the scope of this chapter to report on this pilot study in any detail. Overall, participants agree that they can have an immersive feeling of the scene and the degree of realism is increased. On the other hand, the risk of cognitive overload may also increase. Cognitive overload occurs when a large amount of information that has exceeded an individual's capacity to process (Mayer and Moreno, 2003). Shrivastav et al. (2013) point out that the use of advanced features of educational technologies can induce the risk of cognitive overload, as these features could provide a more complex and information-rich environment. Unfortunately, current research literature cannot yet provide definitive guidelines on the relationship between cognitive overload and VR technology, or whether the adoption of VR technology is likely to enhance the training effectiveness of online RPS for crisis management training.

On the second design principle, all participants agreed that anonymity could encourage positive argument or discussion. To enhance the level of anonymity, the physical layout of the training venue is important. The participants suggested refurnishing the training facility so that the syndicate rooms can be separately located.

Thirdly, in terms of the design of the communication platform in the RPS system, we find that storage size and stability of recording module is very important. Quality of the recording as well as the ease of review can improve the effectiveness in debriefing. Further enhancements can include support for the facilitator in reviewing and analyzing dialogues from previous training exercises using the same scenario. A training database could also be established in future systems for better knowledge management in system design and facilitation.

Fourthly, feedback from our study indicates that the facilitator support aspect of the system can be further enhanced by improving the facilitator user interface to make it more user-friendly and efficient in monitoring the participants' interactions and scenario development. This would avoid the need for external technical support during the training exercise, and hence reduce the possibility of interruption while the facilitator makes sense of the situation. In fact, any interruption for whatever reason could greatly damage the effectiveness of the whole training exercise.

REFERENCES

Bales, R. F. (1950). *Interaction Process Analysis*. Cambridge, MA: Addison-Wesley.

Billings, R. S., Milburn, T. W., & Schaalman, M. L. (1980). A Model of Crisis Perception: A Theoretical and Empirical Analysis. *Administrative Science Quarterly*, *25*(2), 300–306. doi:10.2307/2392456

Boin, A., 't Hart, P., Stern, E., & Sundelius, B. (2005). *The Politics of Crisis Management: Public Leadership under Pressure*. Cambridge, UK: Cambridge University Press. doi:10.1017/CBO9780511490880

Borodzicz, E. P. (2005). *Risk, Crisis and Security Management*. West Sussex, UK: John Wiley & Sons Ltd.

Bostrom, R. P., & Anson, R. G. (1992). *A Case for Collaborative Work Support Systems in a Meeting Environment* (Unpublished working paper). Department of Management, University of Georgia.

Cline, R. J. W. (1994). Groupthink and the Watergate cover up. The illusion of unanimity. In L. R. Frey (Ed.), *Group Communication in Context: Studies of Natural Groups*. Lawrence Erlbaum Associates.

Coombs, T. (2007). *Ongoing crisis communication: Planning, managing and responding*. Thousand Oaks, CA: Sage Publications.

Cornelius, S., Gordon, C., & Harris, M. (2011). Role engagement and anonymity in synchronous online role play. *International Review of Research in Open and Distance Learning, 12*(5), 57–73. doi:10.19173/irrodl.v12i5.923

Dickens, P. (2003). Don't Be Brainwashed by Groupthink. The Scotsman, p. 9.

Emmitt, G. E., & Gorse, C. A. (2006). *Communication in construction teams*. London: Spon, Taylor & Francis.

Flin, R. (1996). *Sitting in the Hot Seat: Leaders and Teams for Critical Incidents*. Chichester, UK: Wiley.

Freeman, M., & Capper, J. M. (1999). Exploiting the web for education: An anonymous asynchronous role simulation. *Australian Journal of Educational Technology, 15*(1), 95–116.

Glaser, R. O. (1993). *Groupthink index: can we manage our agreements? Facilitator guide*. Organization Design and Development.

Gredler, M. E. (1992). *Designing and evaluating games and simulations*. London: Kogan Page.

Hermann, C. (1963). Some consequences of crisis which limit the viability of organizations. *Administrative Science Quarterly, 8*(1), 61–82. doi:10.2307/2390887

Hiltz, S. R. (1978). The impact of a new communications medium upon scientific research communities. *Journal of Research-Communication Studies, 1*, 111–124.

Janis, I. L. (1972). *Victims of Groupthink: A Psychological Study of Foreign Policy Decisions*. Boston: Houghton Mifflin.

Janis, I. L. (1982). *Groupthink* (2nd ed.). Boston: Houghton Mifflin.

Mayer, R. E., & Moreno, R. (2003). Nine ways to reduce cognitive load in multimedia learning. *Educational Psychologist, 38*(1), 43–52. doi:10.1207/S15326985EP3801_6

McGrath, J. E. (1984). Groups: Interaction and Performance. Englewood Cliffs, NJ: Prentice-Hall, Inc.

Mclaughlan, R. G., & Kirkpatrick, D. (2005). *Online text-based role play-simulation: The challenges ahead.* Simulation Industry Association of Australia.

Miranda, S. M. (1994, February). A voidance of groupthink: Meeting management using group support systems. *Small Group Research*, *25*(1), 105–136. doi:10.1177/1046496494251007

Orasanu, J., & Fischer, U. (1997). Finding decisions in natural environments: the view from the cockpit. In C. E. Zsambok & G. Klein (Eds.), *Naturalistic Decision Making*. Mahwah, NJ: Lawrence Erlbaum.

Poole, M. S., & DeSanctis, G. (1992). Micro level Structuration in Computer-Supported Group Decision Making. *Human Communication Research*, *19*(1), 5–49. doi:10.1111/j.1468-2958.1992.tb00294.x

Portney, K. E., & Cohen, S. (2006). Practical contexts and theoretical frameworks for teaching complexity with digital role-play simulations. In S. Cohen, K. E. Portney, D. Rehberger, & C. Thorsen (Eds.), *Virtual Decisions*. Mahwah, NJ: Lawrence Erlbaum.

Rosander, M., Stiwne, D., & Granström, K. (1998). "Bipolar groupthink": Assessing groupthink tendencies in authentic work groups. *Scandinavian Journal of Psychology*, *39*(2), 81–92. doi:10.1111/1467-9450.00060 PMID:9676161

Salas, E., Bowers, C., & Rhodenizer, L. (1998). It Is Not How Much You Have but How You Use It: Toward a Rational Use of Simulation to Support Aviation Training. *The International Journal of Aviation Psychology*, *8*(3), 197–208. doi:10.120715327108ijap0803_2 PMID:11541532

Schneid, T. D., & Collins, L. (2001). *Disaster Management and Preparedness.* New York: Lewis.

Shrivastav, H., & Hiltz, S. R. (2013). Information Overload in Technology-Based Education: A Meta-Analysis. *Proceedings of the 19th Americas Conference on Information Systems. Overload in Technology-Based education*, 1–10.

Sniezek, J., Wilkins, D., & Wadlington, P. (2001). Advanced Training for Crisis Decision Making: Simulation, Critiquing, and Immersive Interfaces. *HICSS, 3*, 3042.

Wills, S., Leigh, E., & Ip, A. (2011). *The power of role-based e-learning: Designing and moderating online role play.* New York: Routledge.

Wills, S., & McDougall, A. (2008). Reusability of online role-play as learning objects or Learning designs. In L. Lockyer, S. Bennett, S. Agostinho, & B. Harper (Eds.), *Handbook of Research on Learning Design and Learning Objects, Issues, Applications and Technologies*. IGI Group. doi:10.4018/978-1-59904-861-1.ch037

Wills, S., Rosser, E., Devonshire, E., Leigh, E., Russell, C., & Shepherd, J. (2009). *Encouraging role based online learning environments by Building, Linking, Understanding, Extending: The BLUE Report*. Australian Learning and Teaching Council.

Winn, W. (1997, January). Advantages of a theory-based curriculum in instructional technology. *Educational Technology*, 34–41.

Chapter 3
Virtual Standardized Patients for Interactive Conversational Training:
A Grand Experiment and New Approach

Thomas B. Talbot
University of Southern California, USA

Albert Skip Rizzo
University of Southern California, USA

ABSTRACT

The USC Standard Patient is a virtual human-based conversational agent serving in the role of a simulated medical patient, also known as a virtual standardized patient (VSP). This research identified deficiencies of extant VSP systems, defined a robust set of requirements, and successfully achieved nearly all of them. Markedly impressive advancements were made in virtual human technology, techniques to apply natural language processing, automated assessment artificial intelligence, and pedagogical design. The effort succeeded with performance parameters of high conversational performance, accurate assessment, and strongly demonstrated user training effect. Although working well within its confined are of expertise, the ability for computers to create authentic mixed initiative conversations remains elusive. This effort leaves behind many lessons for interactive serious games, clinical virtual humans, and conversational virtual human training applications.

DOI: 10.4018/978-1-5225-7461-3.ch003

INTRODUCTION

The advent of Virtual Standardized Patients (VSPs) as a conversational training tool is a recent, yet an evolutionary development from use of human patient actors for the training and assessment of medical interviewing skills. The use of human actors has considerable benefits but at high cost and with narrow availability. Advances with interactive technologies has furthered exploration of computer-based conversational approaches though sometimes with limited success. In this Chapter, we explore a large-scale and well-funded effort by the University of Southern California to make significant advances in VSPs along with the important technical, practical and pedagogical lessons that resulted from their experience. The implications success are relevant to virtual human avatar conversational training of all types and applications, and are certainly not exclusive to medical education.

The VSP itself is a conversational agent and is shown in Figure 1. Typically, the VSP features a three-dimensional avatar which simulates a conversation. With this format, there is typed or speech recognition-based input from the user which is processed by artificial intelligence-based (AI) natural language understanding (NLU) systems. The NLU system interprets the meaning of the user statement and matches it to the post appropriate response possible. In this manner, it is possible to create a simulated doctor-patient conversation, though typically it is limited to one side posing questions and the opposite one responding to them.

In 2013, the University of Southern California (USC) began a nearly eight-million-dollar US Defense Department research project to develop a new type of VSP which promised to overcome the operational limitations of prior approaches and build upon lessons from both failures and successes. The effort is called USC SimCoach Standard Patient Studio (cf. https://standardpatient.org) aka "Standard Patient". Five years, twelve-million-dollars and several studies later, the Standard Patient team is ready to share lessons learned and results of this ongoing experiment.

With the goal to create a viable Virtual Standardized Patient (VSP). The Standard Patent project successfully created a working prototype that is both a VSP experience and authoring tool. The prototype was designed to function through regular web browsers. As it is cloud based; it was modular and capable of multiple types of interactions, including natural language interviews, structured encounters (choice-based), physical exam, medical tests and an interactive after-action report (AAR). The VSP was designed to be physiologically static, as opposed to extant dynamic medical simulations. The authoring system, Standard Patient Studio, is an open-source sharing community that was created to foster a volunteer research base, as a use case exploratorium and for the creation of a critical mass of educational content. Standard Patient cases are modeled closely after human standardized patients, yet are designed for repetitive use for deliberate practice targeting diagnostic interviews.

Figure 1. USC Standard Patient medical interview client
(USC, 2018)

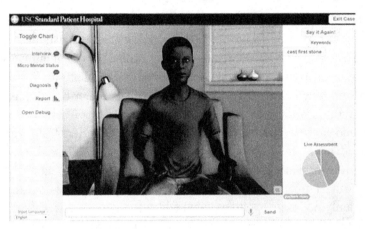

BACKGROUND

An integral part of medical and psychological clinical education involves training in interviewing skills, symptom/ability assessment, diagnosis and interpersonal communication. Students initially learn these skills through a mixture of classroom lectures, observation, and role-playing practice with standardized patients; persons recruited and trained to take on the characteristics of a real patient, thereby affording medical students a realistic opportunity to practice and be evaluated in a simulated clinical environment. This method was first attempted in 1963 by Dr. Howard Barrows at the University of Southern California (1964). Since that time, the use of live actors has long been considered as the gold standard medical education experience for both learning and evaluation purposes (Adamo, 2004; Jack, et al., 2009). Human Standardized Patients (HSPs) are paid actors who pretend to be patients for educational interviews and provide the most realistic and challenging experience for those learning the practice of medicine because they most closely approximate a genuine patient encounter. HSPs are also a key component in the United States Medical Licensing Examination (National Board of Medical Examiners, Philadelphia, PA) Step 2 Clinical Skills exam (cf. http://www.usmle.org). HSP encounters engage clinical skill domains such as social skills, communication skills, judgment, and diagnostic acumen in a real-time setting. Other kinds of practice encounters fall short of this because they either do not force the learner to combine clinical skill domains or they spoon feed data to the student with the practice case that turns the learning more into a pattern recognition exercise rather than a realistic clinical problem-solving experience. The HSP is the only type of encounter where it is up to the learner to naturalistically pose questions to obtain data and information about the case that then needs to be integrated for the formulation of a diagnostic hypothesis and/or treatment plan.

Despite the well-known advantages of HSPs (Howley, et al., 2008; Berkhof, et al., 2011), they are employed all too sparingly. The reason for this limited use is primarily due to the high costs to hire, train and maintain a diverse group of patient actors. Moreover, despite the expense of standardized patient programs, the standardized patients themselves are typically low-skilled actors. Administrators face constant turnover resulting in considerable challenges for maintaining the consistency of diverse patient portrayals for training students. This limits the value of this approach for producing realistic and valid interactions needed for the reliable evaluation and training of novice clinicians. Thus, the diversity of clinical conditions that HSPs can characterize is limited by availability of human actors and their skills. HSPs actors may provide suboptimal variation control and are typically limited to healthy appearing adult encounters. This is even a greater problem when the actor needs to be a child, adolescent, elder, person with a disability or in the portrayal of nuanced or complex symptom presentations.

The situation is even more challenging in the training of students in clinical psychology, social work, and other allied health professions. Rarely are live standardized patients used in such clinical training. Most direct patient interaction skills are acquired via role-playing with supervising clinicians and fellow graduate students, with closely supervised "on-the-job" training providing the brunt of experiential training. While one-way mirrors provide a window for the direct observation of trainees, audio and video recordings of clinical sessions is the more common method of providing supervisors with information on the clinical skills of trainees. However, the imposition of recording has been reported to have demonstrable effects on the therapeutic process that may confound the end goal of clinical training (Bogolub, 1986) and the supervisor review of raw recordings is a time-consuming process that imposes a significant drain on resources.

In this regard, VSPs can fulfill the role of human standardized patients by simulating diverse varieties of clinical presentations with a high degree of consistency, and sufficient realism (Stevens et al, 2009; Rizzo et al., 2011a/b), as well as being always available for anytime-anywhere training. In fact, there is a growing literature on the use of VSPs in the testing and training of bioethics, basic patient communication, interactive conversations, history taking, clinical assessment, and clinical decision-making and initial results suggest that VSPs can provide valid and reliable representations of live patients (Talbot, et al., 2012a; Lok, et al., 2007; Triola, et al., 2006).

The reliability of human standardized patient responses can exceed 90%, but human performance is variable, (Tamblyn, 1991a; Pangaro, 1997). Human raters are also a major source of assessment variability, with one large study demonstrating that raters account for a 20% variability in assessment scores (Tamblyn, 1991b) in addition to inter-site rating differences. Human assessment performance can be improved by moving from rating scales to checklist style assessments. A US military study tracking 40 HSP encounters employed checklist assessments and reported a 13% discrepancy rate upon videotape review (Pangaro 1997.). Even with good verbal accuracy, inconsistencies are noted in how patient actors portray facial & nonverbal expressions and their physical presentation (Baig 2014). This inconsistency or inability to portray specific findings with healthy individuals can lead to significant deviations in learner diagnostic pick-ups between VSPs and SPs. In one study (Wendling 2011), learners were significantly more likely to make the intended diagnosis of Obstructive Sleep Apnea in a VSP (85% to 24%, $p < 0.005$) as compared to a human SP due to the ability for the VSP to consistently demonstrate parameters such as body mass, neck girth and airway appearance.

Fortunately, the use of virtual human characters for training is encouraging. USC experience from multiple virtual human training projects and their associated studies have shown that learners readily accept virtual human (VH) characters in place of human role-players and interact with them in a similar manner. In one representative study, the Immersive Naval Officer Training System (INOTS), a structured encounter simulation, was employed to evaluate naval officer candidates' perceptions of a role-player vs. the VH (Campbell, 2011), where VH received higher ratings than the human in many categories except eye gaze; those categories included engagement, body language, spoken responses, vocal intonation and facial expression. Additionally, physiological data corroborated the self-report data. As far as the participants' emotional experience of the role-play was concerned, there was not a substantial measurable difference between the virtual human and the live human. We know from this and other studies that participants tend to enjoy and find such experiences to be of value (Bergin, 2003; Hays 2012; Poore, 2012).

Problem: The State of Virtual Standardized Patients

Upon the outset of our work, there were two primary problems with VSPs for simulating complex medical interviews: 1) Performance and 2) Content Creation. VSP systems required cumbersome software installation of several different programs that had to work together and such systems generally had poor reliability. Conversational patient interactions varied in quality, though they were often thin and brittle; any deviation from anticipated questions often resulted in non-sensical patient responses.

Furthermore, the VSPs often lacked responses to off-track medical questions; resulting in the learner receiving hints as to being on-track by receiving valid responses. VSPs challenged the natural language understanding (NLU) performance of the time.

When it comes to the medical interview with a VSP, there are two primary modes of interaction. The first style of VSP medical interview is the natural language random-access (NLRA) encounter. NLRA medical interviews allow the learner to ask any question they can come up with in any order. Second, there are structured encounters where the VSP is conversational and the learner interacts by selecting between prepared choices, eliminating the need NLU technology and training language. Both styles of interviews are supported by Standard Patient and each has advantages in various situations.

Content creation workload for VSPs was considerable and required a team of engineers working to build a single case over a four-to-six-month timeframe. Each question/response pair also required language training data, typically 7-15 or more sample questions to pair to each patient response. Thus, a VSP with 250 responses may require 3,000 training language items. With such a degree of effort, the notion of building a critical mass of usable content was unrealistic and cost prohibitive. Additionally, most VSP systems performed at about 65-75% correct responses to user questions, too low for practical use (Patrick, 2008). At that time, the high cost of content creation, limited distribution, poor reliability, and marginal performance rendered a business case for VSPs moot.

A VISION FOR A NEW GENERATION VIRTUAL STANDARDIZED PATIENT

By 2010, several promising technologies were seeing fruition which had potential to make VSPs more practical. First was FLoReS (Morbini et al., 2013), a new NLU system designed to be "Forward Looking & Reward Seeking" offered high performance and was more tolerant of spelling & grammatical variations, and provided a significant boost in language recognition due to its maximum entropy classifier. Contemporary to FLoReS, DARPA funded an online virtual human named SimCoach (Rizzo et al., 2011). SimCoach, seen in Figure 2, was designed to conversationally engage Veterans, seek out mental health risk factors and provide information and referrals to behavioral resources. More importantly, SimCoach was cloud-based and worked on computer web-browsers. No longer would installation or high-performance computing equipment be necessary to use virtual humans. SimCoach allowed for high-volume virtual human content delivery. SimCoach used the FLoReS classifier and contained other novel technologies such as automated non-verbal behavior and emotional expression AI. SimCoach also featured a cloud-based content authoring capability. It was clear that SimCoach had far more potential as a technology platform than as a Veteran's mental health counselor.

The process leading to a new-generation VSP began with a comprehensive assessment of the virtual human technology approaches to date in addition to studying how human standardized patients are employed. We interviewed medical students regarding their HSP encounters and the feedback was surprising. Students saw value in the HSP experience but were also apprehensive, fearing unfair judgment from the patient actor who evaluated them. They strongly expressed a desire for concrete and specific feedback on their performance which they felt was vague – they were looking for actionable feedback to improve their medical interview performance.

On the technical side, it was clear that building each VSP from the ground up would be too time consuming. It was also noted that there was considerable overlap between different VSP patient cases and their topical areas and language training data. Tools like SimCoach and its enabling tech chain seemed like a good fit for a VSP application and would serve as the tech base for Standard Patient. The next step was to create some requirements and then develop strategies to implement those goals with available technology.

Design Requirements

A new generation VSP would require a robust VSP experience with high performance and reliability and be able to respond appropriately more than 90% of the time. The VSP encounters must offer specific and actionable assessment. Content must be

*Figure 2. SimCoach psychological health aid for Veterans
(USC, 2010)*

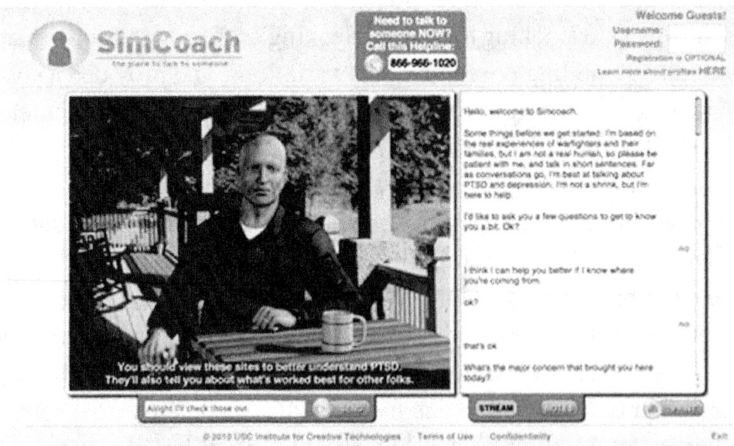

authorable with considerably less effort in less than 10% of the time and not require computer programmers, but be created by medical educators. The system must allow for community-based authoring. Finally, the system must offer broad availability via cloud-based content delivery. For each of these requirements, a technical strategy was then developed:

1. **Robust Functional Experience:** The goal was to make sure that the VSPs conversational domain was wide enough to avoid hinting at the desired question topical areas. It was decided to abandon the practice of creating a new conversation-topic domain database for every new VSP scenario. Instead, we developed a Unified Medical Taxonomy (UMT) whereby all medical cases share the exact same taxonomy. This required a broad and detailed taxonomy to be developed, but once created it would allow every VSP case to answer all medical general questions regardless of the actual condition experienced in the scenario. The UMT, shown in Table 1, evolved into about 750 interview topics and covered all aspects of a typical medical interview. There were additional UMT sections for non-conversational elements such as physical examination (140 tests) and laboratory/radiology (480 tests).

The advantages of the UMT approach are numerous; every case has a broad topical domain area and most importantly it is possible for all cases to share the same language training data. Instead of starting over, every new case that is tested and trained contributes to the NLU training for all cases in our system, thus achieving a large volume of training data (15,000+ items) which greatly enhances the performance of the NLU system. This training data efficiency and accumulated quantity was hypothesized to provide for very high performance. The disadvantage of this UMT approach is flexibility; all cases must employ topics that are built into the system and the system cannot be modified to support scenario-specific and non-medical interview questions.

2. **Rapid Authoring:** We created a web-based authoring tool and portal. The authoring tool included 140 distinct avatars of all ages, sizes and description and was modular in nature. There would be modules for medical interview, choice-based conversations, tests, physical exam and diagnosis/orders. The interface was modeled on easy to use web-based tax preparation software such as TurboTax (Intuit Inc). The interview module authoring included the UMT in tree form, though it separated medical history, review of system and history of present illness into their own tabbed sections. An example is shown in Figure 3. Most taxonomy items included a default response ("I don't have

Table 1. The Unified Medical Taxonomy (abbreviated) formed the structure of the conversational interview system

Medical History (MH)	Review of Systems (ROS)	History of Present Illness (HPI)

Medical History
  - Medications
  - Past Medical History
  - Surgical History
  - Allergies
  - Accidents
  - Preventative Medicine
Social History
  - General
  - Infection risk/exposure
  - Exercise
  - Recreational Drugs
  - Etc...
Relationships
  - Relationships
  - Stressors
  - Support System
Occupational History
  - Profession
  - Education
	General Health & Constitutional
	  - Illness
	  - Fever
	  - Pain
	  - Etc...
	HEENT
	Chest
	  - Cardiac
	  - Respiratory
	  - Etc...
	Vascular
	Skin
	Gastrointestinal
	Genitourinary
	Musculoskeletal
	Endocrine
	Neurological
	Psychiatric
		Narrative State Machine
		  - Chief Complaint
		  - Narrative Progression
		HPI Modifiers
		  - Onset / duration
		  - Progression
		  - Aggravator / alleviator
		  - Previous episode
		  - Etc..
		Social Responses
		Special Responses

30 Topical Areas 221 Items	44 Topical Areas 473 Items	4 Areas 51 Items

diarrhea"), allowing for the author to enter text for the chief complaint and relevant symptoms – thus a viable case can be created by modifying 30-40 items in the authoring tool – the default items would provide credible negative responses to off topic questions. Of note, authors simply entered text of what they wanted the VSP character to say. A system we built called Cerebella would analyze the text and create a video rendering that included contextually appropriate non-verbal behavior. For example, a statement such as "I don't really know" may feature a shoulder shrug. With automated speech, mouth visemes and non-verbal behavior generation, animators and artists would not be required to develop new content. In total, these approaches promised to reduce the development time for a VSP from months to hours.

3. **Community-Based Open-Source Authoring:** To enable this objective, we created a portal and made all content open-source via the Creative Commons 4.0 license. Any content published for consumption would automatically have its source information available to every author on the system. It was hoped that authors could share content with each other and make new content based upon already authored cases.

Figure 3. Screenshot of Standard Patient medical interview authoring module as seen within a web browser

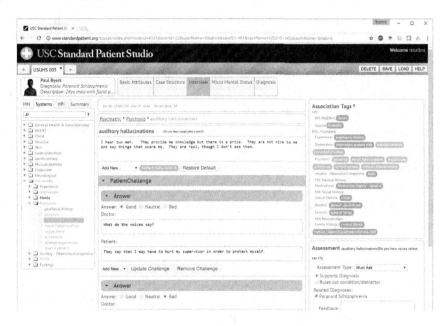

4. **Actionable Assessment:** Specific actionable assessment was a challenging goal that required a new kind of solution. We treated the doctor-patient conversation as a turn-based strategy game whereby the goal is to obtain maximum relevant information return in the fewest number of questions. Under this assessment system, called INFERENCE-RTS, the UMT serves as the structure of the assessment. The author determines which topical areas are important to have been addressed during the medical encounter. The author does this by adding assessment tags to taxonomy items. The tags included green high priority tags (worth 4 points), blue normal priority tags (worth 1 point) and red-flag tags for inappropriate actions. For example, in a patient with pneumonia, the taxonomy item for cough is getting an assessment tag. Assessment tags are called up based on the patient response and not-necessarily the question asked. It is possible to copy existing assessment tags onto multiple responses within the taxonomy; for example; the patient may reveal cough during a response about shortness of breath. Called "association assessment tags," this strategy allows for flexible rewarding of information revealed by the patient regardless of questioning strategy, provided case-relevant information is revealed. The

taxonomy also includes open-ended question items that can help to evaluate if the user is employing an open or closed based questioning strategy (i.e. "Tell me about your cough?" vs "Do you have cough"). Feedback would be provided upon the conclusion of a case. For this purpose, a special feedback item called a 'case mind map' was developed and can be seen in Figure 4. The case mind map is a graphical tree structure that shows assessment tags from the UMT in an organized structure (by topical area). Information that was revealed in the encounter shows up as labelled & and colored tags. Information that was not revealed shows up as grey boxes. Grey boxes may be selected to reveal the missed topic area, author feedback and an example of a question that would lead to this information being revealed. Additionally, right side of the tree is reserved for tags related to the actual condition experienced by the patient (Called "Rule In") and the left side is reserved for tags employed to eliminate possibilities of other conditions that are not present ("Rule Out").

5. **Broad Availability and Compatibility:** Use of the SimCoach platform provided a ready to use web-based capability. The entire system is cloud-based. Since 3D graphics inside web browsers had low adoption and numerous compatibility problems in 2013, virtual patient avatar statements are prerendered onto video. A looping video of the VSP is preloaded and statements by the VSP are streamed down to the web browser in real time. Thus, any web browser capable of viewing online videos are also capable of running the VSP. We employed Flash (Adobe Inc) to display the video content.

Figure 4. The after-action report (AAR) case mind map allows learners to obtain an instant perspective on their performance and explore areas for improvement

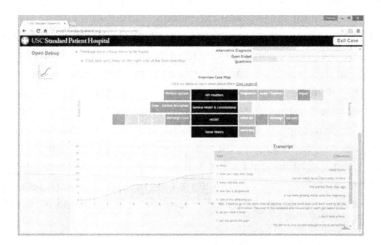

Prototype Development

With these design considerations in mind, our team developed the first prototype during 2013 and 2014 with our development partner, Breakaway Games (Hunt Valley, Maryland) which built all web-based content while the USC Institute for Creative Technologies built out the virtual human and assessment components. The first six months were primarily conceptual with weekly design meetings followed by an eighteen-month development period. The first prototype was shown in the exhibit hall at the Government Showcase at the 2015 International Meeting on Simulation in Healthcare (IMSH). Unbeknownst to the USC team, Breakaway Games entered Standard Patient in the 2015 Serious Games & Virtual Environments Showcase, winning best of show in the competition. This would be the first of at least four international awards eventually won by Standard Patient and this first award was very consequential to its future. A week prior to the IMSH conference, the DoD notified our team that we had not been selected for a four-million-dollar continuation phase. At IMSH, Standard Patient was viewed as a breakthrough and was invited as a demonstration at the closing plenary. Given the unusually high level of excitement and enthusiasm around our prototype, the contest award and feedback from conference attendees, the DoD reevaluated their prior decision and eventually selected our team for the continuation funding.

RESULTS, OUTCOMES AND LESSONS

The educational literature informs us that mastery requires deliberate practice (Ericsson 2004) in both quantity and quality. Standard Patient VSP cases are intended to be repeated multiple times, until each case is mastered (Talbot 2012a). This depends upon repetitive use. The after-action report (AAR) never includes scores, but shows indices that graphically depict progress towards mastery. INFERENCE-RTS AARs provide concrete assessment items to help learners improve with the next attempt of a case. Additionally, the AAR case mind-map allows leaners to randomly explore their case performance (Talbot 2012b). The mind-map provides a 'visual gestalt' that is far cleaner yet more informative than text feedback. It is designed around chunking theory (Gobet 2005) to help learners discover patterns and associations in their diagnostic strategy. If our system worked as designed, we would expect to see an increase in performance because of deliberate practice with our system.

The Exploratory Study

With a functional prototype in 2015, we conducted our first user study with medical students with mixed success. The cloud-based system did function reliably, even with multiple users. This first study employed 105 late second year medical student subjects at USC Keck School of Medicine who were just mere months away from working with live patients. Subjects were divided into four groups which received different conditions. One group received a minimal orientation, a second group received an orientation plus a visual demonstration of the prototype with examples of the types of questions the system can respond to. A third group received group two's orientation plus a demonstration on the use of the AAR stem. Finally, a fourth group received group two's orientation but the AAR report was withheld. With these four groups, it was anticipated that the optimal level of orientation would be determined as well providing a control for the effect of the after-action assessment, so that improved performance with repeated case use could be traced to that assessment report rather than just the repetitive case exposure. The big prize from this study would be demonstration of a training effect. In this study, each subject performed a case three times, so it should be possible to see such an effect.

Results from the study came back with both surveys and testing data. Of greatest concern was that there did not appear to be a discernable pattern between the first and third case repetitions; something entirely unsuspected. After detailed analysis, we determined that the study design was flawed. The study had a case with multiple modules, including physical exam, and that we did not control for the time spent on each case. The subjects varied in time spent between iterations, seemingly randomly, and many subjects spent later iterations exploring the physical exam which was not the focus of our study. We also discovered a scoring exploit by which subjects were improperly credited when asking certain follow up questions. Based on this experience, we learned several useful things. We learned that most case performance happened within 5 minutes of starting the case. The physical exam was not relevant to the case's patient compliant, so we would just provide physical findings instead of providing the rich physical exam module. We knew that we would want to control for time spent on each case repetition.

On the positive side, the survey information was useful. Subjects enjoyed the AAR report and felt that the assessment was actionable; those subjects who did not receive the AAR became frustrated by the system and did not see the point of it, and had a performance decline on the third iteration. We determined that our orientation videos were too long, but it was appropriate to give example of the types of questions to ask and that it was necessary to show how to navigate through the AAR screen. NLU performance was about an 87% appropriate response rate and exploratory study transcript NLU errors were adapted to language training the Standard Patient system.

The Definitive Study

The definitive study looked at subject assessment and performance gains using the VSP prototype. Results were impressive; so much so that we commissioned an independent statistical analysis which confirmed and added statistical evidence to our findings.

This 65-subject study, still using late-second year medical students, had one VSP naïve group with an optimized orientation video. The study was conducted with an optimized, controlled quasi-experimental design protocol that limited the case attempts to five minutes and AAR feedback review to two minutes. There were four sequential case attempts by each subject. In comparison to our exploratory study, the definitive study results showed gains that greatly outpaced performance seen in the earlier effort. This reflects the effects of focused questioning (time limits), an improved orientation, better system performance and better human factor controls.

Study results showed that intentional practice with the VSP prototype resulted in a large training effect as evidenced by large performance score gains. Average performance scores increased by +59% on attempt three and +67% on attempt four. The top quartile demonstrated very impressive performance gains; +147% on attempt three and +160% on attempt four.

Results show reliable gains in performance score, high priority item score and standard priority item score. Subjects increased use of the history of present illness (HPI) open narrative and employed more open-ended questions with each attempt. Subjects required fewer questions to approach a given level of performance with each attempt.

Subjects asked relevant questions earlier in the interview – a trend that continued with each subsequent case attempt. This permitted subjects to ask more questions with each attempt as they tried to perform. Interviewer efficiency improved with each attempt. Subjects asked more questions to rule out alternative diagnoses with each attempt as well. Most performance improvements happened during attempts two and three, with continued but decreasing gains on the fourth attempt.

Overall performance of the NLU system was over 92% correct responses to questions in both the first and fourth case attempt, a new record for VSP systems (Talbot et al, 2017). A transcript review showed that the INFERENCE RTS system automated assessment system performed superlatively and was consistently accurate within 2-4% of actual performance with a slight performance undermeasurement bias.

An independent data analysis was conducted at the University of Minnesota Medical School by Dr. Pamela Andreatta, Associate Professor of Human Performance

Research in Medical and Surgical Education and President of the Society for Simulation in Healthcare (Andreatta, 2016). In this analysis, multivariate tests for "information gain" (Performance Score) confirmed a statistically significant difference between sequential repetitions [$F(3,180) = 69.49$ ($p<0.001$)] with an effect size for tagged items (partial eta squared) of 0.79, which is considered a very large effect. The report states:

The statistically significant differences between repetitions for multiple performance variables provides validity evidence and methodological rigor in the content domain, as well as confirms the sensitivity and validity of the assessment metrics to differentiate between performances.

The report concludes:

The clear evidence supporting the virtual patient system is that there is sufficient precision of measurement to facilitate performance acquisition and maintenance at any level of mastery. This provides an on-demand opportunity for clinicians to acquire interviewing skills, or to rehearse or practice specific interviewing skills that they may not have needed within their clinical practice areas; all prior to engagement with a real patient in an applied clinical context. The advantages for efficiency and accuracy in the applied clinical setting are obvious, but there are concomitant advantages for patient safety and quality of care because history taking is a critical component of developing a differential diagnosis and an informed treatment plan for the patient.

A detailed survey was provided to definitive study subjects. Subjects reported very positive impressions of their orientation, positive sentiment towards ability to interact with the VSP prototype and expressed positive sentiment that the system understood them. They stated that the interaction did not quite feel natural.

We assessed ease of use with the well-regarded System Usability Scale (Brooke, 1996). The study SUS score was 67.65, which places usability in the 'Good' range. This is equivalent to use of a modern cell phone (65.9) and television (67.8). VSP system applicability was highly rated by study participants. The survey expressed high scores and majority favorable opinions for use of the VSP for practice of diagnostic interviewing, preparation for standardized patients, preparation to see real patients and most expressed a desire to practice again with the system.

Negative comments focused on unexpected answers, excessive case attempts (preferring 3 rather than 4) and inability to ask follow-up questions. Positive comments were numerous, describing the VSP prototype as "impressive" and a "valuable learning tool".

Comments included:

The biggest strength is being able to get immediate feedback and knowing which important crucial questions need to be asked in order to rule in and rule out a particular diagnosis.

The end feedback in the report was pretty helpful and helped me differentiate between different similar illnesses.

Feedback regarding the 'naturalness' of the interaction was important to us. We attribute this sentiment to the synthetic voices, the uncanny valley effect (Mori, 1970), lack of topical follow up capability and typed input. Voice input was added to the system after the study.

Overall, system usability, desirability and applicability for training received positive results from this survey. A VSP prototype was capable of being well accepted, easy to use, understanding student language input, and providing a training effect. Students recognize the potential for preparation for standardized patient testing and real patient encounters. The strongest area for natural language VSPs is in diagnostic interviewing skills. The dynamism of character interactions could have been improved, especially if topic-specific follow up questions are enabled.

The Psychiatry Domain

In 2016, we attempted a series of psychiatric interviews in cooperation with the Uniformed Services University of the Health Sciences (USUHS). Research is ongoing, though we found that NLU performance of these cases was significantly lower, hovering between 75-80% correct responses; too low for acceptable routine use. We eventually added additional psychiatry content to the UMT, though that only partially ameliorated the performance. The issue was that psychiatry often involves personal stories and individual factors that bring up questions that don't show up in a list of medical questions of any size. For example, a schizophrenic patient mentions that his supervisor "knows his secret and is after me" – the UMT approach cannot handle questions like "Why is your boss out to get you?"

Based on this experience, we decided to develop the ability to add to the taxonomy for individual cases, though at that cost of having to provide all language training for those items and expect that feature to be available in 2018. For the psychiatry cases, we implemented a live-feedback feature that displayed when assessment tags were earned and showed a pie chart (See Figure 1) to indicate the remaining unexplored content; the response to this feature was enthusiastic and coincided with an improvement in the impression of the scenario seeming natural.

The Spoken Word

We also implemented voice recognition and compared typed vs. spoken interaction in a medical student-run study (Bautista et al., 2016). The results were that spoken interactions seemed more natural to users but speaking resulted in about 5-15% lower NLU performance. About half of that decrease was attributed to voice recognition errors, the rest was because people simply speak differently than they type, even when trying to type conversationally. We subsequently began training spoken input along with the typed input but have not followed up with an additional study. Interestingly, medical students preferred to type to the VSP in order to maintain encounter privacy.

Structured Choice Encounters

We built a robust structured encounter capability with choice-oriented conversations. Called Select-A-Chat, these VSPs can converse about any topic, can exchange initiative with the user and do not require NLU or language training (Talbot, 2016b). Interaction is limited to available choices, however. We had previously been successful with this approach with a forensic interviewing prototype called Virtual Child Witness (John, 2013; John, 2015). With the VSP, we created a number of interesting scenarios including a vaccine resistant parent and a psychiatry antidepressant management simulator (with Emory University). The Select-A-Chat seems to be useful for encounters that don't fit the standard medical interview mold and are well-liked by users; though prospective technology funders appear to be more impressed with NLU systems despite their higher risks, language training requirements and narrower practical domains.

Commercialization

The USC Standard Patient system continues as a freeware open-source content community at the time of this writing. It was commercialized through as spin-off company in 2017 (Medical Mechanica LLC, New Market, MD) and has been used for medical communications and clinical scenario training, primarily employing the Select-A-Chat module. The potential market for medical student applications is fairly small (with 40,000 medical students in the USA), but there is a wider potential customer pool for continuing medical education, nurses, physician assistants and mental health. Other potential applications for the technology include job interviews, difficult conversation practice, leadership skills and personal assistants & health coaches.

Open Source Authoring

The open-sourced authoring community was a mixed success. Several educators created decent content on the system, though they were far rarer than we had assumed they would be. Most educators never attempted to author content or they gave up after an initial try. Creating easy to use tools was not enough. The tools were simple, though those learning to author often required guidance as to how to appropriately use the assessment tags. In the end, it was apparent that case authoring was simply a talent – one that individuals possessed or not. This included an aptitude for creation, writing skills and perseverance. The open source nature of system content was successful and made case sharing possible. One thing we had failed to do was to identify promising content and aggregate it into a critical mass of useful cases, though we intend to rectify that deficiency soon.

Future Advances

Ongoing work with the USC Standard Patient includes keeping up with an evolving internet, which is a significant consideration with any large cloud-based application. The team is building out a robust high-fidelity physical examination for the military. The Perceptive Patient, under development, featuring multimodal sensing of the user's face, linguistic analysis and a lethetic processing model by which the VSP actively judges the human, affecting VSP demeanor and likelihood of providing truthful responses to sensitive questions. Additional work is exploring methods to make these conversational agents physiologically dynamic and even potentially adaptive to the physiological state of the human they are conversing with. Near term work involves improving the basic performance of existing components which still have room for improvement.

SOLUTIONS AND RECOMMENDATIONS

Many useful lessons were gained form the USC Standard Patient experience. Firstly, the development approach was key. At the outset, VSPs were advancing albeit slowly. Standard Patient exceeded prior efforts because it undertook a deep examination of fundamental technologies and the limitations of extant efforts. This was coupled by the availability of new generation technology from our laboratory, but more importantly, a fresh look at the user's needs was essential. With those in hand, an aggressive set of requirements to solve current limitations was coupled with a generous development budget. Each of the major areas of improvement benefitted from a fresh approach grounded in other possibly distantly related success stories.

Frequent and repeat use of research studies and user clinics greatly aided in the improvement of the prototype. Attending conferences with public access to the system also provided good feedback. This frequent contact with reality was sometimes dispiriting but it was necessary to discover what improvements had to happen.

The most important lesson from this experience is that a computer simulation does not have to be an exact facsimile of an analog one to be useful. As an example, real patient and even HSP conversations are much more nuanced and richer that anything the VSP can do. The VSP will never seem as natural or fluent as conversation between humans, and that is fine. With VSP training, the interviews are much shorter and to the point – they are very useful in formulating a set of inquiries based on what the VSP is telling the user. Unlike working with patient actors, VSPs allow learners to see very specific feedback instantly and repeat their encounter immediately; improving along the way. With a HSP, the learner may have a 20-minute session followed by a 10 minute debrief. With a VSP, they will typically conduct the case and have repeated the case 3-4 times within a similar timeframe. That tight feedback loop is amazing and it does a lot for a learner. We've stated that VSPs may never do some things as well as HSPs, but they do other things much better than HSPs ever will; VSP assessments are highly accurate yet are interpersonally nonjudgmental. One major benefit to the VSP is accessibility. Once created, a single VSP case can be distributed to thousands of learners and accessed any time it is desired, greatly lowering the cost of training. HSPs can work with one learner at a time at scheduled place and time, often with considerable support staff.

VSP/HSP comparisons may sometimes be difficult because they are doing somewhat different things and sometimes one modality will be preferable to the other depending on circumstances and objectives. Upon building new computer simulated experiences, it is important to not bind oneself to assumptions and thinking from the methods you are augmenting or replacing.

CONCLUSION

The development of USC Standard Patient was a major undertaking for our laboratory and one that provided many advancements in VSPs as often as it provided lessons learned along with newly identified avenues for advancement. The studies are in and others are underway. The project has six awards under its belt and an expanding portfolio of uses. The true value of VSPs and other Virtual Humans will lie in the quality, effectiveness and scope of the applications built upon the technology. The ultimate judgment for the VSP will be in its utility it finds and the results it generates. Along the way, technology and interactive techniques will improve as well. No development is the final word; the path of progress is never ending.

ACKNOWLEDGMENT

This research was supported by the United Stated Defense Medical Research Development Program (DMRDP) and the US Army Research Laboratory (ARL) [Contract W911NF-14-D-0005].

REFERENCES

Adamo, G. (2003). Simulated and Standardized Patients in OSCEs: Achievements and Challenges 1992-2003. *Medical Teacher*, *25*(3), 262–270. doi:10.1080/0142159031000100300 PMID:12881047

Andreatta, P. (2016). *An Independent Analysis of a Virtual Standardized Patient System*. Unpublished Government Report, directly communicated from author.

Baig, L. A., Beran, T. N., Vallevand, A., Baig, Z. A., & Monroy-Cuadros, M. (2014). Accuracy of Portrayal by Standardized Patients: Results from four OSCE stations conducted for high stakes examinations. *BMC Medical Education*, *14*(1), 97. doi:10.1186/1472-6920-14-97 PMID:24884744

Barrows, H. S., & Abrahamson, S. (1964). The Programmed Patient: A Technique for Appraising Student Performance in Clinical Neurology. *Academic Medicine*, *39*(8), 802–805. PMID:14180699

Bautista, M., Leeds, A., Tokel, T., & Talbot, T. B. (2016). Spoken vs typed questioning in a conversational medical interview with virtual standardized patients. *International Meeting on Simulation in Healthcare*.

Bergin, R. A., & Fors, U. G. (2003). Interactive Simulated Patient—an Advanced Tool for Student-Activated Learning in Medicine and Healthcare. *Computers & Education*, *40*(4), 361–376. doi:10.1016/S0360-1315(02)00167-7

Berkhof, M., Rijssen, H. J., Schellart, A. J., Anema, J. R., & Beek, A. J. (2011). Effective training strategies for teaching communication skills to physicians: An overview of systematic reviews. *Patient Education and Counseling*, *84*(2), 152–162. doi:10.1016/j.pec.2010.06.010 PMID:20673620

Bogolub, E. B. (1986). Tape Recorders in Clinical Sessions: Deliberate and Fortuitous Effects. *Clinical Social Work Journal*, *14*(4), 349–360. doi:10.1007/BF01892595

Brooke, J. (1996). SUS: a "quick and dirty" usability scale. In *Usability Evaluation in Industry*. London: Taylor and Francis.

Campbell, J. C., Hays, M. J., Core, M., Birch, M., Bosack, M., & Clark, R. E. (2011). Interpersonal and Leadership Skills: Using Virtual Humans to Teach New Officers. *Proceedings of the 33rd Interservice/Industry Training, Simulation, and Education Conference (I/ITSEC)*.

Gobet, F. (2005). Chunking Models of Expertise: Implications for Education. *Applied Cognitive Psychology*, *19*(2), 183–204. doi:10.1002/acp.1110

Hays, M. J., Campbell, J. C., Poore, J. C., Webb, A. K., King, T. K., & Trimmer, M. A. (2012). Can Role-Play with Virtual Humans Teach Interpersonal Skills? *Proceedings of the 34th Interservice/Industry Training, Simulation, and Education Conference (I/ITSEC)*.

Howley, L., Szauter, K., Perkowski, L., Clifton, M., & Mcnaughton, N. (2008). Quality of Standardised Patient Research Reports in the Medical Education Literature: Review and Recommendations. *Medical Education*, *42*(4), 350–358. doi:10.1111/j.1365-2923.2007.02999.x PMID:18298448

Jack, B., Chetty, V., Anthony, D., Greenwald, J., Sanchez, G., Johnson, A., ... Culpepper, L. (2009). A Reengineered Hospital Discharge Program to Decrease Rehospitalization: A Randomized Trial. *Annals of Internal Medicine*, *150*(3), 178–187. doi:10.7326/0003-4819-150-3-200902030-00007 PMID:19189907

Lok, B., Ferdig, R. E., Raij, A., Johnsen, K., Dickerson, R., Coutts, J., & Lind, D. S. (2006). Applying Virtual Reality in Medical Communication Education: Current Findings and potential Teaching and Learning Benefits of immersive Virtual Patients. *Virtual Reality (Waltham Cross)*, *10*(3-4), 185–195. doi:10.100710055-006-0037-3

Morbini, F., Devault, D., Sagae, K., Gerten, J., Nazarian, A., & Traum, D. (2013). FLoReS: A Forward Looking, Reward Seeking, Dialogue Manager. *Natural Interaction with Robots, Knowbots and Smartphones*, 313-325. doi:10.1007/978-1-4614-8280-2_28

Mori, M. (1970). The Uncanny Valley. *Energy*, *7*(4), 33–35.

Pangaro, L. N., Worth-Dickstein, H., Macmillan, M. K., Klass, D. J., & Shatzer, J. H. (1997). Performance of "Standardized Examinees" in a Standardized-Patient Examination of Clinical Skills. *Academic Medicine*, *72*(11), 1008–1011. doi:10.1097/00001888-199711000-00021 PMID:9387827

Parsons, T. D., Kenny, P., Ntuen, C. A., Pataki, C. S., Pato, M. T., Rizzo, A., & Sugar, J. (2008). Objective Structured Clinical Interview Training Using a Virtual Human Patient. *Studies in Health Technology and Informatics*, *132*, 357–362. PMID:18391321

Poore, J., Webb, A., Hays, M. J., Campbell, J., Trimmer, M., & Major, L. M. (2012). *Emulating Sociality: A Comparison Study of Physiological Signals from Human and Virtual Social Interactions*. Poster presented at Social & Affective Neuroscience Society Annual Meeting.

Rizzo, A., Kenny, P., & Parsons, T. (2011). Intelligent Virtual Humans for Clinical Training. *International Journal of Virtual Reality and Broadcasting*, *8*(3).

Rizzo, A., Lange, B., Buckwalter, J. G., Forbell, E., Kim, J., Sagae, K., & Kenny, P. (2011). SimCoach: An Intelligent Virtual Human System for Providing Healthcare Information and Support. *International Journal on Disability and Human Development*, *10*(4), 213. doi:10.1515/IJDHD.2011.046

Talbot, T.B., Kalisch, N., Christoffersen, K., Lucas, G., Forbell, E. (2016a). Natural Language Understanding Performance & Use Considerations in Virtual Medical Encounters. *Studies in Health Technology and Informatics, 220*, 407-413. doi:10.3233/978-1-61499-625-5-407

Talbot, T. B., Lyon, T. D., Rizzo, A., & John, B. (2016b). *Virtual Child Witness: Effects of Single and Multiple Use on Performance with Novice and Expert Cohorts in a Structured Virtual Human Interview. Interservice/Industry Training, Simulation, and Education Conference*. I/ITSEC.

Talbot, T. B., Sagae, K., John, B., & Rizzo, A. (2012a). Sorting Out the Virtual Patient: How to Exploit Artificial Intelligence, Game Technology and Sound Educational Practices to Create Engaging Role-Playing Simulations. *International Journal of Gaming and Computer-Mediated Simulations*, *4*(3), 1–19. doi:10.4018/jgcms.2012070101

Talbot, T. B., Sagae, K., John, B., & Rizzo, A. (2012b). Designing Useful Virtual Standardized Patient Encounters. *Interservice/Industry Training, Simulation and Education Conference Proceedings (I/ITSEC)*.

Tamblyn, R. M., Klass, D. J., Schnabl, G. K., & Kopelow, M. L. (1991). Sources of Unreliability and Bias in Standardized-Patient Rating. *Teaching and Learning in Medicine*, *3*(2), 74–85. doi:10.1080/10401339109539486

Tamblyn, R. M., Klass, D. J., Schnabl, G. K., & Kopelow, M. L. (1991). The Accuracy of Standardized Patient Presentation. *Medical Education*, *25*(2), 100–109. doi:10.1111/j.1365-2923.1991.tb00035.x PMID:2023551

Triola, M., Feldman, H., Kalet, A. L., Zabar, S., Kachur, E. K., Gillespie, C., & Lipkin, M. (2006). A Randomized Trial of Teaching Clinical Skills Using Virtual and Live Standardized Patients. *Journal of General Internal Medicine*, *21*(5), 424–429. doi:10.1111/j.1525-1497.2006.00421.x PMID:16704382

Wendling, A., Halan, S., Tighe, P., Le, L., Euliano, T., & Lok, B. (2011). Virtual Humans Versus Standardized Patients: Which Lead Residents to More Correct Diagnoses? *Academic Medicine*, *86*(3), 384–388. doi:10.1097/ACM.0b013e318208803f PMID:21248598

ADDITIONAL READING

Beutler, L. E., & Harwood, T. M. (2004). Virtual reality in Psychotherapy Training. *Journal of Clinical Psychology*, *60*(3), 317–330. doi:10.1002/jclp.10266 PMID:14981794

Bickmore, T., & Giorgino, T. (2006). Health Dialog Systems for Patients and Consumers. *Journal of Biomedical Informatics*, *39*(5), 556–571. doi:10.1016/j.jbi.2005.12.004 PMID:16464643

Bickmore, T. W., Pfeifer, L. M., & Paasche-Orlow, M. K. (2007). Health Document Explanation by Virtual Agents. Intelligent Virtual Agents Lecture Notes in Computer Science, 183-196. doi:10.1007/978-3-540-74997-4_18

Ericsson, K. A. (2004). Deliberate Practice and the Acquisition and Maintenance of Expert Performance in Medicine and Related Domains. *Academic Medicine*, *79*(Supplement), S70–S81. doi:10.1097/00001888-200410001-00022 PMID:15383395

Ezequiel, O., Tibiriça, S., Grosseman, S., & Carvalho, P. M. (2012). Distance Learning and Conceptual Maps During Medical Clerkships. *Medical Education*, *46*(11), 1111–1111. doi:10.1111/medu.12018 PMID:23078699

Hubal, R.C., Kizakevich, P.N., Guinn, C.I., Merino, K.D., West, S.L. (2005). The Virtual Standardized Patient: Simulated Patient-Practitioner Dialogue for Patient Interview Training. Proceedings of Medicine Meets Virtual Reality.

John, B.S., Talbot, T.B., Lyon, T., Rizzo, A. (2015). Virtual Child Witness: Effects of single and multiple use on virtual human interview performance with novice and expert cohorts. Government Report.

John, B.S., Talbot, T.B., Lyon, T., Rizzo, A., Buckwalter, J. G. (2013). Training Effective Investigative Child Interviewing Skills Through Use of a Virtual Child: A Pilot Study Comparing Two Different Skill-Level Groups Performance with a Prototype of the Virtual Child Witness (VCW) Program. In 5th International Pediatric Simulation Symposia and Workshops (IPSSW), 236.

Kenny, P., Parsons, T. D., Gratch, J., & Rizzo, A. (2008). Evaluation of Justina: A Virtual Patient with PTSD. Intelligent Virtual Agents Lecture Notes in Computer Science, 394-408. doi:10.1007/978-3-540-85483-8_40

Kenny, P., Rizzo, A., Parsons, T. D., Gratch, J., & Swartout, W. (2007). A Virtual Human Agent for Training Clinical Interviewing Skills to Novice Therapists. *Annual Review of Cybertherapy and Telemedicine*, *5*, 81–89.

Kenny, P. G., Parsons, T. D., Gratch, J., & Rizzo, A. (2009). Evaluation of Novice and Expert Interpersonal Interaction Skills with a Virtual Patient. Intelligent Virtual Agents Lecture Notes in Computer Science, 511-512. doi:10.1007/978-3-642-04380-2_67

Leuski, A., & Traum, D. (2010). Practical Language Processing for Virtual Humans. *Proceedings of the 22nd Innovative Applications of Artificial Intelligence Conference (IAAI)*, 1741-1747.

Maguire, P., Fairbairn, S., & Fletcher, C. (1986). Consultation Skills of Young Doctors: Benefits of Feedback Training in Interviewing as Students Persist. *British Medical Journal*, *292*(6535), 1573–1576. doi:10.1136/bmj.292.6535.1573 PMID:3719282

Martin, J. M. (2014). *Subject: Emergent Leader Immersive Training Environment (ELITE) Lite Accreditation. U.S. Government Document*. ATZL-CTN-I.

Rizzo, A., & Talbot, T. B. (2015). *Virtual Patients Chapter in Combs D. The Digital Patient*. Wiley.

Rossen, B., Lind, S., & Lok, B. (2009). Human-Centered Distributed Conversational Modeling: Efficient Modeling of Robust Virtual Human Conversations. Intelligent Virtual Agents Lecture Notes in Computer Science, 474-481. doi:10.1007/978-3-642-04380-2_52

Sagae, K., Christian, G., Devault, D., & Traum, D. R. (2009). Towards Natural Language Understanding of Partial Speech Recognition Results in Dialogue Systems. Proceedings of Human Language Technologies: The 2009 Annual Conference of the North American Chapter of the Association for Computational Linguistics, Companion Volume: Short Papers on - NAACL 09, 53-56. 10.3115/1620853.1620870

Stevens, A., Hernandez, J., Johnsen, K., Dickerson, R., Raij, A., Harrison, C., & Lind, D. S. (2005). The Use of Virtual Patients to Teach Medical Students Communication Skills. The Association for Surgical Education Annual Meeting, 191(6), 806-811.

Talbot, T. B. (2013). Playing with Biology: Making Medical Games that Appear Lifelike. *International Journal of Gaming and Computer-Mediated Simulations*, *5*(3), 83–96. doi:10.4018/jgcms.2013070106

Talbot, T.B. (2015). COMRADE: Methods for Adaptive Competency Management and Just-in-Time Clinical Acumen Augmentation. MedSIM Magazine, 8(1).

Talbot, T. B., & John, B. (2013). *Virtual Child Witness*. International Pediatric Simulation Society.

Tokel, T., Talbot, T. B., Bautista, M., & Leeds, A. (2017). *Use of Virtual Standardized Patients for Facilitating Conversational Medical Interviews. Association for Educational Communications & Technology (AECT)*. Conference.

Chapter 4

Investigating Epistemic Stances in Game Play Through Learning Analytics

Mario Martinez-Garza
Independent Researcher, USA

Douglas B. Clark
University of Calgary, Canada

ABSTRACT

The authors apply techniques of statistical computing to data logs to investigate the patterns in students' play of The Fuzzy Chronicles and how these patterns relate to learning outcomes related to Newtonian kinematics. This chapter has two goals. The first goal is to investigate the basic claims of the proposed two-system framework for game-based learning (or 2SM) that may serve as part of a general-use explanatory framework for educational gaming. The second goal is to explore and demonstrate the use of automated log files of student play as evidence of learning through educational data mining techniques. These goals were pursued via two research questions. The first research question examines whether students playing the game showed evidence of dichotomous fast/slow modes of solution. A second research question investigates the connection between conceptual understanding and student performance in conceptually-laden challenges. Implications in terms of game design, learning analytics, and refinement of the 2SM are discussed.

DOI: 10.4018/978-1-5225-7461-3.ch004

INTRODUCTION

Digital games are potentially powerful vehicles for learning (de Freitas; 2018; Gee, 2007; Prensky, 2006; Mayo, 2009; Shaffer, Squire, Halverson, & Gee, 2005; Rieber, 1996; Squire et al., 2003), and numerous empirical studies have linked classroom use of educational games to increased learning outcomes in science (e.g., Annetta, Minogue, Holmes, & Cheng, 2009; Dieterle, 2009; Neulight, Kafai, Kao, Foley, & Galas, 2007; Squire, Barnett, Grant, & Higginbotham, 2004). Several reviews have concluded that game-based learning offers numerous theoretical and practical affordances that can help foster students' conceptual understanding, engagement, and self-efficacy (Aldrich, 2003; Cassell & Jenkins, 1998; Kafai, Heeter, Denner, & Sun, 2008; Kirriemuir & Mcfarlane, 2004; Martinez-Garza, Clark, & Nelson, 2012, Munz, Schumm, Wiesebrock, & Allgower, 2007). That said, not all games effectively support learning for all learners (Young et al., 2012). Clark, Tanner-Smith, and Killingsworth (2015) found favorable support for the use of educational games overall, but particularly in cases where games were augmented through the application of sound learning theory.

While the general question of whether games can provide productive contexts for learning is approaching consensus, *how* and *why* and *when* games work are more open questions. The effectiveness of game-based learning has been attributed to many causes (Linehan, Kirman, Lawson, & Chan, 2011; Dondlinger, 2007), including constructs as varied as fun, feedback, engagement, flow, problem-solving, narrative, etc. Several scholars have proposed design principles to optimally leverage some or all of these constructs (e.g., Annetta, 2010; Kelle, Klempke, & Specht, 2011; Tobias & Fletcher, 2007; Plass, Homer, & Kinzer, 2014). Also, educational games claim a broad spectrum of possible learning outcomes (Martinez-Garza, Clark, & Nelson, 2013b). Educational researchers have a vast space of explanations, design principles, and observed outcomes for game-based learning available, which in combination with the broad range of gaming genres, gaming populations, and technology platforms, creates a wide and constantly changing space of inquiry that resists generalized claims. Furthermore, digital games also present unique assessment challenges. Since games often incorporate novel student activities for which there are no well-established existing measurement methods, measures often need to be developed along with the game in an iterative fashion (Harpstead, Myers, & Aleven, 2013). Thus, some scholars have called for increased methodological rigor and emphasis on usable (i.e., generalizable) knowledge in educational games research (Dede, 2011; Foster & Mishra, 2008).

Regardless of the variations in theoretical framing, methods, or learning outcomes, the common denominator of all game-based learning research is the act of students' play. A general claim of game-based learning research can be phrased as "if a student plays this particular game, they will learn this particular thing." And while much inquiry into game-based learning is directed towards explicating other issues that influence and structure educational gaming (e.g., design considerations, materials and curricula to support educational games, and detection of learning outcomes), less attention is paid to the particulars of play itself, i.e., what choices the student has available, what informs those choices, and what feedback the game offers in response. Generally speaking, the act of play as the central driver of learning is somewhat under-examined in the educational gaming literature. Among the possible reasons for this lack of focus are (1) the general difficulty of observing, encoding, and analyzing play systematically, and (2) the limitations of general theoretical frameworks that might help operationalize play in meaningful actionable ways.

Previous educational research efforts that analyzed digital gameplay at the individual level have relied primarily on observational methods (e.g., Annetta, Minogue, Holmes, & Chang, 2009; Hou, 2012; Sengupta, Krinks, & Clark, 2015). Observational studies that aim for thick description (Geertz, 1973) of gamers at play explicate this richness and often succeed in building strong cases for learning (e.g., Squire, DeVane, & Durga, 2008). However, investigations of play that use a student's *in situ* performance as an indicator of the learning are generally limited in scope and scale by the costs and demands of observation and coding. A possible way to address this limitation involves the use of log file data (Slater, Joksimović, Kovanovic, Baker, & Gasevic, 2017). Students' actions within the game environment, when recorded and compiled, can potentially produce a rich and detailed account that can be productively analyzed using methods of statistical computing (Martinez-Garza, Clark, & Nelson, 2012). These statistical computing methods, variously known as *learning analytics* (LA), or *educational data mining* (EDM), could be used not only for assessment of learning, but also to find underlying structure and regularity in students' play that may inform meaningful generalizations about what constitutes learning through play in a particular game environment. Using a combination of log file data and learning analytics, educational games scholarship is working to potentially transcend the limitation of cost, time, and human effort without abandoning deep qualitative analysis (Berland, Baker, & Blikstein, 2014; Hooshyar, Yousefi, & Lim, 2018; Kinnebrew et al., 2017; Rowe et al., 2017).

OBJECTIVE

This paper has two goals. The first goal is to investigate the basic claims of the Two-System Framework of Game-Based Learning (Martinez-Garza & Clark, 2016), a cognitive perspective that may serve as part of a general-use explanatory framework for educational gaming. The second goal is to explore and demonstrate the use of educational data mining techniques on automatically collected log files of students' play. The data mining techniques featured in this paper could potentially find general use, and this paper aims at offering a demonstration of plausible methods and processes that are suited for the specific challenges of game play data.

The context for this research is an educational game intended to help middle school students develop a better understanding of Newtonian kinematics. Among its other functionalities, this particular game stores all student actions and collects them in a central database. The Conceptual Framework section describes this game, titled *The Fuzzy Chronicles,* in some detail. Then, a summary of the Two-System Framework (or 2SM) is presented, followed by specific discussion of the implications of the 2SM in the context of *The Fuzzy Chronicles.* A brief overview of current research that makes use of log files from digital educational environments as evidence rounds out the Conceptual Framework section.

Plan of Work

After laying out the necessary groundwork, we articulate the goal of investigating the central claims of the 2SM more specifically in two research questions. Research Question 1 (RQ1) asks, "can the two epistemic stances theorized in the 2SM be observed through the study of log files gathered from student play?" The epistemic stances described in the 2SM are best imagined as styles or strategies of play, and thus, a more targeted approach is warranted to investigate the effects of these styles on specific conceptual understandings that gameplay intends to promote. Research Question 2 (RQ2) provides this specificity by asking, "Do differences in gameplay in the specific game situations correlate with differences in performance on a conceptual knowledge test?" Each question is investigated in its own section, with separate Results and Discussion subsections. In the Conclusions, we outline some of the opportunities and difficulties of using educational data mining on digital game play logs, future directions for this kind of research, and also propose improved design factors for educational games that might better promote students' behaviors during play to more closely align with those behaviors found linked to positive learning outcomes.

CONCEPTUAL FRAMEWORK

Overview of the Game Environment: The Fuzzy Chronicles

For this study, we used the educational game titled *The Fuzzy Chronicles*, codenamed EPIGAME (Clark, 2012; Clark, Sengupta, Brady, Martinez, & Killingsworth, 2015). *The Fuzzy Chronicles* is the third iteration of the SURGE line of digital games intended to help students advance their understanding of Newtonian kinematics. *The Fuzzy Chronicles* (hereafter, EPIGAME) takes the form of a series of puzzles presented as a science fiction adventure. Students play as the space navigator Surge, who must find and rescue space capsules piloted by *Fuzzies*, adorable but somewhat hapless creatures who are stranded in space. In order to accomplish these rescues, the student must navigate Surge's spaceship through a two-dimensional spatial grid (see Figure 1 and Figure 2) by tracing a *Trajectory* to the stationary Fuzzy, then placing *Actions* at *Waypoints* along that Trajectory. Most Actions take the form of *Boosts* that propel Surge's ship in one the four cardinal directions with an amount of force that the student chooses. Gameplay is divided into *Levels*, each comprising a separate navigational and/or rescue challenge. All Levels have a *Start Point* and an *End Gate,* and may also optionally contain obstacles, such as impenetrable *Nebulas* and *Radiation*, as well as *Velocity Gates* and *Mass Gates* that impede Surge's progress. These Gates signal an attribute of Surge's capsule (i.e., a specific velocity or mass) that the student is required to match before the Gate will open. Colliding with a Nebula, a Radiation field, or a Gate causes the destruction of the Surge capsule and any rescued Fuzzies, and failure of the Level.

The interactive structure of EPIGAME has two phases - a *planning phase* and an *action phase*. In the planning phase, students decide their trajectory and place their actions appropriately. The student signals the end of the planning phase by hitting the *run lever*, thus starting the action phase. In this phase, Surge's capsule follows the student's plan, which may result either in a successful navigation to the end gate and the rescue of any stranded Fuzzies or the destruction of Surge's capsule. If successful, the student moves on to the next level. If the student is not successful and Surge's capsule is destroyed, they are returned to the planning phase in order to change the planned trajectory and/or add or remove actions before triggering a new action phase. Together, a planning phase and its resultant action phase are called an *attempt* (which may be successful or unsuccessful).

In theory, a student may complete the game having needed only one attempt (i.e., one planning phase and one action phase) per level. In reality, students often require multiple attempts before they successfully advance. In a given level, the student is free to construct a plan for the entire trajectory for the entire level and place all necessary actions before first activating of the run lever. Alternatively,

Figure 1. Anatomy of an EPIGAME level. (1) Start Point (2) Velocity Gate (3) Laser Deactivator (or "Button") (4) Nebula (5) Matching Button and Laser (note the green color of both) (6) End Gate (7) available Actions

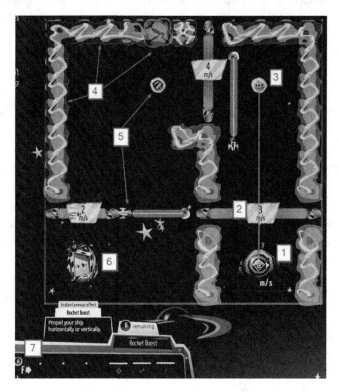

students may choose to segment the trajectory and place only a few actions at a time, thereby solving the level incrementally (i.e., draw part of a trajectory, place a few actions, activate the Run Lever, see what happens, and adjust and extend the trajectory and actions iteratively through multiple cycles of attempts). The game neither suggests nor encourages either approach, so a student may select whichever method they find more suitable.

A full game of EPIGAME as designed for this study consists of 32 levels of generally increasing complexity. Each subsequent level typically requires more actions than the previous ones, as it contains more challenges and obstacles, and demands more effort by the player to plan and strategize for success. Because of this, it is likely that any students of EPIGAME will find at least one level that requires multiple attempts in order to succeed. Some levels, particularly near the end of the game, allow only a very limited margin of error. Therefore, progress in the game requires the student to be persistent at times, take several different approaches when

Figure 2. An attempt in process. The student is setting direction (8) and force (9) parameters on an action. The student has set a trajectory (10) through several waypoints (a-e). To begin the attempt, the student presses the launch lever (11)

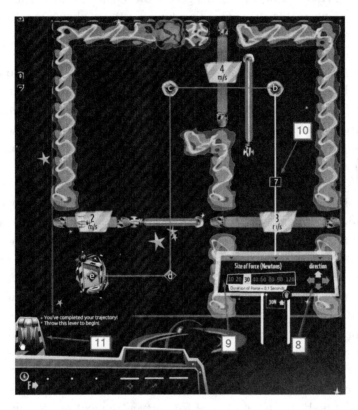

faced with apparently insurmountable levels of difficulty, and explore and experiment with different combinations of actions to find a correct solution for each level.

The Two-System Framework of Game-Based Learning

A goal of this paper is to investigate a theory of game-based learning called the Two-Stance Model framework, or 2SM (Martinez-Garza & Clark, 2016). The 2SM framework seeks to support a more sophisticated understanding of how and what people learn from digital games. It was motivated by the contrast between (a) recent scholarship that finds uneven evidence of the measurable learning outcomes of digital game play (de Freitas, 2018; Young et al., 2012) and (b) the observation that students inhabit rich ecologies of knowledge about the games they play (Gee, 2007) that include often-impressive feats of cognition.

Many digital games can be accurately described as software models of scientific phenomena encased within game-like structures that are intended to increase student engagement. In the case of educational games, the intention is that students develop an understanding of the principles that underlie these phenomena through the thoughtful and purposeful exploration of their scientific models. The premise of the 2SM framework is that students of educational games do not necessarily form accurate mental analogues of the software models that drive the phenomena they experience in-game (i.e., the encased "simulation"); rather, they create a second-order model (as in, a model of a model of a phenomenon) that is oriented towards explaining the functioning of the encased simulation, predicting its future states, and allowing the student to feel that they understand the simulation or game, and has some measure of control over it.

Students might have two distinct goals when interacting with a game's encased simulation. The first involves developing their second-order model to better understand the simulation and use it as a laboratory to investigate the objects and relationships within the simulation. The second goal involves executing various game actions to manipulate the simulation to create the desired state (i.e., success). These two sets of goals imply different forms of thinking about the information being presented by the digital game. Our hypotheses are that (a) the first goal prioritizes or incentivizes an inquiry stance oriented towards the purposeful and systematic investigation of the operating principles of the encased simulation and that (b) the second goal prioritizes or incentivizes a heuristic-driven problem-solving stance oriented towards efficiently achieving the player's goals. A student in the inquiry stance (or "learner" stance) might probe the simulation for information that confirms their understanding. A student in the problem-solving stance (or "player" stance) might only engage in exploratory actions and observe whether these actions lead to positive results.

These two stances can be conceptualized further using features from the two-system model of cognition (Evans, 2008). Two-system models of cognition distinguish between effortless thought, or "intuition", and deliberate purposeful "reasoning". These modes of cognition are neutrally labeled as System 1 and System 2, respectively. The former is described as fast, automatic, associative, emotional, and opaque; the latter as slower, controlled, serial and self-aware. In the 2SM framework, System 1 is associated with the "player" stance and System 2 with the "learner" stance.

Under this framework, when a person begins play, the game might suggest a goal to the player, immediately triggering a self-query, "how do I achieve this goal?" The self-query shifts the person towards the learning stance, and in response to the query a second-order model is constructed. This model is tuned and revised so that it consistently predicts which actions would effectively move the state of the game closer to the goal state. Alternatively, a player can "black-box" the game's encased simulation and rely on mental shortcuts, or heuristics. These heuristics are rendered as execution steps ("Do X so that Y happens") and enacted in the simulation through the game's interface. Heuristics that prove effective are reinforced and actions that have a negative effect are rephrased as avoidance steps ("Don't do X so that Y doesn't happen"). With repeated reinforcement, effective rules are matched to the context cues from the environment and stored as conditionals, i.e., "In situation Z, if you want Y to happen, do X." These conditionals, or *rules*, are easy to remember, quick to access, and require nearly no cognitive effort to execute: they fit the functional definition of heuristics.

Whenever the student finds herself in a situation that is covered by a stored rule, she will in most cases default to doing what that rule stipulates. When in unfamiliar territory, the student must shift to a learner stance, reinstate the second-order model, and use it to make new predictions. If the student always knows a rule that applies, the model is most likely deactivated and the student will default to System 1-style processing, or fast, effortless, intuitive heuristics. Thus, through play, a person gathers three forms of knowledge about the game: (a) the conditions that the game presents, (b) a set of heuristics, or rules of action with activation criteria that match these conditions, and (c) a second-order mental model, i.e., an idiosyncratic explanation of how the game systems produce the observed conditions. In the case of educational gaming, these three forms of knowledge combine to form part of the learning benefit that students may develop from playing the game.

The 2SM is a novel application of the two-system theory of reasoning to educational games. There are suggestive findings from adjacent programs of research that have examined forms of reasoning within and around digital learning environments supporting the validity of the 2SM (e.g., Parnafes & diSessa, 2004; Gijlers & de Jong, 2013). One of the goals of this paper is to explore the fundamental claims of the 2SM, namely that traces of students' System 1 and System 2 reasoning can be observed during play, and that preference for one stance over another has a significant effect on learning. These possible effects are explored in more detail in the following section.

Implications of the 2SM for Learning

In the 2SM, stances are defined as collections of resources (Hammer & Elby, 2003). The framework stipulates that the two stances are associated with cognitive processes described in the two-system theory of cognition (Sloman, 1996; Stanovich, 1999; Kahneman, 2003; Evans, 2008). Thus, a stance or collection of resources organized around System 1 would be optimized for processing speed and effortless thought, while a stance organized around System 2 would be primed for information use and deliberative reasoning. Stances, like resources, are cued around task demands. Certain tasks are structured in a way that discourages analytic reasoning (e.g., driving a car), while others, like academic writing, are less amenable to quick, associative thinking. That said, human beings are generally biased towards System 1 reasoning as an effort-saving and time-saving strategy (Reyna & Ellis, 1994).

The question then becomes, which of the two stances is most conducive to learning? Intuitively, it would seem that the effortful, analytic processes described as System 2 that drive the learner stance would be preferred over faster, less deliberate thinking. This would be particularly true in the case of games that are *conceptually integrated* (Clark & Martinez-Garza, 2012) because such games are designed in such a way that thinking about game rules and challenges closely parallels thinking about science concepts and relationships. However, it is uncertain whether an educational game can sustain System 2-type processing over long periods. First, students will tend to find ways to save time and effort when negotiating cognitively-demanding challenges, i.e., the "cognitive miser" of Fiske and Taylor (1991). Secondly, players facing a game they consider *too* challenging may simply disengage, thus negating any educational benefit the game might offer. Thus, a "happy medium" may be more desirable in which players both (a) reflect deeply about concepts and ideas represented in the game and (b) put their understanding into practice in motivating and interesting ways.

EPIGAME has some features aimed at achieving this "happy medium". It is intended to invite learners to think and reason about the concepts and relationships the game portrays and not to merely passively experience them. Players of EPIGAME encounter obstacles and situations of increasing difficulty that are designed not only to provide opportunities for learning but also to adapt to players' increasing knowledge and proficiency over the course of the game. Ideally, students encounter EPIGAME game levels whose difficulty matches but does not significantly exceed their own skill - this alignment keeps interest and engagement high even in the face of ostensibly higher cognitive demands (cf. "flow" in Csikszentmihalyi, 1991). But this adaptation is not perfect: students may encounter game levels that are too difficult or too easy. The goal then is ultimately not to shield students from difficulty but to provide enough scaffolding and feedback so that the *perceived* difficulty remains manageable.

We propose that a student's response to perceived difficulty cues the stances. Which stance is cued depends largely on each student's developing understanding of the concepts and relationships underlying the game. Early in the game, the perceived difficulty may be influenced by the student's prior experience with similar games or familiarity with the game's targeted concepts and relationships. Thus, the student's *prior knowledge* of the game or the principles behind the game's encased simulation may also be a significant factor that cues and organizes the stances. For instance, students with low prior knowledge might prefer a slower, more methodical approach, while students who feel confident in their understanding might play faster, and with less tentativeness, because they may have a more detailed and functional internal model. Later in the game, once all students have had similar opportunities to engage with the game's challenges, these differences might not be so stark, or they may disappear altogether. Therefore, it becomes important to examine the students' gameplay to ascertain how the game's varying set of structures and experiences influence students' learning.

Learning Analytics in Educational Gaming

Digital environments that promote learning should prompt a change in student behavior within that environment. If an educational game is designed in such a way that students are able to apply what they learn in the context of the game, then these changes in behavior should be reflected not only in external measures of learning but in play itself. If so, then these changes are potentially recoverable and traceable from log data *post hoc* (cf., Slater, Joksimović, Kovanovic, Baker, & Gasevic, 2017). However, changes in student behaviors that signal learning can be easily lost in the vastness and complexity of the available data, since even comparatively simple games allow for a broad range of student interactions. Methods based on learning analytics (LA) can provide researchers with tools to classify, predict, and discover latent structural regularities even in data sets as voluminous and idiosyncratic as gameplay logs (e.g., Berland et al., 2014; Hooshyar et al., 2018; Kinnebrew et al., 2017; Rowe et al., 2017). LA techniques cannot only help us characterize and describe learning behavior, but they can also deploy Markov-type approaches, such as Bayesian knowledge tracing and performance factors analysis, to provide some insight into latent student knowledge. Interestingly, these Markov-type models could be used for prediction and not just description; for example, they could be used to guide adaptive scaffolding and feedback. That said, while more research is required for these applications to achieve their full promise, significant ongoing work is already exploring and refining the use of learning analytics on data logs from educational environments.

The use of in-game performance data as evidence of learning outcomes has been proposed by Shute (Shute & Ventura, 2013) and others. Shute and colleagues proposed that a learner's actions within the game environment can be used as a form of assessment when evaluated against an evidence model, as per the evidence-centered design (ECD) assessment framework (Mislevy, Almond, & Lukas, 2003). Under this framework, evidence models are preceded by activity models, which are contextualized and tailored to the particular affordances and constraints of the learning environment. One implementation of EDC which seems particularly suited to educational games, "stealth assessment", aims to collect model data directly from the learning environment, bypassing the need for overt knowledge testing that may detract from the play experience. Using this methodology, Shute and Ventura have measured both learning of specific knowledge, e.g., as qualitative physics (Ventura, Shute, & Small, 2014), and also broad cognitive skills and traits, such as persistence (Ventura, Shute, & Zhao, 2013) and 21st-century skills (Shute, 2011).

Activity models can become highly complex, especially in the case of games in which many different interactions are possible. This complexity often leads to a large number of observable variables, which in turn complicates the task of formalizing them into an evidence model. For this reason, researchers have found value in machine-learning (ML) techniques of computational statistics that can make finding patterns and relationships between large numbers of variables more tractable. Examples of educational games where researchers have used ML techniques to analyze student performance data along an EDC paradigm are the investigation of systems thinking in *SimCityEDU* (Mislevy et al., 2014) and inquiry skills in *Mission Biotech* (Lamb, Annetta, Vallett, & Sadler, 2014). ECD models that are focused on content-specific outcomes that apply ML techniques are also feasible, such as the investigation of student learning of biological processes of stem cells in *Progenitor X* (Halverson & Owen, 2014); of fraction arithmetic in *Save Patch* (Kerr & Chung, 2012) and of Newtonian mechanics in *Impulse* (Rowe, Asbell-Clarke, & Baker, 2015). There are several more exemplars of ML techniques that are used to characterize students' performance in digital environments, although these focus either on learning environments that are simulation-based (rather than game-like) or do not align exactly with an EDG paradigm. Researchers have successfully applied ML techniques, for example, to describe (a) students' science inquiry activity in *Science Assessments* (Gobert, Sao Pedro, Baker, Toto, & Montalvo, 2012) and in *Virtual Performance Assessments* (Baker & Clarke-Midura, 2013; Clarke-Midura & Dede, 2010); (b) students' developing engineering thinking in *Nephrotex* (Chesler et al., 2015); and (c) students' understanding of genetics in *BioLogica* (Buckley et al., 2004).

RESEARCH QUESTIONS

The groundwork laid thus far has discussed the 2SM as a theoretical perspective for examining gameplay and discussed learning analytics as an approach to analyzing gameplay through data logs. The next step is to articulate the specific hypotheses and the kinds of evidence that might support them. As mentioned in the Objective section, this paper has two research questions, which we expand upon in greater detail in the following paragraphs.

Question 1: Can the Two Stances of the 2SM, as Specified by the Framework, Be Detected in Game Play Data?

The first question is intended to test a cornerstone claim of the 2SM, while also evaluating whether the 2SM is a useful lens for interpreting game play data as recorded in The Fuzzy Chronicles. The hypothesis is that gameplay logs exhibit an underlying interpretable structure when features relevant to the 2SM are selected and analyzed. In the case of the null hypothesis, there will be no such observable structure, or it will not be easily interpretable, or the structures revealed will not correlate significantly with learning outcomes.

Question 2: How Do Changes in Students' Functional Understanding of the Game Relate to Performance on a Test of Conceptual Understanding?

The second question refers to the feasibility of directly assessing students' emergent understanding of the concepts of Newtonian kinematics represented in The Fuzzy Chronicles based on their solutions to small, localized challenges. Each maneuver the students are asked to make in EPIGAME (starting and stopping, changing directions, keeping to a set velocity, picking up or throwing an object, etc.) is designed to highlight a particular physics concept or principle. By identifying and analyzing students' actions with regard to challenges *of the same type,* both within a student and over time, or between students, we can better understand how these challenges focus thought and learning for individual students. Since EPIGAME is intended to be a conceptually-integrated game (Clark & Martinez-Garza, 2012), the hypothesis is that improved performance in these conceptually-laden challenges indicates a greater understanding of the underlying principles of Newtonian kinematics. If the null hypothesis is true, variations in student performance will not correlate significantly with learning outcomes.

METHODS

Studies and Participants

To investigate the research questions, we performed two experimental runs using EPIGAME in the months of March and April 2015. The first run was used to address possible confounds as well as pilot the gameplay data "pipeline," or the entire process of collecting, collating, testing, and analyzing EPIGAME logs. We report on study 1, the pilot study, only briefly as foundation and comparison for study 2.

The second study, which is the focus of the current manuscript, deployed the full data analytic process to investigate both research questions. The two studies used the same EPIGAME version, the same assessments, and had roughly the same duration.

Study 1 (Pilot Study)

The participants were 86 9th-grade students from a public high school in Middle Tennessee. In this study, the students were divided into four groups, each randomly assigned into a Solomon four-group design (Solomon, 1949) (Figure 3). The 4-group Solomon experimental design was used in order to obtain a test of the internal validity of the posthoc effect sizes and test for interactions between the pre-test and the intervention. The two non-treatment groups participated in their normal classroom curriculum on the topic of force and motion, while the treatment groups only played the game for three 90-minute sessions. Approximately 20 minutes were reserved at the beginning and end of the entire study for a 21-item multiple-choice test intended to assess the students' conceptual and qualitative understanding of Newton's First and Second Law. Two of the groups, one treatment and one non-treatment, completed pre-tests; all four groups completed post-tests 5 days after the experiment began.

Our initial conjecture, in line with the 2SM, was that high pre-test score indicating a high prior conceptual understanding of physics would enable students to form more advanced play strategies. The use of these strategies would then be reflected in post-test gains. However, students might also be primed by the relationships and situations that appear in the pre-test, and post-test gains might correspond not to differences in gameplay or in prior knowledge, but in a testing effect. Thus, the goal of Study 1 was (1) to determine whether the version of EPIGAME was effective as a learning experience, (2) to investigate any possible testing effects. The statistical treatment of the four-group design that allows this disentanglement can be found in Braver and Braver (1988):

Two-way within-subjects ANOVA (Table 1) performed on the assessment data showed that students in Study 1 made significant pre-post gains ($F = 10.61$, df $= 104$, $p < 0.01$), with no strong evidence in favor of testing effects ($F = 1.11$, df $= 104$, $p = 0.29$) or interactions between pre-test scores and treatment ($F = 0.36$, df $= 104$, $p = 0.55$). This represents strong evidence that whatever knowledge students are bringing into gameplay was not gleaned from the pre-test, nor did the pre-test prime students as to which relationships or interactions were important and thus biasing performance in the post-test.

Figure 3. The Solomon 4-group design
Graphic from Braver & Braver (1988)

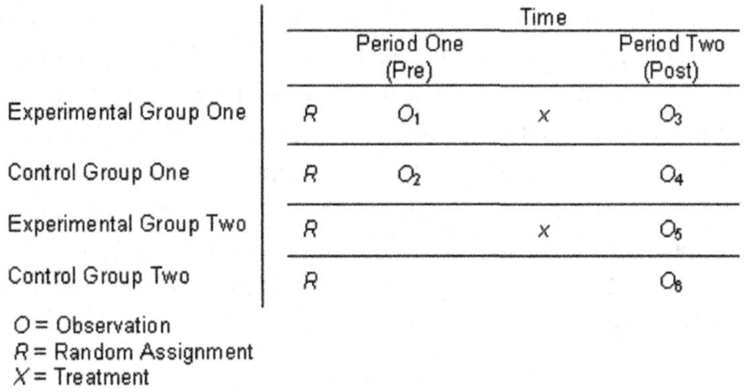

		Time	
		Period One (Pre)	Period Two (Post)
Experimental Group One	R	O_1	x	O_3
Control Group One	R	O_2		O_4
Experimental Group Two	R		x	O_5
Control Group Two	R			O_6

O = Observation
R = Random Assignment
X = Treatment

Table 1. Two-way within-subjects analysis of variance for Study 1

Effect	DF_n	DF_d	F	p	ges
Effect of pretest	1	104	1.1161	0.29	0.0106
Effect of treatment	1	104	10.614	0.002 **	0.0926
Pretest x Treatment	1	104	0.3552	0.55	0.0034

Study 2 (Research Study)

Study 1 helped to discard two competing hypotheses: that EPIGAME is not effective as a learning tool, and thus no patterns or changes in gameplay affect learning, and that pre-testing rather than gameplay is the source of any observed pre- to post-test gains. The remaining hypothesis, that differences in gameplay are indeed the source of pre- to post-test gains, is the focus of Study 2. In this second study, 123 7th grade students from a public middle school in Middle Tennessee used the EPIGAME software as part of their normal classroom instruction for five consecutive class periods lasting 45 minutes each.

As in the prior study, each student had their own computer and was specifically instructed to avoid sharing information. They could provide encouragement or hints in lieu of direct assistance, and researcher help was provided to students who appeared intractably stuck, were having technical issues, or had urgent questions about the game interface.

As in Study 1, approximately 20 minutes were reserved at the beginning and end of the intervention for a 21-item test of conceptual understanding of force in motion. All students who were present at the first and last day of the intervention were asked to complete the assessment. The pre-post assessment data was anonymized and students with missing pre- or post-test scores were dropped from the study. In the case of students with complete pre- and post-test scores, a unique ID was generated for each; that unique ID was used to link the assessment data with the game play data.

Of the 123 students who participated in the study, 104 provided both pre- and post-tests. A matched-pairs *t*-test showed a statistically significant increase in test performance ($t = 11.702$, df $= 103$, $p < 0.0001$) (Figure 4). The value of Cohen's *d* suggests a large effect size ($d = 1.62$).

Emulating the Evidence-Centered Design Approach

In the Learning Analytics in Educational Gaming section (above), a significant portion of the reviewed research that used learning analytics to make sense of students' process or log data used an evidence-centered design (ECD) framework for assessment as well. ECD offers several advantages for this form of research, *viz.*:

1.   The Student Model serves to constrain the number of latent variables that the ML algorithm must infer, aiding in model fit.

Figure 4. Boxplot of pre- and post-test results for Study 2

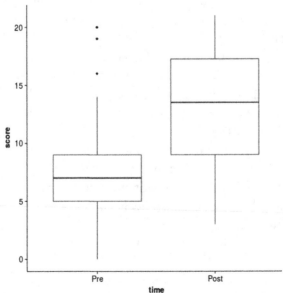

2.   The Evidence Model provides identification rules and ready-made coding schemes, boosting the interpretability of the final model.
3.   The Task Model pre-selects observed variables that are likely to be significant, obviating the need for dimensionality-reducing steps, such as a Principal Components Analysis to help reduce the number of observed variables to a tractable number.

Considering these advantages, it is clear that learning analytics and ECD processes are well-suited for each other. Unfortunately, it is likely unworkable to apply the ECD framework retrospectively, as the products of ECD are intended to address the specific purposes of that particular assessment (Mislevy, Almond, & Lukas, 2003). Thus, the goal would be to emulate some useful features of ECD, such as the student model and the evidence model. The student model can be operationalized in terms of the hypothesized dynamics of the 2SM. The evidence model would then map these dynamics into the observable variables. The end result would not be nearly as robust as the full ECD evidentiary argument, but would at least qualify as a cognitive model of task performance, or an illustration of the thinking processes underlying the knowledge and skills students apply *in vivo* when solving educational tasks in a specific domain (Leighton & Gierl, 2007).

An important feature of learning analytics and machine learning methods is that they generally cannot produce results that have inherent meaning. Unlike statistical treatments of parametric data such as pre- and post-test results, in which a statistically-significant result indicates a change in the participants' behavior along a measured construct, machine learning and data-mining algorithms generate descriptions of likely patterns and structures present in the data. It is up to the analyst to interpret what those patterns and structures mean and evaluate whether or not they support the proposition being researched (Vellido, Martin-Guerroro, & Lisboa, 2012).

Ideally, the interpretation of patterns and structures revealed by learning analytics are supported by robust theory. That is, features discovered in the data align with existing constructs and relevant explanations for the learning phenomena being studied. In this case, the proposed interpretive lens is provided by the 2SM. Under the 2SM framework, students use collections of resources, or stances, that organize around the cognitive processes that are optimized for fast ("player") or slow ("learner") processing. And so, the first task is to theorize how these stances would manifest as students play EPIGAME, i.e., how the "fast" and "slow" resources would affect gameplay. Evoking the evidence-centered design paradigm, we will call this operationalization the "student model". The second task is then to create an "evidence model," that is, to deduce how the actions and strategies defined in the student model will appear in the gameplay data logs. The goal of the evidence model is to select, from all the information contained in the logs, which pieces of data are most likely to characterize the operations defined in the student model.

The Student Model

The trial-based dichotomous pass/fail task structure of EPIGAME suggests two general strategies for arriving at a solution, one mainly using "fast" processing, and the other using "slow" processing. These strategies, or modes, are:

1. Additive-Iterative Mode, in which a student solves a level through a step-by-step iterative accumulation of actions, each checked for efficacy in a separate attempt.
2. Solve-and-Debug Mode, in which an entire solution is drafted whole-cloth, then corrected only if and as necessary.

While both of these approaches imply that the learner is *thinking,* they differ in what students are thinking *with,* and what they are thinking *toward.* A student using the Additive-Iterative Mode does not necessarily have to have a working knowledge of the game's concepts and relationships in mind; all they require is that EPIGAME provide an unambiguous signal that each added action is a step towards a solution (which EPIGAME provides, in the way of visually-clear animations, e.g., of Surge's capsule exploding or of the Exit Gate being activated). The Additive-Iterative Mode can be thought of as related to Parnafes and diSessa's (2004) "constraint-based thinking." Furthermore, a Solve-and-Debug approach necessitates that the student has a vision of a solution. Armed with a good working knowledge of the rules of operation, a student might feel more capable of taking more actions within each trial because they have a reasonable expectation that those actions will be effective. The Solve-and-Debug Mode can be thought of as related to Parnafes and diSessa's (2004) "model-based thinking."

Evidence Model

The two strategies described above represent the best estimate of the forms of play that students are most likely to use. While these forms of play sound very different mechanistically, it is useful to think of them as opposite ends along a continuum. On one end of this continuum, the Solve-and-Debug Mode is slow to plan, is more likely to be correct, and if it is not, it may require only small, effective fixes. On the other end, the Additive-Iterative Mode is fast, less likely to be correct since a student using this mode may not always define a full solution, and the iterative fixes are more error-prone. Thus, the differences between these two approaches may be captured with only a few contrasting parameters (Table 2).

The first and third parameters, *Response time* and *Actions per attempt*, are straightforward and directly observable in the data. A longer Response Time indicates slower, more deliberate processing; shorter Response Time corresponds to quick decision-making. Similarly, the number of Actions per attempt is likely specific to each Mode: more Actions taken in the same attempt implies a more elaborate, thought-out plan, while fewer Actions might indicate iterations or corrections.

The second parameter, *Error rate*, will have to be computed from other variables. Broadly speaking, the difference in Error rate between the two Modes represents the willingness of students to accept failed Attempts. Failure during an Attempt is more or less required in the Additive-Iterative Mode, since a student may consider failure as a "partial success" if it creates a baseline upon which they can iterate. A student using this Mode may also create a partial solution with some set of parameters they know, and guess at the remaining parameters, counting on the fact that the game will provide actionable feedback. Alternatively, failed Attempts when using the Solve-and-Debug mode are more likely to be unintentional or unforeseen mistakes, rather than intentional probes or guesses. Students using the Solve-and-Debug mode seek to avoid error rather than accept it as inevitable. Thus, the Error rate parameter should incorporate information on how often students fail a level repeatedly, as this continued error would indicate unsuccessful guessing and/or low-information processes such as exhaustive testing of all the available actions.

Treatment of the EPIGAME Logs

The data analysis of EPIGAME logs from Study 2 proceeded in four phases:

1. data normalization and integrity checks,
2. variable selection and dimensionality reduction,
3. clustering of student gameplay data and sequence mining, for RQ 1, and
4. contextual feature mapping, for RQ 2.

Table 2. Forms of solution and their likely parameters

Parameters	Additive-Iterative	Solve-and-Debug
Response time	Low	High
Error rate	High	Low
Actions per attempt	Low	High

Phase 1: The initial corpus of gameplay, recovered directly from the classroom server, was composed of 16,239 records. Each record described one particular student's attempt to solve one particular level. The version of The Fuzzy Chronicles used in this study had 32 levels, so each student produced an average of 132 attempts, approximately 4 attempts per level. Each record also contained a JSON object detailing the specific parameters of the attempt the student performed, such as where on the map an action was placed, how much time the student took to plan their actions, and which values the student chose for each parameter of each action. The dataset contained approximately 1.1 million of these gameplay parameters.

We then extracted a set of variables to help characterize each attempt. Broadly speaking, we extracted two kinds of variables: observed and derived variables. *Observed* variables are characteristics of gameplay directly recorded by the EPIGAME software, such as planning time. *Derived* variables are those discovered through logical tests or comparisons performed on observed variables, akin to a coding scheme. A total of 23 observed and derived variables were defined, each capturing an element or aspect of gameplay (see Appendix for a complete description of these variables). These 23 variables were selected on the basis of their ability to describe differentially the parameters for the forms of solution described in Table 2.

Phase 2: Generally, when using LA techniques, it is most desirable to have a data set with the smallest, most meaningful set of variables possible. Datasets with large numbers of variables are computationally very expensive to process, and such data is vulnerable to a variety of phenomena that distort results and complicate these types of analyses. In order to select only the most meaningful variables, we performed a Principal Components Analysis (PCA) on the dataset (16,239 attempts x 23 variables) using the *FactoMineR* software for *R* (Husson, Josse, Le, and Mazet, 2007). The PCA returned 3 components with eigenvalues greater than 1, with a total of 72.1% variance explained by those three components. The full results of the PCA are included in Table 3 (below). The variables associated with the components were:

1. Component 1:
   a. *tl.Modifys*, a count of how many modifications a student made to the parameters of placed Actions, e.g., changing a Boost from 10N to 20N increases *tl.Modify* by 1.
   b. *tj.Adds*, a count of how many Waypoints were added to the Trajectory.
   c. *planningTime.log*, the observed time students spend planning and placing elements, in seconds, logarithmically transformed to amplify the difference between shorter and longer planning times.
   d. *eff.actions.added*, a derived variable counting how many new Actions were executed effectively on a given attempt compared to the previous attempt.

2. Component 2:
   a. *par*. A model-based effectiveness score derived from a Markov-chain model of the combined series of outcomes of all the students' plays of each level. Each student generated a chain of Attempts for each level, and each attempt had a particular outcome, e.g., one Attempt ends in a navigation error, then two Attempts ended at Velocity Gates, then the next Attempt ended at the Success Gate. This chain of Attempts captures each student's transversal of a level. When all students' chains of Attempts for a given level are taken together, we can use a Markov-chain model to calculate the probability that a student will transition from one outcome to another on a per-attempt basis. The model is then used to calculate *par,* which is the posterior probability of a Success state occurring randomly at the end of an Attempt given the state at the end of the previous Attempt (as in, e.g., golf, "the chance of making par"). These probabilities can range from (0,1], with 0, or no chance of success on the next attempt, being indicative of random play, and 1, or certainty of success in 1 more attempt, indicating expert play. In other words, the *par* metric asks, "if this student were playing totally randomly – that is, following only the transitions observed for all students as a whole - given that their last attempt ended in a certain outcome, what is the probability that they will find the Success Gate through sheer chance in one more attempt?"[1] An important property of this metric is that it penalizes very long chains of Attempts and rewards navigating to the Success Gate on the first Attempt.
   b. *par.delta.sqrt*. The change in the value of the *par.sqrt* metric from attempt *n*-1 to *n* for the current level and student, square-root transformed.
3. Component 3:
   a. *is.abort*, an observed variable that tests whether or not the student manually aborted the attempt using the Abort button.
   b. *fail.same,* a derived variable that tests, if an Attempt was failed, whether or not a student failed that Attempt at the same place on the map as the immediately-previous Attempt *and* whether both Attempts failed for the same reason.

Since *par.sqrt* and *par.delta.sqrt* were linear combinations of each other, *par. sqrt* was discarded in favor of *par.delta.sqrt*, which had the higher squared cosine for Component 2. At this point, further treatment of the data followed the line of inquiry specific to each research question. Relevant details can be found in their respective sections below.

Table 3. Results of the Principal Components Analysis

	Component				
	1	**2**	**3**	**4**	**5**
Modifications to Timeline	0.4746	0.0015	0.0000	0.0001	0.0014
Additions to Trajectory	0.4173	0.0078	0.0000	0.0001	0.0000
Effective Actions added	0.1787	0.0000	0.0014	0.2471	0.0000
Par metric (square root transformed)	0.0345	0.4694	0.0000	0.0000	0.0005
Change in Par metric from previous Attempt	0.0001	0.7498	0.0000	0.0002	0.0005
Planning time (log transformed)	0.3297	0.0028	0.0000	0.0274	0.0000
Test of consecutive similar failure	0.0854	0.0048	0.1082	0.0000	0.0890
Test whether Level was aborted	0.0000	0.0014	0.6434	0.0000	0.0220

Note: values are given as squared cosines

RESULTS RQ1: CAN THE TWO STANCES OF THE 2SM BE DETECTED IN GAMEPLAY DATA?

The main claim of the 2SM is that the stances organize around fast- and slow-processing mechanisms, so we tested the data for play strategies that embody fast and slow play. After the dimensionality reduction process above, we are left with a manageable number of variables which are nonetheless theoretically significant and useful in describing these strategies.

Clustering

The next step in the analysis is to examine the dataset to determine whether students' play has some latent order or structure that can be brought into focus using our theoretically-relevant variables. To find this possible structure, we will use *clustering*, an unsupervised classification method. The goal of a clustering algorithm is to find the groups of observations whose features are more similar within-group than with regard to the data at large. Since this technique is unsupervised, we do not provide a pre-determined classification scheme for the software to "learn"; the rationale for this choice is that if a clustering algorithm returns a reasonably-interpretable set of clusters and these clusters were created by interactions between theoretically-significant variables, then that is a solid indication that the theory describes latent structures of the data.

With the final list of seven variables already selected, we proceeded to create a similarity matrix using Gower's coefficient to account for the mixed data types. Then, we performed affinity propagation clustering with the resulting similarity matrix. Affinity propagation (AP) is a clustering method that takes as input measures of similarity between pairs of data points and simultaneously considers all data points as potential exemplars (Frey & Dueck, 2007). This method was selected as preferable to the more conventional k-means/k-medoids method because of its ability to produce a set of meaningful exemplars for each cluster – a vital consideration given the variation possible between attempts and the need to later interpret the characteristics of each cluster reasonably.

The AP clustering algorithm converged on a set of 145 "proto-clusters" after 260 iterations. These "proto-clusters" were then collapsed using an agglomerative method akin to hierarchical clustering. The resulting cluster dendrogram is given in Figure 5. The lower segment of each line indicates a separate proto-cluster, and the height of the joint between two proto-clusters indicates how similar they are, with greater height indicating more similarity between the clusters being joined.

Visual inspection of the cluster dendrogram suggested that a "cut" at 0.905 altitude would reduce the number of clusters to a manageable six. This clustering solution was codenamed *part.6*. The "goodness of fit" of an AP clustering solution is difficult to ascertain via standard methods such as Rand coefficients because AP clustering does not necessarily aim to produce compact clusters. Rather, it seeks to maximize the "representativeness" of the chosen exemplars. In order to determine the adequacy of the *part.6* solution, we created a heat map from the similarity matrix (Figure 6).

Figure 6 shows the degree of dissimilarity between Attempts as a heatmap. The heatmap is 16239 (the number of Attempts) cells by 16239 cells, and each cell is colored by the similarity between the row Attempt and the column Attempt. White means highly similar Attempts, dark orange indicates most dissimilar Attempts. The intention of the heatmap is to show how similar the clusters were within and how distinctive they were without. Cluster 2 (in yellow) was the least similar one (i.e., it contains more orange cells, indicating within-cluster dissimilarity), where Clusters 1 and 4 are very similar within members. Cluster 5 is somewhere in the middle, and Clusters 3 and 6 are too small to show structure at this resolution. We iterated on the *part.6* solution several times in an attempt to resolve Cluster 2 (corresponding to the yellow region) into 3+ smaller clusters as suggested by the heat map, but no satisfactory solution was found that preserved the other clusters, and so the *part.6* solution prevailed. The distribution of Attempts across the six clusters of the *part.6* solution are given in Figure 7.

Figure 5. Cluster dendrogram of the AP clustering result

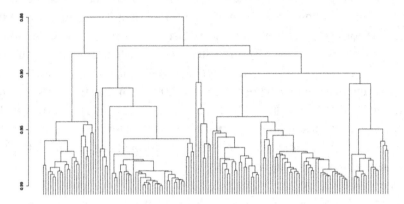

Figure 6. Heat map of the similarity matrix, along with the dendrogram of the part.6 clustering solution. According to the dendrogram, Clusters 2 (yellow) and 5 (blue) are most similar, while Cluster 4 (cyan) is the most distinct

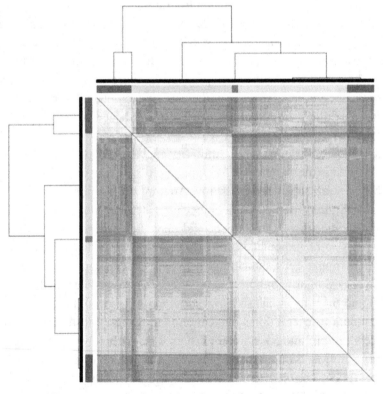

*For a more accurate representation see the electronic version.

Before proceeding to the sequence mining, we studied the properties of the *part.6* clustering. As noted above, the preliminary variable reduction performed through PCA left us with only 7 theoretically-significant variables out of the original 26. The *part.6* solution represents a mathematical arrangement of students' attempts that have some similar structure in terms of these 7 variables. Figure 8, below, shows a generalized pairs plot (Emerson et al., 2012) that helps visualize how the structure of each cluster responds to each of the feature variables.

From each of the clusters, we visually examined the exemplar chosen by the AP clustering algorithm, the two nearest neighbors to the exemplar, and two random members of that cluster. The 5 members of each cluster were interpreted, both by themselves and in the context of the sequence of level attempts in which they occurred. Based on this analysis, we labeled the clusters qualitatively according to a general description of the students' actions therein:

- **Cluster 1 (in red): *ABORTS*.** Students recognize that the level is going to fail and press the "Abort the Mission" button to preserve the momentum of play rather than allow the simulation to end on its own.

Figure 7. Histogram of the distribution of Attempts across part.6 clusters

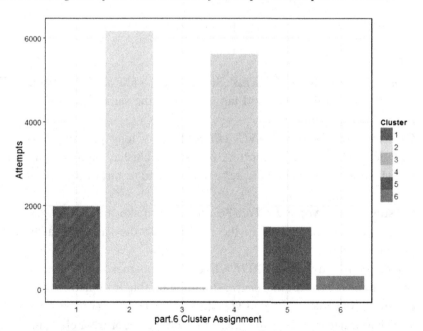

For a more accurate representation see the electronic version.

Figure 8. Generalized pairs plot (Emerson, et al., 2012) of the 7 theoretically-significant variables with the highest eigenvalues, plotted against each other, and classified according to the part.6 solution (rightmost column)

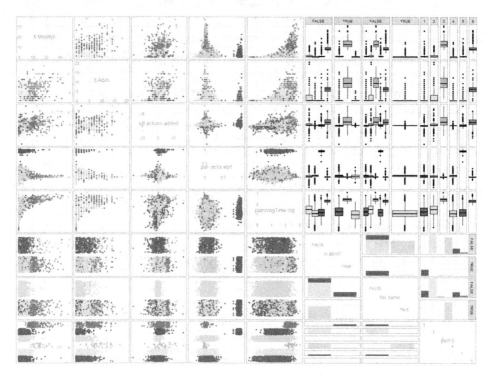

- **Cluster 2 (in Yellow):** *TINKER*. Students add a few actions, advance a little further along in the level, and fail, but not in the same place on the map as the previous Attempt
- **Cluster 3 (in Green):** *LONG ABORTS*. Very long planning episodes (> 100 seconds) that end in Abort. A very sparse cluster, barely distinguishable from Cluster 1. Possibly indicates a deletion and restart of the solved level in progress.
- **Cluster 4 (in Cyan):** *FUTILITY*. Students make a few changes but fail exactly in the same place in the map against the same obstacle as their previous attempt.
- **Cluster 5 (in Dark Blue):** *WINNING*. Students make one or more changes or additions that result in a successful attempt, thus completing the level.
- **Cluster 6 (in Pink):** *PLANNING*. Students spend a long time and add actions as well as trajectory elements (i.e., added both categories of elements). These attempts are occasionally successful, but not always.

Further investigation revealed that cluster assignments have some structure both in terms of *when* they occur in the order of play (i.e., early levels vs. later levels in Figure 9) and in terms of learning outcomes of the student that produced them (i.e., in terms of pre-post learning gains in Figure 10).

As we can see, the relative distribution of the cluster assignments may be sensitive to the learning outcome of the student (Figure 10). In other words, the levels played by students at a given level of pre-post test performance may have a different ratio of cluster assignments than those of students at a different level of performance. The different frequency profiles in Figures 5 and 6 suggest, furthermore, that the differences are not entirely due to how far students progress into the game. It follows that the *part.6* cluster solution provides not only a set of meaningful code assignments that describe students' play but also that these assignments are related somehow to learning outcomes. Figure 10 further suggests that cluster patterns evolve as students progress through the game.

Sequence Mining

Sequence mining is a way to find patterns in ordered data, such as words in a sample of natural language or genes in a protein. The main requirement is that the order

Figure 9. Frequency of part.6 cluster assignment by level. Graph shown is smoothed via local least-squares regression fitting (α=0.65)

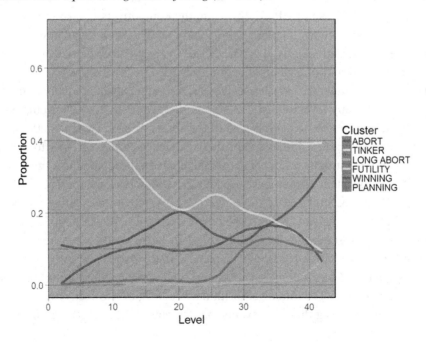

Figure 10. Frequency of part.6 cluster assignment by pre-post test score gain

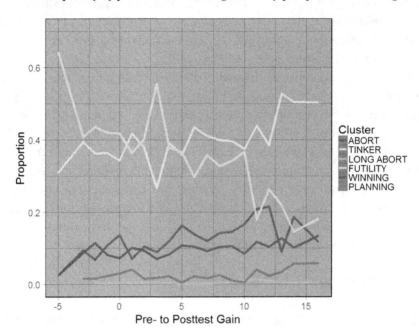

of the components is as significant, or more significant, than their frequencies. The question sequence mining asks is, "given a set of items that form sequences, what are the most common smaller sequences to be found within and across those sequences?" In the case of EPIGAME data, the components to be sequenced are cluster membership codes; in other words, our goal is to investigate how students' actions, described individually in general terms by the clustering procedure, appear in succession as a part of a chain of actions intended to solve a level.

The dataset contained 2730 such sequences, meaning that the students' combined attempts to solve any level totaled 2730, or an average of 22.2 levels attempted per student. Each sequence was comprised of the series of each student's attempts to solve a single level; thus, the length of these sequences ranged from 1 to 140, the minimum and maximum number of consecutive attempts recorded in a single level. To perform the sequence mining, we used the *TraMineR* package for *R* (Gabadinho, Ritschard, Muller, & Studer, 2011). This package can calculate the relative importance of *subsequences* of elements within the element chains of sequence data. The relative importance of subsequences is measured not in terms of their frequency but in terms of "support", or the fraction of sequences in the overall sample that contain that subsequence. More salient subsequences will appear within more sequences than less salient ones. The mining algorithm was configured to seek only first-order subsequences, meaning that only events that happen consecutively are considered to be in sequence, and the minimum support level was set at 0.01; in other words, to qualify for analysis, a subsequence had to be supported by at least 27 sequences. An additional parameter was set so that the support of subsequences of *n* identical codes would be consolidated across all sequences found in one or more identical codes. The algorithm returned 47 candidate subsequences, which were then ordered by support. The results of the sequence mining are given in Figure 11, below:

The height of the bars in the graph indicate the support for that subsequence, and they are ordered by decreasing support. Support for the unitary subsequences, e.g., (TINKER), the most common one, are quite high since, for example, a sequence of (TINKER) - (TINKER) - (TINKER) can claim the subsequence (TINKER) a total of 6 times. This means that our data contained a high proportion of sequences containing long chains of TINKER, and similarly high proportions of chains of FUTILITY. The high support value of WINNING is to be expected since 97% of all sequences end with WINNING, which is how students advance in the game after all.

To investigate the relationship between play sequences and learning, we then classified students according to their pre-post test performance. Since the group of students as a whole gained significantly in their pre- to post-test scores, we chose a classification strategy that would qualify their gains relative to the overall increase in scores. The resulting classification scheme is summarized in Table 4 (below). The "High Prior" group consisted of students who scored in the upper quartile in both pre- and post-tests. The "Low Prior" group is likewise formed of students who scored in the bottom quartile of the pre- and post-test. A third group, "Learned" contains students whose pre-test scores were in the lower three quartiles but who improved their score by at least one quartile. A fourth group, "Null", collected students whose

Figure 11. The 25 highest-supported subsequences. Numbers in parenthesis indicate cluster assignment of the sequenced items, following the part.6 solution (above)

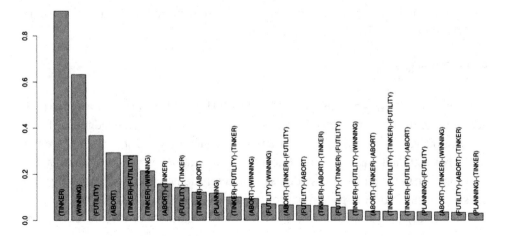

pre-test was in the higher three quartiles but did not show a significant increase in their scores. The number of students in each classification was 14, 13, 23, and 54, respectively.

These assignments were used as discriminant groups so that each detected subsequence's support could be tested for correlation with learning outcomes via a Chi-square test. Table 5 contains the 18 subsequences with the highest Chi-square statistic. Support for these subsequences thus varies by discriminant group in a statistically significant way. The graph of the resulting support values for each subsequence according to the student classification group is provided in Figure 12 (below).

In Figure 12, red bars indicate subsequences with significantly less support than under the assumption of independence. Conversely, blue-colored bars indicate significantly more support. Sequences in white show no statistical significance across all four groups. These significances are computed at the 0.01 level; light-blue and light-red bars indicate significance at the $p = 0.05$ level. For significance testing, the p-values were Bonferroni-corrected for multiple comparisons. This correction increases the probability of false negatives, but protects against incorrectly rejecting the null hypothesis, i.e., that the support values for the subsequences do not vary across discriminant groups.

This group-discriminant sequencing analysis suggests that students in the High Prior knowledge group have sharply fewer FUTILITY subsequences, fewer TINKER-FUTILITY and FUTILITY-TINKER, ABORT-TINKER, TINKER-FUTILITY-TINKER, and FUTILITY-TINKER-FUTILITY cycles, and substantially more PLANNING chains. Conversely, students with Low Prior knowledge are more likely to present longer FUTILITY chains and more TINKER-FUTILITY cycles. These students are also more likely to follow FUTILITY with ABORT, ostensibly because they recognize the probable outcome of that attempt would also have been FUTILITY. Students in the middle two quartiles who do demonstrate a relative increase in their conceptual understanding also show more FUTILITY chains and slightly more TINKER-FUTILITY chains.

RQ1 Discussion

The sequence analysis reveals that students with High or Low Prior knowledge play very differently than their peers. Students who have High Prior knowledge plan more and exhibit very few sequences of attempts in which they are stuck. They are not as likely to attempt small iterative fixes, preferring more complex and thought-out solutions. On the other hand, if students consistently demonstrate repeated failure on the same obstacle over large numbers of attempts, such as in a FUTILITY sequence, it is less likely that they improved their learning, regardless of their level of prior

Table 4. Classification of Students by relative pre-post gains

Pre-Test Score (Quartile)	Post-Test Score (Quartile)		
	1st	*2nd – 3rd*	*4th*
1st	Low Prior	Learned	Learned
2nd – 3rd	Null	Null	Learned
4th	Null	Null	High Prior

Table 5. Sequence analysis by discriminant group

Subsequence	*p*	Chi-Sq	Support by Group			
			High Prior	Learned	Low Prior	Null
(WINNING)	0.0000	115.71	0.42	0.60	0.81	0.69
(FUTILITY)	0.0000	113.28	0.17	0.32	0.54	0.43
(TINKER) – (FUTILITY)	0.0000	98.56	0.11	0.24	0.45	0.34
(FUTILITY) – (TINKER)	0.0000	33.92	0.06	0.13	0.22	0.17
(TINKER) – (FUTILITY) – (TINKER)	0.0000	32.16	0.03	0.09	0.15	0.12
(PLANNING) – (WINNING)	0.0001	29.05	0.04	0.01	0.00	0.01
(PLANNING)	0.0003	26.88	0.19	0.12	0.08	0.10
(FUTILITY) – (TINKER) – (FUTILITY)	0.0006	25.28	0.01	0.05	0.10	0.07
(FUTILITY) – (ABORT) – (TINKER)	0.0006	25.28	0.02	0.04	0.10	0.04
(ABORT) – (TINKER)	0.0013	23.77	0.09	0.15	0.23	0.17
(ABORT) – (TINKER) – (FUTILITY)	0.0021	22.78	0.02	0.06	0.12	0.08
(FUTILITY) – (ABORT)	0.0051	20.89	0.04	0.06	0.14	0.07
(ABORT)	0.0178	18.25	0.22	0.28	0.36	0.32
(TINKER) – (ABORT) – (TINKER) – (FUTILITY)	0.0560	15.79	0.01	0.02	0.06	0.03
(TINKER) – (WINNING)	0.0983	14.55	0.15	0.23	0.28	0.22
(LONG ABORT)	0.1368	13.80	0.03	0.02	0.01	0.01
(FUTILITY) – (WINNING)	0.1510	13.57	0.03	0.07	0.08	0.09
(TINKER)	0.1528	13.54	0.86	0.90	0.94	0.92

Figure 12. Sequencing analysis by group

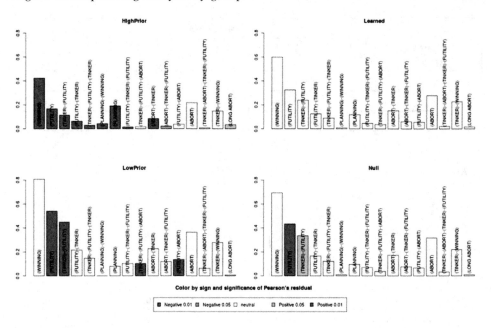

knowledge. No particular way of playing, or subsequence exhibited by students in the *Learned* group, seems to correlate with relative learning gains independently of prior knowledge.

This finding suggests that students' gameplay choices are strongly influenced by their prior knowledge: *High Prior* knowledge students played a very *different game* than their *Low Prior* peers. The former group approached the game as a "planning game," preferring the creation of complete solutions that required only small adjustments, making full use of the Solve-and-Debug strategy hypothesized in the Student Model. The latter group likely saw the game as a "guess and check game" or "tweaking game", where solutions emerged gradually out of extended iterating cycles of more-or-less purposeful trial-and-error, described earlier as an Additive-Iterative strategy.

Why are students in the *Low Prior* group more likely to use the Additive-Iterative strategy? From the Two-System Framework perspective, these students could be said to prefer low-effort, low-information, control-oriented processing strategies. Students who play in the Additive-Iterative mode are more reliant on feedback from the game, since such feedback, rather than evaluation of internalized models, represents their main source of information about how the game operates. The 2SM conceptualizes these as being closer to the Player Stance. On the other hand, students who play the "planning game" can rely more on their own ability to visualize and predict how the game will respond to their input, and thus probably require less feedback from "tweaking" or "guessing and checking." This correlates well with the general descriptions in the 2SM of the Learner Stance.

RESULTS RQ2: GAME/TEST PERFORMANCE RELATIONSHIPS

The main learning goal of EPIGAME is to help students build a deeper understanding of Newtonian kinematics. Thus, the game's rules and systems deal with inertia and the relationship between force and velocity. Ideally, as students improve their ability to solve inertial challenges, their conceptual understanding, per an external measure, should likewise improve. From the previous analysis (see Question 1 section, above), we know that students with different degrees of prior knowledge approach the game differently and play in sharply different ways. In terms of Question 2, we investigated whether these differences in performance on the tests correlate with differences in gameplay in the specific game situations intended to help students develop concepts of inertia.

The first step in this analysis was coding the conceptual challenges. Each challenge is a situation on the game map where a student has to apply one or two maneuvers to advance past that situation. The selected challenges all deal with *inertia* and/or *Newton's second law of motion*. These concepts can be portrayed in EPIGAME in one of four ways:

1. The student must navigate Surge from rest up to a certain velocity by applying an unbalanced force (Figure 13). There are 46 such challenges, and they were coded as *fromStop*.
2. The student must bring Surge from a constant velocity to a stop by applying one or more forces opposed to the direction of motion (35 challenges, coded as *toStop*). (Figure 14)
3. The student must increase the velocity of Surge to a certain level while Surge is in motion by applying an unbalanced force in the direction of motion (4 challenges, coded as *speedUp*). (Figure 15)
4. The student must decrease the velocity of Surge to a certain level while Surge is in motion by applying an unbalanced force opposite the direction of motion (5 challenges, coded as *slowDown*). (Figure 15)

Through visual inspection of the levels, we identified the location and type (*fromStop, toStop, speedUp,* or *slowDown*) of the conceptual challenge. Only the first 90 challenges students encounter while playing EPIGAME were coded. The rationale for this limit is that the conceptual nature of these challenges changes in

Figure 13. A fromStop challenge. Students begin motion from rest at point B and navigate toward C

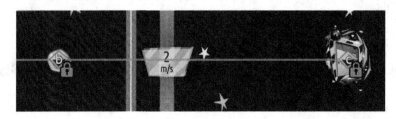

Figure 14. A toStop challenge. Students must completely stop at B before proceeding to C

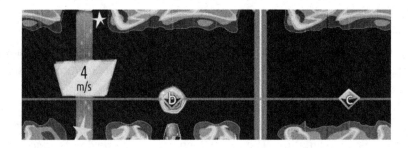

Figure 15. A slowDown (left) and a speedUp challenge (right). In both cases, the student must apply an unbalanced force at B

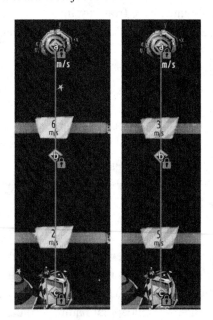

the latter levels, first when changes in mass are introduced, and then when students have to deal with forces applied in action-reaction pairs. Thus, the first 90 challenges students encounter before these increases in complexity are the most conceptually similar and can be safely compared. Furthermore, these first 90 challenges are where we might be most likely to see trajectories of improvement because it tracks students from the beginning of the game where the learning curve may prove the clearest.

To analyze these first 90 challenges, the overall gameplay dataset was filtered through a conditional join in order to identify which attempts ended at one of the coded challenges. A total of 2175 attempts were identified. Later, we decided to reduce the sample to 1282 attempts corresponding to the first 15 challenges of each type, under the rationale that the unbalanced number of challenges per type (e.g., 46 *fromStop* vs. 4 *slowDown*) would likely lead to problems with the model fit if we used the challenge type as a covariate.

Next, we proceeded to fit a generalized linear model to the data. Since the dependent variable is a count comprised of positive whole numbers only, a Poisson regression would be most appropriate. However, the data showed considerable overdispersion, and thus a negative binomial regression was chosen.

Generalized Linear Model

The statistics of the generalized linear model are provided in Table 6. In this model, the High Prior classification and *fromStop* challenge type are the model references. The statistically significant predictors of student errors per Conceptual challenge are Challenge instance, and as noted, the type of challenge is not a statistically significant predictor. Furthermore, a previous iteration of the model showed that the interaction terms of the predictors were also not statistically significant. From these results, we concluded that the variables best suited to predict the number of errors students commit are the number of similar challenges already faced and the students' prior knowledge.

RQ2 Discussion

The generalized linear model fitted to the challenge data confirms the hypothesis that students tend to make fewer errors on a challenge each successive time they encounter a challenge of the same type. More surprising is that the *mean* number of errors can also be predicted on the basis of a student's prior knowledge grouping. In other words, the first 15 times students face challenges of a given type, students who score highly on the pre-test are likely to commit as few as half as many errors as students who did not score highly.

Figure 16. Mean errors per student per Conceptual challenge. Student achievement groups are in columns. Challenge types are in rows

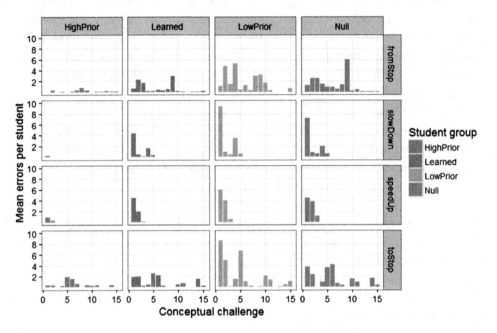

Table 6. Coefficients of the negative binomial regression model

	Dependent Variable: Number of Errors per Challenge		
	Estimate	**Std. Error**	***p*-value**
Challenge instance	-0.064***	0.008	*>0.001****
Learned	0.484***	0.148	*0.001****
Low Prior	0.744***	0.153	*>0.001****
Null	0.654***	0.140	*>0.001****
slowDown Challenge	0.112	0.090	*0,21*
speedUp Challenge	0.008	0.093	*0.93*
toStop Challenge	0.040	0.067	*0.55*
Constant	1.117***	0.150	*>0.001****
Observations	1,282		
Log Likelihood	-3,221.669		
theta	1.371***	0.066	
Akaike Inf. Crit.	6,459.338		
Note:	****p<0.01*		

A possible explanation is suggested by the bar chart matrix on Figure 16. We can see there that students in the High Prior column make fewer errors overall, but more importantly, commit nearly no errors the first time they face a challenge of a given type. Students in other groups commit at least 3 errors on average and often more. Given their lack of familiarity with EPIGAME, it would seem reasonable that High Prior students would make at least a few errors when they initially encounter a challenge, while they internally navigate how their understanding of physics does or does not apply to the situations and rules of the game. However, the near-total absence of errors on initial contact with challenge types suggests that High Prior students *already know* something directly relevant to these challenges.

There are at least two other sources of knowledge besides any prior EPIGAME experience that students might be drawing on when they face new challenges. First, they may be drawing on inferences made from the pre-test. However, we demonstrated in Study 1 that EPIGAME and the EPIGAME assessment are free of testing effects (see Methods section), so a "priming" effect is unlikely. The other source might be the tutorial animations embedded in EPIGAME. There are two types of tutorials. At levels 1, 4, 8, 10 and 11, the tutorial animations are essentially *worked examples*. Students watch as the Mentor character demonstrates skills such as how to apply forces, how to draw Waypoints, and how to start the trial. These animations are intended to guide students as they learn the game's interfaces, design conventions, etc. On the other hand, the tutorials at levels 2 and 7 are *contrasting cases* (Figure 17). These animations take the form of experiments; a challenge is approached with several combinations of parameters, of which only one is correct. The student must deduce from this demonstration *why* that particular maneuver was effective. While the "worked example" tutorials show the *hows* of EPIGAME, the "contrasting case" tutorials show the *whys*.

Our explanation for the low rate of error of High Prior knowledge students during initial trials relative to their lower-prior-knowledge peers is grounded in the 2SM. The 2SM defines two broad classes of knowledge regarding "how to play": heuristics and internalized models. The "worked example" tutorials, with their emphasis on how to execute specific maneuvers, have more "heuristicness" than "modelness". Conversely, the "contrasting cases" tutorial focus strongly on the variables and relationships at play, suggesting more model quality. It may be that the main difference between High Prior students and their peers is *which form of the tutorial* they chose to focus on. Since each form of tutorial primes a different form of knowledge about "how to play", students with a strong preference for one form of tutorial over the other may approach the game with different kinds of knowledge and therefore play in different ways. And in fact, these differing styles of play do emerge (see Question 1), with High Prior students showing a marked preference for slow, deliberate play and a small tolerance for error. In contrast, students in the

Figure 17. A "contrasting case" tutorial. The use of 10N and 30N are both incorrect for a 2m/s Velocity Gate

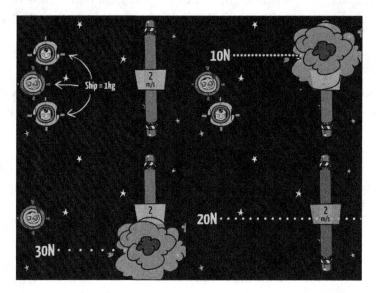

Low Prior and Null learning groups prefer iterative, "tweaking" gameplay that is inherently more fast-paced, yet they tend to accrue errors at each challenge, often as many as 10, 20 or more (see Figure 16). In summary, it may be that the tutorials, as necessary parts of the game experience, can "prime" the 2SM stances according to (a) the forms the tutorials take (prescriptive vs. descriptive) and (b) how salient and useful the student finds the information presented in the tutorials themselves.

OVERALL CONCLUSIONS

This study was designed to explore two primary questions. First, can the two stances of the 2SM specified in the framework be detected in gameplay data? Second, how do changes in students' functional understanding of the game relate to performance on a test of conceptual understanding? Related to these two questions, a third implicit question explored the viability of our approaches to data-mining and learning analytics of game-play data to explore the two explicit research questions. In the following sections, we analyze the two research questions in terms of the overarching implications for the 2SM. Next, we consider the overarching implication for the design of digital games to support conceptual learning. Finally, we close with an examination of the third implicit questions about the viability and generalizability of our approaches to data-mining and learning analytics of game-play data to explore theoretical questions about learning.

What the Findings Say About the 2SM

The 2SM is intended as a general-purpose framework for student cognition during gameplay; it is comprehensive yet not intended to be specific to any kind of game or any target domain. Because of this generality, it requires many constructs and mechanisms to explain phenomena of play. Furthermore, these constructs and mechanisms are mostly latent, existing only in the student's mind and perhaps only for brief moments of time. For these reasons, it is unlikely that a single study, however ambitious, could prove the 2SM as a theory.

The findings in this paper suggest that the basic underpinnings of the 2SM pass muster, for the most part. We see the indicia of both fast, low-information play and slow, deliberative play. More importantly, these styles of play co-vary strongly with learning outcomes, indicating that fast styles of play may not support students in developing knowledge of a form transferable beyond to the game, in this case, focusing on Newtonian kinematics. Some students perseverate, however, in guess-and-check iteration, relying entirely on the game to provide the necessary feedback, instead of using all available information to infer some generalizable rule they can use to increase their effectiveness. We can see from the Contextual Mapping analysis that some students never seem to stop making errors in parts of the game relating to a specific concept, even when they've already cleared a similar challenge 10 times or more. Essentially, these students never switch to a more model-oriented thoughtful stance. Conversely, some students begin in a more thoughtful stance and remain in that stance throughout play.

Although we find evidence supporting the existence of the two stances and their general outlines, the findings do not support the hypothesized swapping back and forth between stances. Related to this absence of stance switching, the finding that prior knowledge strongly influences play, even in the early stages, is problematic in terms of the 2SM. First, because it inverses the proposed way that stances get cued. In the original framing of the 2SM, the Learner Stance is cued by a task that is too demanding, where the student has no fast effortless rule to apply. However, the results in this paper strongly support the claim that the opposite may be true, or that perceived high task demands cue the Player stance as an effort-saving strategy that is ultimately maladaptive in terms of learning. The second challenge to the 2SM comes from the necessity of having students "learn to play" the game before they actually "play" it. This instructional phase and its consequences were not addressed originally in the 2SM. Yet as we have discussed previously, the Tutorial materials and other instructional affordances might bias students towards one form of reasoning or another, independently of how the student would otherwise organize their epistemic Stance.

These findings suggest that revisions of the 2SM are warranted in at least two lines. On one hand, (1) the role of prior knowledge as an epistemic resource, largely ignored in the original framing. The 2SM envisions a student with well-defined goals for play but a "blank slate" in terms of pre-existing knowledge about the game. Further research that specifically targets the effect of prior knowledge, and of knowledge gleaned early in play from tutorial materials is warranted, and those findings integrated into the 2SM. Another possible revision involves (2) the issue of task demands and their possible role in cueing other resources, such as mastery or performance orientations (Pintrich, 2000). The 2SM does not explicitly consider whether a student finds a given game situation "easy" or "difficult"; rather it only considers what epistemic resources the student has at hand, such as heuristics and second-order models. Yet the findings of this study highlight that Player Stance related patterns of play may also be a coping strategy to deal with game situations students find too difficult. For the 2SM to properly account for these coping strategies, a study might be designed where versions of the game of various difficulty levels are assigned to students at different levels of achievement, either by pre-test score or by an automated adaptive functionality.

Implications for Game Design

The results of the gameplay data analysis from RQ1 support the notion that patterns of play related to the Player Stance are not optimal for learning. Students who persist in fast strategies are not likely to improve their learning relative to their peers, and students who make the highest relative gains do not prefer fast strategies overall. The analysis shows that a tolerance or preference for Attempt sequences with a high reliance on FUTILITY are associated with lower learning outcomes.

In the 2SM framework, multiple FUTILITY attempts with low average time per attempt can be understood as a strategy for obtaining feedback from the game's model as a way to avoid having to use slower, more intensive reasoning processes such as the second-order model. The goal of this strategy is to serve the student's agency and sense of control and preserve the momentum of play. It may be that the Player Stance helps students remain motivated and engaged even in the face of failure, and long after the novelty of the game has worn off. Yet, as we have seen, in the case of EPIGAME, the Player Stance and its associated play strategies are associated with lower learning gains. This warrants the question, can the Player Stance be disrupted in order to promote learning? Or in the context of EPIGAME, can a student playing the "tweaking game" be nudged towards playing the game more as a "planning game?" Can a game be designed in such a way that this "nudge" occurs automatically?

In the case of EPIGAME, the tutorials might provide a clue as to how this "nudge" can occur early in play (see Question 2), and we can envision a functionality that provides this "nudge" in a just-in-time fashion. This hypothetical feature would depend on having a method to detect whether or not a student has settled in a Player Stance. This "detector" could be built upon the analysis described in RQ1: the game could use a similar process of unsupervised clustering we used to arrive at the *part.6* solution as a guide to classify students' actions in real time, and then detect the sequences of play which, as we have seen, are not strongly associated with learning. This added functionality would allow specific feedback to be provided to students early in their play before they commit to playing a "tweaking game" (c.f. Clark, Martinez-Garza, Biswas, Leucht, & Sengupta, 2012). Lastly, if the game can be made so that, once it has gathered enough student data to predict a student's play characteristics, the game can modulate its difficulty to make sure that the student faces challenges appropriate to their level of skill and knowledge, while compensating for the tendency of students to choose low-effort strategies if doing so preserves the momentum of play. These three additional functionalities could all be potentially very powerful ways to promote student learning with games, and they are all made possible by an expanded understanding of how students actually play.

These findings should also motivate discussion about how much and what kinds of support students should receive during game-based learning opportunities. Lower-performing students' over-reliance on fast strategies might be more of an adaptive response to being forced to play a game that is too difficult as opposed to an intentional strategy choice in response to their perceptions of what the game is about. In this case, automated feedback and adaptation as discussed above would also be useful. Students who are facing intractable difficulty could be detected and helped automatically. Perhaps students perseverating in fast strategies are doing so transgressively (see Aarseth, 2007) as a rejection of the game's challenge and a personal disinvestment from the game's outcomes. This low-effort position is radically different from the low-ability position described above, but in terms of data logs, it would look similar. The analytics used in this study are not well-suited to detect the difference between low effort and low ability, although some scholars have had success with specific detection algorithms for disengagement in the context of science simulations (Gobert, Baker, & Wixon, 2015).

In this study, as in much of classroom-based educational game research, we relied on pre-existing classroom norms for expectations on student behavior and effort. Also, in the classroom phase of this study we relied on the presence and expert eye of the teacher to help identify and gently correct students who were off-task and offer guidance to those few students who may have found the game too demanding. We observed and respected these practices while fully knowing that their effects would disturb the central assumption that the data logs record students' actions *and only students' actions*. This tension points to an inherent limitation of the data logging approach. Data logging can only account for what happens within the student-computer interaction, and classroom technology use often involves, or even privileges, person-to-person interactions. It is during these kinds of interactions that teachers and often peers help students make sense of the game when the game itself doesn't offer the necessary scaffolds, whether motivational or content-related. These interactions may have effects on participating students' play that would be captured by data logging but would be difficult for LA techniques to correctly explain or attribute. It may be that future work that harnesses data log analytics for adaptive feedback might approach, or perhaps even duplicate, the classroom teacher's ability to identify apathy and helplessness in the classroom context, or the knowledgeable peer willingness to dispense timely hints. Until that time, however, we accept some imperfection and "mangling" of the record and look for opportunities to more deeply integrate log-based analytics with observational and grounded methods.

Regardless, in order to access the potential and intended benefits of an educational game, students must first *learn to play* the game itself. This step can easily be glossed over during design; when it comes to introducing unfamiliar digital games into the classroom, we might hold the notion that young students can simply "pick it up" and "figure it out", since they may already be "gamers". Thus, materials intended to help students orient themselves in the game environment and learn how to reach gameplay goals may not receive as much design attention as they otherwise would. Furthermore, when games are used in an educational setting, these materials compete for classroom time with the main game, where the target curricular material is most likely to reside. Ideally, we would prefer if students spend only a little time "learning to play" and as much time as possible simply "learning."

Our findings problematize these design assumptions. First, as shown, prior knowledge can structure gameplay to a great extent (see RQ1 analyses). Students who enter the game experience with a good working knowledge of the concepts and relationships are less reliant on feedback-driven and iterative "tweaking" styles of play. Second, the analysis also suggests that the way the game teaches students to play, by following a procedure or operationalizing a relationship, may also be an important influence on students, even when this learning is focused squarely on game-specific knowledge and not on curricular concepts and relationships.

If prior knowledge and differential use of tutorial materials can structure and influence play and, thus, learning, then a greater emphasis must be placed on game functionality that supports students who do not initially enjoy or leverage these advantages. For example, lack of prior knowledge can be addressed with *scaffolding*, and gameplay difficulty can be adapted to reduce repeated error. These and other measures should be considered as means to ensure that all students can access substantially similar game experiences and with this, hopefully, more equitable positive learning outcomes.

Data-Mining and Learning Analytics as a Tool

The work described in this paper has followed a methodology that is not limited to investigating EPIGAME logs. The general methodology is versatile and feasible for use in other contexts. Starting from a robust and detailed record of students' interactions with a digital environment and a theoretical framework that supports conjectures as to why certain patterns of action create opportunities for the desired change, researchers can define the important features of those patterns and then use those features to investigate the data record using whatever LA techniques are most appropriate for that particular type of data.

A more novel focus of this analysis, which is highlighted in Research Question 2, is that it aims to track the development of students' conceptual understanding at the level of particular concepts of inertia using finer-grained observations centered on particular gameplay regions. These regions are intended to highlight specific content, and thus student performance in these regions is more closely tied to conceptual understanding than gross-level summative measures. These summative measures have been successfully used in the past and may be appropriate and sufficient for some research questions. However, the use of finer-grained contextual data offers the advantage of supporting claims of students' conceptual understanding of individual concepts such as inertia or First Law rather than broad performance constructs, such as knowing how to play EPIGAME.

This is not to say that the EPIGAME data structure and focus and the associated analyses are universal. The trial-retrial structure of gameplay and the grain size of the data capture are not necessarily common to all educational games. The specific combination of play structure and grain size warranted the sequence mining and contextual feature mapping. Other digital environments will have different interactive structures, and thus algorithms and techniques possibly better suited to the questions being asked. Fortunately, the state of the art of learning analytics is increasing both the accessibility and variety of statistical computing software, making it suitable for a wider variety of data structures, game mechanics, and learning foci.

One thing that will likely remain invariant, however, is the expertise of the analyst and their familiarity with the context and the data. In this paper, our own long association with EPIGAME data and our observations accumulated over multiple opportunities to facilitate students' play of EPIGAME facilitated the creation of the derived variables, the process of interpreting the *part.6* clustering, and the use of sequencing as a way to add meaning to the cluster assignments. It is unlikely that this kind of intimate understanding of the affordances and constraints of particular games and data can be substituted by generic software although it can, perhaps, be supplemented. Until that time, however, the skill of the analyst, as in all interpretative observational methods of research, will be crucial to success.

ACKNOWLEDGMENT

The research reported here was supported by the Institute of Education Sciences, U.S. Department of Education, and the National Science Foundation through grants R305A110782 and 1119290 to Vanderbilt University. The opinions expressed are those of the authors and do not represent views of the Institute, the U.S. Department of Education, or the National Science Foundation.

REFERENCES

Aarseth, E. (2007). I fought the law: Transgressive play and the implied player. *Situated Play. Proc. DiGRA*, 24-28.

Annetta, L. A. (2010). The "I's" have it: A framework for serious educational game design. *Review of General Psychology*, *14*(2), 105–112. doi:10.1037/a0018985

Annetta, L. A., Minogue, J., Holmes, S. Y., & Cheng, M.-T. (2009). Investigating the impact of video games on high school students' engagement and learning about genetics. *Computers & Education*, *53*(1), 74–85. doi:10.1016/j.compedu.2008.12.020

Baker, R. S., & Clarke-Midura, J. (2013). Predicting successful inquiry learning in a virtual performance assessment for science. In S. Carberry, S. Weibelzahl, A. Micarelli, & G. Semeraro (Eds.), *User Modeling, Adaptation, and Personalization* (pp. 203–214). Berlin: Springer. doi:10.1007/978-3-642-38844-6_17

Berland, M., Baker, R. S., & Blikstein, P. (2014). Educational data mining and learning analytics: Applications to constructionist research. *Technology, Knowledge, and Learning*, *19*(1-2), 205–220. doi:10.100710758-014-9223-7

Braver, M. W., & Braver, S. L. (1988). Statistical treatment of the Solomon four-group design: A meta-analytic approach. *Psychological Bulletin, 104*(1), 150–154. doi:10.1037/0033-2909.104.1.150

Buckley, B. C., Gobert, J. D., Kindfield, A. C. H., Horwitz, P., Tinker, R. F., Gerlits, B., ... Willett, J. (2004). Model-based teaching and learning with Biologica™: What do they learn? How do they learn? How do we know? *Journal of Science Education and Technology, 13*(1), 23–41. doi:10.1023/B:JOST.0000019636.06814.e3

Chesler, N. C., Ruis, A. R., Collier, W., Swiecki, Z., Arastoopour, G., & Shaffer, D. W. (2015). A novel paradigm for engineering education: Virtual internships with individualized mentoring and assessment of engineering thinking. *Journal of Biomechanical Engineering, 137*(2), 024701. doi:10.1115/1.4029235 PMID:25425046

Clark, D. B. (2012). *Designing Games to Help Players Articulate Productive Mental Models* [Video file]. Keynote commissioned for the Cyberlearning Research Summit 2012 hosted by SRI International, the National Geographic Society, and the Lawrence Hall of Science with funding from the National Science Foundation and the Bill and Melinda Gates Foundation, Washington, DC. Retrieved from https://www.youtube.com/watch?v=xlMfk5rP9yI

Clark, D. B., & Martinez-Garza, M. (2012). Prediction and explanation as design mechanics in conceptually-integrated digital games to help players articulate the tacit understandings they build through gameplay. In C. Steinkuehler, K. Squire, & S. Barab (Eds.), *Games, learning, and society: Learning and meaning in the digital age.* Cambridge, MA: Cambridge University Press. doi:10.1017/CBO9781139031127.023

Clark, D. B., Nelson, B. C., Chang, H.-Y., Martinez-Garza, M. M., Slack, K., & D'Angelo, C. M. (2011). Exploring Newtonian mechanics in a conceptually-integrated digital game: Comparison of learning and affective outcomes for students in Taiwan and the United States. *Computers & Education, 57*(3), 2178–2195. doi:10.1016/j.compedu.2011.05.007

Clark, D. B., Sengupta, P., Brady, C., Martinez-Garza, M., & Killingsworth, S. (2015). Disciplinary Integration in Digital Games for Science Learning. *International STEM Education Journal, 2*(2), 1-21. Retrieved from http://www.stemeducationjournal.com/content/pdf/s40594-014-0014-4.pdf

Clarke-Midura, J., & Dede, C. (2010). Assessment, technology, and change. *Journal of Research on Technology in Education*, *42*(3), 309–328. doi:10.1080/15391523.2010.10782553

Corbett, A. T., & Anderson, J. R. (1994). Knowledge tracing: Modeling the acquisition of procedural knowledge. *User Modeling and User-Adapted Interaction*, *4*(4), 253–278. doi:10.1007/BF01099821

Csikszentmihalyi, M. (1991). *Flow: The Psychology of Optimal Experience* (1st ed.). Harper Perennial.

de Freitas, S. (2018). Are games effective learning tools? A review of educational games. *Journal of Educational Technology & Society*, *21*(2), 74–84.

Dede, C. (2011). Developing a research agenda for educational games and simulations. In S. Tobias & J. D. Fletcher (Eds.), *Computer Games and Instruction* (pp. 233–247). Charlotte, NC: Information Age Publishing.

Dondlinger, M. J. (2007). Educational video game design: A review of the literature. *Journal of Applied Educational Technology, 4*(1), 21-31.

Emerson, J. W., Green, W. A., Schloerke, B., Crowley, J., Cook, D., Hofmann, H., & Wickham, H. (2012). The Generalized Pairs Plot. *Journal of Computational and Graphical Statistics*, *22*(1), 79–91. doi:10.1080/10618600.2012.694762

Evans, J. S. B. T. (2008). Dual-Processing Accounts of Reasoning, Judgment, and Social Cognition. *Annual Review of Psychology*, *59*(1), 255–278. doi:10.1146/annurev.psych.59.103006.093629 PMID:18154502

Foster, A., & Mishra, P. (2008). Games, Claims, Genres and Learning. In R. E. Ferdig (Ed.), *Handbook of research on effective electronic gaming in education* (pp. 33–50). Hershey, PA: Information Science Reference. doi:10.4018/978-1-59904-808-6.ch002

Frey, B. J., & Dueck, D. (2007). Clustering by passing messages between data points. *Science*, *315*(5814), 972–976. doi:10.1126cience.1136800 PMID:17218491

Gabadinho, A., Ritschard, G., Müller, N. S., & Studer, M. (2011). Analyzing and Visualizing State Sequences in R with TraMineR. *Journal of Statistical Software*, *40*(4), 1–37. doi:10.18637/jss.v040.i04

Gee, J. P. (2007). What Video Games Have to Teach Us About Learning and Literacy (2nd ed.). New York, NY: Palgrave Macmillan.

Geertz, C. (1973). Thick Description: Towards an Interpretive Theory of Culture. In *The Interpretation of Cultures* (pp. 3–30). New York, NY: Basic Books.

Gijlers, H., & de Jong, T. (2013). Using Concept Maps to Facilitate Collaborative Simulation-Based Inquiry Learning. *Journal of the Learning Sciences*, *22*(3), 340–374. doi:10.1080/10508406.2012.748664

Gobert, J. D., Sao Pedro, M. A., & Baker, R. S., Toto, E., & Montalvo, O. (2012). Leveraging educational data mining for real-time performance assessment of scientific inquiry skills within microworlds. *Journal of Educational Data Mining*, *4*(1), 111–143.

Halverson, R., & Owen, V. E. (2014). Game-based assessment: an integrated model for capturing evidence of learning in play. *International Journal of Learning Technology*. Retrieved from http://www.inderscienceonline.com/doi/abs/10.1504/IJLT.2014.064489

Hammer, D., & Elby, A. (2003). Tapping Epistemological Resources for Learning Physics. *Journal of the Learning Sciences*, *12*(1), 53–90. doi:10.1207/S15327809JLS1201_3

Harpstead, E., Myers, B. A., & Aleven, V. (2013). In search of learning: facilitating data analysis in educational games. In *Proceedings of the SIGCHI Conference on Human Factors in Computing Systems* (pp. 79–88). New York, NY: ACM. 10.1145/2470654.2470667

Hooshyar, D., Yousefi, M., & Lim, H. (2018). Data-Driven Approaches to Game Player Modeling: A Systematic Literature Review. *ACM Computing Surveys*, *50*(6), 90. doi:10.1145/3145814

Hou, H. T. (2012). Exploring the behavioral patterns of learners in an educational massively multiple online role-playing game (MMORPG). *Computers & Education*, *58*(4), 1225–1233. doi:10.1016/j.compedu.2011.11.015

Husson, F., Josse, J., Le, S., & Mazet, J. (2015). *FactoMineR: Multivariate Exploratory Data Analysis and Data Mining*. Retrieved from http://CRAN.R-project.org/package=FactoMineR

Kahneman, D. (2003). Maps of Bounded Rationality: Psychology for Behavioral Economics. *The American Economic Review*, *93*(5), 1449–1475. doi:10.1257/000282803322655392

Kerr, D., & Chung, G. K. W. K. (2012). Identifying key features of student performance in educational video games and simulations through cluster analysis. *Journal of Educational Data Mining, 4*(1), 144–182.

Kinnebrew, J. S., Killingsworth, S. S., Clark, D. B., Biswas, G., Sengupta, P., Minstrell, J., ... Krinks, K. (2017). Contextual Markup and Mining in Digital Games for Science Learning: Connecting Player Behaviors to Learning Goals. *IEEE Transactions on Learning Technologies, 10*(1), 93–103. doi:10.1109/TLT.2016.2521372

Lamb, R. L., Annetta, L., Vallett, D. B., & Sadler, T. D. (2014). Cognitive diagnostic like approaches using neural-network analysis of serious educational videogames. *Computers & Education, 70*, 92–104. doi:10.1016/j.compedu.2013.08.008

Leighton, J. P., & Gierl, M. J. (2007). Defining and evaluating models of cognition used in educational measurement to make inferences about examinees' thinking processes. *Educational Measurement: Issues and Practice, 26*(2), 3–16. doi:10.1111/j.1745-3992.2007.00090.x

Linehan, C., Kirman, B., Lawson, S., & Chan, G. (2011). Practical, Appropriate, Empirically-validated Guidelines for Designing Educational Games. In *Proceedings of the SIGCHI Conference on Human Factors in Computing Systems* (pp. 1979–1988). New York: ACM. 10.1145/1978942.1979229

Martinez-Garza, M., Clark, D. B., & Nelson, B. C. (2013). Digital games and the US National Research Council's science proficiency goals. *Studies in Science Education, 49*(2), 170–208. doi:10.1080/03057267.2013.839372

Martinez-Garza, M. M., Clark, D., & Nelson, B. (2013). Advances in Assessment of Students' Intuitive Understanding of Physics through Gameplay Data. *International Journal of Gaming and Computer-Mediated Simulations, 5*(4), 1–16. doi:10.4018/ijgcms.2013100101

Martinez-Garza, M. M., & Clark, D. B. (2017). Two systems, two stances: a novel theoretical framework for model-based learning in digital games. In P. Wouters & H. van Oostendorp (Eds.), *Instructional Techniques to Facilitate Learning and Motivation of Serious Games* (pp. 37–58). Cham, Switzerland: Springer; doi:10.1007/978-3-319-39298-1_3

Mislevy, R. J., Almond, R. G., & Lukas, J. F. (2003). A brief introduction to evidence-centered design. *ETS Research Report Series, 2003*(1), i–29. doi:10.1002/j.2333-8504.2003.tb01908.x

Mislevy, R. J., Oranje, A., Bauer, M. I., von Davier, A., Hao, J., Corrigan, S., ... John, M. (2014). *Psychometric considerations in game-based assessment* (white paper). Retrieved from http://www.instituteofplay.org/work/projects/glasslab-research/

Parnafes, O., & diSessa, A. (2004). Relations between Types of Reasoning and Computational Representations. *International Journal of Computers for Mathematical Learning*, *9*(3), 251–280. doi:10.100710758-004-3794-7

Pintrich, P. R. (2000). Multiple goals, multiple pathways: The role of goal orientation in learning and achievement. *Journal of Educational Psychology*, *92*(3), 544–555. doi:10.1037/0022-0663.92.3.544

Plass, J., Homer, B., & Kinzer, C. (2014). *Playful Learning: An Integrated Design Framework* (White paper #02/2014). Games for Learning Institute. doi:10.13140/2.1.4175.6969

Prensky, M. (2006). *Don't bother me Mom - I'm learning!: how computer and video games are preparing your kids for twenty-first century success - and how you can help!* Paragon House. Retrieved from http://www.worldcat.org/isbn/1557788588

Reyna, V. F., & Ellis, S. C. (1994). Fuzzy-trace theory and framing effects in children's risky decision making. *Psychological Science*, *5*(5), 275–279. doi:10.1111/j.1467-9280.1994.tb00625.x

Rieber, L. P. (1996). Seriously considering play: Designing interactive learning environments based on the blending of microworlds, simulations, and games. *Educational Technology Research and Development*, *44*(2), 43–58. doi:10.1007/BF02300540

Rowe, E., Asbell-Clarke, J., & Baker, R. S. (2015). Serious games analytics to measure implicit science learning. In C. S. Loh, Y. Sheng, & D. Ifenthaler (Eds.), *Serious Games Analytics* (pp. 343–360). Springer International Publishing. doi:10.1007/978-3-319-05834-4_15

Rowe, E., Asbell-Clarke, J., Baker, R. S., Eagle, M., Hicks, A. G., Barnes, T. M., ... Edwards, T. (2017). Assessing implicit science learning in digital games. *Computers in Human Behavior*, *76*, 617–630. doi:10.1016/j.chb.2017.03.043

Sengupta, P., Krinks, K. D., & Clark, D. B. (2015). Learning to Deflect: Conceptual Change in Physics during Digital Game Play. *Journal of the Learning Sciences*, *24*(4), 638–674. doi:10.1080/10508406.2015.1082912

Shaffer, D. W., Squire, K. D., Halverson, R., & Gee, J. P. (2005). Video games and the future of learning. *Phi Delta Kappan, 87*(2), 104–111. doi:10.1177/003172170508700205

Shute, V., & Ventura, M. (2013). *Stealth assessment: Measuring and supporting learning in video games*. Cambridge, MA: MIT Press.

Shute, V. J. (2011). Stealth assessment in computer-based games to support learning. In S. Tobias & J. D. Fletcher (Eds.), *Computer Games and Instruction* (Vol. 55, pp. 503–524). Charlotte, NC: Information Age Publishing. Retrieved from http://pdf.thepdfportal.net/PDFFiles/6536.pdf

Slater, S., Joksimović, S., Kovanovic, V., Baker, R. S., & Gasevic, D. (2017). Tools for educational data mining: A review. *Journal of Educational and Behavioral Statistics, 42*(1), 85–106. doi:10.3102/1076998616666808

Sloman, S. A. (1996). The empirical case for two systems of reasoning. *Psychological Bulletin, 119*(1), 3–22. doi:10.1037/0033-2909.119.1.3 PMID:8711015

Solomon, R. L. (1949). An extension of control group design. *Psychological Bulletin, 46*(2), 137–150. doi:10.1037/h0062958 PMID:18116724

Squire, K. D., DeVane, B., & Durga, S. (2008). Designing centers of expertise for academic learning through video games. *Theory into Practice, 47*(3), 240–251. doi:10.1080/00405840802153973

Stanovich, K. E. (1999). *Who is rational? Studies of individual differences in reasoning*. Mahwah, NJ: Lawrence Erlbaum Associates.

Tobias, S., & Fletcher, J. D. (2007). What Research Has to Say about Designing Computer Games for Learning. *Educational Technology, 47*(5), 20–29.

Vellido, A., Martin-Guerroro, J. D., & Lisboa, P. (2012). Making machine learning models interpretable. *Proceedings of the 20th European Symposium on Artificial Neural Networks, Computational Intelligence and Machine Learning (ESANN)*, 163–172.

Ventura, M., Shute, V., & Small, M. (2014). Assessing persistence in educational games. *Design Recommendations for Intelligent Tutoring Systems*, 93-101.

Ventura, M., Shute, V., & Zhao, W. (2013). The relationship between video game use and a performance-based measure of persistence. *Computers & Education*, *60*(1), 52–58. doi:10.1016/j.compedu.2012.07.003

Wickham, H. (2014). Tidy data. *Journal of Statistical Software*, *59*(10), 1–23. doi:10.18637/jss.v059.i10 PMID:26917999

Young, M. F., Slota, S., Cutter, A. B., Jalette, G., Mullin, G., Lai, B., ... Yukhymenko, M. (2012). Our Princess Is in Another Castle: A Review of Trends in Serious Gaming for Education. *Review of Educational Research*, *82*(1), 61–89. doi:10.3102/0034654312436980

APPENDIX

Observed and Derived Variables in the Epigame Log Data

Table 7. Catalog of variables in the Study 2 dataset

Variable Name	Meaning	Type	Notes
Student ID		Identification	Anonymized to a serial number
Experiment ID		Identification	
Date and Time		Identification	
Step Visit	Number of times student has visited that Level (step)	Observed	
Attempt		Observed	Only Attempt = 1 was used
attemptTrial	Order of this Attempt within a series of Attempts (i.e., a Trial)	Observed	
totalTrials	Combined number of Attempts in all Trials of this Level by this student	Observed	
endState	Did the player succeed (=1), fail (=0), or abort (=2)?	Observed	
endScore	Score obtained by that student at the end of that Trial	Observed	
scoreImproved	Did the student increase their Score this Attempt?	Derived	
trialTime	Length of time a between this Attempt and the end of the previous Attempt	Observed	Incorrectly named in software, should be "attemptTime"
actionsUsed	How many Actions were placed on Waypoints during the Planning Phase	Observed	
isExit	Did the student leave the Level after this Attempt?	Observed	
timeLine	Position of the time cursor on the Timeline at level end	Observed	More relevant in the Timeline version of EPIGAME. Students in the present studies did not have access to the time cursor.
attemptTrial.max	Maximum value of the variable attemptTrial for that student for that level	Derived	
p.attemptTrial	Measure of **p**rogress of Attempts within the Trial	Derived	Calculated as (attemptTrial / attemptTrial.max)
p.totalTrials	Measure of progress of Attempts within the combined chain of Attempts over all Trials	Derived	Calculated as [attemptTrial + (sum of all attemptTrial.max of all previous trials) / totalTrials]
ending.event	The state of the game that caused the Level to end.	Observed	Allowed states: Success Gate, Navigation Error, Mass Gate collision, Velocity Gate collision, Laser collision, Abort.
ended.at.action	Number of actions that fired successfully	Observed	
Par	Model-derived metric of effectiveness.	Derived	See "Treatment of EPIGAME logs" for a complete description.
planningTime	Duration of the Planning Phase	Observed	
tl.Adds	Addition of Actions to the Timeline	Observed	

continued on following page

Table 7. Continued

Variable Name	Meaning	Type	Notes
tl.Deletes	Deletion of Actions from the Timeline	Observed	Very rare (mean = 0.05 deletions per Attempt)
tl.Modifys	Modification of parameters of Actions already in the Timeline	Observed	
tl.Moves	Actions moved within the Timeline	Observed	Very rare (mean = 0.17 moves per Attempt)
added.Tl.Total	Sum of Timeline Adds, Deletes, Modifys and Moves	Derived	
tj.Adds	Waypoints added to the Trajectory	Observed	
tj.Modifys, tj.Moves, tj.Deletes	Analogous to the Timeline (prefix: tl.) count variables	Observed	These variables exist in the record but no instance of these types of events was recorded.
locX, locY	Coordinates of Surge's spaceship when an event or Action occurred	Observed	
fail.same	Did this Attempt fail at the same location, for the same reason?	Derived	
eff.actions.added	How many Actions fired in this Attempt compared to the number that fired in the preceding Attempt?	Derived	Could be negative.
par.delta	Difference in the par metric between this Attempt and the previous one	Derived	
par.sqrt, par.delta.sqrt	Square-root transformations of the par and par.delta variables	Derived	
is.abort	Did the student press the Abort button before the level otherwise ended?	Derived	The software also registers the Abort button press in the endState variable.
ActionLog	Combined variable that registers the Actions applied to Surge during the Attempt	Observed	Includes position, type, and location of each Action applied
EventLog	Combined variable that registers important moments of gameplay not caused by Actions	Observed	Not fully functional in this version of EPIGAME
Serial	Serial number of the Conceptual challenge	Derived (from ActionLog)	
failed.to	In case of failure of a Conceptual challenge, the specific action the student did not do	Derived (from ActionLog)	Possible values: fromStop, toStop, speedUp, slowdown
is.colinear	Does this Conceptual challenge also require students to execute a turn?	Derived (from ActionLog)	
constant.mass	Do students have to account for changes to Surge's mass during the Conceptual challenge?	Derived (from ActionLog)	Only Conceptual challenges that pass this test were analyzed here
Pre, Post	The student's pre- and post-test scores, respectively	Observed	
bin.1	Classification of students according to beginning and ending quartile in assessment score	Derived	See "Question 1: Sequence Mining" for detailed description of this classification

[1]The key insight that led to the development of the *par* metric was the observation that the transition probabilities described in the Markov-chain model (i.e., the probability of a certain outcome for an Attempt given the outcome of the previous Attempt) were closely related to both the spatial layout of each level and the number of times that students had encountered that level's challenges before. For example, in the EPIGAME level pictured in Figure 1, we would expect to see the transition probability of Velocity Gate to Navigation Error to be high, because the layout of the level places a 90-degree turn after a Velocity Gate, and both challenges are likely to cause player errors. Conversely, we would expect the transition from Navigation Error to Success Gate to be very low, since there is at least one obstacle between the last 90-degree turn and the Gate. Few students would be able to follow up a Navigation error with a clean transversal of the Laser and Velocity Gates.

Furthermore, a given outcome can transition into *itself*, indicating an outcome that is very often repeated across students and chains of Attempts. Higher "self-transitions" probabilities are more common when new game elements are introduced, and students make repeated attempts to advance past the new challenges. Self-transitions generally become rarer, however, as students gain more proficiency in dealing with each challenge, i.e., from one level to the next.

Chapter 5

If the Gear Fits, Spin It Again!
Embodied Education, Design Components, and In-Play Assessments

Mina C. Johnson
Arizona State University, USA & Embodied Games, USA

David Birchfield
SmalLab Learning, USA

Colleen Megowan-Romanowicz
American Modeling Teachers Association, USA

ABSTRACT

To understand how students learn while engaged in active and embodied science games, two gears games were created. Would students' gear switching skills during the game be correlated with pre- and post-knowledge tests? Twenty-three seventh graders, playing as dyads, used gestures to manipulate virtual gears in the games. The Microsoft Kinect sensor tracked arm-spinning movements. Paper and pencil gear knowledge tests were administered before and after. In Game 1 (the easier one), the in-game switching data was significantly negatively correlated with only pretest gear knowledge. In Game 2 (the harder one), switching was negatively associated with both pre- and posttests. Negative correlations mean that fewer switches were used and that demonstrated better knowledge of mechanical advantage. In-game process data can provide a window onto learner's knowledge. However, the games need to have appropriate sensitivity and map to the learner's ZPD. In ludo (or in-process) data from videogames with high sensitivity may attenuate the need for repetitive traditional knowledge tests.

DOI: 10.4018/978-1-5225-7461-3.ch005

INTRODUCTION

The use of immersive games as learning tools has become more accepted in classrooms, and their value has been verified (Merchant, Goetz, Cifuentes, Keeney-Kennicutt, & Davis, 2014). This chapter is an update to the 2015 article called, *If the Gear Fits, Spin It*. This chapter version includes a simpler interpretation in the discussion section, more insights on game design, and some updated references to augmented and virtual realities (AR/VR).

While much research supports the assertion that serious games can be more effective in terms of learning (d = 0.29, p < .01) and retention (d =0.36, p < .01), than conventional instruction methods (Wouters, Nimwegen, Oostendorp, & van der Spek, 2013), others have found more limited results in academic domains (Young et al., 2012). The Embodied Games lab has published primarily on mixed reality games and simulations, we have consistently observed that when a comparative class is instructed using game components versus more traditional pedagogies, then the game-based class more often produces better learning outcomes (Johnson-Glenberg, Birchfield, Koziupa, & Tolentino, 2014; Johnson-Glenberg & Megowan-Romanowicz, 2017). The field of STEM and learning games includes domain such as: computer science (Papastergiou, 2009), engineering (Coller & Shernoff, 2009) (Coller & Scott, 2009) and the biological sciences (Lui et al., 2014), to name a few. Coller and Scott (2009) report that the students who were randomly assigned to the videogame-based course showed deeper learning compared to the traditional class students (both groups spent the same amount of time on their course work). A metaanalysis from Young et al. (2012) found evidence for positive effects of videogames on language learning, history, and for exergaming, though they also report *little support for the academic value of videogames in science and math* (Young et al., 2012).

In this reprint of the original article, it is worthy to introduce and explore the concept that not all serious games are created equally. The first author can state unequivocally that she has designed and created games that fall along a spectrum of lame to excellent. Part of the noise in discerning the worth of videogames on STEM learning, and the difficulty in interpreting meta-analyses on games and learning, is that well designed games are lumped together with poorly designed games. In addition, the field still debates the difference between simulations and games. E.g., we opted to call our game-like activities *simulations* in Johnson-Glenberg and Megowan-Romanowicz (2017). Mishra, Anguera, and Gazzaley (2016) succinctly state the obvious.

Scientists are not typically the most proficient video game developers. "Games" developed to accomplish cognitive training goals are frequently limited to the layering on of simple graphic skins and low-level reward to standard cognitive task paradigms. This gamification approach often involves sprinkling game elements on top of low-engaging cognitive tasks, creating slightly less boring exercises, which may be a factor driving the negative findings that have dominated the field. (p. 214.)

It takes a team to create good games, and educators and scientists are not professional game designers. Those of us who trained as learning scientists or educators and wish to create serious games need to pair with professional game designers. In the early days of reviews, it was difficult to find professional grade learning games, but there may be a critical mass now. If the newer meta-analyses were to only include game content that has been designed by small teams of experts, then the field may begin to see more consistent, and positive results on the effects of games for learning. In addition, the field needs more articles that mesh rigorous randomized control trial (RCT) data and quasi-experimental data with clear advice on design for learning. To that end, this article will expand on how gameplay components correlate with traditional knowledge tests, and will end with a set of design guidelines. It is also necessary to understand how some long-held traditions in the entertainment game domain may not translate well into the education game domain. Some of the more established award mechanisms used in entertainment games, e.g., leaderboards and badges, may not be appropriate for classroom environments. A 6-week long study by Hanus and Fox found that the two traditional entertainment game "payoffs" of 1) a public board displaying all scores (called a leaderboard) and 2) the awarding of completion badges might actually hinder learning by negatively affecting intrinsic motivation (Hanus & Fox, 2015).

More research needs to be conducted to understand which components of educational videogames are felicitous to learning. This lab is focused on understanding how embodiment might affect learning during an active STEM game and we continue to develop and explore new methodologies and statistics for mining in-game player data and making sense of the information generated by the learner during gameplay. One gameplay modality that may hold potential for learning is that of embodied learning. "Embodied games" is a category of videogames that incorporates gesture into the act of learning.

Embodiment theory proposes that cognition is deeply rooted in the body's interactions with the environment and that cognition is for action in the world (Wilson, 2002). As evidence, Hauk et al. (2004) describe fMRI experiments that demonstrate that when reading words related to action, areas in the brain are activated in a somatotopic manner. For example, reading "lick" activates motor areas that control the mouth, whereas reading "pick" activates areas that control the hand. This activation is part of a network representing 'meaning' or semantics. The study was done on adults and thus demonstrates that the mappings do not fade once stable comprehension is attained, that is, motor codes are still activated during linguistic comprehension long after the meaning has become stable or automated (Hauk, Johnsrude, & Pulvermüller, 2004). If cognition and the body are deeply and irrevocably connected, then perhaps all cognition, even abstract thought, is embodied (Glenberg, Witt, & Metcalfe, 2013). If this is true, then it seems prudent to design learning games that take advantage of how the body moves to reify concepts to be learned.

Embodied Educational Games

Creating educational games that are also embodied may be especially useful for topics that have traditionally been "tough to teach". This lab focuses on science for several reasons. First, it is a closed problem space, there is usually one answer, so it is a less ambiguous space to design for. Second, computer-aided instruction can be used to facilitate comprehension of content that is not readily apparent to human perceptual systems. This means making the macro (e.g., astronomy) and the micro (e.g., bacteria, or the genome) accessible or what some term, making the unseen seen. With the advent of affordable VR, others are pushing for VR in education to be used to take advantage of the fantastical (Slater & Sanchez-Vives, 2016). Third, an informed citizenry is crucial; there is concern that too many students are leaving the science pipeline around middle school. Games may be a way to engage and retain youth in the sciences. Games offer students an opportunity for stepping out of their usual identities and trying on new ones. When a learner is able to take on the "identity" of an expert (Shaffer et al., 2009), s/he can begin to feel and react like an expert. If the expert is a scientist then the learner might show outcomes like volunteering more answers in class, mentoring others, or spontaneously writing a letter to the a city's mayor about zoning laws learned in the game (Squire & Klopfer, 2007).

Gestures. Gestures may facilitate novices on their journey to becoming experts. By definition a novice is someone whose knowledge is fragmented. The "knowledge in pieces" paradigm (DiSessa, 1988), posits that learners as novices do not yet hold a coherent whole model, they perhaps have pieces that do not fit together. They understand that gears spin and can aid in "work", but do not understand how the input diameter of a gear train affects the work performed. By adding the extra modality of gesture in engaging embodied games, we may aid in the creation of coherent knowledge structures for these novices. The mental model might cohere better.

Other educational researchers have been supporting the use of movement, or body-based metaphors, in learning before motion capture and games were added to the mix (Nathan et al., 2014). Indeed, Cook and Goldin-Meadow (Cook & Goldin-Meadow,

2006) manipulated children's gesture during instruction on new mathematical concepts. The children who were prompted to gesture while learning retained the knowledge they had gained better than the children who were not prompted. Cook et al. postulate that gesturing serves a causal role in learning, perhaps by giving learners an alternative, embodied way of representing new ideas. Goldin-Meadow states, "…perhaps it is the motor aspects of gesture that are responsible for the cognitive benefits" (Goldin-Meadow, 2011). She also posits that gestures may help to "off-load" cognition. Nathan and Alibali (Nathan et al., 2014) found a significant relationship between action and cognition and experimenter's language (i.e., prompts and hints) as participants learned geometry proofs. Education could benefit from having more body-based, gesture-oriented games. However, game designers need a set of guidelines to help them design such games. One set has been proposed by Lindgren and Johnson-Glenberg (2013), and this chapter ends with a reiteration of the set proposed in 2015.

How can embodiment affect education? The goal was to create a game that would add a meaningful motor trace to the act of learning, in this way the game might enhance encoding and retention. The game should not activate just any motor trace, the game should activate a trace that contains overlap with the content to be learned. This overlap has been called gestural congruency (Black, Segal, Vitale, & Fadjo, 2012; Segal, Black, & Tversky, 2010). The physical gesture should match the abstract content to be learned.

This lab has attempted to be systematic when designing games and follows the tenets mentioned in the Discussion section and further extrapolated in our other articles (Johnson-Glenberg, Birchfield, et al., 2014; Lindgren & Johnson-Glenberg, 2013). It should be noted that games can be either low or high on the embodiment spectrum and several taxonomies have emerged that attempt to "quantify" the amount of embodiment in educational content (Johnson-Glenberg, 2017; Johnson-Glenberg & Megowan-Romanowicz, 2017; Skulmowski & Rey, 2018).

As an example of a high embodied gesture that overlaps very physically with the concept to be learned, consider the *Alien Health* game (Johnson-Glenberg, Savio-Ramos, & Henry, 2014). In that game using the *Kinect* sensor, the virtual food item is grasped by the learner's hand and placed close to the avatar's mouth, as opposed to merely hitting an "eat" button. That is, the human player makes the motion of bringing the virtual item to his/her mouth as the *Kinect* maps and makes the virtual object move on screen toward the avatar mouth. As a more conceptual example, consider, moving the hand "up" to connote the concept of "more". In one of our new VR games with hand controls, the player raises the physical hand upwards; in real time as the hand moves the virtual graph begins filling upwards with either numbers or the amount of butterflies collected. This is a kinesthetic prediction task, players are showing a numerical amount not by writing down symbols or speaking language, but by using the body. As the player lowers the hand, that action simultaneously lowers the graph (Johnson-Glenberg, submitted).

Gesture also implies that the body is being active. Therefore, these are sometimes referred to as active games. The increased sensorimotor input that occurs during active, high embodied learning may also positively affect learning. Better learning outcomes are reported in an RCT study on the electric field (Johnson-Glenberg & Megowan-Romanowicz, 2017). The groups that had agency over the content (could move content on screen with either their hands or tracking of the knees) learned significantly more than the group that interacted in a low embodied manner or with only text and symbols.

The genesis. For over a decade, members of the lab have been designing learning games and simulations for mixed and augmented reality (MR and AR) platforms. The term 'mixed reality' was first used by Milgram and Kishino (Milgram & Kishino, 1994) to connote realities that have been projected or used virtual overlays, although aspects of the real world were still present. (This distinguishes it from immersive VR where a 360° headset insures there is no intrusion of the real world.) The first three authors have published extensively on the MR platform called *SMALLab* (Situated Multimedia Arts Learning Lab). The *SMALLab* motion-capture platform uses 12 ceiling-mounted infrared *Optitrack* cameras to track players while holding a rigid body trackable object. The experience feels immersive because the projected floor and tracked space is large (15 x 15 X 15 feet). The players can see the outside world and that also makes it collaborative. (Videos can be found at www.smallablearning. com.) Entire classrooms can sit around the projected perimeter and observe and interact with active students in the space. When learning in this MR platform was compared with traditional instruction (teacher and content held constant) significant gains, and several trends, were seen that favored the MR platform (Johnson-Glenberg, Birchfield, et al., 2014; Johnson-Glenberg, Birchfield, Megowan-Romanowicz, Tolentino, & Martinez, 2009; Johnson-Glenberg, Birchfield, Megowan-Romanowicz, & Uysal, 2009)

As Connolly et al. (Connolly, Boyle, MacArthur, Hainey, & Boyle, 2012) noted, newer platforms like mobile, virtual worlds, and augmented reality mobile kits will continue to come to market and should have profound effects on educational gaming. With the advent of more cost-effective sensors, several of us opted to focus on designing educational content for smaller sensors like the Microsoft *Kinect*'s joint tracking system. The original *Kinect* (*Kinect 360*) was used in this study. It captured up to 20 joints on the body at approximately 30 frames per second.

Game Design

This chapter reports findings on two science games. The first game was easier to play, it was called Tour de Force; the second game was more difficult, it was called the Winching Game. These were part of a series of six short games created to help middle school students understand how simple machines, gears and levers, worked. The topic of simple machines is attractive because several parts of the body can simulate the action of gears or levers (the arm is a natural lever). After the topic space was chosen we needed to reframe it through the epistemology of children's scientific thinking. The design was premised on the concept of naïve science learners from diSessa's theory (diSessa, 1988) that human knowledge consists of many, loosely organized, fragmented pieces of knowledge. These building blocks of understanding are called phenomenological primitives (p-prims) (diSessa, 1988). They are small knowledge elements whose origins stem from repeated abstractions of very familiar events. We hold that these familiar events are experienced in an embodied manner at the earliest age. For example, many students come to kinematics and other science topics with misconceptions, i.e., that force is not an action with an equal and opposite reaction.

In a *SMALLab* sponsored summer camp, 17 middle schoolers helped to pilot many of the study's test items (see test as Appendix of the original article). Approximately 95% of students incorrectly answered that the largest input gear in a gear train would always lift the largest and heaviest item. When queried why, they replied with a variant of, "bigger is always better" - unpublished data - (Johnson-Glenberg, 2012). With repeated exposure to appropriate games, leveled content, and scaffolded discovery from the teacher, the goal was to re-organize a student's network of fragmented knowledge elements into a coherent and correct (more expert-like) model. The students may need to "experience" how the construct is incorrect and why. They may need to use *physical* body actions to *virtually* manipulate smaller and larger objects to really understand why their current gear mental model is incorrect. With this experience, and a new motor memory trace, students' knowledge structures may over time begin to resemble experts' knowledge structures.

The Beauty of Gears

To understand gears, we wanted to encourage students to explore the relationships between a number of *embodiable* concepts including gear size, speed of rotation, and direction. One challenge we confronted was how to embody the idea of diameter (size) and mechanical advantage when two gears interact. The first few questions on the test were designed to measure students' conceptual coherence and were influenced by an early study by Metz (1985). Her participants worked with a set of physically manipulable gears fashioned with a wooden crank. Two of the gears were marked with the form of a man. When a marked gear was turned clockwise, the man pictured on it somersaulted feet-first. Participants were instructed to arrange articulating gears so that they could "make the two men somersault in the same direction." Via trial and error, participants learned the relationship of parity between gear elements. E.g., if there were an odd number of gear elements between the marked gears, then the two marked gears turned in the same direction. Eleven and 12 years-olds were able to understand this rule. The Metz study demonstrates that students are able to construct complex knowledge through the direct manipulation of physical systems. Our goal was to preserve the powerful learning that can occur via this type of physical embodied experience and integrate it into the affordances of digital media in a game-like manner.

Gears also afford the concept of mechanical advantage (MA). A robust energy concept is central to an understanding of all science and MA as well. Although energy is often treated as if it were a straightforward and easily defined quantity, energy is notoriously difficult for people to understand. The third author was a physics teacher for 25 years and often her high school and college students confounded energy with the concepts of force and power (and even speed). [1]

Gears are a good choice for study, besides being able to be embodied, they involve both mathematical and scientific concepts. Gears require the application of both descriptive and causal conceptual models. Their motion and action are familiar (bicycles, pulleys, etc.) and easy to visually perceive because there is no hidden mechanism at work, but gears also reveal stubborn misconceptions regarding both simple (e.g., size, speed, and direction) and complex (e.g., mechanical advantage) constructs. In the games for this series, students were only exposed to double gear systems. There was one input gear and one output gear; players controlled the input gear's diameter. The output gear size was always preset and constant throughout the game. The mechanical advantage construct is a ratio, and it is Output to Input, or O:I. That is, diameter of the output gear divided by the diameter of the input gear.

The lab created a series of six simple machines games, three of these were games on levers. The three lever games were of such short duration (less than one minute each and only resulted in two lengths of the arm being captured by the sensor) that a meaningful frequency of change in a lever game was difficult to extract. Thus, we focus on only the gears games for this paper which had three unique diameters. Figure 1 shows the standard stance for the gears games with the arm extended out in front. Turning the whole arm (that is revolving the wrist joint around the shoulder joint) would make the input gear spin in the same direction and would control the input gear's diameter size.

Figure 1.
Videos of the two games are at: Tour de Force at https://www.youtube.com/watch?v=kSsiJZOUKt4
The Winching game https://www.youtube.com/watch?time_continue=1&v=NHLwQ8kZQ5A
Or at https://www.embodied-games.com/games/ at the bottom of page, under video highlights.

Research Questions. The test covered a range of gear concepts. We wanted to know how in-game play would correlate with both pretest and posttest knowledge. In the case of manipulating the bikes up hills of varying slopes, a student who understands that a smaller gear will get the bike up a steeper hill is one who does not show uncertainty about gear size as the hills change slope. That student will not bounce around trying many different gear diameters. Our hypothesis was that the students who were confused about the optimal gear diameters for mechanical advantage (MA) would be the ones who switched gear size more often. In addition, those who switched gear size more often during play would be the ones who demonstrated the lowest scores on the traditional paper and pencil knowledge pretests. This means there should be a negative correlation between number of gear switches and scores on the pretest, demonstrating that those who started with lower prior knowledge would probably not perform as well during gameplay.

Regarding the correlations for a posttest, we considered this study to be exploratory. Poor in-game performance could translate to poor posttest performance if the game is sensitive to, and calibrated for, specific knowledge structures that might be altered by posttest. On the other hand, the game is played in pairs (dyads) and dyadic performance would affect play in ways we were uncertain about. This study represents our first explorations of how dyads perform in front of a class in an active and observed-over-time game. The issue of how to design games that gather meaningful knowledge information during play (sometimes called in-process) is a timely one, because if serious "construct sensitive" games that gather meaningful in-game data that predict the amount of content learned can be created, then educators will not be forced to waste learners' class time giving repetitive or summative paper/pencil posttests.

METHODS

Participants

Participants were 23 7th graders from a middle school with 160 students in urban CA. The study began with 25 participants, but two (one from each class) were absent the day of the posttest, or their in-process data were corrupted. Fifty percent at the school received financial aid and 52% of the students were described as "people of color" by the Principal. There were 11 females in the two classes. There were no significant knowledge test differences due to gender. Two science classrooms were used in the study and the same teacher covered the same content in both classes.

Procedure

The entire study was a seven day-long intervention on Simple Machines. The study began with the concept of gears and then moved onto levers. There were three class sessions during which instruction was focused on gears. On Day 1, the pretest was given and then students played the Ratio Match gears tutorial game to get used to the arm spinning mechanic. On Day 2, students played the easier Tour de Force game, and on day 3, they played the more difficult Winching game. On day 4, students took the gears posttest and then continued on with the levers content. Participants were quasi-randomly assigned to dyads (more on this in the Discussion section).

The classroom lessons were co-designed with two science teachers, the project's lead programmer, a cognitive psychologist, an experienced game designer, and a physics subject matter expert. The classroom teacher in this study was engaged and very innovative, e.g., he brought in his own manipulatives like planks and bricks for levers, and his own bicycle to demonstrate gears. Thus, the content for the week of lessons was not solely based on the supplied *Kinect* games, the teacher interspersed short lectures that he devised. The teacher was provided with a scripted guide for the *Kinect*-based games, which he followed closely.

Day 1- Gears Tutorial Game. Student dyads took turns learning the mechanics of the *Kinect* using the Gear Ratio Tutorial Game that Dr. Birchfield designed. Two players either volunteered or were asked to come to the front of the room. The regular classroom projector projected the image (approximately 80 inch diagonal) on the wall. The dyad would stand in front of the *Kinect* sensor with their backs to the class and practice matching gear diameters in this sandbox-style tutorial game. (Video available https://www.youtube.com/watch?v=kSsiJZOUKt4&feature=youtu.be.)

Figure 2 shows the screenshot of the tutorial *Ratio Match* game. The *Kinect* is tracking two key joints on each players' bodies, i.e., the wrist and shoulder. The shoulder is the pivot point. Revolving the wrist joint around the shoulder joint creates one of three preset diameters on the screen.

The input gear rotates in real time with the player, and in the same direction as the player's arm. This is a strong example of gestural congruency. The virtual input gear diameter snaps to three different sizes. If a player makes a very wide circle around the shoulder joint it will result in the largest gear diameter of 12- the outer, red area. In Figure 2, the players are being prompted to match to a ratio, in this case an input size of 12, and the output gear on the inside is locked at a diameter of 5. Thus, 12:5 is the target ratio. The player that first completes two revolutions with an input maintained at the largest size 12 revolution will win the point. The game ends when the 45 second timer runs out. The total number of matches are presented in the boxes on top. (Note: we did not gather in-process data on this short tutorial.) Every student in the two classes was able to engage in this sand-box tutorial.

Day 2 - Tour de Force Game. On the second day, dyads played the *Tour de Force* biking game. The teacher first asked for volunteers and then the non-volunteering students were placed together in dyads. Thus, dyads were "quasi-randomly" assigned; they were not preset. Friends often chose each other in the early rounds. The game had a cut-off play time of 240 seconds. On average the last player usually crossed the finish line by two minutes (120 seconds). Figure 1 showed a player with her arm

Figure 2.

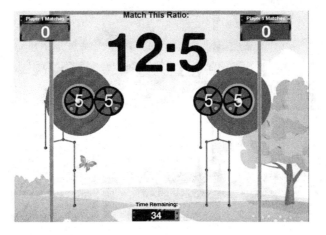

out in front as she turned the input gear on the pink bike on the top of the screen, the bike is going up a small hill. The second player is lagging behind on the green bike.

As players came to the front of the class, the experimenter entered their subject IDs into the computer from a prepopulated list of students. The size of the input gear, as measured via distance from the wrist to the shoulder pivot point, would vary (snap to) three sizes. The diameter changes were time stamped and mapped to subject ID. Figure 3 shows a close up of the opening screenshot.

Players are also able to see statistics on their performance such as input force, output force, kilometers per hour, and time played so far. At the beginning of the lesson the teacher guided student exploration of the equation: *Work = Force X Distance*. The lecture included the concept that there was a limited amount of input force, that is, they had only so much effort they could exert on the input gear. There were three input gear sizes to choose from in this game: 4, 5, and 16. The winner was the one who crossed the finish line first. To be the fastest, a player needed to show facility with critical constructs associated with the input gear (the pedal gear). They needed to quickly deduce that on the flat section of the race course the largest gear (size 16) should be used. Then, on the steep hill sections, the smallest gear (size 4) should be switched to for optimal performance. The gear switch needs to be well-timed and maintained as long as the player was on that specific terrain. If the player was not generating enough output force the bike would remain stationary. It did not slide backwards.

A learner who understood (intuited) mechanical advantage would exhibit both a very fast time *and* a minimal amount of gear switching. The biking course had 16 waypoints, that is, places where the hill slope could change. All participants played

Figure 3.

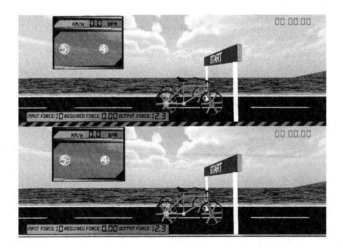

on the same default course with the same hills. On the far right in Figure 3, you can see the beginning of a small hill.

Configuration Panel - Tour de Force. Because we strive for players to also be creators, or generative in the games, a configuration panel, accessed with the key strokes "ctrl c" was included. The panel (see Figure 4) allowed for the slopes of the hills to be varied by altering the Y coordinates. In this way slopes that were impassable could be created and discussion could occur around math concepts like graphing, mechanical advantage, and game design, e.g., what makes for a "fun" and challenging game, versus a simply frustrating experience (not being able to ascend a hill of 80°). Pedal force (input force) and bike weight could also be altered in a different section of the configuration panel. (In the Discussion section we explore why this was never used.)

Profile of the Player. Players come to games with varying amounts of prior knowledge, both in terms of comfort with game play and knowledge of the content to be learned.[2] Regarding prior content knowledge, middle schoolers often approach gear trains with a knowledge structure that includes a misconception regarding diameter and which size input gear would be most efficacious given the circumstances. One way we measured whether they understood that they needed a smaller input gear to get up a steeper hill was via the number of diameter switches they made during play. Students often attempted many different gear diameters before they began to address their most common misconception - "bigger is always better". The students who either understood mechanical advantage on the bike gear train, or who could

Figure 4.

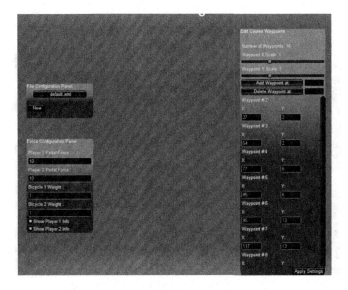

use the formula of the ratio of O:I (output to input) made the switch quickly to the smallest input gear size and stuck with it until they had reached the top of the hill. At the top, when the course would flatten, players who got it would switch adroitly back to the bigger gear and maintain that diameter for optimal speed until the next waypoint.

Students who did *not* understand the concept of smaller gears for steeper hills would bounce around trying the three different sizes of input gear until the bike finally moved. We labeled them the "Bouncers". The students who were more efficient, and consistently demonstrated they got it - were labeled the "Got its". It appeared that all students attacked the first couple of hills with the type of exploration technique commonly seen in mastering new games, but the Bouncers never really moved from exploration to "exploitation" during these games. We wanted to know if some of this behavior could be captured via in-process data and if overall number of switches would correlate with other subject variables like prior knowledge.

Day 3. The Winching Game - On the third day, dyads played the Winching Game. (See Figure 5.) The goal was to lift boulders of varying weight (force) from a pit onto a conveyor belt. The player with the most boulders lifted when the timer buzzed at 90 seconds won. In Figure 5, the input gear is the black circle on top. The output gear was locked at always be set at 5. Students needed to understand how to change the size of the input gear to efficiently winch up the larger boulders. The input gear sizes were set to 5, 7 or 9.

Winching is harder. This game was more difficult than the previous biking one because the input gear now moved in *two* directions. Spinning to the right would hoist the cable up, and spinning to the left would drop the cable back down to get the next

Figure 5.

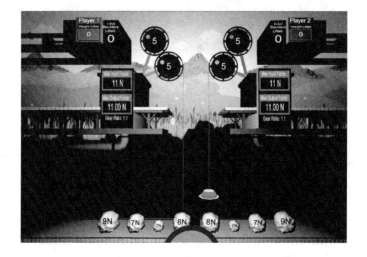

boulder. The optimal diameter for the input gear changed with each boulder's mass (see the bottom of Figure 5). Players needed to deduce that a smaller diameter was needed for the heavier boulders. Because the game is timed, players need to rapidly lower the cable (with magnetic head) down and it was always best to do that with the largest diameter. Boulders were randomly seeded at the bottom of the screen and moved on a second conveyor belt, they ranged in weight from 2 Newtons (N) to 9 N for this game. A Newton is a measure of force and can be thought of as 0.22 lb. One of the constraints was that the largest input gear would *not* lift the largest boulder. The boulder could not be moved no matter how rapidly the player spun his or her arm, a new diameter had to be chosen. The player with the most boulders at the end of the timed cycle was the winner.

Configuration Panel - Winching Game - This game also included a configuration panel for user-created content. Users could alter start conditions varying in weight ranges and preset output gear diameters, etc.; however, that panel was not used during this study.

Measure

Gears Knowledge Measure. This measure was an experimenter-designed test created with several middle school teachers and a physics subject matter expert. (See test in original article.) It was pilot-tested to be age-appropriate. There were 13 items to be answered on the gears test, either multiple choice, open-ended, or fill in the blank items. The very last item queried students to choose the correct relatively-sized gear to winch up objects of varying mass. The maximum score achievable on this subtest was 54 points. Multiple choice questions were worth three points and open-ended questions ranged from zero to five points. It included both near and far transfer items. The invariant test is the same from pretest to posttest. There were not ceiling effects as the highest score achieved on the posttest was 37.

The Gears Lessons: Learning Goals

The instructional goals in the teacher's guide were:

1. Understand energy interactions in terms of transfer and storage
2. Develop a concept of work as a mechanism for energy transfer
3. Apply the concept of conservation of energy
4. Understand and demonstrate comprehension of calculations of the efficiency of a simple machine, specifically mechanical advantage via game play
5. Define and show comprehension of mechanical advantage (*the factor by which the input force is multiplied by the use of a machine to transfer energy*)

Results

Knowledge test. All results were run with SPSS v22. All alphas levels were set to .05 and were two-tailed.

Pretest and Classroom Differences. The two classes differed significantly on gears knowledge pretest. The teacher was surprised by this result because he had been teaching the students for four months and stated the two class skill-levels were equally matched. He hypothesized the difference in pretest may have been due to a before and after lunch distinction. The AM class scored 20.08 (SD 6.56), and the PM class scored 12.08 (SD 9.89) on the pretest. An independent t test revealed a significant difference, $t_{(22)} = 2.32 \, p = .03$. (Note, the classroom scores by posttest were no longer significantly different by class, $t_{(22)} = 1.57 \, p < .14$, and a General Linear Model analysis using the interaction of time by class was not significant, $F_{(1,20)} = .08$.) Thus, the decision was made to combine the classes into one dataset to increase overall power for the study since all students received the exact same instruction by the same teacher.

Combined classrooms - Posttest. As a combined group, the gears knowledge test results for the 23 participants were: pretest $M = 16.81$ (*SD* 8.89); posttest $M = 21.19$ (*SD* 7.90). This gain was significant on a paired t test: $t_{(22)} = 2.33, p = .03$. The effect size was medium. Cohen's d is typically reported in the cognitive sciences, it is the mean difference between scores divided by the pooled average of the pretest and posttest standard deviations, $d = .52$.

In-Process Gameplay Analyses – Tour de Force – Entire Sample. Our hypothesis was that the students who were more efficient with their gear changes, that is, the "Got Its" with fewer switches during game play, would do better on the paper and pencil test. The metric used was gear diameter switches - the average frequency of change of gear size during play. The game cut off after four minutes of play. During the first round of play students interacted with the *Tour de Force* game for a mean of 78.41 seconds (Range = 32 to 190, $SD = 36.37$ seconds). Students averaged 72.27 gear switches ($SD = 41.52$ switches). The prediction was that the "Got Its" who understood mechanical advantage would use fewer switches and would cross the finish line faster. This was evident with the entire sample. Overall those with shorter times used fewer switches, $r(22) = .82 \, p < .001$. But, were these faster players the winners within their dyads?

Tour de Force - Dyadic Analysis. Tour de Force lent itself to analyses using the pair of players (the dyad) as the unit of analysis because the game course did not alter between dyads. We saw that if the winner was faster, the loser was comparatively faster as well within the whole sample. Thus, partnerships affected play across the sample. However, we only had 11 dyads on the day Tour de Force was played. (We only used first time play data and one student went twice, with a first time player and so we did not include that dyad.) We note that statistical power is an issue in the following analyses, indeed, *G Power* (v 3.1) provides an estimate of only .26 to find significance at a .05 alpha level using a .50 effect size; if we wanted .80 power we would need 34 pairs.

With more pairs, we would be able to consider using other types of analyses like Hierarchical Linear Modeling (HLM). Although the case could be made that these data are not traditionally nested. HLM assumes the structure of the data are nested at a level we never considered in this small study, e.g., teacher, school, or district. It may be the case that position of play (first or last pair to play after observing) had an effect on scores and time, but we did not store those data. We do consider the paired to be linked, or yoked, within their game space. In this manner each dyad player is not independent (i.e., one wins – ergo the other *must* lose). An analysis of interest might be whether the number of gear switches separating the winner versus loser within dyad was significantly different, and that analysis was run.

Analyzing the set of first-time play dyads, the winner switched frequency of gear diameters on average 51.91 times (SD= 20.67), the loser switched 91.55 times (SD= 53.13). When students were analyzed as the winner (coded as 1) and loser (coded as 0) within dyads, the frequency of switch between players was correlated as well, r = .68, p =.02. Faster dyads had fewer switches overall and some of the losers in a faster dyad would have been the winners in a slower dyad. This supports the hypothesis that partners affected each other's' play.

We wanted to know if the difference between switches was statistically significant regardless of whether the yoked pair were in a relatively faster or slower dyad. Using a *paired* t-test within dyad we account for some variance between dyads. But because this may seem controversial, we also ran independent t tests. The paired t test revealed that the difference between the winners' and losers' switch frequency was significant, see Table 1, p = .01, with a large effect size (Cohen's d) of .95. Independent and bootstrap analyses are also reported and were also significant supporting the hypothesis that winners used significantly fewer switches within play, Bootstrap t = 2.03, bias = -.02, p = .03 (SE = 11.70).

In Gameplay and the Knowledge Test. The next question was whether the winners in the game showed greater gains on the knowledge posttest. The effect of change on test scores was moderate, d = .56. See Table 1. The inferential paired t test was not statistically significant because we only had 8 dyads in that analysis (several players missing data or posttest knowledge scores). We note again the power issue, but the direction of the t value would support the hypothesis that winners in the game dyad did better on the knowledge posttest than the losers within a dyad. There was a sort of "switchover" seen as well. That is, the dyad losers did better on the pretest (by two points on average) but *worse* on the posttest (again by two points on average). This may suggest that in-game processes were capturing knowledge as it changed.

Winner and loser knowledge pretests were not significantly different within dyad (paired *t* value < .80), perhaps suggesting that friends who score similarly on tests often choose each other to play with. The amount of switching was not significantly correlated with pretest scores within dyads, *r* < .25.

Tour de Force Gameplay and Knowledge Test - Whole sample. Using the sample as a whole group, we had predicted a negative correlation such that the students who made fewer gear switches would have higher test scores. There was significant evidence of this on the pretest, *r* = -.41, *p* = .05; however, at posttest this negative correlation did not hold, *r* = .12, *p* = .29, NS.

The Harder Game - In Process Analyses – Winching Game – Whole sample. In the Winching Game was reported to be somewhat more difficult than the first game. During the Winching Game the students lifted on average 17.7 rocks (*SD* = 8.47). All teams played for the same amount of time (90 seconds).The range of gear size switches was 43 – 140; *M* = 75.28 (*SD* = 27.61). The number of gear switches was not predictive of number of rocks successfully lifted, *r* = -.10. Although, in this small sample we still see that the valence is negative.

Gameplay and Knowledge Test - Winching Game - Whole Sample. We predicted a negative correlation between number of switches and test scores, such that the students who made fewer switches, would have higher test scores. We saw some evidence of this on the pretest, *r* = -.26 (NS) and stronger evidence on the posttest, *r* = -.37, *p* = .07, which represents a statistical trend.

We did not run the same of sort of comparative dyadic analysis on this game because each player within each dyad was confronted with a different game course. That is, rock sizes were randomly seeded for each game and for each player on the bottom conveyor belt. It was possible for three rocks of the same size to come out in a row making one player's task much easier than the other player's task. This is different than the Tour de Force Game where the hill series never varied within or between dyads.

Table 1. Paired and Independent t Tests Comparing Dyadic Winners and Losers

Dyad Comparison	df	M Difference (SD)	Cohen's d	t Test sig. Level
# of Gear Switches (Loser - Winner)	10	39.65 (41.91)	.95	Paired = 3.14** *p* = .013**
				Independent = 2.03 *p* = .032*
Knowledge Test Gains Score (Loser Gain – Winner Gain)	8	- 5.78 (10.40)	.56	Paired =- 1.67 *p* = .13

DISCUSSION

Both the gears Winching Game and Tour de Force Game were designed as playful environments for students to practice and demonstrate their understanding of gear trains and mechanical advantage. On average the two classes demonstrated statistically significant gains in learning on the knowledge posttest after the intervention. The games were embodied and innovative; they used the *Kinect* sensor as the input device so the body could mimic the tool of instruction (a spinning gear or a pumping lever). Our goal was to make the learners' movements map to the content to be learned with gestural congruency. We mined student performance during gameplay to explore how "physical" arm rotations and "virtual" gear diameter shifts related to dyadic performance and on more traditional paper and pencil tests.

In the game Tour de Force, the faster students were always the winners in the dyad and the faster students also used significantly fewer gear switches (at least in nine of the 11 Tour de Force dyads). A key research question is whether in-process gameplay correlates with performance on more traditional tests. The results here also suggest that outcomes may depend on the difficulty of the game. In the easier Tour de Force game where arm spin rotation was only in one direction, the "Got Its" did significantly better on the pretest (as would be predicted). However, the players' in-game performance was not predictive of posttest, that is, students' knowledge post-intervention was not correlated with diameter gesture-choices during learning. Perhaps because Tour de Force was rather easy to master and all students got the basics by the end of the race course, so it lacked precision as a predictive tool.

For the more difficult Winching Game, the valences of the pretest and posttest correlations remained negative, as we had predicted. By posttest the better learners were generally using fewer switches representing a trend for more learning ($p < .07$). Thus, there is some evidence that in-game performance on appropriately calibrated (i.e., harder, more effortful) games can reveal a learner's profile. These findings suggest that when students are in a more challenging game, one that might match their Zone of Proximal Development (Vygotsky, 1978), they might exhibit patterns of movement that suggest ongoing comprehension. The negative correlations support the hypothesis that the "Got It" players, the ones who rapidly understood how mechanical advantage worked during the game, also showed greater gains on the posttest. These were the ones who could see a larger boulder coming down the belt, switch expeditiously to a smaller input gear to grab it, and then switch back to a larger gear (and use a different direction) to spin the cable back down to grab another boulder.

In Tour de Force, within a dyad, the winners in the dyads did not start with statistically higher pretest scores (as a simplistic prior knowledge-based hypothesis might predict). However, when the winners took the posttest they did on average have higher *posttest scores* than the dyadic losers. This suggests that the game may have been capturing some moments where knowledge may have "switched over", that is, a time when pretest was no longer the sole predictor of performance – at some point during the three day intervention a *different sort of learning* may have been occurring that was not contingent on the previous knowledge the student arrived to the task with. Or, it may be that the quasi-random nature of the dyadic pairings added too much noise, e.g., "smarter kids hang together" so there was self-selection bias. In addition, the smarter, more confident, friend pairs were usually the first to volunteer, so that when whole group correlations are run many nuances are lost. The later-playing students could have benefitted from observing earlier rounds, although we did note some boredom in the class by the very end. A final, equally speculative, assumption might be that the paper and pencil static test may be capturing a different sort of declarative, or crystalized, knowledge that is very different from what gestures can show. Gestures can reveal knowledge that is internalized, but not captured on other types of tests or present in speech acts (Goldin-Meadow, 2014). We have recently begun to gather movement data using a touch-sensitive assessment tool, a large *WACOM Pro* tablet (Johnson-Glenberg & Megowan-Romanowicz, 2017), these sorts of gesture-based assessments show promise for more sensitive analyses of gains on embodied educational applications.

Larger studies are needed, as well as low-embodied control groups. Nonetheless, this study represents a start in gathering the sorts of effect sizes and results that can be expected in embodied multi-media science games. Learning scientists have speculated for years regarding the constraints associated with gathering validity and reliability on gameplay data. One timely question, given a test-besotted school environment, would be: "Is it possible to gather valid knowledge information about comprehension in-vivo during gesture-based gameplay?" Our results suggest *"yes"*, in-process data can be predictive of knowledge – if the games are in a cognitively appropriate zone of playability. If this is the case, then why should we force students to work through lengthy paper and pencil tests post-gameplay? If a student demonstrates in real time that s/he has mastered the concept, then a traditional multiple-choice type test need not be administered (Gee & Shaffer, 2010).

Game design principles. With this revision, the guidelines which had first been listed in the introduction have now been moved to the discussion section. The first author has just submitted an article for design practices using hand controls in VR for education (Johnson-Glenberg, submitted), as well as a chapter (Johnson-Glenberg, 2017). The six principles listed below are core and appear in all newer sets. Although this first set (from 2015) for mixed reality does have a have a special emphasis on "social". The socio-collaborative component is very important in education, but we note it is still expensive to make synchronous, social VR environments.

The tenets remain. Designers should strive to make games:

1. **Embodied**: Include as much "gestural congruency" as possible
2. **Socio-Collaborative:** Build games that encourage discourse with others. This series of games used dyads (pairs of students), but it also gave the observing students tasks to keep the whole class engaged
3. **Generative**: Also called Active. Learning games should encourage learners to be physically active. When learners manipulate content on screen in realtime that also gives them ownership and agency over the lesson
4. **Immediate Performance Feedback:** Feedback should not be intrusive, constant, or too negative. Low stakes failure should be built into the beginning to encourage exploration
5. **Cycle of Expertise:** Level up in difficulty as the player shows competence. If the funds are available, make your game adaptive with branches of difficulty
6. **Include User-Created Content:** This is last because it is difficult to do. Ideally students should be contributors and not just passive consumers of media. E.g., these games included in-game editors that allowed students to create personalized virtual race courses for their peers. This is highly generative and we have seen that it encourages students to take 'ownership' of the content (Johnson-Glenberg, Birchfield, et al., 2014). (The teacher did not use them in this study.)

LIMITATIONS AND FUTURE DIRECTIONS

The *Kinect* sensor was used as the input device; however, these sorts of movement and data-driven decision analyses can be accomplished with other technologies (e.g., the *Leap Motion*, embedded blob detection cameras, tracking on latest generations of immersive VR headsets with hand controls). This lab focuses on games that use as much sensori-motor activity as possible, so the whole arm is used to spin a gear, but perhaps circling the finger to spin a gear on a tablet may be just as effective? The amount of sensorimotor activation is a question for future studies. We agree with Nathan et al.'s (2014) observation in a paper that also assessed gear knowledge. The authors state that "...grounding actions may be most effective when the underlying mathematical ideas...align with the physical and spatial relation..." (p.192). Nonetheless, the gesture they used of "tapping on" virtual gears to learn the parity rule, may not have been as powerful as using a full-arm gesture to simulate turning the virtual gears in real time, as we did in our study.

New assessment metrics. This emerging field of game analyses is in need of more adroit, more sophisticated inferential tools. We were uncertain how to deal with the dynamic fluxes occurring over the class-long hour of play. For example, many of the beginning-of-play dyads were not truly randomly assigned (e.g., friends), but the end-of-play dyads were randomly assigned by the teacher from a pool without replacement. Perhaps we could add a decay function to an analysis to account for increasing randomness or independence of the pairs? Additionally, the end-of-play dyads, who may have been more introverted, observed more bouts of play before their turns. In this manner, one might expect the end-of-play dyads to pick up faster on the optimal mechanical advantage gear switch. Anecdotally, this was not seen in either the gears or levers games. The end-of-play dyads were generally composed of the slower and poorer performing players. One hypothesis is that they are the more uncertain students, and observation can only take you so far in an active game. For future studies, teachers might use random number generated pairs for play. We could also include a metric to assess students' self-efficacy, self-regulation (likelihood to persist) or goal structure (performance vs. mastery) with respect to learning games.

Clearly this exploratory study needs more dyads for power considerations. In addition, with a longer time series Hurst exponents and other persistence measures could have been reliably gathered. Hurst exponents are interesting measures for predictivity in a time series. As an example, in a social experiment with children, DiDonato (DiDonato et al., 2012) showed that when young children demonstrated flexibility and nonpersistence (as in, a Hurst exponent closer to .5 which connotes more randomness and less pink noise), the exponent was a positive indicator for later behaviors. They found that preschool children who were more gender flexible with play partners during earlier play showed better positive adjustment on several sociability scales six months later. In the learning and computer aided instruction literature, Snow et al. (Snow, Allen, Jacovina, & McNamara, 2015) investigated how log data can be used as a proxy for self-regulated learning and agentic behavior. Specifically, they identified patterns of behaviors that indicated controlled and ordered processes as students made choices through two computer-based tutors using various dynamic time series methodologies (i.e., Hurst, Entropy, Random Walks).

The Hurst exponent from a time series is certainly a more nuanced metric than the measures of central tendency used in this paper. With a longer series than the few minutes of play, perhaps a delta of variance may have emerged as a meaningful change over time metric. We will borrow terminology from Stafford and Dewar (Stafford & Dewar, 2013) who categorized players as either *Explorers* (what we might call Bouncers) or *Exploiters* (what we call the Got Its). Stafford and Dewar gathered statistics on hundreds of thousands of on-line players on a simple perceptual/motor game called *Axon*. They first binned players into percentile groups based on variance during first five times of play (higher variance = *explorers*) and then correlated that with subsequent performance data (plays six through 10: $r = .59$, p <.0001). The Explorers were not overly concerned with getting it right the first few times they played. Explorers moved all over the screen and spaced their practice sessions out. The Exploiters massed their practice sessions and were primarily goal-driven. *Explorers did better* at later gameplay even though all players practiced the same amount of time. This is an in-game metric that tells us something about the player profile over time. In the Tour de Force game, performance through gameplay like latency-to-switch-for-hill could reveal intriguing dynamic player profiles over time of play.

Prior Knowledge. We are interested in the construct of prior knowledge and how it interacts with intervention. Low and moderate pre-intervention knowledge students may be able to learn more in an embodied game because the learning is not driven primarily by language or memorizing symbols. These students may demonstrate higher gains when in an embodied condition. On the other hand, it may be the case that using the body is overwhelming at first, sensory overload may occur. Low prior knowledge learners might actually benefit from a symbolic tutorial before attempting an embodied session. We should also gather spatial abilities. The new 3D tools will be interesting to work with and prior spatial skills may interact with learning. Jang, Vitale, Jyung, and Black (2016) found that low spatial ability participants learned more from a direct 3D manipulation condition compared to the low spatial, yoked group in the observe condition (topic: functioning of the inner ear). Our study, unfortunately, did not have the power to run aptitude by treatment interactions (Cronbach & Snow, 1977).

Transfer. Transfer remains a thorny issue. In a relevant gears example, Dixon and Dohn (Dixon & Dohn, 2003) directly instructed participants to use the alternation (parity) strategy on a structurally analogous task in which balance beams were connected end-to-end in a series. Participants were asked to predict whether the last balance beam in the series would go up or down, given the movement of first beam. After being instructed on alternation and solving 10 problems using alternation, participants were given gear-train system problems. Despite immediate prior mastering of the alternation strategy, participants showed no evidence of transfer. Their median discovery trial did not differ from that of uninstructed participants. In our study, the final test question (item 10) asked about relative input gear size when winching up objects of varying masses. On the pretest only three participants chose the correct answer for the heaviest object (the mattress, 13%), on the posttest only six chose the correct answer (25%, paired t <.80, NS). This was not the sort of robust transfer gain we had hoped to see. It reminds us that teachers may still need to be very explicit with students about what was learned, and perhaps remind students to transfer and apply the MA knowledge to other similar content.

Adaptivity. For future design, we will work towards tracking behavior and integrating what we know about in ludo performance and placing learners in appropriate levels. If the student is a Bouncer and remains a Bouncer throughout several games, then the system should be able to place the student into a tutorial that goes over the concept of MA again, or flag the teacher to come and make sure the student fully understands the mechanics of the physical gameplay and/or the concepts.

Observation as an IV. Many of our games are designed with a performative aspect. The student(s) go to the front of the class to play and demonstrate their knowledge. There may be effects related to position or time of play. As in, the final students have observed more play and seen the mistakes of the earlier players so they should be at some advantage. Previous ranked player analyses have not shown a significant difference due to time of play (Johnson-Glenberg & Hekler, 2013), although that was also a small n study. We do know that after 20 minutes of observation the students who have already played these short games begin to get restless. We now recommend that teachers use these short games as "stations", and not make the entire class watch for more than six or so sessions.

Students as Creators. Finally, we are excited about building in-game editors and allowing students to alter gameplay for peers. We would like to understand why the configuration panels were not fully used. For the final few instructional minutes of the Tour de Force game, the teacher demonstrated to the students the panel. He changed the Y axis on one hill so that the extremely steep hill would be impossible to ascend. However, the teacher did not let the students explore this on their own; he did not encourage them to build or sketch out separate race courses for different teams to play. One idea for the next classroom instantiation is for us to include some locking code in the game that will not advance after five play sessions unless some of the hill parameters are altered and played through. Teachers often report feeling a press to get through topics and so changing around the game and going deeper to explore different start states may feel like a luxury to them. A hypothesis worth testing is whether students in the "creator condition" retain more information than those who never alter the game.

CONCLUSION

Two games called Tour de Force and the Winching Game were designed to instruct middle schoolers in the concepts associated with gear trains. Learners used the body to map the relatively abstract concept of mechanical advantage to physical, kinesthetic sensations. The games used the *Kinect* sensor as the input device to track the changing diameter of the player-created input gear. Paper and pencil tests were administered before and after the game intervention and significant gains in learning were made. In addition, dyadic data were gathered during play regarding amount of gear switches made during play on the easier game. Data were examined to understand student movement performance and explore how the arm rotations and gear diameter shifts related to scores on more traditional tests. Negative correlations were predicted, such that, players with fewer gear changes would score higher on the tests. The valence and magnitude of the correlations between gear switches varied between the two games. For the easier first game, movement data significantly negatively predicted pretest score, but not posttest score. For the more difficult second game, The Winching Game, gear switches were negatively associated with both pre- and posttests.

These exploratory data provide a window onto how students might perform on traditional tests. One take-away for our lab was that not all embodied games are created equal, even though the same team created the games and play-tested them with several students. We at first thought the games were of equal difficulty. However, the "in the wild" classroom students reported that the Winching Game was more difficult to master. It may be that the predictive effects of games emerge only from a game that is sufficiently challenging, or in the learner's appropriate Zone of Proximal Development (ZPD) (Vygotsky, 1978). If a game is too easy, it has low sensitivity, then being a winner or loser in a dyad will not reveal much about differences in comprehension. We also make note that the game might be capturing a different sort of knowledge than the crystalized paper and pencil test. Goldin-Meadow contends learners' gestures "precede, and predict" the acquisition of structures in speech (Goldin-Meadow, 2014). Thus, the learner may be understanding the concept and gesturing adroitly in the game, but still not be able to demonstrate that comprehension on a symbolically-oriented assessment measure.

Although the study sample size was small for inferential statistics, effect sizes that might be associated with short in-class, embodied games are reported. One primary goal is to use immediate game-style feedback to attenuate the need to give repetitive, time-wasting paper and pencil tests. We find this to be a promising intersection of gesture-based STEM instruction and in ludo assessments.

REFERENCES

Black, J. B., Segal, A., Vitale, J., & Fadjo, C. L. (2012). Embodied cognition and enhancing learning and motivation. In D. Jonassen & S. Land (Eds.), *Theoretical foundations of learning environments*. New York: Routledge.

Coller, B., & Scott, A. A. (2009). Effectiveness of using a video game to teach a course in mechanical engineering. *Computers & Education*, *53*(3), 900–912. doi:10.1016/j.compedu.2009.05.012

Connolly, T. M., Boyle, E. A., MacArthur, E., Hainey, T., & Boyle, J. M. (2012). A systematic literature review of empirical evidence on computer games and serious games. *Computers & Education, 59*(2), 661–686. doi:10.1016/j.compedu.2012.03.004

Cook, S., & Goldin-Meadow, S. (2006). The Role of Gesture in Learning: Do Children Use Their Hands to Change Their Minds. *Journal of Cognition and Development, 7*(2), 211–232. doi:10.120715327647jcd0702_4

Cronbach, L., & Snow, R. (1977). *Aptitudes and Instructional Methods: A Handbook for Research on Interactions*. New York: Irvington.

DiDonato, M. D., Martin, C. L., Hessler, E. E., Amazeen, P. E., Hanish, L. D., & Fabes, R. A. (2012). Gender consistency and flexibility: Using dynamics to understand the relation between gender and adjustment. *Nonlinear Dynamics Psychology and Life Sciences, 16*(2), 159–184. PMID:22452931

diSessa, A. (1988). Knowledge in pieces. In G. Forman & P. B. Pufall (Eds.), *Constructivism in the Computer Age*. Hillsdale, NJ: Lawrence Erlbaum Associates.

Dixon, J. A., & Dohn, M. C. (2003). Redescription disembeds relations: Evidence from relational transfer and use in problem solving. *Memory & Cognition, 31*(7), 1082–1093. doi:10.3758/BF03196129 PMID:14704023

Gee, J. P., & Shaffer, D. W. (2010). Looking where the light is bad: Video games and the future of assessment. *EDge, 6*(1), 2–19.

Glenberg, A. M., Witt, J. K., & Metcalfe, J. (2013). From the revolution to embodiment: 25 years of cognitive psychology. *Perspectives on Psychological Science, 8*(5), 573–585. doi:10.1177/1745691613498098 PMID:26173215

Goldin-Meadow, S. (2011). Learning through gesture. *Wiley Interdisciplinary Reviews: Cognitive Science, 2*(6), 595–607. doi:10.1002/wcs.132 PMID:24187604

Goldin-Meadow, S. (2014). Widening the lens: What the manual modality reveals about learning, language and cognition. *Philosophical Transactions of the Royal Society, Biological Sciences., 369*(20130295).

Hanus, M., & Fox, J. (2015). Assessing the effects of gamification in the classroom: A longitudinal study on intrinsic motivation, social comparison, satisfaction, effort, and academic performance. *Computers & Education, 80*, 152–161. doi:10.1016/j.compedu.2014.08.019

Hauk, O., Johnsrude, I., & Pulvermüller, F. (2004). Somatotopic representation of action words in human motor and premotor cortex. *Neuron, 41*(2), 301–307. doi:10.1016/S0896-6273(03)00838-9 PMID:14741110

Jang, S., Vitale, J., Jyung, R., & Black, J. (2016). *Direct manipulation is better than passive viewing for learning anatomy in a three-dimensional virtual reality environment* (Vol. 106). Academic Press.

Johnson-Glenberg, M. C. (2012). *Pilot study with SMALLab summer camp attendees.* Unpublished.

Johnson-Glenberg, M. C. (2017). Embodied education in mixed and mediated realities: Principles for content design. In D. Liu, C. Dede, & J. Richards (Eds.), *Virtual, Augmented, and Mixed Realities in Education* (pp. 193–218). Springer Verlag. doi:10.1007/978-981-10-5490-7_11

Johnson-Glenberg, M. C. (submitted). *Immersive VR and education: Embodied design principles that include gesture and hand controls.* Academic Press.

Johnson-Glenberg, M. C., Birchfield, D., Koziupa, T., & Tolentino, L. (2014). Collaborative embodied learning in mixed reality motion-capture environments: Two science studies. *Journal of Educational Psychology, 106*(1), 86–104. doi:10.1037/a0034008

Johnson-Glenberg, M. C., Birchfield, D., Megowan-Romanowicz, M. C., Tolentino, L., & Martinez, C. (2009). Embodied Games, Next Gen Interfaces, and Assessment of High School Physics. *International Journal of Learning and Media, 1*(2). doi:10.1162/ijlm.2009.0017

Johnson-Glenberg, M. C., Birchfield, D., Megowan-Romanowicz, M. C., & Uysal, S. (2009). SMALLab: Virtual geology studies using embodied learning with motion, sound, and graphics. *Educational Media International, 46*(4), 267–280. doi:10.1080/09523980903387555

Johnson-Glenberg, M. C., & Hekler, E. B. (2013). Alien Health game: An embodied, motion-capture exer-game teaching nutrition and *MyPlate. Games for Health Journal, 6*(2). doi:10.1089/g4h.2013.0057

Johnson-Glenberg, M. C., & Megowan-Romanowicz, M. C. (2017). Embodied science and mixed reality: How gesture and motion capture affect physics education. *Cognitive Research: Principles and Implications, 2*(24). doi:10.118641235-017-0060-9 PMID:28603770

Johnson-Glenberg, M. C., Savio-Ramos, C., & Henry, H. (2014). "Alien Health": A nutrition instruction exergame using the *Kinect* sensor. *Games for Health Journal: Research, Development, and Clinical Applications, 3*(4), 241–251. doi:10.1089/g4h.2013.0094 PMID:25083315

Lindgren, R., & Johnson-Glenberg, M. C. (2013). Emboldened by embodiment: Six precepts regarding the future of embodied learning and mixed reality technologies. *Educational Researcher, 42*(8), 445–452. doi:10.3102/0013189X13511661

Lui, M., Kuhn, A., Acosta, A., Niño-Soto, M. I., Quintana, C., & Slotta, J. D. (2014). Using mobile tools in immersive environments to support science inquiry. *CHI '14 Extended Abstracts on Human Factors in Computing Systems, 978,* 403-406. doi:10.1145/2559206.2574796

Merchant, Z., Goetz, E. T., Cifuentes, L., Keeney-Kennicutt, W., & Davis, T. J. (2014). Effectiveness of virtual reality-based instruction on students' learning outcomes in K-12 and higher education: A meta-analysis. *Computers & Education, 70,* 29–40. doi:10.1016/j.compedu.2013.07.033

Metz, K. (1985). The development of children's problem solving in a gears task: A problem space perspective. *Cognitive Science, 9*(4), 431–471. doi:10.120715516709cog0904_4

Milgram, P., & Kishino, A. F. (1994). Taxonomy of mixed reality visual displays. *IEICE Transactions on Information and Systems, E77-D*(12), 1321–1329.

Mishra, J., Anguera, J. A., & Gazzaley, A. (2016). Video Games for Neuro-Cognitive Optimization. *Neuron, 90*(2), 214–218. doi:10.1016/j.neuron.2016.04.010 PMID:27100194

Mislevy, R. J., Behrens, J. T., DiCerbo, K. E., & Levy, R. (2012). Design and discovery in educational assessment: Evidence-centered design, psychometrics, and educational data mining. *JEDM-Journal of Educational Data Mining, 4*(1), 11–48.

Nathan, M. J., Walkington, C., Boncoddo, R., Pier, E. L., Williams, C. C., & Alibali, M. W. (2014). Actions speak louder with words: The roles of action and pedagogical language for grounding mathematical reasoning. *Learning and Instruction, 33,* 182-193.

Papastergiou, M. (2009). Digital Game-Based Learning in high school Computer Science education: Impact on educational effectiveness and student motivation. *Computers & Education, 52*(1), 1–12. doi:10.1016/j.compedu.2008.06.004

Segal, A., Black, J., & Tversky, B. (2010). *Do Gestural Interfaces Promotoe Learning? Congruent Gestures Promote Performance in Math.* Paper presented at the 51st Meeting of the Psychonomic Society Conference, St. Louis, MO.

Shaffer, D., Hatfield, D., Svarovsky, G., Nach, P., Nulty, A., Bagley, E., ... Mislevy, R. (2009). Epistemic Network Analysis: A Prototype for 21st Century Assessment of Learning. *International Journal of Learning and Media*, *1*(1).

Skulmowski, A., & Rey, G. D. (2018). Embodied learning: Introducing a taxonomy based on bodily engagement and task integration. *Cognitive Research*, *3*(1), 6. doi:10.118641235-018-0092-9 PMID:29541685

Slater, M., & Sanchez-Vives, M. V. (2016). Enhancing our lives with immersive virtual reality. *Frontiers in Robotics and AI*, *3*(74). doi:10.3389/frobt.2016.00074

Snow, E. L., Allen, L. K., Jacovina, M. E., & McNamara, D. S. (2015). Does agency matter?: Exploring the impact of controlled behaviors within a game-based environment. *Computers & Education*, *26*, 378–392. doi:10.1016/j.compedu.2014.12.011

Squire, K., & Klopfer, E. (2007). Augmented Reality Simulations on Handheld Computers. *Journal of the Learning Sciences*, *16*(3), 371–413. doi:10.1080/10508400701413435

Stafford, T., & Dewar, M. (2013). Tracing the trajectory of skill learning with a very large sample of online game players. *Psychological Science*. doi:10.1177/095679761351146

Vygotsky, L. S. (1978). *Mind in Society: The Development of Higher Psychological Processes*. Cambridge, MA: The Harvard University Press.

Wilson, M. (2002). Six views of embodied cognition. *Psychonomic Bulletin & Review*, *9*(4), 625–636. doi:10.3758/BF03196322 PMID:12613670

Wouters, P., Nimwegen, C., Oostendorp, H., & van der Spek, E. (2013). A meta-analysis of the cognitive and motivational effects of serious games. *Journal of Educational Psychology*, *105*(2), 249–265. doi:10.1037/a0031311

Young, M. F., Slota, S., Cutter, A. B., Jalette, G., Mullin, G., Lai, B., ... Yukhymenko, M. (2012). Our Princess Is in Another Castle: A Review of Trends in Serious Gaming for Education. *Review of Educational Research*, *82*(1), 61–89. doi:10.3102/0034654312436980

ENDNOTES

[1]   Energy is usually defined simply as "the ability to do work", a more general and useful definition is "the ability to cause a change". One reason to use the more general definition is that the term work is one that is often misunderstood as well. There are two things that can be done with energy: it can be stored and/or it can be transferred. The transfer of energy by means of work happens by exerting a force on something across some distance. The product of the input force and the distance travelled is the work done on the object. Working is the mechanism for energy transfer. Simple machines (e.g., levers and gears) are devices that make work easier by changing the magnitude and/or direction of a force and the displacement of the object to which the force is applied. This allows for useful work to be done on some object that would be difficult, or impossible, to accomplish otherwise. Examples of tasks that are hard for humans to do alone are lifting heavy boulders, moving pianos up stairs without pulleys or planes, and cycling up very steep hills.

[2]   Mislevy, et al. (2012) make intriguing points about how game designers and statisticians can work together in designing games to mitigate some of the prior gameplay knowledge that surely adds noise to all knowledge gain scores. They stress how the assessment design framework called Evidence Centered Design (ECD) can complement game design principles, so that designers can address assessment criteria such as reliability and validity jointly with game criteria like engagement and interactivity in mind (Mislevy, Behrens, DiCerbo, & Levy, 2012).

Regarding prior gameplay knowledge, we posit that the gameplay mechanism in this study was novel for all participants since the *Microsoft* Kinect for *XBOX* suite at the time did not have any products similar to our gears games when eth study ran. It was novel, yet intuitive; players did not need to use cognitive resources to recall the affordances of buttons A and B on a remote.

Chapter 6

Monster Mischief:
A Game–Based Assessment of Selective Sustained Attention in Young Children

Karrie E. Godwin
Kent State University, USA

Derek Lomas
IO Delft University of Technology, The Netherlands

Ken R. Koedinger
Carnegie Mellon University, USA

Anna V. Fisher
Carnegie Mellon University, USA

ABSTRACT

Selective sustained attention, or the ability to allocate perceptual and mental resources to a single object or event, is an important cognitive ability widely assumed to be required for learning. Assessing young children's selective sustained attention is challenging due to the limited number of sensitive and developmentally appropriate performance-based measures. Furthermore, administration of existing assessments is difficult, as children's engagement with such tasks wanes quickly. One potential solution is to provide assessments within an engaging environment, such as a video game. This chapter reports the design and psychometric validation of a video game (Monster Mischief) designed to assess selective sustained attention in preschool children. In a randomized controlled trial, the authors demonstrate that Monster Mischief is significantly correlated with an existing measure of selective sustained attention (rs ≥ 0.52), and more motivating for young children as almost three times more children preferred Monster Mischief to the existing measure.

DOI: 10.4018/978-1-5225-7461-3.ch006

INTRODUCTION

Cognitive tests can provide a wealth of data. This data is beneficial not only for research scientists but also for practitioners as performance on cognitive tests can be used for diagnostic purposes. However, if participants do not complete the assessment batteries, the utility of such tests are limited. This issue is especially pertinent for young children as their enthusiasm and engagement with cognitive assessments can wane rapidly. The gamification (Deterding Deterding, Dixon, Khaled, & Nacke, 2011) of cognitive tests is one promising strategy for increasing the utility of cognitive assessments. While the simple addition of game-elements to assessments may have some value, games offer the potential to provide a richer space of assessment tasks (Holmgård, Togelius, & Henriksen, 2016). Thus, creating valid game-based assessments has considerable potential value for researchers, practitioners, and the educational system at large.

While games have been used extensively to provide intrinsic motivation for learning (Malone, 1981; for review and meta-analysis see Clark et al., 2013), there have been comparatively few studies demonstrating *both* the validity of games as assessments and empirical validations demonstrating that game-based assessments improve children's intrinsic motivation. MacPherson and Burns (2008) explicitly compared game-like versions of assessments of working memory and processing speed to traditional assessments; but they did not assess whether the games improved player affect or motivation. There have also been several ambitious efforts to design batteries of game-based assessments for a range of neuropsychological constructs (including Aalbers et al., 2013; Delgado et al., 2014; Méndez et al., 2015; Rosetti et al., 2017). In many cases, these research efforts have demonstrated that games can serve as reliable assessments that correlate well with traditional neuropsychological assessments (or even predict psychiatric diagnoses like ADHD). But across these studies, no comparison was made to determine if the game-based assessments enhanced player affect or motivation. However, work by Attali and Arieli-Attali (2015) found that the addition of game-like points to an online math assessment somewhat improved task likability for middle school students while having no effect on the accuracy of responses. In a recent review of the literature on cognitive assessment and training games (Lumsden, Edwards, Lawrence, Coyle, & Munafò, 2016), only one study (Prins et al., 2011) reported behavioral measures (more voluntary completion and fewer absences) to validate the enjoyability of their game; however this was a working memory training game that was compared to a working memory training exercise. A related line of research has investigated how game data can be used to generate evidence of ability, as in Shute's (2011) notion of "stealth assessments" or other investigations of the psychometrics of games (GlassLab, 2014). Despite the limited evidence, game-based assessments (Mislevy et al., 2012) may have the potential to support higher levels of user enjoyment while preserving assessment validity. Accordingly, we sought to redesign an existing measure of attention as an engaging video game that would maintain sufficient validity as an assessment while also increasing children's motivation.

In what follows, we provide a brief overview of selective sustained attention, its development, and how it is traditionally measured. We then discuss the design of *Monster Mischief,* a video game to assess selective sustained attention, and present the results from an experimental study examining the validity of *Monster Mischief* and its potential effect on children's enjoyment and motivation. We close by discussing the limitations of the work as well as future directions.

Selective Sustained Attention

Attention is multidimensional and encompasses a diverse set of psychological constructs, including (but not limited to) orienting, selection, shifting, maintenance, and executive attention (see Colombo & Cheatham, 2006; Gitelman, 2003; Fisher & Kloos, 2016; Posner & Petersen, 1990). The present work focuses on selective sustained attention which is defined as: "a state of engagement that involves narrowed selectivity and increased commitment of energy and resources on the targeted activity … and that primarily enhances information processing in that system" (Setliff & Courage, 2011, p. 613). Selective sustained attention is important because the ability to selectively allocate attentional resources is commonly hypothesized to aid learning (e.g., Carroll 1963; Bloom, 1976; Oakes, Kannass, & Shaddy, 2002). As stated by Oakes and colleagues (2002), "if attention were constantly reoriented to every new event, it would be difficult ... to learn about any single object or event" (p.1644). In accordance with this assertion, prior research has implicated selective sustained attention in task performance (e.g., Choudhury & Gorman, 2000; DeMarie-Dreblow & Miller, 1988), academic achievement (e.g., Duncan et al. 2007; for review see Goodman, 1990), and learning outcomes (e.g., Fisher, Thiessen, Godwin, Dickerson, & Kloos, 2013; Fisher, Godwin, & Seltman, 2014; Yu & Smith, 2012).

Theoretical Perspectives on Selective Sustained Attention

There has been a long tradition in the cognitive psychology literature of distinguishing between two modes of attention regulation. One mode refers to regulation that is said to be top-down, controlled, and endogenous (i.e., arising from within the organism); whereas the other mode is commonly referred to as bottom-up, automatic (or in some cases automatized through extensive practice), and exogenous (i.e., arising from outside the organism) (e.g., Jonides, 1981; Miller & Cohen, 2001; Posner, 1980; Pashler, Johnston, & Ruthruff, 2001; Schneider & Shiffrin, 1977). In the present paper, we are adopting the developmental framework of attention regulation put forth by Ruff and Rothbart (1996). This framework builds upon the dual-mode of attention regulation suggested by the above theories. Specifically, according to Ruff and Rothbart (1996) the state of selective sustained attention can be obtained through two distinct systems: an orienting system and an executive control system. Under the orienting system, selective sustained attention is driven by exogenous factors such as the saliency of the stimuli including characteristics such as the brightness or contrast of the stimuli as well as motion. Thus, exogenously driven selective sustained attention is considered largely an automatic process driven by the physical characteristics of the environment or the stimulus (Bornstein, 1990; Ruff & Rothbart, 1996). Under the executive control system, selective sustained attention is driven by endogenous factors; in other words the focus of attention is directed internally based on the individual's desires, interests, and goals (Colombo & Cheatham, 2006; Posner & Petersen, 1990; Posner & Rothbart, 2007). The two systems are said to be neurally and anatomically distinct, with the orienting system involving areas within the parietal lobe, superior colliculus, and lateral pulvinar nucleus of the thalamus, and the executive system involving areas within the prefrontal cortex (PFC) and anterior cingulate gyrus (for review see Fisher & Kloos, 2016).

In the present paper we focus on endogenously driven selective sustained attention as prior research suggests that endogenously regulated selective sustained attention may be particularly important for learning in education settings (Erickson, Thiessen, Godwin, Dickerson, & Fisher, 2014). In education settings children need to attend to an externally-prescribed learning objective, but often face multiple sources of distraction (Godwin, Almeda, Seltman, Kai, Skerbetz, Baker, & Fisher, 2016). Children who are better able to endogenously regulate their attention may be more likely to maintain focus on the learning objective in the face of distractions and thus have better learning outcomes.

Development of Selective Sustained Attention

The orienting and executive control systems follow different developmental trajectories. The orienting system matures during infancy. In contrast, the executive control system follows a more protracted developmental course continuing to mature into adolescence (Diamond, 2002; Luna, 2009; Posner & Rothbart, 2007). Thus, early in life selective sustained attention is driven by exogenous factors, later in development endogenous factors become more instrumental (Diamond, 2006; Colombo & Cheatham, 2006; Oakes, Kannass, & Shaddy, 2002; Ruff & Rothbart, 1996).

Marked improvements in selective sustained attention are seen throughout early childhood: For example, 21-month-old children can only engage in episodes of selective sustained attention for approximately 2 minutes, in contrast children 5 to 6 years of age are able to engage in episodes of selective sustained attention for 9 minutes or more (Choudhury & Gorman, 2000; Ruff & Lawson, 1990; Sarid & Breznitz, 1997; for review see Fisher & Kloos, 2016). However, these estimates likely reflect the upper limit of children's ability to maintain attention on a single activity, as selective sustained attention was assessed during free play (or other self-directed activities), rather than within structured learning contexts where a child's attention span may be far shorter (e.g., Geary, 2011). As children advance through early and middle-childhood, selective sustained attention continues to improve and children become less susceptible to distraction (Ruff & Rothbart, 1996; Ruff & Capozzoli, 2003) and they develop the ability to produce and utilize effective attention strategies (DeMarie-Dreblow & Miler, 1988).

Children's ability to endogenously regulate selective sustained attention is hypothesized to be related to two core executive functions, namely inhibitory control and working memory (Miyake, Friedman, Emerson, Witzki, Howerter, & Wager, 2000). Endogenously driven selective sustained attention is related to inhibitory control, as the successful completion of tasks often requires inhibiting extraneous information or events (Ruff & Rothbart, 1996). Similarly, endogenously driven selective sustained attention requires sufficient working memory in order to maintain an active representation of task goals (Colombo & Cheatham, 2006).

Measurement of Selective Sustained Attention

Selective sustained attention in infants is typically assessed using eye gaze and physiological measures such as heart rate (for review see Fisher & Kloos, 2016; Richards, 2003). To measure selective sustained attention in toddlers and young children, researchers commonly utilize play-based measures of selective sustained attention (see Ruff & Rothbart, 1996). Studies relying on play-based measures of selective sustained attention use extensive coding protocols in which the child's eye gaze, facial expression, posture, and activity level are coded. For example, selective sustained attention entails several behavioral signatures such as looking at the object of interest with an intent facial expression, leaning toward the object, and engaging in minimal extraneous body movements (Choudhury & Gorman, 2000; Godwin & Fisher, In press; Oakes, at al., 2002; Ruff & Capozzoli, 2003; Ruff & Rothbart, 1996; Tellinghuisen, Oakes, & Tjebkes, 1999).

Performance-based measures of selective sustained attention are commonly administered to older children and adults (Fisher & Kloos, 2016). The most widely used performance-based assessment of selective sustained attention is the Continuous Performance Test (CPT; Rosvold, Mirsky, Sarason, Bransome, & Beck, 1956). In the CPT, participants are presented with a stream of visual stimuli over a prolonged period of time (e.g., up to 40 minutes). Participants are asked to respond by pressing a button when the target appears and withhold a response for non-targets. Targets occur infrequently, and thus require the participant to maintain a state of prolonged vigilance. The CPT is considered inappropriate for use with preschool children due to the long task durations and limited familiarity with the task stimuli (e.g., letters and numbers). Child-friendly adaptions to the CPT have been pursued in which the task duration is shortened and the stimuli are altered to include highly familiar objects. However, these adaptions have met with limited success as recent research has documented that young children typically fail to reach the minimum performance criteria (for review see Fisher & Kloos, 2016). Thus, preschool children are in a measurement gap as they are too old for the physiological measures utilized with infants and toddlers and too young for the performance-based measures typically employed with older children and adults (Fisher & Kloos, 2016). In order to mitigate the measurement gap, Fisher, Thiessen, Godwin, Kloos, and Dickerson (2013) developed *Track-It*, a computer-based task designed to assess selective sustained attention in young children

Track-It Assessment of Selective Sustained Attention in Young Children

Track-It (Fisher et al., 2013) is a performance-based measure of selective sustained attention that was designed to be an isomorphic yet developmentally appropriate version of the *Multiple Object Tracking* (MOT) task (Pylyshyn & Storm, 1988; Yantis, 1992). Performance on the *Track-It* task is dependent upon a subject's ability to sustain attention to a target object over time while ignoring distractors.

The *Track-It* assessment (see Figure 1) consists of a set of distractor objects and a target that move along random trajectories across a computer screen for a pre-determined period of time (prior studies have used trial durations of 10 and 30 seconds) and then disappear. The subject's task is to identify the location where the target object disappeared. Prior research utilizing *Track-It* revealed that performance on this assessment was significantly related to children's learning scores in a classroom-like setting (Fisher et al., 2013). Specifically, children who were better able to track a target object amidst distractors were also likely to obtain higher scores on the classroom learning task ($r = 0.53$, $p = 0.01$). This finding highlights the important contribution of selective sustained attention on children's academic performance.

Track-It is unique in its ability to assess within a single task both exogenous and endogenously-driven selective sustained attention by manipulating the different types of distractors deployed in the task (e.g., homogenous and heterogeneous distractors). In the heterogeneous distractors condition the distractors are all distinct from the target and from each other (e.g., red triangle, green diamond, blue square). In this condition, *Track-It* performance is hypothesized to reflect endogenously-driven selective sustained attention. The task requires effortful control of attention as the target and distractors are equally salient and thus there is no contextual support. In the homogenous distractor condition, the distractors are distinct from the target (e.g., yellow circle) but identical to one another (e.g., red triangles). In this condition, *Track-It* performance is hypothesized to reflect both endogenous as well as exogenously-driven selective sustained attention as the task still requires effortful control; however, there is contextual support within the task as the target is unique from all distractors and therefore more salient. Due to our interest in endogenously-driven selective sustained attention, we utilized the heterogeneous distractors condition in the present study.

Although *Track-It* provides a sensitive and developmentally appropriate measure of selective sustained attention in children three to five years of age, children's engagement with the task wanes quickly. Therefore, we sought to investigate whether it was possible to redesign *Track-It* as an engaging video game that would also maintain sufficient validity as an assessment while increasing children's motivation.

Figure 1. Schematic of the Track-It Game

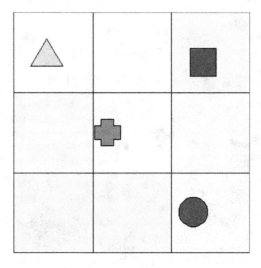

Design of Monster Mischief

The version of the *Monster Mischief* game described in this paper is a performance-based measure of endogenously regulated selective sustained attention. *Monster Mischief* was designed to closely mirror the original heterogeneous condition of the *Track-It* assessment while providing motivational design elements that were intended to sustain students' intrinsic motivation to participate and play the game. *Monster Mischief* (See Figure 2) features a set of colorful "monsters" that run around various settings (e.g., a play room filled with toys) and hide behind an assortment of objects (e.g., a toy chest). This design feature stands in contrast to *Track-It* which utilized simple shapes which were presented on a 3x3 grid.

The target character is indicated at the beginning of the trial by a glowing circle that encompasses the target. Children must click on the target character to initiate the trial. Then, the target and distractor monsters run around the screen until they hide behind an array of objects in the room (such as a toy chest or a rocking horse). If the player successfully clicks on the target's hiding spot, the character reveals itself and gives the player a jewel. The present study seeks to determine whether the design elements of *Monster Mischief* increase children's engagement and motivation to play the instructional game, while still maintaining the validity of the measure.

Figure 2. Schematic of the Monster Mischief video game. The target monster is highlighted in yellow at the beginning of each trial

The *Monster Mischief* game was designed to have a parallel structure to the *Track-It* assessment (see below for details). Thus, we expected the following pattern of results: Performance on *Monster Mischief* should be statistically equivalent to an existing assessment of selective sustained attention (i.e., *Track-It;* Hypothesis 1), and Performance on *Monster Mischief* should be significantly correlated with an existing assessment of selective sustained attention (i.e., *Track-It;* Hypothesis 2).

In order to create the parallel structure between *Monster Mischief* and *Track-It*, we engaged in an iterative design process that was driven by the goal of having *Monster Mischief* require equivalent cognitive processes as *Track-It*. This equivalency should occur when both tasks can be described by the same abstract description: a target object was visually indicated to the user among 3 other objects; all objects then moved randomly about the screen for a period of time and then disappeared. The user was then required to identify the target object's location and to discriminate the target object from other objects. Any task that is reasonably designed to fit this description might be expected to have the same face validity. This abstracted equivalent task structure is akin to having the same game mechanic, with different game aesthetics (Hunicke et al., 2004). As a step in our design process, we articulated the mapped relations between the game and the assessment. The key components of the *Track-It* task were incorporated into the *Monster Mischief* game to ensure alignment and to equate *Track-It* and *Monster Mischief* on the level of task difficulty. For example, the games were equated as closely as possible on the following parameters: the number and type of distractors, the movement paths of the target and distractors, the number of test trials, the number of test locations, and the number of lures included in the memory check; see Table 1 for additional details on the alignment between *Track-It* and *Monster Mischief*. It is important to note that one parameter, trial duration, was not directly aligned between *Track-It* and *Monster Mischief*. Specifically, *Monster Mischief* had a slightly longer trial duration than *Track-It*. The longer duration of the test trials in *Monster Mischief* compared to *Track-It* was a design choice. This decision was based on the concern that *Monster Mischief* might not be as attentionally demanding as *Track-It* due to the changes in the surface features of the task which were intended to make *Monster Mischief* more engaging for young children. Consequently a slightly longer trial duration was selected for *Monster Mischief*.

Engagement and Motivation

The primary design objective of *Monster Mischief* was to retain the features of the *Track-It* task within a video game design that would be more engaging and motivating for the children to play; see Table 2 for the full list of the motivational design elements. Thus, children should choose to play and report liking *Monster Mischief* more than the existing selective sustained attention assessment (i.e.,

Table 1. Alignment between Track-It and Monster Mischief

	Track-It	Monster Mischief
Distractors (Number and Type)	3 unique distractors	✔
Motion (Target/Distractor motion path)	Randomized path	✔
Trials (Number)	5 trials (1 practice trial and 4 test trials)	✔
Trial Duration	Approximately 10s	Approximately 20s
Test Locations (Hiding locations)	9 potential locations (3x3 grid)	✔
Memory Assessment (Number of lures)	3	✔

Track-It; Hypothesis 3). Video games are intrinsically motivating (Ryan, Rigby, & Przybylski, 2006); thus, incorporating game design features into an experimental task was hypothesized to increase student engagement and motivation. In *Monster Mischief*, we sought to increase the attractiveness of the game as well as its capacity to support child engagement over time through intrinsic fantasy, narrative-driven curiosity, as well as achievement motivation.

Prior research has demonstrated that introducing fantasy elements can increase the "motivational appeal" of an activity (Malone, 1981, Parker & Lepper, 1992). The *Monster Mischief* game presents the assessment task as an intrinsic part of a fantasy context: the point of the tracking task is to retrieve jewels stolen by the monsters. The game narrative is hypothesized to increase players' curiosity to discover what will happen over time (Malone, 1981; Loewenstein, 1994), thus helping to maintain children's engagement.

The *Monster Mischief* game also supports achievement motivation (Eccles & Wigfield, 2002; Ryan, Rigby, & Przybylski, 2006) by providing players with a clear goal (viz., click on the hiding location of the monster that stole the jewel), a visual reward for attaining the goal (viz., an animation of a magical jewel flying into the score board) and a small cost for failing to attain the goal (viz., seeing an animation of the mischievous monster emerging from its hiding location and giggling); See Figure 3. In contrast, *Track-It* does not provide children with positive or negative feedback that might support achievement motivation. Further, the *Monster Mischief* map was used to provide a set of more distal goals, including: obtaining the maximum number of gems, unlocking all available levels, clearing the clouds from the map, reaching the castle). No such goal structure was available in *Track-It*.

Table 2. Motivational Design Elements of Monster Mischief compared to Track-It

	Monster Mischief	**Track-It**
Targets	Cute animated "monsters"	Simple shapes
Background	The game takes place in colorful settings that are familiar to young children (e.g., a play room)	9x9 grid
Test locations	Characters hide behind the objects in the room (e.g., the characters disappear behind the toys in the play room)	The shapes disappear in one of the 9 squares
Feedback	If the child finds the hiding location of the target character, the character emerges from behind the object and gives the child a jewel. If the child selects the wrong location, the target character emerges from the correct location and giggles.	No feedback is provided
Backstory	At the beginning of the game the mischievous monsters take jewels from the castle. The child's task is to find where the characters are hiding in order to collect all of the jewels.	No backstory
Overarching Goal	Collect all of the jewels at each level of the game. Within each level, the number of jewels the child has earned is displayed at the top of the screen. A map marks the child's progress across the game levels.	None

EXPERIMENTAL EVALUATION OF MONSTER MISCHIEF

The three aforementioned hypotheses were tested in an experimental study of *Monster Mischief* (originally described in Godwin, Lomas, Koedinger, & Fisher, 2015). Specifically, after designing a functional version of the *Monster Mischief* game, we conducted an experimental study to assess the validity of the *Monster Mischief* game as an assessment of endogenously driven selective sustained attention by comparing children's performance on *Monster Mischief* to their performance on the *Track-It* assessment in the Heterogeneous Distractors condition. Additionally, we examined whether design elements of *Monster Mischief* increased children's engagement and motivation to play the video game.

Method

Participants

Thirty preschool children were recruited to participate in the present study. Three children were ultimately excluded from the study: 1 child was excluded due to non-compliance with experimenter instructions, 1 child was excluded due to an interruption in the testing session (i.e., a fire drill), and 1 child was excluded due

Figure 3. Schematic of the motivation and engagement design features included in Monster Mischief: a fantasy context (Panel A); clear goal (click on the hiding location of the monster that stole the jewel; Panel B), goal structure for more distal goals (Monster Mischief map; Panel C), positive feedback (a visual reward, a jewel, for attaining the goal; Panel D), and negative feedback (monster emerging from its hiding location and giggling; Panel E).

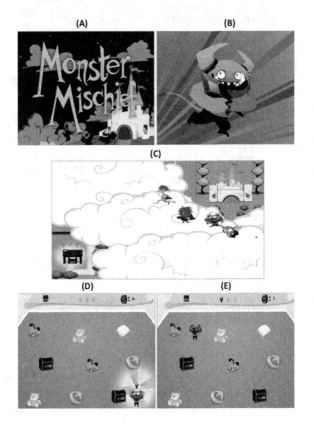

to experimenter error. The final sample included 27 children. The mean age was 4.50 years ($SD = 0.31$ years). Children ranged in age from 4.08 years to 5.00 years.

Study Design

Children were tested individually by the first author of this paper or a hypothesis blind research assistant in a room adjacent to the child's classroom. The entire testing session lasted approximately 15 minutes. The testing session was divided into three phases. In Phase 1, children played 5 trials of either *Track-It* or *Monster Mischief*. In Phase 2, children played 5 trials of the alternate game. In Phase 3, children were given a choice of playing either *Track-It* or *Monster Mischief*. Children's game choice in Phase 3 was recorded as an index of children's motivation. Game choice has been successfully used as a measure of motivation in the prior literature (Parker & Lepper, 1992). Additionally, after each game children were asked to rate how much they liked each game using a 5-point scale (i.e., the *Smile Scale*; see appendix). The order in which the games were presented was counterbalanced across participants (i.e., whether *Track-It* or *Monster Mischief* was presented first).

Measures

Track-It Task: Children completed 5 trials of the heterogeneous condition of the *Track-It* task, 1 practice trial and 4 test trials. Each trial lasted for approximately 10 seconds. On each trial, children saw four objects (e.g., simple shapes) moving on a computer screen: a target object and three unique distractors. The objects move across a 3x3 gird and land on one of nine locations. Each grid location was marked in a pastel color to assist children in reporting the last location visited by the target. For each trial, the target object and the distractors are randomly selected from an array of simple shapes. Children are asked to watch a particular object (i.e., target object) while ignoring the rest of the objects (i.e., the distractors). When the objects stop moving and disappear from the computer screen, children are asked to identify the location last visited by the target object; see Figure 1. After each trial, a memory check is administered to ensure that children were tracking the intended target. In the memory check, children are presented with an array of four objects (i.e., the target and three lures) and asked to identify the specific object they were tracking. For both the tracking portion of the task and the memory check, children can provide a verbal or non-verbal response (i.e., point to the location/object). Overall, *Track-It* provides two performance indices: Attention (indicated by the accuracy of identifying the last location visited by the target) and Memory (indicated by the accuracy of identifying the target object on the memory check). Please note that a new feature, error analysis, is now available in the most recent software update of *Track-It* (Kim, Vande Velde, Thiessen, & Fisher, 2017)

   Monster Mischief Game: Children completed 5 trials of the *Monster Mischief Game*, 1 practice trial and 4 test trials. Each trial lasted for approximately 20 seconds. In the *Monster Mischief Game*, children see a set of cute and friendly monsters (one target and three distractors). During the game, the characters run around various settings (e.g., a play room) and hide behind common objects; see Figure 2. At the beginning of the trial, one of the characters is identified as the target (i.e., the target character is encircled by a glowing ring). At the end of the trial, all of the characters hide behind various objects (e.g., disappear behind a toy chest, rocking horse, etc.). If the child correctly identifies the target character's hiding spot (by clicking on the appropriate object), the target character will reveal itself and the child will earn a jewel. At the end of each trial a memory check is administered. Children are presented with an array of four characters (i.e., the target and three lures) and asked to identify the specific character they were tracking. For both the tracking portion of the task and the memory check, children can provide a verbal or non-verbal response (i.e., point to the location/character). Similar to *Track-It*, *Monster Mischief* provides Attention and Memory measures.

Due to constraints relating to school policies regarding how long children may be absent from the classroom while participating in research, administering additional test trials was not possible within the allotted time frame. Thus, within a single testing session children were only able to complete 10 trials, 5 trials of *Monster Mischief* and 5 trials of *Track-It*.

Smile Scale: Before starting the experiment proper, children were introduced to the *Smile Scale*. The *Smile Scale* is a child friendly version of a 5-point likert scale (Read & MacFarlane, 2006). The *Smile Scale* includes five faces (images were obtained from the Google search engine) that exhibit a range of facial expressions from a big frown to a big smile. Children were given three practice items (e.g., *"Which face should I point to if I told you I really like to Jump Rope"*). The practice items were included to ensure that the children understood how to use the scale. See the appendix for the scale, script, and practice trials that were used to familiarize children with the *Smile Scale*.

Game Choice: After playing both games, children were presented with a piece of paper that included a screen shot of each game. The screen shots served as a memory cue for the children. Children were told that they only had a few minutes left before they would return to class and so the child could choose which game he or she wanted to play. After children made their selection, they were asked to provide a rationale for their choice (e.g., *"Great, why did you choose the _____ game?"*). The child's response was recorded. Then, the child played one trial of the game he or she selected.

RESULTS

On both *Track It* and *Monster Mischief*, children obtained high Memory scores ($M = 0.91$, $SD = 0.19$, range 0.25-1.00 and $M = 0.86$, $SD = 0.21$, range 0.25-1.00, respectively). This suggests that children accurately encoded the identity of the target object, which is a necessary precondition for successfully tracking a target object moving amidst distractors. Children also achieved relatively high Attention scores ($M = 0.74$, $SD = 0.26$, range 0.25-1.00 and $M = 0.73$, $SD = 0.28$ range 0.00-1.00, for *Track-It* and *Monster Mischief* respectively); see Figure 4.

Figure 4. Mean Attention and Memory scores for the Track-It task and the Monster Mischief Game. Error bars represent the standard errors of the means. Standard errors of the means are as follows, Attention: Track-It = 0.05, Monster Mischief = 0.053; Memory Check: Track-It = 0.035, Monster Mischief = 0.041

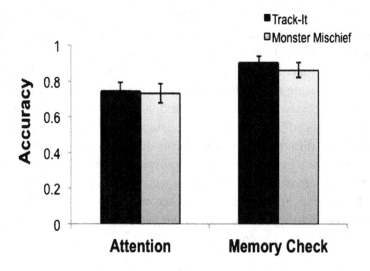

Concurrent Validity of Monster Mischief

In order to determine the validity of *Monster Mischief* and thereby test Hypotheses 1 and 2, we examined the performance alignment between *Monster Mischief* and the *Track-It* task. Children's performance on the memory check for the *Track-It* task and the *Monster Mischief* game were not significantly different from each other (paired samples $t(26) = 1.22, p = 0.23$ *ns*). A test of equivalence was also conducted using Weber and Popova's (2012) Paired-Samples Equivalence Procedure in order to ascertain whether memory performance was statistically equivalent in *Monster Mischief* and *Track-It*. The minimum substantial effect ($\Delta = 0.5$) was selected based on Cohen's (1988) guidelines for a medium effect. The equivalence test was statistically significant suggesting that the memory demands of the two games are comparable; $t(26) = 1.22, p = 0.025$. Statistical equivalence could not be confirmed using more conservative (i.e., smaller) effect size levels ($\Delta = 0.3$ or 0.1 both *ps* > 0.27). However, the failure to find evidence of equivalence at these more conservative levels should be interpreted with caution due to the small sample size utilized in the present paper and the known power problems of equivalence tests (see Weber & Popova, 2012). Children's memory check scores on the two games were also found to be significantly correlated ($r = 0.52, p = 0.006$), suggesting that these measures tapped reliable individual differences in memory encoding.

Similarly, there was no significant difference on the Attention scores of *Track-It* and *Monster Mischief* (paired samples $t(26) = 0.20$, $p = 0.84$ *ns*). A test of equivalence was also performed in order to determine whether children's attention scores in *Monster Mischief* and *Track-It* were statistically equivalent. The minimum substantial effect ($\Delta = 0.5$) was again selected based on Cohen's (1988) guidelines for a medium effect. Children exhibited equivalent attention performance indicating that the difficulty level of the two games is comparable; $t(26) = -0.20$, $p = 0.001$. Akin to the results for children's memory performance statistical equivalence could not be confirmed using more conservative effect size levels ($\Delta = 0.3$ or 0.1, $ps = 0.053$ and 0.35 respectively). Children's attention scores on the two games were also significantly correlated ($r = 0.62$, $p = 0.001$), suggesting that these measures tapped reliable individual differences in endogenously driven selective sustained attention.

The results of the paired sample t-tests, equivalence tests, significant correlations between *Monster Mischief* and *Track-It*, along with the face validity of *Monster Mischief* (due to the high degree of similarity across the two tasks) provide converging evidence for the validity of *Monster Mischief* as an assessment of endogenously driven selective sustained attention.

Comparison of Enjoyment and Motivation

Smile Scale: The *Smile Scale* was included in the present study to test Hypothesis 3 by quantifying how much children enjoyed each game. We hypothesized that that children should report liking *Monster Mischief* more than the existing selective sustained attention assessment and thus the *Smile Scale* scores should be higher for *Monster Mischief* than *Track-It*.

The *Smile Scale* was incorporated after data collection commenced. As a result, data for 18 of the 27 children were obtained. From this limited dataset, children tended to report that they liked both the *Track-It* task and the *Monster Mischief* game. For the *Track-It* task the average score on the *Smile Scale* was 4.50 (*SD* = 0.79). Similarly, on the *Monster Mischief* game, children's average score on the *Smile Scale* was 4.44 (*SD* = 0.86); paired sample $t(17) = 0.22$, $p = 0.83$ *ns*. Failure to observe any significant differences on the *Smile Scale* may be due to social desirability effects, namely children may have been hesitant to report that they did not like either one of the games. Additionally, children only completed 5 trials of each game. It is possible that differences may emerge if playtime were extended. For example, with more prolonged exposure the novelty of both tasks may wane. However, children's engagement in *Monster Mischief* may be maintained due to the incorporation of the motivational design elements. In contrast, engagement in *Track-It,* which lacks these game features, may decline. In general, children did not tend to utilize the entire *Smile Scale*, resulting in a truncated range of scores. For both games, the scores on the *Smile Scale* ranged from 3 (i.e., "*the game is just okay*") to 5 (i.e., "*I really liked the game*"). Enjoyment was not found to be related to children's performance on *Track-It* or *Monster Mischief*, as *Smile Scale* ratings were not significantly correlated with children's attention performance scores (both $rs < 0.28$, $ps > 0.26$ *ns*). This pattern of result may be due in part to the truncated range in children's *Smile Scale* scores as the limited variability in children's *Smile Scale* ratings makes it more difficult to detect an association between enjoyment and children's performance.

Game Choice: To further test Hypothesis 3, children's game choice patterns were analyzed to determine if children would choose to play *Monster Mischief* more than the existing selective sustained attention assessment. After playing both games children were asked to choose which game they wanted to play for the remainder of the testing session (*Track-It* or *Monster Mischief*).

The vast majority of children selected the *Monster Mischief* game as their free-choice game option. In fact 74% of children (20 out of 27) selected *Monster Mischief* while only 26% of children (7 out of 27) selected the *Track-It* task. Children selected *Monster Mischief* as their free-choice game more than would be expected by chance (0.50). The cumulative binomial probability that 20 or more of the 27 children would select *Monster Mischief* as their free-choice game was 0.0095. Additionally, children's game choice was not related to their attention performance on *Track-It* or *Monster Mischief* (both $rs < 0.115$, $ps > 0.567$ *ns*).

After children made their selection, they were asked to provide a rationale for their choice (e.g., "*Great, why did you choose the _____ game?*"). The child's response was recorded and the child then played one trial of the game they selected. Children's responses were analyzed. Many children had trouble providing a rationale for their game selection. For the 7 children who selected *Track-It* as their free-choice, 1 child gave no response, 1 child indicated that they did not know why they selected the game, and 3 children reported that they selected *Track-It* because they simply "*liked*" the game. The remaining 2 children reported that their game selection was based on aspects of the game (e.g., "*they* [the shapes] *move*"; "*because we didn't do all of the shapes*"). Of the 20 children who selected *Monster Mischief*, 13 children stated that they selected the game simply because they "*liked it*" or reported that the game was "*fun*". The remaining 7 children indicated that they selected *Monster Mischief* due to novelty or various game design elements (e.g., "*because they* [the monsters] *pop out at you*"; "*because I like castles*"; "*because it's so much fun – the monsters hide*"; "*because we only played 2 or 3 monsters and I want to play the purple one*").

Finally, we examined whether children's free-choice was influenced by the order in which the tasks were presented. Recall that the presentation order of *Track-It* and *Monster Mischief* was counter-balanced, such that some children played *Track-It* first and some children played *Monster Mischief* first. It is possible that children may exhibit a preference to switch from the game that they had just played; therefore, we examined whether children were more or less likely to exhibit this 'switch preference' when the last game they played was *Monster Mischief* vs. *Track-It*. When *Monster Mischief* was the second game children played, children were unlikely to exhibit a switch preference towards *Track-It:* only 36% (5 of 14) of the children chose to switch to *Track-It,* while 64% (9 of 14) of children went against switching and chose to play *Monster Mischief* again. In contrast, when *Track-It* was the second game children played, only 15% (2 of 13) of the children chose to play *Track-It* again, while the majority of children exhibited a preference to switch to *Monster Mischief* (85% or 11 of 13); see Figure 5. The association between switch preference and game type (*Track-It* or *Monster Mischief*) was statistically significant; Fisher's Exact test $p = 0.0183$. Overall, this analysis indicates that children were less likely to exhibit a preference to switch away from the game they just played when *Monster Mischief* was administered last, but more likely to show a switch preference when *Track-It* was administered last. This finding points to *Monster Mischief* as the more appealing choice over *Track-It*.

Learning Curve Analysis

A learning curve analysis was conducted to examine whether the task provides some context for learning. Learning curves are defined as changes in task performance over

Figure 5. Children's free-choice game selection as a function of the order in which the assessments were presented (i.e., Monster Mischief first followed by Track-It or Track-It first followed by Monster Mischief)

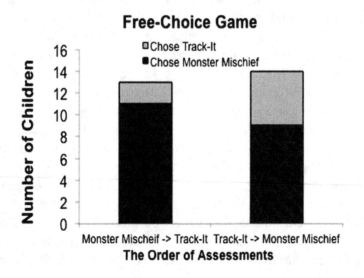

opportunities (Ritter & Schooler, 2001). In Figure 6, the average success rates for the memory check and locating the target are presented over the four experimental trials in both *Track-It* and *Monster Mischief*. For reasons discussed in the Method section, only four test trials of each game were administered. With only four trials, there is little data that might demonstrate a significant learning curve. Regular improvements in performance over each trial are observed in children's *Monster Mischief* performance; however, in a single factor regression model predicting student performance, the trial opportunity number was an insignificant predictor of success (*Track-It:* $p = 0.70$; *Monster Mischief:* $p = 0.33$). Future studies involving a greater number of trials will be necessary to identify significant learning curves, if any.

CONCLUSION

In conclusion, this study designed and evaluated *Monster Mischief*, a video game for the assessment of selective sustained attention. Motivational design elements were incorporated to create a video game that was engaging and motivating to young children. We then conducted an experimental study to test the validity of *Monster Mischief*. A valid game-based assessment of endogenously driven selective sustained

Figure 6. Learning Curve Analyses for the Track-It task (Panel A) and the Monster Mischief Game (Panel B). In both panels, the top line shows the success rate for identifying the correct location of the hidden target across each task opportunity (i.e., Attention score), while the bottom line shows the success rate for correctly remembering which target was being tracked (i.e., Memory Check). Error bars represent the standard errors of the mean

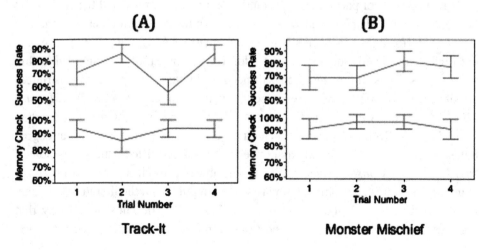

attention would show an equivalent level of performance to an existing assessment, would be significantly correlated with performance on the existing assessment, and be more enjoyable than the existing assessment. The findings from the present experiment largely align with the expected pattern of results. Specifically, the results of the present study suggest that we successfully created a video game that was of comparable difficulty level to the *Track-It* task. Additionally, performance on *Track-It* and *Monster Mischief* was significantly correlated. Children also exhibited a preference for *Monster Mischief* over *Track-It* when asked what game they would like to play again, presumably due to the addition of motivational design elements. However, there were no significant difference in enjoyment observed from the results of the *Smile Scale*.

Limitations

Overall, the *Monster Mischief* video game shows potential as an engaging assessment of children's selective sustained attention; however, it is important to note several limitations of the present study. First, we examined the relationship between children's performance in *Monster Mischief* and the heterogeneous condition of *Track-It*. Currently, it is unknown whether *Monster Mischief* can be adapted to measure exogenously driven selective sustained attention as well. Akin to *Track-It*, the ideal assessment would enable the measurement of both endogenous and exogenous factors within a single task or game to provide a more comprehensive analysis of the development and contribution of each type of selective sustained attention. Second, although we compared *Monster Mischief* to *Track-It*, it would also be beneficial to determine if children's performance on *Monster Mischief* is related to other measures of attention and if it is predictive of other cognitive abilities (e.g., inhibitory control).

A related issue of particular importance concerns the strength of the correlation between *Monster Mischief* and *Track-It*. Although the correlation between the two attention performance measures is respectable ($r = 0.623$), the two measures are not highly correlated, suggesting that additional information is contained within these scores. Thus, future research will need to distinguish among three different possibilities: (1) *Track-It* measures selective sustained attention better than *Monster Mischief*, (2) *Monster Mischief* measures selective sustained attention better than *Track-It*, or (3) Both tasks measure selective sustained attention to a similar degree but each task reflects variability associated with task-specific features (e.g., longer trial duration in *Monster Mischief*). No task is able to provide a pure measure of the construct of interest, a problem known as "task impurity" in the literature (Miyake, Friedman, Emerson, Witzki, Howerter, & Wager, 2000). Thus, it is likely that performance on *Monster Mischief* (and *Track-It*) reflects selective sustained attention as well as other cognitive abilities and task artifacts. Thus, future research examining the validity of these measures may help adjudicate between the possibilities listed above.

Third, extensions to this work are warranted as it is critical to assess children's performance and engagement in *Monster Mischief* over more extended periods of play and across time. With this groundwork in place, we can also begin to collect additional data on the psychometric utility of a broader range of difficulty factors in the game. Lastly, additional research is needed to fully validate *Monster Mischief* as a reliable measurement tool. For example, the reliability of the game should be assessed either through test-retest reliability (comparing the correlation of student performance over multiple testing sessions) or by introducing multiple items with variable difficulty and reporting on the reliability of the different items (i.e., Cronbach's Alpha). Difficulty can be manipulated in *Monster Mischief* and *Track It*, by varying several parameters including: speed, number of distractors, number of hiding locations, and the trial duration (i.e., the amount of time before the target hides/disappears).

Reflections on Games for the Assessment of Sustained Selective Attention

A common principle in instructional design (and assessment design) is to avoid extraneous cognitive load; that is, designs should avoid unnecessary flourishes (seductive details; Mayer, Griffith, Jurkowitz, & Rothman, 2008) that might distract from the intended task performance. Because game designs often contain a great deal of flourish, this can be a point of design conflict between game designers and other stakeholders (psychologists, instructional designers, etc). For instance, even a game element as basic as "competition" was found to have negative consequences for learning (Deleeuw & Mayer, 2011).

In the case of *Monster Mischief*, however, the design intent calls for extraneous cognitive load to be added to the intrinsic cognitive load of the core task (tracking an individual target). Extraneous cognitive load, in this case, was germane to the assessment of selective sustained attention. As distracting design elements were a desirable part of the game's design intent, we built in "extraneous" game elements as parameters of the overall task design in order to provide a richer spectrum of difficulty. By making distracting elements as optional and flexible parameters, future experiments can be designed to measure their impact on player performance. This implies that the assessment of certain cognitive skills, such as those associated with inhibiting distraction, may be particularly well-suited for game-based assessment.

Future Directions

During the development of *Monster Mischief*, we produced three additional game mechanics that could be employed in future research. These game mechanics were intended to increase the difficulty of the game in order to use the game with a wider age range of children and to explore whether *Monster Mischief* could be adapted to evaluate additional aspects of attention such as divided attention. The additional game mechanics include: coins, fireworks, and cloud mode. Each mechanic is discussed briefly below.

Coin Mechanic: When coins are turned on, a random number of coins (0-3) may appear in random locations, for a random period of time before disappearing (see Figure 7). If a player clicks on a coin, it flies up to the scoreboard and is added to their score. The rationale for this mechanic is to divide a player's attention between the primary task (tracking the monster that stole the jewel) and a secondary task (collecting coins). With the addition of the coins mechanic, the experience of gameplay appeared to be more difficult (easier to lose track of the target monster and erroneously select the wrong hiding location or target object). This mechanic is designed to provide a child-friendly means of assessing multi-tasking performance (Fischer, Morrin & Joslyn, 2003), which is currently measured through various assessments such as the Six Elements task (Siklos, & Kerns, 2004), the Gatekeeper task (Heathcote et al., 2014) and the Multiple Errands task (Logie, Trawley & Law, 2011).

Firework Mechanic: Young children often have trouble reorienting to a task and returning to a state of focused attention after attention has been disrupted (DiLalla & Watson, 1988). Thus, the firework mechanic was specifically designed to distract players and, therefore, provide a parameter that might permit an assessment of distractibility. When the firework mechanic is turned on, small red fireworks appear at random (location and time) and then pop with a shower of sparks (See Figure 8).

Cloud Mode: When cloud mode is turned on, there are no specific objects behind which the monsters hide – they simply disappear (See Figure 9). Then, players have to click on the area where the target monster disappeared without the aid of visual landmarks. In this mode, we can measure the visual-spatial accuracy of a player's response (where accuracy is defined as 100% minus the percent error, where percent error is calculated as the distance between x,y coordinates of the clicked location and the actual location, divided by the x,y dimensions of the screen). The rationale for this mechanic is to provide a more nuanced measure of success (degree of accuracy instead of correct/incorrect) and to increase difficulty by removing memorable landmarks.

Figure 7. Schematic of the coin mechanic in the Monster Mischief video game. During the trial, a random number (0-3) of coins appear and the player aims to collect the coins before the coins disappear while also continuing to track the target monster. The number of coins the player collects is tallied in the scoreboard at the top of the screen.

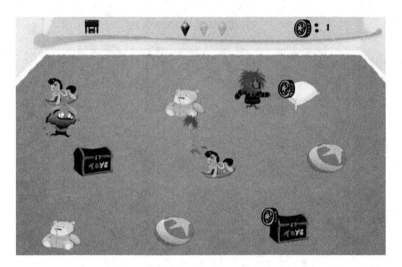

In addition to the above mechanics, there are several difficulty parameters that exist within both *Track-It* and *Monster Mischief*. These include the number and variety of distractors, the duration of average tracking time, and the speed of movement. Maximum difficulty would be expected to occur under the following conditions: maximum number of distractors all having the same character shape as the target monster, maximum movement speed and trial duration, employing cloud mode, incorporating the coin and firework mechanics (maximum number of coins/fireworks). Successful performance at this maximum difficulty level would correspond to the measurement ceiling of a player's ability. Procedurally generated variations in the task design space could be produced and randomly assigned to future players, potentially in an online setting. Regression analysis of task parameter variations could then be used to characterize the expected difficulty of different design configurations (Lomas, Patel, Forlizzi, & Koedinger, 2013), which may be useful for constructing multiple test forms with a broad range of difficulty.

Future work should also explore the game as an instructional tool that may help train children's selective sustained attention capacity and reduce their susceptibility to distractions. Presently, it is an open question whether a cognitive skills game for children could both assess selective sustained attention and also help improve it, akin to the cognitive skills training games that are currently popular for adults (e.g.,

Figure 8. Schematic of the firework mechanic in which a firework appears in a random location (Panel A) and after a period of time pops (Panel B) thereby testing participants' distractibility

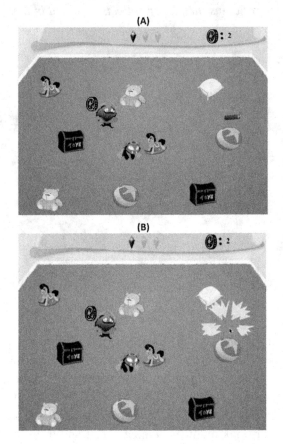

Lumosity, Posit Science and Akili). The makers of cognitive skills training games claim that improving performance on an assessment of a cognitive skill could broadly transfer to other activities (e.g., one could improve working memory by practicing a game which tests one's working memory). Although it is well documented that transfer of skills from one context to another is quite difficult (e.g., Perkins & Solomon, 1988). Thus, it is perhaps not surprising that such claims have come under scrutiny (FTC, 2016).

Research examining whether training can enhance children's executive functioning, a related cognitive skill set, point to reasons to be cautious. As noted previously, executive function skills are a set of high-level cognitive processes. Executive functioning plays a significant role in student performance, providing a better predictor of school readiness than IQ, and is related to various indicators of success

Figure 9. Schematic of cloud mode in which visual landmarks of the monsters' potential hiding locations have been removed. Instead, the monsters simply disappear after a period of time

in life (Diamond, 2013). Additionally, executive functioning may be hampered in certain vulnerable populations such as children living in poverty (Johnson, Riis, & Noble, 2016), which is a complex and urgent issue that affects 1 in 5 children in the United States (DeNavas-Walt and Proctor, 2015). Based on findings such as these, researchers are interested in studying the feasibility of improving children's executive functions which may help mitigate the negative effects of poverty and reduce the achievement gap. In relation to working memory, researchers have found minimal support that cognitive training is effective; training benefits seem limited to near transfer (i.e., other working memory tasks) as opposed to far transfer--no apparent training benefits for academic outcomes (For review see Redick, Shipstead, Wiemers, Melby-Lervag, & Hulme, 2015). Interestingly, inhibitory control may be *less* amenable to training than working memory (for review see Diamond, 2012). For example, Thorell, Lindqvist Bergman Nutley, Bohlin, and Klingberg (2009) found that preschool children exhibited initial training benefits *only* for specific inhibitory control tasks, no evidence of narrow transfer, and no evidence of transfer to other executive function tasks.

According to Diamond (2012) guiding principles for training executive function include recommendations to incorporate opportunities for repeated practice as well as leveled difficulty progressions in order to see continued improvement. These recommendations may also be germane for skills training targeting attention and can be readily incorporated in cognitive skills games. Consequently, cognitive skills training games such as *Monster Mischief* may be well suited to seamlessly incorporate these recommendations into the game design. Thus, future work will need to determine whether a cognitive skills training game like *Monster Mischief* could yield improvements in attention that transfer to real world educational contexts. Nevertheless, the potential gains that could be achieved from such an intervention warrant further empirical work. Ultimately, a video game like *Monster Mischief* might be used to test the hypothesis that cognitive skills practice can increase the attention span of young children and decrease their susceptibility to distractions. Accordingly, it is of interest to explore whether interventions could be created to help support the development of selective sustained attention in young children.

ACKNOWLEDGMENT

We would like to thank Tara Helfer and Jeremy Galante for their help with illustrations and animation. We also thank Sharan Shodhan for game programming. We thank the children, parents, teachers, and staff at the Children's School and Baldwin United Methodist Church Preschool who made this work possible. This work was supported in part by a Graduate Training Grant by the Department of Education (R305B090023).

REFERENCES

Aalbers, T., Baars, M. A. E., Rikkert, M. G. M. O., & Kessels, R. P. C. (2013). Puzzling with online games (BAM-COG): Reliability, validity, and feasibility of an online self-monitor for cognitive performance in aging adults. *Journal of Medical Internet Research*, *15*(12), e270. doi:10.2196/jmir.2860 PMID:24300212

Attali, Y., & Arieli-Attali, M. (2015). Gamification in assessment: Do points affect test performance? *Computers & Education*, *83*, 57–63. doi:10.1016/j.compedu.2014.12.012

Bloom, B. S. (1976). *Human Characteristics and School Learning*. New York: McGraw-Hill.

Bornstein, M. H. (1990). Attention in infancy and the prediction of cognitive capacities in childhood. In J. Enns (Ed.), *Development of Attention: Research and Theory*. Elsevier. doi:10.1016/S0166-4115(08)60448-3

Carroll, J. B. (1963). A model of School Learning. *Teachers College Record, 64,* 723–733.

Choudhury, N., & Gorman, K. (2000). The relationship between attention and problem solving in 17–24 month old children. *Infant and Child Development, 9,* 127–146. doi:10.1002/1522-7219(200009)9:3<127::AID-ICD225>3.0.CO;2-5

Clark, D., Tanner-Smith, E., Killingsworth, S., & Bellamy, S. (2013). *Digital Games for Learning: A Systematic Review and Meta-Analysis (Executive Summary).* Menlo Park, CA: SRI International.

Colombo, J., & Cheatham, C. L. (2006). The emergence and basis of endogenous attention in infancy and early childhood. In R. Kail (Ed.), *Advances in Child Development and Behavior* (Vol. 34, pp. 283–310). Oxford, UK: Academic Press. doi:10.1016/S0065-2407(06)80010-8

Deleeuw, K. E., & Mayer, R. E. (2011). Cognitive consequences of making computer-based learning activities more game-like. *Computers in Human Behavior, 27*(5), 2011–2016. doi:10.1016/j.chb.2011.05.008

DeMarie-Dreblow, D., & Miler, P. H. (1988). The development of children's strategies for selective attention: Evidence for a transitional period. *Child Development, 59*(6), 1504–1513. doi:10.2307/1130665 PMID:3208562

DeNavas-Walt, C., & Proctor, B. D. (2015). Income and poverty in the United States: 2014. *US Census Bureau, Current Population Reports.* Retrieved from: https://www.census.gov/content/dam/Census/library/publications/2015/demo/p60-252.pdf

Deterding, S., Dixon, D., Khaled, R., & Nacke, L. (2011, September). From game design elements to gamefulness: defining gamification. In *Proceedings of the 15th international academic MindTrek conference: Envisioning future media environments* (pp. 9-15). ACM. 10.1145/2181037.2181040

Diamond, A. (2002). Normal development of prefrontal cortex from birth to young adulthood: Cognitive functions, anatomy, and biochemistry. In D. T. Stuss & R. T. Knight (Eds.), *Principles of frontal lobe function* (pp. 466–503). London, UK: Oxford University Press. doi:10.1093/acprof:oso/9780195134971.003.0029

Diamond, A. (2006). The early development of executive functions. In E. Bialystok & F. Craik (Eds.), Lifespan Cognition: Mechanisms of Change (pp. 7-95). Oxford University Press. doi:10.1093/acprof:oso/9780195169539.003.0006

Diamond, A. (2012). Activities and programs that improve children's executive functions. *Current Directions in Psychological Science, 21*(5), 335–341. doi:10.1177/0963721412453722 PMID:25328287

Diamond, A. (2013). Executive functions. *Annual Review of Psychology, 64*(1), 135–168. doi:10.1146/annurev-psych-113011-143750 PMID:23020641

DiLalla, L. F., & Watson, M. W. (1988). Differentiation of fantasy and reality: Preschoolers' reactions to interruptions in their play. *Developmental Psychology, 24*(2), 286–291. doi:10.1037/0012-1649.24.2.286

Duncan, G. J., Dowsett, C. J., Claessens, A., Magnuson, K., Huston, A. C., Klebanov, P., ... Japel, C. (2007). School readiness and later achievement. *Developmental Psychology, 43*(6), 1428–1446. doi:10.1037/0012-1649.43.6.1428 PMID:18020822

Eccles, J. S., & Wigfield, A. (2002). Motivational beliefs, values, and goals. *Annual Review of Psychology, 53*(1), 109–132. doi:10.1146/annurev.psych.53.100901.135153 PMID:11752481

Erickson, L. C., Thiessen, E. D., Godwin, K. E., Dickerson, J. P., & Fisher, A. V. (2014). Endogenously- but not Exogenously-driven Selective Sustained Attention is Related to Learning in a Classroom-like Setting in Kindergarten Children. In P. Bello, M. Guarini, M. McShane, & B. Scassellati (Eds.), *Proceedings of the 36th Annual Conference of the Cognitive Science Society* (pp. 457-462). Austin, TX: Cognitive Science Society.

Fischer, S. C., Morrin, K. A., & Joslyn, S. (2003). *Measuring Multi-tasking Ability.* Report prepared for the Office of Naval research by Anacapa Sciences, Inc.

Fisher, A. V., Godwin, K. E., & Seltman, H. (2014). Visual environment, attention allocation, and learning: When too much of a good thing may be bad. *Psychological Science, 25*(7), 1362–1370. doi:10.1177/0956797614533801 PMID:24855019

Fisher, A. V., & Kloos, H. (2016). Development of selective sustained attention: The Role of executive functions. In L. Freund, P. McCardle, & J. Griffin (Eds.), *Executive function in preschool age children: Integrating measurement, neurodevelopment and translational research.* APA Press. doi:10.1037/14797-010

Fisher, A. V., Thiessen, E., Godwin, K., Kloos, H., & Dickerson, J. P. (2013). Mechanisms of focused attention in 3- to 5-year-old children: Evidence from a new object tracking task. *Journal of Experimental Child Psychology, 114*(2), 275–294. doi:10.1016/j.jecp.2012.07.006 PMID:23022318

FTC. (2016, January 5). *Lumosity to pay $2 million to settle FTC deceptive advertising charges for its "Brain Training" program* [Press release]. Retrieved from https://www.ftc.gov/news-events/press-releases/2016/01/lumosity-pay-2-million-settle-ftc-deceptive-advertising-charges

Geary, K. E. (2011). *The impact of choice on child sustained attention in the preschool classroom* (Unpublished Thesis). Louisiana State University, Baton Rouge, LA.

Gitelman, D. R. (2003). Attention and its disorders: Imaging in clinical neuroscience. *British Medical Bulletin*, *65*(1), 21–34. doi:10.1093/bmb/65.1.21 PMID:12697614

Glasslab. (2014). *Pyschometric Considerations in Game-Based Assessments*. White Paper Released by Glasslab, 160.

Godwin, K. E., Almeda, M. V., Seltman, H., Kai, S., Skerbetz, M. D., Baker, R. S., & Fisher, A. V. (2016). Off-task behavior in elementary school children. *Learning and Instruction*, *44*, 128–143. doi:10.1016/j.learninstruc.2016.04.003

Godwin, K. E., & Fisher, A. V. (in press). Wiggleometer: Measuring selective sustained attention in children. *Proceedings of the 40th Annual Meeting of the Cognitive Science Society*.

Godwin, K. E., Lomas, D., Koedinger, K. R., Fisher, A. V., (2015). Monster Mischief: Designing a video game to assess selective sustained attention. *International Journal of Gaming and Computer-Mediated Simulations: Assessing human Capabilities in Video Games and Stimulations*, *7*(4), 18-39.

Goodman, L. (1990). *Time and learning in the special education classroom*. SUNY Press.

Heathcote, A., Eidels, A., Colman, J., Watson, J., & Strayer, D. (2014). Multi-tasking in working memory. *Proceedings of the Annual Meeting of the Cognitive Science Society*, 601–606.

Holmgård, C., Togelius, J., & Henriksen, L. (2016). *Computational Intelligence and Cognitive Performance Assessment Games. Computational Intelligence and Games*. CIG.

Hunicke, R., LeBlanc, M., & Zubek, R. (2004). MDA: A formal approach to game design and game research. In *Proceedings of the Workshop on Challenges in Game AI, 19th National Conference on Artificial Intelligence*. AAAI Press.

Johnson, S. B., Riis, J. L., & Noble, K. G. (2016). State of the art review: Poverty and the developing brain. *Pediatrics*, *137*(4), 1–16. doi:10.1542/peds.2015-3075 PMID:26952506

Jonides, J. (1981). Voluntary vs. Automatic control over the mind's eye's movement. In J. B. Long & A. D. Baddeley (Eds.), *Attention and Performance IX*. Hillsdale, NJ: Lawrence Erlbaum Associates.

Kim, J., Vande Velde, A., Thiessen, E., & Fisher, A. V. (2017). Variables Involved in Selective Sustained Attention Development: Advances in Measurement. *Proceedings of the 39th Annual Meeting of the Cognitive Science Society*, 670-675.

Loewenstein, G. (1994). The Psychology of curiosity: A review and reinterpretation. *Psychological Bulletin*, *116*(1), 75–98. doi:10.1037/0033-2909.116.1.75

Logie, R. H., Trawley, S., & Law, A. (2011). Multitasking: Multiple, domain-specific cognitive functions in a virtual environment. *Memory & Cognition*, *39*(8), 1561–1574. doi:10.375813421-011-0120-1 PMID:21691876

Lomas, D., Patel, K., Forlizzi, J. L., & Koedinger, K. R. (2013). Optimizing challenge in an educational game using large-scale design experiments. In *Proceedings of the SIGCHI Conference on Human Factors in Computing Systems* (pp. 89-98). ACM. 10.1145/2470654.2470668

Lumsden, J., Edwards, E. A., Lawrence, N. S., Coyle, D., & Munafò, M. R. (2016). Gamification of Cognitive Assessment and Cognitive Training: A Systematic Review of Applications and Efficacy. *JMIR Serious Games*, *4*(2), e11. doi:10.2196/games.5888 PMID:27421244

Luna, B. (2009). Developmental changes in cognitive control through adolescence. *Advances in Child Development and Behavior*, *37*, 233–278. doi:10.1016/S0065-2407(09)03706-9 PMID:19673164

Malone, T. (1981). Toward a theory of intrinsically motivating instruction. *Cognitive Science*, *5*(4), 333–369. doi:10.120715516709cog0504_2

Mayer, R. E., Griffith, E., Jurkowitz, I. T. N., & Rothman, D. (2008). Increased Interestingness of Extraneous Details in a Multimedia Science Presentation Leads to Decreased Learning. *Journal of Experimental Psychology. Applied*, *14*(4), 329–339. doi:10.1037/a0013835 PMID:19102616

McPherson, J., & Burns, N. R. (2008). Assessing the validity of computer-game-like tests of processing speed and working memory. *Behavior Research Methods*, *40*(4), 969–981. doi:10.3758/BRM.40.4.969 PMID:19001388

Méndez, A., Martín, A., Pires, A. C., Vásquez, A., Maiche, A., González, F., & Carboni, A. (2015). Temporal perception and delay aversion: A videogame screening tool for the early detection of ADHD. *Revista Argentina de Ciencias del Comportamiento, 7*(3).

Miller, E. K., & Cohen, J. D. (2001). An integrative theory of prefrontal cortex function. *Annual Review of Neuroscience, 24*(1), 167–202. doi:10.1146/annurev. neuro.24.1.167 PMID:11283309

Mislevy, R. J., Corrigan, S., Oranje, A., DiCerbo, K., Bauer, M. I., von Davier, A., & John, M. (2016). Psychometrics and game-based assessment. *Technology and Testing: Improving Educational and Psychological Measurement*, 23-48.

Miyake, A., Friedman, N. P., Emerson, M. J., Witzki, A. H., Howerter, A., & Wager, T. D. (2000). The unit and diversity of executive functions and their contributions to complex "frontal lobe" tasks: A latent variable analysis. *Cognitive Psychology, 41*(1), 49–100. doi:10.1006/cogp.1999.0734 PMID:10945922

Oakes, L., Kannass, K. N., & Shaddy, D. J. (2002). Developmental changes in endogenous control of attention: The role of target familiarity on infants' distraction latency. *Child Development, 73*(6), 1644–1655. doi:10.1111/1467-8624.00496 PMID:12487484

Parker, L., & Lepper, M. (1992). Effects of fantasy contexts on children's learning and motivation: Making learning more fun. *Journal of Personality and Social Psychology, 62*(4), 625–633. doi:10.1037/0022-3514.62.4.625 PMID:1583588

Pashler, H., Johnston, J. C., & Ruthruff, E. (2001). Attention and performance. *Annual Review of Psychology, 52*(1), 629–651. doi:10.1146/annurev.psych.52.1.629 PMID:11148320

Perkins, D. N., & Salomon, G. (1988). Teaching for transfer. *Educational Leadership, 46*(1), 22–32.

Posner, M. I. (1980). Orienting of attention. *The Quarterly Journal of Experimental Psychology, 32*(1), 3–25. doi:10.1080/00335558008248231 PMID:7367577

Posner, M. I., & Petersen, S. E. (1990). The attention system of the human brain. *Annual Review of Neuroscience, 13*(1), 25–42. doi:10.1146/annurev.ne.13.030190.000325 PMID:2183676

Posner, M. I., & Rothbart, K. R. (2007). Research on attention networks as a model for the integration of psychological science. *Annual Review of Psychology, 58*(1), 1–23. doi:10.1146/annurev.psych.58.110405.085516 PMID:17029565

Prins, P. J., Dovis, S., Ponsioen, A., ten Brink, E., & van der Oord, S. (2011). Does computerized working memory training with game elements enhance motivation and training efficacy in children with ADHD? *Cyberpsychology, Behavior, and Social Networking, 14*(3), 115–122. doi:10.1089/cyber.2009.0206 PMID:20649448

Pylyshyn, Z. W., & Storm, R. W. (1988). Tracking multiple independent targets: Evidence for a parallel tracking mechanism. *Spatial Vision, 3*(3), 179–197. doi:10.1163/156856888X00122 PMID:3153671

Read, J. C., & MacFarlane, S. (2006) Using the fun toolkit and other survey methods to gather opinions in child computer interaction. *Proceeding of the 2006 conference on Interaction design and children - IDC '06*, 81. 10.1145/1139073.1139096

Redick, T. S., Shipstead, Z., Wiemers, E. A., Melby-Lervag, M., & Hulme, C. (2015). What's working in working memory training? An educational perspective. *Educational Psychology Review, 27*(4), 617–633. doi:10.100710648-015-9314-6 PMID:26640352

Richards, J. E. (2003). The development of visual attention and the brain. In The cognitive neuroscience of development. East Sussex, UK: Psychology Press.

Ritter, F., & Schooler, L. (2001) The learning curve. International Encyclopedia of the Social and Behavioral Sciences, 8602–8605.

Rosetti, M. F., Gómez-Tello, M. F., Victoria, G., & Apiquian, R. (2017). A video game for the neuropsychological screening of children. *Entertainment Computing, 20*, 1–9. doi:10.1016/j.entcom.2017.02.002

Rosvold, H. E., Mirsky, A. F., Sarason, I., Bransome, E. D., & Beck, L. H. (1956). A Continuous performance test of brain damage. *Journal of Consulting Psychology, 20*(5), 343–350. doi:10.1037/h0043220 PMID:13367264

Ruff, A. H., & Lawson, K. R. (1990). Development of sustained, focused attention in young children during free play. *Developmental Psychology, 26*(1), 85–93. doi:10.1037/0012-1649.26.1.85

Ruff, H., & Capozzoli, M. (2003). Development of attention and distractibility in the first 4 years of life. *Developmental Psychology, 39*(5), 877–890. doi:10.1037/0012-1649.39.5.877 PMID:12952400

Ruff, H. A., & Rothbart, M. K. (1996). *Attention in early development: Themes and variations*. New York, NY: Oxford University Press.

Ryan, R. M., Rigby, C. S., & Przybylski, A. (2006). The motivational pull of video games: A self-determination theory approach. *Motivation and Emotion, 30*(4), 347–365. doi:10.100711031-006-9051-8

Sarid, M., & Breznitz, Z. (1997). Developmental aspects of sustained attention among 2- to 6-year-old children. *International Journal of Behavioral Development, 21*(2), 303–312. doi:10.1080/016502597384884

Schneider, W., & Shiffrin, R. M. (1977). Controlled and automatic human information processing: I. Detection, search, and attention. *Psychological Review, 84*(1), 1–66. doi:10.1037/0033-295X.84.1.1

Setliff, A. E., & Courage, M. L. (2011). Background television and infants allocation of their attention during toy play. *Infancy, 16*(6), 611–639. doi:10.1111/j.1532-7078.2011.00070.x

Shute, V. J. (2011). Stealth Assessment in Computer-Based Games To Support Learning. *Computer Games and Instruction*, 503–524.

Siklos, S., & Kerns, K. A. (2004). Assessing multitasking in children with ADHD using a modified Six Elements Test. *Archives of Clinical Neuropsychology, 19*(3), 347–361. doi:10.1016/S0887-6177(03)00071-4 PMID:15033221

Tellinghuisen, D. J., Oakes, L. M., & Tjebkes, T. L. (1999). The influence of attentional state and stimulus characteristics on infant distractibility. *Cognitive Development, 14*(2), 199–213. doi:10.1016/S0885-2014(99)00002-7

Tenorio Delgado, M., Arango Uribe, P., Aparicio Alonso, A., & Rosas Díaz, R. (2014). TENI: A comprehensive battery for cognitive assessment based on games and technology. *Child Neuropsychology*, 1–16. PMID:25396766

Weber, R., & Popova, L. (2012). Testing equivalence in communication research: Theory and application. *Communication Methods and Measures, 6*(3), 190–213. doi:10.1080/19312458.2012.703834

Yantis, S. (1992). Multielement visual tracking: Attention and perceptual organization. *Cognitive Psychology, 24*(3), 295–340. doi:10.1016/0010-0285(92)90010-Y PMID:1516359

Yu, C., & Smith, L. B. (2012). Embodied attention and word learning by toddlers. *Cognition, 125*(2), 244–262. doi:10.1016/j.cognition.2012.06.016 PMID:22878116

APPENDIX

Introduction of the Smile Scale

During this game I will ask you a couple questions using a special scale. Here is how it works. See all the faces [point to the faces on the scale]? See how some of the faces are frowning and some are smiling? Look at this face [point to face 1]. This face is making a **big** frown - that means I really **don't** like something. This face has a **little** frown [point to face 2] – that means I **dislike** something a **little bit**. Look at this face [point to face 5]. This face has a **big** smile - that means I **really like** something. This face has a **little** smile [point to face 4] – that means I like something a **little bit**. Look at this face [point to face 3], this face is **not** smiling **or** frowning so that means I think something is **just okay**.

Practice Items

1. *"Which face should I point to if I told you that I **really don't like** brussels sprouts?"*

[Wait for child's response]
    "Yes, I would point to the face making a big frown *[point to face 1]* because I really don't like brussels sprouts." *[Or:* "That's a good guess, but I would point to the face making a big frown *[point to face 1]* because I really don't like brussels sprouts."*]*

2. "Okay, try this one - which face should I point to if I told you that I **really like** to jump rope?"

Figure 10.

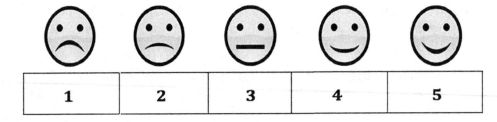

[Wait for child's response]

"Yes, I would point to the face making a big smile *[point to face 5]* because I really like to jump rope." *[Or:* "That's a good guess, but I would point to the face making a big smile *[point to face 5]* because I really like to jump rope."*]*

3. "Okay let's do one more. Which face should I point to if I told you I think the color green is **just okay**?"

[Wait for child's response]

"Yes, I would point to this face that is not smiling or frowning *[point to face 3]* because that means I think something is just okay." *[Or:* "That's a good guess, but I would point to this face that is not smiling or frowning *[point to face 3]* because that means I think something is just okay."*]*

"All right we will use this again in a little bit but now we are going to play some computer games"

Rating each game using the Smile Scale:

Okay, now I want you to point to the face that shows me what you thought about this game: Remember this face means you **really don't like** this game [point to 1], this face means you **disliked** this game **a little** [point to 2], this face means you thought the game was **just okay** [point to 3], this face means you **liked** the game **a little** [point to 4], and this face means you **really like the game** [point to 5]. Okay what did you think about the game - *whatever you think is fine.*

Chapter 7

A Digital Game for Undergraduate Calculus:
Immersion, Calculation, and Conceptual Understanding

Yu-Hao Lee
University of Florida, USA

Norah E. Dunbar
University of California – Santa Barbara, USA

Keri Kornelson
University of Oklahoma, USA

Scott N. Wilson
University of Oklahoma, USA

Ryan Ralston
University of Oklahoma, USA

Milos Savic
University of Oklahoma, USA

Sepideh Stewart
University of Oklahoma, USA

Emily Ann Lennox
University of Oklahoma, USA

William Thompson
University of Oklahoma, USA

Javier Elizondo
University of Oklahoma, USA

ABSTRACT

This study has two goals: first, to investigate the effectiveness of using a digital game to teach undergraduate-level calculus in improving task immersion, sense of control, calculation skills, and conceptual understanding, and second, to investigate how feedback and visual manipulation can facilitate conceptual understanding of calculus materials. One hundred thirty-two undergraduate students participated in a controlled lab experiment and were randomly assigned to either a game-playing condition, a practice quiz condition, or a no-treatment control condition.

DOI: 10.4018/978-1-5225-7461-3.ch007

The authors collected survey data and behavioral-tracking data recorded by the server during gameplay. The results showed that students who played the digital game reported highest task immersion but not in sense of control. Students in the game condition also performed significantly better in conceptual understanding compared to students who solved a practice quiz and the control group. Gameplay behavioral-tracking data was used to examine the effects of visual manipulation and feedback on conceptual understanding.

INTRODUCTION

Calculus is the foundation for higher-level mathematics in disciplines such as physics, engineering, and economics. Calculus is not only important for understanding more advanced courses in school, it is also a significant predictor of one's earnings at work beyond school (Rose & Betts, 2004). However, several studies have reported a disconnect between the calculus that students learned in classrooms and students' ability to apply calculus concepts to other disciplines and to utilize calculus outside of schools (Lesh & Zawojewski, 2007). Students often fail to transfer their calculus knowledge because they lack hands-on experiences of applying their understanding to solving authentic problems; in fact, around 70% of problems in one calculus textbook are solved by mimicking the examples shown in the textbook (Lithner, 2004). This might cause students to be less motivated to learn because they do not understand the value of calculus in real-world applications. Studies have shown that students who experienced problem-solving scenarios in pre-calculus classes have better conceptual understanding of calculus applications, can identify and use appropriate resources, and are more motivated to take an active role in learning calculus (Stanley, 2002). Learning across multiple contexts (e.g., different media or different problem context) can also promote transfer because students can compare their experiences to abstract general concepts and construct a flexible understanding that can be applied to different contexts (Bransford, Brown, & Cocking, 1999).

Digital games have been proposed as an effective way to promote students' conceptual understanding of abstract knowledge and problem-solving transfer (Boyle, Connolly, & Hainey, 2011; Garris, Ahlers, & Driskell, 2002; Gee, 2007). Modern digital games can facilitate meaningful problem-solving experiences for students, allowing them to visualize abstract concepts and situate the concepts in different contexts to gain a better understanding (Squire, 2003). They can provide immediate, or just-in-time feedback for students to assess and adjust their process (C.-Y. Lee & Chen, 2009). Games encourage players to form initial hypotheses, test them, observe the outcome, and revise their hypotheses. This process is similar to the process of experiential learning (Kolb & Kolb, 2005). In other words, digital game can simulate authentic problems for students to apply their calculus knowledge. They also allow students to visualize and actively manipulating factors to construct a flexible mental model which improves transfer across contexts.

While many studies have examined the use of digital games to enhance mathematics education, most of them focus on primary to secondary school mathematics or drill-and-practice for mathematical calculations (e.g., Ke, 2008a, 2008b; Mayo, 2009). Few studies have investigated using digital games to facilitate undergraduate-level mathematics, especially calculus, which is a complex foundational concept that affects student performance in more advanced courses. A major challenge of designing a calculus game is balancing the complex concepts and skills while keeping students immersed in the game. In this study we developed a game to teach undergraduate-level calculus called *Mission Prime* which is based on mathematical education principles.

The primary goal of this study is to compare the effects of a digital game to teach university-level calculus to a traditional method of solving practice questions and a no-treatment control group. A secondary goal is to investigate (if any) what affordances of the game promote students' conceptual understanding. We used behavioral-tracking data of player actions during gameplay to investigate whether the affordances of digital games to provide feedback and visual manipulation improved students' conceptual understanding of calculus. The study design is a controlled lab experiment with random assignment that employs both pre- and post-test questionnaires paired with server-based player behavioral data to examine the following general research questions:

1. Is playing a calculus video game more effective in promoting conceptual understanding than traditional practice questions or no-treatment?
2. Is playing a calculus video game more effective in promoting calculation skills than traditional practice questions or no-treatment?
3. Is the experience of playing a calculus game more immersive than traditional practice questions or no-treatment?
4. Do the number of feedback provided by the video game and the ability to manipulate visual representations improve students' conceptual understanding of the content mathematics?

THEORETICAL BACKGROUND

Promoting calculus transfer

Traditional mathematics courses are designed to guide students through a sequence of modules that makes up complex mathematical concepts. Students are introduced to one small module at a time and are expected to be able to piece together the modules and understand how the modules fit together to form a bigger picture. However, student may fail to realize the bigger picture and are left with isolated, incomplete understanding of the concepts (Tall, 1991). Even students who do well in mathematics classes may understand equations as symbol manipulation and fail to realize its relation to real-life problems and applications (Siegler, 2009). This may be a reason that can explain why many STEM educators feel that students are under-prepared in their calculus training and fail to understand its application in other disciplines (Lesh & Zawojewski, 2007).

The major goal in the calculus education reform since the 80s is to shift from the traditional focus on memorization and calculation techniques to promote conceptual understanding and focus on calculus applications. Many mathematics educators argue that in order to reach this goal, mathematics course should be designed the opposite way around (Kaput, 1994; Tall, 1991), meaning that students are first exposed to authentic application problems so that they can develop a need for learning the concepts. Then the complex systems are broken down into smaller modules facilitated by visual aids for students to manipulate and observe (Disessa & Sherin, 2000; Kaput, 1994). This type of design situates the mathematics concepts within authentic problems, allowing students to take on a more active role in knowledge construction (Oehrtman, 2009). This may facilitate a better appreciation of concepts and promote transfer between contexts.

Several studies have tested the effects of teaching mathematics through authentic problems and visual manipulations. For example, Stanley (2002) provided students with real-life problems such as designing drug dosage or developing a saving plan. She then asked them to work in groups to solve these problems using calculus. The study found that although the students did not perform better in quizzes than students who were not exposed to real-life problems, but the students who solved real-life problems were more motivated, were better at identifying appropriate resources, and had a better understanding of calculus applications. Another study by Kidron and Zehavi (2002)found that using software to display dynamic graphics helped students visualize the mathematical processes and gave meaning to the abstract concepts.

Using Digital Games to Promote Calculus Education

Digital games have been proposed as effective means for teaching mathematics because of several unique affordances. Digital games can (a) provide meaningful problems in situated contexts for players to solve (Gee, 2007; Steinkuehler & Duncan, 2008), (b) allow players to visualize complex systems and manipulate dynamic factors (Shaffer, 2006), (c) present multiple representations to demonstrate the underlying concepts (Betz, 1995), (d) give immediate performance or formative feedback for players to track the progress or adjust their hypotheses (Delacruz, 2012), and (e) promote sense of immersion and motivations (Squire et al., 2003).

Educators have been experimenting with using digital games for education for quite some time. "Edutainment," or the combination of education with entertainment was a concept that was thought as the future of education in the 80s. However, poor design that merely masks practice-and-drill with animations has earned edutainment a sour reputation for being neither effective education nor entertaining (Van Eck, 2006). As digital games progressed from simple games to games that can simulate complex systems and engage players in dynamic relations, so has research on the affordances of digital games and how to utilize them for education (Charsky, 2010). A recent study found that when used appropriately, even a practice-and-drill game can be designed to motivate students to learn mathematics (Ke, 2008a).

Many studies have empirically examined the use of digital games to enhance mathematics education, but most of those studies focused on primary or secondary school education with mixed results. Meta-analyses and systematic reviews of games for education generally attribute the mixed results to small sample sizes and the lack of control groups in many studies (Connolly, Boyle, MacArthur, Hainey, & Boyle, 2012). Cordova and Lepper (1996) found that students who learned through a game in mathematics classes outperformed students in classes that did not incorporate games. They also found that the sense of control, challenge, curiosity and the ability to situate knowledge into context increased students' intrinsic motivation. Another study compared classrooms that used a game to teach ninth-grade algebra and those that did not, the findings showed that students who used the games outscored students that did not participate in the ETS algebra assessments (Morgan & Ritter, 2002). Spotnitz (2001) examined the effect of a mathematics game on forth to sixth-grade students' intrinsic motivation, self-efficacy, task involvement, and performance. After four weeks of 30-minute sessions, students answered a questionnaire along with a mathematics quiz. The study found that students who learned through the game reported higher intrinsic motivation, self-efficacy, and task involvement. Although there was significant improvement between the pre and post-test, students who played the game did not perform significantly better than students who received a traditional education. Similarly, Ke (2008a) also found that student was more motivated and engaged when using digital games, yet they did not perform significantly better when assessed with traditional paper-and-pencil tests. We hypothesize that students in the game condition would report higher immersion and sense of control, but we believe the effects on improving calculation skills can go either way, and thus pose it as a research question.

H1. Participants in the game condition report higher immersion than (a) the practice quiz condition and (b) the no-treatment control condition.

H2. Participants in the game condition report higher perceived control than (a) the practice quiz condition and (b) the no-treatment control condition.

RQ1. Will participants in the game condition perform better in calculation skills than (a) the practice quiz condition and (b) the no-treatment control condition?

While the evidence on digital games' ability to improve mathematics calculation skills are mixed, studies have shown that it may be effective in promoting higher-order metacognition and deep conceptual understanding. For example, Liang and Zhou (2009) conducted a qualitative assessment of students' experience with a mathematics game and their academic performance. They found that students who used the game reported more positive attitudes towards mathematics. The students also felt that the feedback provided by the games helped them develop a sense of responsibility for their own learning and correct their mistakes without fear of embarrassment. More importantly, the students felt that they have a better understanding of how mathematics is connected to their everyday life when learning through the games. Another study by Lopez-Morteo and López (2007) used a game-like computer supported system to engage students in mathematics. They found that students who used the game-like system gained a positive attitude towards mathematics, which is a significant predictor of mathematics performance. Students in the experiment also appreciated the system for presenting theorems and problems from multiple perspectives, allowing them to understand that "mathematics are more than counting numbers" (p.636). Because problem-solving experiences and multiple representations were argued to promote deep conceptual understanding of mathematics (Kaput, 1994; Tall, 1991), we hypothesize that students who played the calculus game would have better conceptual understanding than students who received a traditional practice quiz or received no treatment.

H3. Participants in the game condition perform better in conceptual understanding than (a) the practice quiz condition and (b) the no-treatment control condition.

In addition to comparing the effectiveness of a calculus game to traditional methods of education, we are also interested in examining which features of the game would facilitate students' conceptual understanding. As suggested by Anderson, Greeno, Reder, and Simon (2000), to promote effective learning, it is crucial to examine the students' learning activities and cognitive procedures to gain a deeper understanding of how students are learning from our educational design. We use in-game behavioral tracking data to observe student activities in the game and test the hypotheses that games promote conceptual understanding through providing feedback and allowing students to manipulate visual representations.

211

H4. Visual manipulation positively predicts conceptual understanding among participants in the game condition.

H5. Number of feedback positively predicts conceptual understanding among participants in the game condition.

METHOD

Experiment Design

A between-subject experiment design was used to test the hypotheses and research questions. 132 students were recruited from Calculus II classes at a large Midwestern university using extra credits as incentives. When participants arrived at the lab, after giving informed consent, they were administered a short online survey measuring their attitude towards mathematics, the number of calculus classes that they have taken, and basic demographics including age, gender, and department majors. Next, the participants were randomly assigned to one of the three conditions (game, practice quiz, control). Of the three conditions, the digital game group was asked to play a calculus game until they finished all the scenarios or until one hour had elapsed; the practice quiz group received a calculus practice quiz for them to solve in one hour; the third group control group did not receive any treatment before the measurements and played the game after they completed all the questionnaires. An hour was used because the game was designed to be used as support material in an undergraduate Calculus classroom. Therefore it had to fit within a class period. After the stimulus, the participants' calculation skills and conceptual understanding were measured using a paper-and-pencil calculus test designed by members of the research team from the Mathematics department. The participants' perceived immersion and sense of control were measured with a subset of the cognitive absorption scale developed by Agarwal and Karahanna (2000). While the game group played the game, we tracked their behaviors in the game including the frequency of different actions, the number of feedback they received, the duration of time on each action and scenario, whether they used the visual manipulation function, and how long they spent manipulating the visual representations.

After removing seven participants who did not complete the study, a total of 125 participants were included in the analyses with 50 in the game condition, 38 in the practice quiz condition, and 37 in the control condition. The average age of the participants was 19.39 years old ($SD=2.57$). There were more male participants ($n=77, 65.8\%$) than female ($n=40, 34.2\%$), and the majority were university freshman ($n=97, 82.9\%$), perhaps due to recruitment from calculus courses which are often required foundational courses in many STEM departments.

The Game: Mission Prime

The game used in this study is a game developed by the research team to enhance the learning experience of undergraduate calculus to first-year students and sophomores. The project is part of a university-wide initiative to incorporate technology into foundational STEM courses to enhance student learning. For calculus, we designed a game called *Mission Prime*. In the game, the players' goal is to help set up a space colony using their knowledge of optimization, one of the key concepts in calculus. In each scenario, players are given a problem such as maximizing the interior of a fence with limited resources. The player will be able to select objects, adjust viable parameters, view the problem space from multiple perspectives, and ultimately select the mathematical 'tools' necessary to solve the given problem.

The goal of the game is to train students to: (a) Identify the type of problem, (b) model the problem, (c) select the appropriate resources to solve the problem, (d) set up a function to solve the problem, and (e) find a correct answer to the problem. The game instruction focuses on the identifying, modeling, selecting tools, and setting up a function to solve the problems. Calculations were not emphasized in favor of deeper, perhaps more conceptual understanding of the problem.

The players were asked to assemble a function to solve the problem out of a set of formulae provided. For example, in a scenario the players were asked to construct a hydraulic generator and the player must figure out the dimensions (see Figure 1). Once the function is built out of these various components the player will be able to perform various operations on it and observe the final output. If the function yields the correct answer, the player will complete the scenario. If the function yields an incorrect answer, the player will be given feedback and will be asked to modify the function until the right answer is found. This design allowed players to focus on learning the conceptual framework of the problem without having to memorize formulae and perform calculations. During the problem-solving process, players can manipulate the visual representation of the objects, rotate their view of the problem space, and switch between two-dimensional and three-dimensional perspectives to help them come up with a solution to the problem (see Figure 2).

Each scenario in the game represents a new problem that is built on previous learning. This design allows players to learn the concepts through multiple representations and allow the players to incorporate new mathematical concepts with their existing mental representations as they progress.

The game *Mission Prime* was designed with mathematical educational theories in mind. Students were given an application problem to facilitate purposeful engagement, and each scenario is a different representation of the basic concept of optimization. Visual aids were given that allow students to move around and observe.

Both performance and formative feedback were given to help students keep track of their progress and adjust their actions.

Measurements

Conceptual understanding. Calculus conceptual understanding was measured by two open-ended questions developed by members of the research team from the Mathematics department. The first question asked participants to describe "What do you think are the important concepts in optimization?" and the second question asked participants to explain "how and why we use the derivative to solve optimization problems?" The open-ended questions were scored by the researchers according to a scoring rubric while blind to the experimental conditions. The scores ranged from 0 to 4 on each question and were averaged to gain a general calculus concept score. The average score across the conditions was 1.66 ($SD=1.15$).

Calculation skills. Calculus calculation skills were measured using two quiz questions to test the students' ability to solve an optimization problem. Each of the two questions requires two answers for width and height, which result in four answers. Each of the answers was scored 0 for incorrect answers and 1 for correct answers; the scores were aggregated to create a calculation score that ranged from 0 to 4. The average score across the conditions was 1.30 ($SD=1.37$).

Figure 1.

Figure 2.

Immersion. Perceived immersion was measured by a subset of the cognitive absorption scale developed by Agarwal and Karahanna (2000). The subscale consisted of five Likert-type items that asked participants to rate how much they agree with the statements (e.g., "While I was engaged with the training tool, I was able to block out most other distractions."). The items were reliable with Cronbach's α=.91.

Sense of control. Sense of control was measured by another subset of the cognitive absorption scale which consisted of three Likert-types items (e.g., "When I was engaged with the training tool, I felt in control."). The items were reliable with Cronbach's α=.85."

Game behavioral-tracking data: Feedback and visual manipulation. We measured number of feedback and duration of visual manipulation in each scenarios using unobtrusive behavioral-tracking from the game server. A major advantage of using behavioral data is that the measurement is unobtrusive. Thus the player will not feel threated when making mistakes and spending large amount of time on manipulating the visual representations (Y.-H. Lee, Heeter, Magerko, & Medler, 2012). Behavioral-tracking also allowed us to gain exact frequency and duration of actions without the potential problem of having human observer errors (Heeter, Lee, Medler, & Magerko, 2013). These behavioral data also gave the game development team insights into parts of the game that players were having trouble in and improve the game in future iterations. Players received both performance and formative feedback when they submit a decision in the game, the performance feedback tells the players if they are correct or not. The formative feedback tells players how they can improve. Duration of visual manipulation tracks how much time each player spends on manipulating the visual representation in each scenario.

RESULTS

Equivalence Between Groups

The current experiment used random assignment at the subject level to establish equivalence between groups. Until recently, many education studies have used group-level assignment to compare different treatments. A problem with group-based assignment is that the different natural groups (i.e., classes or schools) may have different instructors, use different materials, and consists of students from different departments which can confound the effect. Another potential threat of group-level assignment is selection bias. That is, researchers may intentionally assign their preferred treatment to classes with better performances in the first place. Because of the potential biases in group-based assignments, the Institute for Education Sciences advocates expanding research on practical programs using experiments with random assignments (Simpson, Lacava, & Graner, 2004).

Random assignment at the subject level, if implemented correctly, can ensure that the third variables which may cause a difference in the effects are evenly distributed between the experimental groups. A random assignment also ensures that the researcher cannot manipulate the results by intentionally assigning certain subjects to specific groups. While random assignment at the subject level is assumed to establish equivalence between groups, we conducted Chi-square tests on the sex, age, and number of Calculus courses taken to establish equivalence between groups. Chi-square results showed that there was no significant difference regarding sex ($X^2 = .03, p = .987$), age ($X^2 = 17.21, p = .372$), and number of Calculus courses taken ($X^2 = 10.26$, $p = .114$), suggesting that the three experiment groups are equivalent and the difference in results can be attributed to the different experimental treatments.

Immersion

Hypothesis 1 posited that participants in the game condition report higher perceived immersion in the task than the practice quiz condition and the control condition. We conducted one-way Analysis of Variance (ANOVA) to test the hypothesis. Experiment conditions were used as the independent variable, and perceived immersion was the dependent variable.

The result showed that there was a significant difference between the three conditions, $F(2, 122)=4.77$, $p=.010$, eta squared$=.07$ in perceived immersion. Post-hoc comparison with Tukey HSD showed that the game condition ($M=5.67$, $SD=1.05$) reported significantly more immersed in the task than the practice quiz condition ($M=4.90$, $SD=1.26$) and the control condition ($M=5.04$, $SD=1.50$). The practice quiz condition was not significantly different from the control condition ($p=.873$). The result was consistent with hypothesis 1. The findings indicate that participants felt more immersed in playing the game than doing practice quiz.

Sense of Control

Since digital games can facilitate self-paced learning that may increase students' sense of control in their learning progress and results, hypothesis 2 posited that participants in the game condition would report a higher sense of control than participants in the other two experimental conditions. We conducted a similar ANOVA to test the hypothesis, this time with a sense of control as the dependent variable. The results showed that unlike what we hypothesized, there was no significant difference between the conditions in their sense of control, $F(2, 122)=1.22$, $p=.300$. Participants in the game condition ($M=4.60$, $SD=1.47$) did not report a higher sense of control than the practice quiz condition ($M=4.85$, $SD=1.16$), nor the control condition ($M=4.33$, $SD=1.55$). The result was not consistent with hypothesis 2.

Calculus Calculation Skills

Research question 1 asked whether the game will improve students' calculation skills over the traditional practice quiz or no treatment. To test this research question, we conducted an Analysis of Covariance (ANCOVA). Experiment condition was entered as the independent variable, and the calculation skill score was used as the dependent variable. Since number of calculus classes taken would potentially affect one's calculation skills, we controlled for the number of calculus classes taken as a covariate.

The result showed that there was no significant difference between the three conditions, $F(2, 113)=.20$, $p=.818$. This suggests that the game condition ($M=1.30$, $SD=1.57$) did not perform significantly better than the homework condition ($M=1.39$, $SD=1.28$) or the control condition ($M=1.18$, $SD=1.17$) in terms of calculation skills. The findings indicate that playing an hour of the game was not more effective in improving the students' calculation skills than doing practice quiz or no treatment at all. A surprising finding was that the practice quiz did not outperform the control group in terms of calculation skills, perhaps because the practice quiz did not help students retrieve relevant knowledge and improve their calculation skills.

Conceptual Understanding

One of the key arguments for using digital games for mathematics education is that it has the potential to facilitate conceptual understanding. Hypothesis 3 posited that participants in the game condition would perform better than the homework and control condition in their understanding of calculus concepts. We conducted another ANCOVA similar to the one for calculation skills, this time with conceptual understanding as the dependent variable. The result showed that there was a significant difference between the three conditions, $F(2, 113)=5.22$, $p=.007$, eta squared$=.08$. The post-hoc comparison showed that the game condition ($M=2.10$, $SD=1.26$) was significantly higher than the practice quiz condition ($M=1.57$, $SD=1.04$) and the control condition ($M=1.32$, $SD=1.01$). Again, the practice quiz condition was not significantly different from the control condition ($p=.747$). The data were consistent with hypotheses H3a and H3b. The findings indicate that the game was more effective in improving students' understanding of calculus concepts than doing one hour of practice quiz or no treatment at all.

Feedback, Visual Manipulation and Conceptual Understanding

Literature suggests that games promote conceptual understanding through giving players feedback and the affordance of visual manipulations (e.g., Delacruz, 2012; Tall, 1991). Hypotheses 4 and 5 focused on the game condition to investigate whether number of feedback and visual manipulations predicts conceptual understanding. After removing seven participants who were either idling during the gameplay or did not play for the required duration, a total of 44 participants were included in the analyses. Because not all the participants were able to complete all the scenarios within the one hour experiment time, we focused on analyzing player behavioral data in the first scenario, which is where players learn the mechanics of the game and the basic concepts. On average, players received 37.72 feedback ($SD=45.43$, ranging from zero to 195) about their performance and how to correct their mistakes. On average, the students in the game condition spent an average of 18.57 ($SD=19.57$) seconds on active visual manipulation in scenario 1. We define "actively used" as usage beyond the required usage in the tutorial phase of scenario 1.

In order to test hypotheses 4 and 5, we conducted a hierarchical regression. Total time spent on scenario 1 was controlled in the first block because total time in the scenario is positively correlated with number of feedback and duration in visual manipulation. The independent variables were number of feedback and duration of active visual manipulations. Conceptual understanding was entered as the dependent variable. The overall model was significant, $F(3, 29)= 2.67$, $p=.031$, $adj\,R^2 =.11$.

Visual manipulation was not a significant predictor of conceptual understanding, $\beta=-.09$, $t=-.52$, $p=.607$. Which suggest that increased time spent in visual manipulation did not significantly predict better conceptual understanding. The result was not consistent with hypothesis 4. Further examining the distribution of scores indicated an inverse u-curve between the duration of visual manipulation and conceptual understanding. Students who did not spend time (i.e., duration = 0) in visual manipulation had the largest variance in terms of conceptual understanding, $M=3.11$, $SD=1.02$. Perhaps because this subgroup consists of students who had better conceptual understanding, to begin with and did not need the visual aide and also consists of students who simply did not pay attention to the game and did not improve their conceptual understanding. For the students who did use the visual manipulation function, there was a positive correlation between visual manipulation and conceptual understanding between 1 to 12.94 seconds, this positive trend reversed after 12.94 seconds, in which increased time spent on visual manipulation beyond 12.94 seconds reduced conceptual understanding.

Number of feedback was a significant predictor of conceptual understanding, but in the opposite direction, $\beta=-.40$, $t=-2.36$, $p=.023$. The result was not consistent with hypothesis 5. The finding suggests that students who were exposed to more feedback actually performed worse in the conceptual understanding. This may be because players only received feedback when they make a mistake. Therefore the number of feedback may also be an indication of the players' performance. When we eliminated students with extremely high number of feedback (i.e., outliers with more than 50 feedback) in the first scenario ($n=8$) from the analysis, number of feedback did not negatively predict conceptual understanding, suggesting that the students with an extremely high number of feedback may have skewed the analyses.

GENERAL DISCUSSION

This study was designed with two main goals in mind. The first goal was to compare the effectiveness of a digital game approach to a traditional approach in promoting calculus conceptual understanding, calculation skills, and sense of immersion and control among undergraduate students. The second goal was to examine actual behavioral data to test whether the affordances digital games to support visual manipulation and feedback improved students' conceptual understanding of calculus.

In line with previous literature (e.g., Ke, 2008a, 2008b; Kebritchi, Hirumi, & Bai, 2010; Kim & Chang, 2010; Liang & Zhou, 2009; Ota & DuPaul, 2002), we found that students felt more immersed in the task when learning through the game in comparison to doing practice quizzes or no treatment. Digital games communicate through designed problems that invite players to solve with limited resources (Gee,

2007). In other words, digital games can facilitate what Siegler (2009) calls *purposeful engagement*. When students understand the purpose of learning, they are more likely to allocate attention to the task and cognitively process the information because they are motivated to solve the problems. Previous literature also suggests that students felt more ownership and responsibility for their learning (Liang & Zhou, 2009). However, in our study, the students who played the game did not report a higher sense of control than the students who solved the practice quiz.

Previous studies on using digital games for mathematics education have shown mixed results in its effectiveness to promote calculation skills (see Connolly et al., 2012 for review). Our result showed that students who played the game did not perform better than students who solved a practice quiz or received no treatment at all. This may be because the game Mission Prime was designed to promote conceptual understanding and intentionally deemphasized calculation and formula memorization in the game. However, had the game required more calculation, the calculation could potentially decrease players' sense of immersion because the gameplay flow would be constantly interrupted by calculations. What was surprising was that the paper-and-pencil practice quiz did not improve calculation skills than no treatment. The most common instructional goal of practice quizzes in education is to let students practice and refresh their memory of materials that they learned in class (Cooper, Robinson, & Patall, 2006). A practice quiz can also act as a self-assessment for the student to understand how well they understand. However, students may not benefit from practice quiz alone. Without guidance or feedback to help students understand how well they are doing, and how to correct their mistakes and improve, students cannot learn from doing quizzes. Instead, students may feel demotivated because they do not see the purpose of the practice quiz.

In terms of promoting conceptual understanding, our results found that undergraduate students who played the game had deeper conceptual understanding than students who solved a practice quiz or no treatment. Mathematics educators have argued that in order to promote conceptual understanding of calculus, it is suggested that calculus could be taught by providing students with a general understanding of its application, and then supporting self-paced learning through feedback and visual representations (e.g., Disessa & Sherin, 2000; Kaput, 1994; Tall, 1991). Digital games can afford this type of educational design by providing meaningful problem for students to solve, constant feedback on the students' process, and allow students to manipulate multiple visual representations that explain the underlying concepts.

Next, we focused on the game condition to investigate whether the number of feedback messages received and duration of visual manipulations predicted better conceptual understanding. Our analyses using behavioral-tracking data of the students' behavior during gameplay found that duration of visual representation manipulation was not a significant predictor of conceptual understanding. When we further examined the data, we found an inverse u-curve among students who actively used the visual manipulation function. Duration spent on visual manipulation was positively correlated with better conceptual understanding to a point (around 12.94 seconds), beyond that point, more time spent on visual manipulation decreased conceptual understanding. There are several potential explanations for this outcome. First, perhaps a moderate amount of visual aid helps students understand the underlying concepts and how it is applied, but excessive time spent on visual manipulation may distract students and impede their understanding. Another potential explanation is that the students who spent a large amount of time on visual manipulation were the ones who could not figure out how to play the game and spent large amount of time exploring all the different functions.

The results also showed that number of feedback predicted conceptual understanding, but in the opposite direction. That is, students who received large numbers of feedback performed worse in conceptual understanding. One possible explanation of this finding is that in the game, feedback appears after the player has made an incorrect attempt. Therefore, a large number of feedback may also indicate that the player is performing poorly and that the feedback was not effective in improving the player's understanding. Another possible explanation is that some students were simply trying random combinations without putting much thought into reading the feedback. For example, one student received as much as 195 feedback in first scenario alone. Because these students were not cognitively processing the feedback message, their understanding may not have improved.

Overall, we found that students reported the gameplay experience as more immersive than traditional practice quiz, and students who played the game also gained a deeper understanding of the underlying concepts that were used to solve the problems in the game. There was no significant difference in terms of improving calculation skills. When examining what caused students in the game condition to have better conceptual understanding, behavioral-tracking data revealed that the students who actively manipulated the visual representation performed better when asked to explicate their understanding of the concepts, but only to a certain point. This finding partially supports theories that argued for the game affordances of manipulating visual representations and that presenting abstract mathematical concepts through multiple representations may promote a deeper understanding of the concepts and its applications.

Limitations

This study was conducted in a controlled laboratory setting with random assignment. Therefore, external factors such as teachers' ability, classroom environment, duration of the class, etc. were controlled in the experiment. As previous researcher has argued, the effectiveness of digital games in classroom education largely depends on the dynamics between the learners, the instructors, curriculum design, and the game design (Ke, 2008a). The findings from this study are the results of comparing the digital game approach to practice quiz and no treatment approach in isolation and should be generalized with caution. In a classroom setting, students may be able to seek additional support from their instructors or fellow students, which may supplement the game or practice quiz to improve learning effect. Other students in the classroom may distract players of the game or students may feel fatigued because of the long duration of classes, which may decrease the effect of the game or the practice quiz. By eliminating these external factors that can influence the students' performance, we can focus on comparing the two different approaches and its affordances.

Due to resource and time constraints, students in this study only played the game once for an hour in the laboratory. Longer gameplay time and repeated play may increase the effectiveness of digital game-based learning.

The participants in this study were recruited from calculus classes; they have already learned the materials covered in the game and the practice quiz in the previous semester. Therefore the results should be interpreted as the effect of using a digital game or practice quiz to rehearse and enhance calculus classroom education, not the effect of using digital games or practice quiz as an initial learning approaches.

CONCLUSION

Few studies have examined the application of digital game-based learning in undergraduate-level mathematics education; fewer studies have examined the actual gameplay processes to identify affordances of digital games that promote deep cognitive understanding of mathematics. Findings from this study suggest that a well-designed digital game can be used to promote student motivation and conceptual understanding in undergraduate-level calculus education. Some mathematics educators have argued that a problem-based learning approach and visual manipulations can motivate learners to take on an active role in learning, and through manipulating and experimenting with visual representations, construct a deep understanding of the underlying concepts (C.-Y. Lee & Chen, 2009; Stanley, 2002; Tall, 1991). This study shows that digital games may provide meaningful problems that immerse students in mathematical problems. The findings marginally support that manipulation of visual representations may predict better conceptual understanding of the mathematics and its application, but only to a certain extent, excessive visual representation may distract learners and disrupt conceptual understanding.

Does this imply that digital games will always improve conceptual understanding over traditional approaches? Not necessarily. The effect of any educational design is ultimately determined by the interaction between the instructor, learner, content, and context. While some instructors can effectively incorporate digital game-based learning into their course design, others may be able to motivate authentic learning and conceptual understanding without using digital games. Future studies should test the effects of digital games in conjunction with traditional approaches, and replicate the study in a classroom setting to observe how students and instructors interact with the new medium, especially if the digital games are designed to target persistent problem areas in undergraduate calculus education.

Future instructional game designers also need to put more efforts into making sure students understand the affordances and feature of the game that support learning. For example, while the game Mission Prime provided the function of visual manipulation, not all the students actively used the function. Findings suggest that students who actively used the function performed better in conceptual understanding to a point. A challenge for instructional games at more advanced mathematical levels is the balance between maintaining engagement in the game and attaining complex learning goals. Mission Prime intentionally emphasized conceptual understanding of optimization over computations, in part to maintain game engagement. If learning goals are more computational in nature, a game would necessarily require creative design solutions so that performing computations does not disrupt gameplay.

REFERENCES

Agarwal, R., & Karahanna, E. (2000). Time flies when you're having fun: Cognitive absorption and beliefs about information technology usage. *Management Information Systems Quarterly*, 24(4), 665–694. doi:10.2307/3250951

Anderson, J. R., Greeno, J. G., Reder, L. M., & Simon, H. A. (2000). Perspectives on learning, thinking, and activity. *Educational Researcher*, 29(4), 11–13. doi:10.3102/0013189X029004011

Betz, J. A. (1995). Computer games: Increase learning in an interactive multidisciplinary environment. *Journal of Educational Technology Systems*, 24(2), 195–205. doi:10.2190/119M-BRMU-J8HC-XM6F

Boyle, E. A., Connolly, T. M., & Hainey, T. (2011). The role of psychology in understanding the impact of computer games. *Entertainment Computing*, 2(2), 69–74. doi:10.1016/j.entcom.2010.12.002

Bransford, J. D., Brown, A. L., & Cocking, R. R. (1999). *How people learn: Brain, mind, experience, and school.* National Academy Press.

Charsky, D. (2010). From edutainment to serious games: A change in the use of game characteristics. *Games and Culture, 5*(2), 177–198. doi:10.1177/1555412009354727

Connolly, T. M., Boyle, E. A., MacArthur, E., Hainey, T., & Boyle, J. M. (2012). A systematic literature review of empirical evidence on computer games and serious games. *Computers & Education, 59*(2), 661–686. doi:10.1016/j.compedu.2012.03.004

Cooper, H., Robinson, J. C., & Patall, E. A. (2006). Does homework improve academic achievement? A synthesis of research, 1987–2003. *Review of Educational Research, 76*(1), 1–62. doi:10.3102/00346543076001001

Cordova, D. I., & Lepper, M. R. (1996). Intrinsic motivation and the process of learning: Beneficial effects of contextualization, personalization, and choice. *Journal of Educational Psychology, 88*(4), 715–730. doi:10.1037/0022-0663.88.4.715

Delacruz, G. C. (2012). Impact of incentives on the use of feedback in educational videogames: CRESST report 813. National Center for Research on Evaluation, Standards, and Student Testing, 1-18.

Disessa, A. A., & Sherin, B. L. (2000). Meta-representation: An introduction. *The Journal of Mathematical Behavior, 19*(4), 385–398. doi:10.1016/S0732-3123(01)00051-7

Garris, R., Ahlers, R., & Driskell, J. E. (2002). Games, motivation, and learning: A research and practice model. *Simulation & Gaming, 33*(4), 441–467. doi:10.1177/1046878102238607

Gee, J. P. (2007). *Good Video Games + Good Learning: Collected essays on video games, learning and literacy* (Vol. 27). Peter Lang. doi:10.3726/978-1-4539-1162-4

Heeter, C., Lee, Y.-H., Medler, B., & Magerko, B. (2013). *Conceptually meaningful metrics: Inferring optimal challenge and mindset from gameplay. In Game Analytics* (pp. 731–762). Springer.

Kaput, J. J. (1994). The representational roles of technology in connecting mathematics with authentic experience. *Didactics of mathematics as a scientific discipline,* 379-397.

Ke, F. (2008a). A case study of computer gaming for math: Engaged learning from gameplay? *Computers & Education, 51*(4), 1609–1620. doi:10.1016/j.compedu.2008.03.003

Ke, F. (2008b). Computer games application within alternative classroom goal structures: Cognitive, metacognitive, and affective evaluation. *Educational Technology Research and Development*, *56*(5-6), 539–556. doi:10.100711423-008-9086-5

Kebritchi, M., Hirumi, A., & Bai, H. (2010). The effects of modern mathematics computer games on mathematics achievement and class motivation. *Computers & Education*, *55*(2), 427–443. doi:10.1016/j.compedu.2010.02.007

Kidron, I., & Zehavi, N. (2002). The Role of Animation in Teaching the Limit Concept. *International Journal of Computer Algebra in Mathematics Education*, *9*(3), 205–227.

Kim, S., & Chang, M. (2010). Computer Games for the Math Achievement of Diverse Students. *Journal of Educational Technology & Society*, *13*(3), 224–232.

Kolb, A. Y., & Kolb, D. A. (2005). Learning styles and learning spaces: Enhancing experiential learning in higher education. *Academy of Management Learning & Education*, *4*(2), 193–212. doi:10.5465/amle.2005.17268566

Lee, C.-Y., & Chen, M.-P. (2009). A computer game as a context for non-routine mathematical problem solving: The effects of type of question prompt and level of prior knowledge. *Computers & Education*, *52*(3), 530–542. doi:10.1016/j.compedu.2008.10.008

Lee, Y.-H., Heeter, C., Magerko, B., & Medler, B. (2012). Gaming mindsets: Implicit theories in serious game learning. *Cyberpsychology, Behavior, and Social Networking*, *15*(4), 190–194. doi:10.1089/cyber.2011.0328 PMID:22165916

Lesh, R., & Zawojewski, J. (2007). Problem solving and modeling. Second handbook of research on mathematics teaching and learning, 2, 763-804.

Liang, X., & Zhou, Q. (2009). Students' experiences of mathematics learning in technology integrated classrooms. *Teaching and Learning*, *5*(1), 62–74.

Lithner, J. (2004). Mathematical reasoning in calculus textbook exercises. *The Journal of Mathematical Behavior*, *23*(4), 405–427. doi:10.1016/j.jmathb.2004.09.003

Lopez-Morteo, G., & López, G. (2007). Computer support for learning mathematics: A learning environment based on recreational learning objects. *Computers & Education*, *48*(4), 618–641. doi:10.1016/j.compedu.2005.04.014

Mayo, M. J. (2009). Video games: A route to large-scale STEM education? *Science*, *323*(5910), 79–82. doi:10.1126cience.1166900 PMID:19119223

Morgan, P., & Ritter, S. (2002). *An experimental study of the effects of Cognitive Tutor® Algebra I on student knowledge and attitude*. Pittsburgh, PA: Carnegie Learning, Inc.

Oehrtman, M. (2009). Collapsing dimensions, physical limitation, and other student metaphors for limit concepts. *Journal for Research in Mathematics Education*, 396–426.

Ota, K. R., & DuPaul, G. J. (2002). Task engagement and mathematics performance in children with attention-deficit hyperactivity disorder: Effects of supplemental computer instruction. *School Psychology Quarterly*, *17*(3), 242–257. doi:10.1521cpq.17.3.242.20881

Rose, H., & Betts, J. R. (2004). The effect of high school courses on earnings. *The Review of Economics and Statistics*, *86*(2), 497–513. doi:10.1162/003465304323031076

Shaffer, D. W. (2006). *How computer games help children learn*. Macmillan. doi:10.1057/9780230601994

Siegler, R. (2009). *Implications of cognitive science research for mathematics education*. Academic Press.

Simpson, R. L., Lacava, P. G., & Graner, P. S. (2004). The No Child Left Behind Act Challenges and Implications for Educators. *Intervention in School and Clinic*, *40*(2), 67–75. doi:10.1177/10534512040400020101

Spotnitz, S. (2001). *Intrinsic motivation in students with learning disabilities as examined through computer based instruction in mathematics* (Unpublished thesis). Columbia University.

Squire, K. (2003). Video games in education. *International Journal of Intelligent Games & Simulation*, *2*(1), 49–62.

Squire, K., Jenkins, H., Holland, W., Miller, H., O'Driscoll, A., Tan, K. P., & Todd, K. (2003). Design Principles of Next-Generation Digital Gaming for Education. *Educational Technology*, *43*(5), 17–23.

Stanley, S. S. (2002). Revitalizing precalculus with problem-based learning. *The Journal of General Education, 51*(4), 306–315. doi:10.1353/jge.2003.0016

Steinkuehler, C., & Duncan, S. (2008). Scientific habits of mind in virtual worlds. *Journal of Science Education and Technology, 17*(6), 530–543. doi:10.100710956-008-9120-8

Tall, D. (1991). *Advanced mathematical thinking* (Vol. 11). Springer. doi:10.1007/0-306-47203-1

Van Eck, R. (2006). Digital game-based learning: It's not just the digital natives who are restless. *EDUCAUSE Review, 41*(2), 16.

Chapter 8

"Nervousness and Maybe Even Some Regret":
Videogames and the Cognitive-Affective Model of Historical Empathy

Liz Owens Boltz
Michigan State University, USA

ABSTRACT

Historical empathy has increasingly been recognized as a multidimensional construct that involves both cognitive and affective dimensions. Research suggests that engaging learners with diverse historical perspectives in activities like debate, writing, and role play can be more effective for historical empathy than traditional instruction. Although several studies have investigated the effectiveness of these strategies, little is known about the effectiveness of games in promoting historical empathy. Through observation, recorded game play, and semi-structured interviews, this chapter examined how historical empathy manifested as eighth graders played a videogame about World War I (Valiant Hearts). The findings indicate that specific elements of game play may foster particular dimensions of historical empathy better than others, and that some dimensions tend to arise spontaneously while others require (or even resist) prompting.

DOI: 10.4018/978-1-5225-7461-3.ch008

INTRODUCTION

Wineburg (2001) has written that mature historical knowing can teach us "to go beyond our own image to go beyond our brief life, and to go beyond the fleeing moment in human history into which we have been born" (p. 19). Entertaining and understanding perspectives outside of our own, and coming to know others, can be a difficult endeavor whether those others lived hundreds of years ago or are currently seated across the aisle from us. Engaging with history offers opportunities to develop the kind of dispositions that allow us to better perceive the experiences of others (Wineburg, 2001). In the context of history education, this construct is generally identified as *historical empathy*: Understanding the historical context, attitudes, cultural norms, belief systems, and other factors that may have shaped the actions of people and institutions in the past.

The persistence of traditional instructional approaches tends to encourage students to rely on history texts to provide answers to historical questions (Wineburg, 1991; Yeager, Foster, Maley, Anderson, & Morris, 1998). On the other hand, students exposed to rich, multimodal activities are more likely to not only recognize multiple perspectives but see the value of doing so (Brooks, 2009; Lévesque, 2008; Levstik & Barton, 2011). Similarly, students who actively engage with different points of view in activities such as historical debate tend to have greater understanding of historical context and stronger perspective taking abilities (Jensen, 2008).

By fostering awareness that diverse and contradictory viewpoints existed within past societies just as they do today, historical empathy can encourage students to examine how their own values have been shaped by societal and historical contexts (Russell, 2011). Such awareness has implications beyond the classroom in the development of engaged citizens able to acknowledge the merits of differing opinions within a pluralist democracy (Barton & Levstik, 2004).

Although research has investigated the effectiveness of activities like debate, role play, and writing/reflection (Levstik & Barton, 2011)—only a few studies have explored the potential of videogames in this regard. Videogames are immersive, multimodal experiences involving text, video, music, and imagery, and many current titles allow players to engage with content from more than one perspective. As such, they may offer affordances to prepare learners to engage in historical empathy— giving players the ability to look "through the eyes of people in the past" (Levstik & Barton, 2011, p. 121).

This study seeks to contribute to our understanding of those affordances. Through observation, recorded game play, and semi-structured interviews, I examined how children demonstrate historical empathy in a videogame that allows them to play from multiple perspectives, and whether particular types of game play tend to elicit historical empathy more often than others.

LITERATURE REVIEW

Educators have increasingly recognized that learners are left out of the interpretive process when history is put forward as a metanarrative to be memorized (Levstik & Barton, 2011). History, many argue, is not an inert chronicle of events but rather more like what documentary filmmaker Ken Burns has described as a dynamic chorus of voices (Ward & Burns, 1994). Current trends in history and social studies education urge educators to avoid universal, unchallenged metanarratives, instead promoting dialogue that engages with diverse viewpoints and encourages historical thinking (Russell, 2011). These skills and dispositions have genuine relevance in democratic education, as they are crucial to the development of critical consciousness necessary for informed political engagement.

Historical Empathy

Learners tend to ascribe past actions they don't understand to inferiority, stupidity, or moral deficit—limiting their ability to understand why people in the past acted as they did (Lee & Ashby, 2001). Historical empathy, in contrast, can help learners gain a better understanding of how perspectives, intentions, beliefs and contexts shaped the actions of people and groups in the past (Ashby & Lee, 1987). As such, it facilitates awareness and understanding of alternate perspectives.

Contemporary research suggests that historical empathy involves both the cognitive exercise of recognizing the perspectives of others as well as affective engagement, or caring with and about people in the past (Barton & Levstik, 2004) and is therefore an activity that requires "imaginative intellectual and emotional participation" (p. 207). This imaginative process should be supported and informed by historical contextualization grounded in evidence (Lévesque, 2008). History education, in this view, entails more than taking on the perspective of another person—it requires the recognition of a multiplicity of historically contextualized perspectives and a sense of "care" that involves an emotional connection with the past. Importantly, forms of caring lead to more active engagement and interest in historical subjects and figures.

Following in this line of thinking, Endacott & Brooks (2013) proposed an updated theoretical model for historical empathy as a dual-dimensional, cognitive-affective construct, noting that such a view is widely accepted in psychological approaches to empathy. Unlike everyday empathy, however, historical empathy is historically situated. As such, it involves three interrelated elements: Historical contextualization, perspective taking, and affective connection.

Historical contextualization requires an understanding of the historical context, attitudes, cultural norms, and belief systems that may have shaped the actions of people and institutions in the past, as well as other events and perspectives relevant to

Figure 1. Theoretical model for historical empathy
(Endacott & Brooks, 2013)

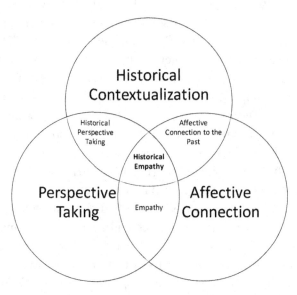

a particular time period. *Perspective taking* is trying to understand what a historical person or group may have thought, and why they acted as they did, based on their lived experience, beliefs, and attitudes. Finally, an *affective connection* involves finding common ground between the lived experience of a person in the past and one's own similar (yet different) experiences, beliefs, and affective responses to situations and events.

Videogames for Learning

History is a content area for which videogames have shown a good deal of potential. For one, the gaming industry has continually shown great enthusiasm for commercial games with historical context. Many best-selling videogames, such as the *Civilization* and *Assassin's Creed* series, contain socio-historical themes. Researchers have recognized that this medium provides a "dynamism and capacity for interaction with socio-historical facts…that would be impossible to achieve any other way" (López & Cáceres, 2010, p. 1344). Squire's (2011) work with students playing *Civilization III*, for example, showed that although students initially interpreted historical game events in terms of their preexisting notions of colonization, playing the game fostered more nuanced, expanded understandings of history. Encouraging players to reflect on their game play and to compare a game's representation of history to primary and secondary sources also has the potential to help learners achieve more sophisticated understandings (Charsky & Mims, 2008).

Emerging research investigating the use of videogames to promote historical empathy has begun to offer promising results. In their study of the game *Mission US: For Crown or Colony* (a web-based educational adventure game set in pre-Revolutionary War Boston), Schrier, Diamond, and Langendoen (2010) found that many students developed richer understandings of the motivations and context behind historical characters' alignment with Loyalist or Patriot causes, demonstrated an affective connection to the past, and were better able to provide explanations of different perspectives. The researchers noted that many students were able to "identify emotionally with at least some of the characters and develop feelings about how they were treated and what became of them" (Schrier et al., 2010, p. 267).

A more recent study of the same game (Diamond, 2012) used player think-alouds, semi-structured interviews, and game play observations to investigate how 8th graders demonstrated historical empathy. The findings indicated that, after playing the game, learners developed more nuanced and context-driven understandings of the characters and that players with greater prior knowledge of the time period were better prepared for the types of game activity that might lead to historical empathy.

As research in this field continues, there appears to be a need for future studies to explore the potential that more robust videogames—those not developed primarily for educational purposes—may hold for historical empathy (see Diamond, 2012). This leads to the primary research questions for this study:

1. In what ways does historical empathy manifest through play of a commercial videogame?
2. Do some components of the videogame appear to elicit evidence of historical empathy more frequently than others?

METHODS

The Videogame

The videogame used in this study was *Valiant Hearts: The Great War* (Ubisoft, 2014), a World War I themed game available across a variety of platforms that was developed in consultation with historians from Mission Centenaire, the French Commission overseeing the WWI centenary commemorative program (Zimet, 2012). Somewhat atypically for a war-themed game, *Valiant Hearts* combines features of the adventure and puzzle videogame genres and uses relatively simple mechanics, potentially making it more appealing to a wider audience (including less experienced players or those not attracted to first-person shooters). Facts and archival photographs that contextualize the experiences of the war can be unlocked as the game progresses; additionally, collectible artifacts (accompanied by description) can be discovered throughout the game environment. Players experience multiple perspectives, including both soldiers and civilians. Diary entries can be unlocked as play progresses, revealing the main characters' motivations and feelings. In sum, the game balances educationally relevant content with entertainment value, is easy to learn to play, and incorporates elements from different game genres. As such, it has potential to serve as a conduit for players of varying levels of experience to engage with a complex and multifaceted historical period, and seemed an appropriate choice of game for this study.

Research Design

This study maintained a qualitative focus consistent with the nature of my research questions. My research design was informed by Endacott's (2010) call for future research on historical empathy to employ methods that capture learners' stream of consciousness, allowing us to see more of their meaning-making and decision-making processes and by Squire's (2006) argument that research must account for the mechanisms by which players interpret meaning from the experiences they have in videogames. Therefore, through a case study approach, I collected a rich set of qualitative data to develop an in-depth understanding of the case in an effort to illuminate the central research questions (Creswell, 2008).

Sample

Participants for this study were recruited via email using a purposeful sampling strategy (Creswell, 2008). Because of the large amount of qualitative data to be collected and the exploratory nature of my research questions, only 4 participants were involved in the study. I recruited participants from the Midwestern United States in same-gender pairs (two self-identified as female, two as male) with the objective of encouraging more interaction and conversation. In the background survey, all participants self-identified as White. The resulting group of participants offered opportunities to compare and contrast across similar cases; by collecting a rich set of qualitative data, I hoped to better illuminate the central research questions (Creswell, 2008). In all coding and data analysis, participant names were replaced with pseudonyms to ensure confidentiality (see Table 1 for participant information).

Data Sources

Data collected for this study included a background survey / pre-test; game play (which included player statements, recorded observations, and game play data; and

Table 1. Self-Reported Participant Demographic Information

	Age	Gender Identity
Deanna	13	F
Beverly	13	F
Julian	13	M
Miles	14	M

a post-test. I used different means of data collection to help inform a more in-depth understanding of the central phenomenon (Creswell, 2008).

The background survey collected basic information including age, gender identification, and grade level. It included Likert-scale questions asking students to rate their frequency of game play and how much they liked social studies/history. In the pre-test, participants answered 5 multiple-choice and 2 true-false questions that assessed their declarative knowledge of WWI. These questions assessed, for example, participants' awareness of the countries involved in WWI, changes in numbers of women entering the workforce as a result of the war, and the weapons/technologies used at the time. This pre-test was modeled on the one used by Diamond (2012), and adapted for the WWI time period.

The use of *Valiant Hearts,* which allows players to inhabit the roles of four different fictional characters (based on historical evidence and artifacts) was a response to Endacott's (2010) suggestion that future research should examine historical empathy with different historical figures, rather than the well-known characters who are typically represented in textbooks and documentaries. Given that players can inhabit characters that would have been marginalized during that time period (including Anna, a woman; and Freddy, a Creole-American), the use of this game also seeks to address the call for history education to incorporate the viewpoints of individuals who have traditionally been excluded or stereotyped due to their race, gender, class, or other factors (Russell, 2011).

The game play observation sessions were held in the summer of 2015 in a lab setting. Each participant pair played *Valiant Hearts* on a Windows-based laptop for one 2-hour session. Participants took turns as the active player so that each spent a similar amount of time controlling the game. The sessions were recorded on video, including recordings of the laptop screen during game play, to collect observational data characterizing the way students play the game, the choices made during game play, and to examine any evidence of students who struggled with game mechanics. At specific points, I used a semi-structured interview protocol to encourage participants to reflect on their experiences, their awareness of the historical context, the characters they had encountered and inhabited, and the content of the game level. For example, after playing as the character of Freddy, I began by asking general questions (modeled on the protocol used in Diamond, 2012) such as: "Can you describe Freddy's situation, or what he was dealing with?" and "What were his reasons for being in the war? How do you know?" I then moved to more specific questions related to historical empathy (modeled on Endacott, 2010) including: "What can you tell me about Freddy's beliefs, values, and what was important to him?" "Do you think everybody believed these things at the time, or were there people that may have had different perspectives?" "How might Freddy's perspective have influenced his decisions in the game's story?" At the end of the game play session, I asked participants general questions about their experience and what they learned from playing the game.

The post-test included the same questions as the pre-test, with the addition of an open-ended question asking participants to reflect on what (if any) historical content and/or characters in the game made an impression on them. I compared post- and pre-test responses to see if any shifts occurred in content knowledge, historical contextualization, and/or historical empathy.

Data Analysis

My analysis was guided by a constant comparative method (Corbin & Strauss, 2008) in which I systematically identified and coded incidents, compared them for similarities and differences, and aggregated conceptually similar incidents together. Similar incidents were then labeled using higher-level descriptive themes. Approaching the data in this way allowed me to identify the unique properties and dimensions of each theme to distinguish them from each other. Importantly, this process also incorporated theoretical comparisons. Drawing from existing literature on historical empathy, I used informed induction to guide my initial coding process, facilitating a focus that extended beyond mere description to the level of abstraction (Corbin & Strauss, 2008).

Established practices in discourse analysis guided my process for segmenting data. Individual sentences or phrases spoken by participants during game play, as often happens in conversation and discussion, were often part of a larger chain of thoughts and statements. As participants spoke, shifts frequently occurred between the pair (including instances in which one might finish the other's sentence, add to it, or correct it) and between participant and researcher before participants stopped speaking and/or returned to game play. This type of discourse, involving inherently contextualized units of language production, has been described as utterances (Schiffrin, 1994). Statements, or adjacent chains of statements relating to an event, idea, prompt, or game play event, were considered utterances for the purposes of this study, and used as the unit of analysis.

I began by reviewing all of the video recordings carefully to get a sense of the data, taking some initial notes about what it showed. I then began my initial round of coding by identifying historical discourse in the think-aloud statements and semi-structured interviews. Historical discourse included statements relating to the historical content of the game; statements relating to history in a general sense; statements relating to the game's historical characters; statements relating to how it might have felt, or what it would have been like, to be one of the characters or to live during the time period in which the game is set; and statements relating to how technology, communication, etc. were different during the game's historical time period than they are today.

I continued this process by identifying game discourse, which was separate and distinct from historical discourse. Game discourse included statements relating to the game (mechanics, genre, difficulty, etc.) that were not directly related to its specific historical content or characters but could potentially reflect the players' level of engagement with the game. I then transcribed all data identified in the mutually exclusive categories of historical discourse and game discourse. Utterances identified as historical discourse and as non-historical, game-related discourse were pulled out and coded as such.

I had previously identified the following game components in the game *Valiant Hearts*: Action/Adventure, Puzzle, Cut Scene, Historical Fact, Diary Entry, and Artifact. Some of these elements are relatively specific to this particular game; others are more common and generally recognized components found in videogames:

- *Action/Adventure* entails taking action within the game; for example, hiding while German patrol passes by, or running across a battlefield trying to avoid enemy fire.
- *Puzzles* often involve a single correct answer or a set of steps that must be completed in the correct order (Tekinbas & Zimmerman, 2003); for example, turning the nozzles on a variety of underground pipes in order to disable a gas leak.
- A *Cut Scene* is an animated sequence that moves the plot forward and helps to explain the characters' backgrounds, motivations, and inner thoughts (Tekinbas & Zimmerman, 2003).
- *Historical Facts* are unlocked during game play in *Valiant Hearts*; each includes an archival photograph and related historical facts; for example, a photograph of a soldier wearing a mask, and a text description of the use of the first chlorine gas attack in 1915.
- *Diary Entries* contain a short written diary entry from one of the game's main characters, often related to their feelings and motivations—such as an entry from Anna expressing her desire to help as many of the wounded as possible.

- *Artifacts* are collectible historical items hidden throughout the game environment. Once collected, the game interface displays an image of the Artifact as well as a description; for example, a deck of cards and an explanation that soldiers played games to alleviate boredom in the trenches.

I performed a content analysis to determine which game components players had encountered when (or immediately prior to) engaging in historical or game discourse. I also flagged utterances as either prompted or unprompted: I coded statements that were elicited by my questions as prompted; spontaneous, unsolicited statements that participants made on their own while playing the game were coded as unprompted.

I continued to use an informed inductive process to code utterances in the data. I carefully reviewed the transcripts and video, developing categories, and revised them through an iterative process in order to reduce overlap and redundancy, in keeping with a constant comparative method. My resulting final themes thus included a combination of emergent categories and categories rooted in existing theoretical frameworks for historical empathy.

Building upon my initial coding criteria, historical contextualization also included utterances relating to contextual details (such as technology, communication, transportation, etc.) that tend to shape historical events, actions, and attitudes. Perspective taking included statements that indicated participants were thinking about what a character's experiences may have been like, what their motives might have been, and an awareness of the "otherness" of that historical character (in other words, a sense that the historical character was differentiated from the player). Affective connection incorporated utterances that reflected participants' recognition of the emotional states of game characters (an essential step in identifying with their feelings and the situations they faced), as well as evidence that the participants cared about the game's historical characters and what became of them. Consistent with previous research, codes for the dimensions of historical empathy were not mutually exclusive.

To establish reliability, I conducted an inter-rater agreement check. After reviewing my coding manual and discussing the coding scheme with an independent rater, I randomly selected 20% of the transcribed utterances. After the rater and I independently coded this selection, I calculated reliability using two indices: the kappa coefficient and percent agreement. The average kappa coefficient for our inter-rater reliability check was .9287, and the overall percent agreement was 99.28%. These statistics indicated that overall agreement was quite high. All disagreements were negotiated and resolved.

RESULTS

Data captured in the background survey reflected recent history/social studies grades that ranged from Julian's A to Deanna's B-. On a scale of 1 to 4, the majority of participants reported that they "know some things about WWI" (3 on the Likert scale). In terms of preferences for history on a scale of 1 to 4, the majority reported "I like social studies/history" (a 3 on the Likert scale). Videogame experience was rated on a scale of 1 to 4. The majority of participants chose 3 on the scale ="I play videogames often (once a week or so)" except for Beverly, who reported that she has "only played videogames a few times" (a 2 on the scale). The results of the background survey are summarized in Figure 2.

The open-ended and short answer questions on the pre- and post-tests were intended to gauge participants' sense of historical empathy and their awareness of the differing perspectives existing during a given time period. I had planned to analyze these responses interpretively, using existing rubrics for historical empathy as a guide. Given the brevity of these responses, however, they provided limited insight into participants' sense of historical empathy. This data was nonetheless retained as a potential source of triangulation to support the other data collected in this study.

Figure 2. Participants' Self-Reported Knowledge, Preferences, and Experience

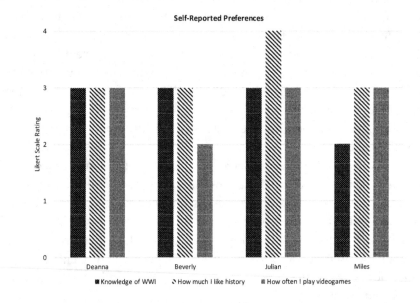

Research Question 1: In What Ways Does Historical Empathy Manifest Through Play of a Videogame?

Due to its highly contextual and multifaceted nature, attempts to quantify or measure the non-linear and evolving process of negotiating historical empathy can be problematic (Endacott & Brooks, 2018). Indeed, it is a complex construct that has been difficult for researchers to characterize even in structured educational settings. Such studies (such as Endacott, 2014) tend to follow a defined instructional model to scaffold students through the process of negotiating historical empathy. Therefore, examining how it may manifest through videogame play—in the context of this study, as a relatively isolated activity without instruction—presented some unique challenges.

Endacott (2014) has posited that "historical empathy is always an iterative process of building and connecting knowledge" (p. 6). The spirit of this argument, combined with an acknowledgement of the affordances and constraints of videogames, informed the broader way in which I operationalized the dimensions of historical empathy in this study. As mentioned previously, my initial coding criteria was rooted in existing theoretical and empirical literature. Taking into account the content of the game and the idea that historical empathy involves connecting knowledge led to some slight adjustments, I expanded the criteria for historical contextualization to include utterances that address relevant contextual details (such as technology, communication, transportation, etc.) that tend to shape historical events, actions, and attitudes. For perspective taking, I included statements that indicated participants were thinking about what a character's experiences may have been like, what their motives might have been, and an awareness of the "otherness" of that historical character (in other words, a sense that the historical character was differentiated from the player). I also expanded the criteria for affective connection to incorporate utterances that reflected participants' recognition of the emotional states of game characters (an essential step in identifying with their feelings and the situations they faced), as well as evidence that the participants cared about the game's historical characters and what became of them. Consistent with previous research, codes for the dimensions of historical empathy were not mutually exclusive. Indeed, in keeping with Endacott & Brooks' (2013) Venn diagram, I expected to see overlaps between the three dimensions of historical empathy.

In addition to the initial codes described above, I also identified several emergent themes and sub-themes from the data. Since a major goal of this study was to explore what historical empathy looks like in videogame play, it was important to consider patterns that appeared to shape participants' experience of playing *Valiant Hearts*. Within the category of historical discourse, the emergent themes I identified included stereotypes (with sub-themes for applying and recognizing stereotypes), knowledge application (with sub-themes for accurate and inaccurate/lacking), and engagement with historical content. Table 2 lists and describes each theme.

Of the historical discourse themes I identified, historical contextualization, perspective taking, accurate knowledge application, and engagement with historical content appeared most frequently. Table 3 summarizes number of times each code appeared, as well as the way each was distributed across the three prompting categories.

Table 2. Description of Emergent Historical Discourse Themes

Theme	Description
Stereotypes	Utterances relating to stereotypes
Applying stereotypes	Applying stereotypes to individuals or groups represented in the game; oversimplifying historical characters or groups
Recognizing stereotypes	Noticing/identifying stereotypes within the game
Knowledge application	Evidence of participants' content knowledge
Accurate	Applying relatively accurate content knowledge
Inaccurate or lacking	Applying inaccurate content knowledge, or indicating a lack of content knowledge
Engagement with historical content	Indicating a sense of interest in, or curiosity about, the historical content of the game

Table 3. Number of Times Each Historical Discourse Theme Appeared (by Prompting Category)

Themes	Unprompted	Prompted During Game	Prompted in Post-Game Interview
Historical empathy			
Historical contextualization	29	48	18
Perspective taking	10	23	51
Affective connection	18	5	16
Stereotypes			
Applying	8	1	0
Recognizing	1	3	0
Knowledge application			
Accurate	35	35	17
Inaccurate/lacking	2	11	6
Engagement with historical content	40	21	14

Some relevant utterances may help to illustrate these historical discourse themes. An example of applying stereotypes occurred when the character of Emile—who was being held captive in a German camp when it was attacked—had to pull a German soldier from the rubble. Upon realizing that the game required her to rescue an enemy, Deanna's response was, "Okay, I'm supposed to help this demon person." Participants also recognized stereotypes while playing, as when Miles commented that many Germans in the game were depicted as "kinda evil," and Julian noticed that their frequent associations with drunkenness and alcohol were "almost stereotypical." Evidence of background knowledge being brought to bear on the game experience came about when participants applied relatively accurate content knowledge—for example, when Julian mentioned a relevant detail he had learned prior to playing: "One of the cool things about trenches that I learned, it was because of this war that the French and British put helmets into their uniforms, because there were so many head injuries in the trenches." In contrast, evidence of a participant's lack of background knowledge arose when Beverly asked, "Was this the time of The Holocaust, too?" indicating that she was confusing WWI with WWII. Finally, an example of engagement with historical content occurred when the topic of trench warfare appeared to arouse Julian's curiosity, sparking the question, "I just wonder what, for the guys who made it through most of the war, like what did their back structure look like? Because before the British and French put helmets into their uniforms, to not get head wounds you had to be crouching the entire time."

One trend that can be seen in this data is the role of prompting in relation to utterances coded for each dimension of historical empathy. Historical contextualization utterances tended to be prompted during the game, perspective taking utterances tended to be prompted in the post-game interview, and affective connection utterances generally arose unprompted during game play. Utterances relating to historical contextualization and affective connection were more likely than perspective taking to come up unprompted during game play.

An example of a prompted utterance, co-coded for all three dimensions of historical empathy, occurred in the post-game interview. After they had finished playing the game, I asked Julian and Miles to describe what it was like to live as a soldier in WWI based on what they experienced in the game:

Julian: Well I think there would be, in the beginning I think there would be a little bit of pride. Because, because like war was like a big thing to do, like to go fight in a war. But towards the end I think there would be, because it was dragging out so long, I think there would be nervousness, and...
Miles: Maybe even, like, some regret.

In this instance, Julian showed an awareness of the public sentiment surrounding the war, as well as recognition that those perspectives were not monolithic and may have shifted (Endacott, 2010). Both Julian and Miles also seemed mindful of the emotional impact the experience may have had on individual soldiers. This confluence of all three dimensions seems less likely to have been elicited during game play, or unprompted; asking the question appeared to encourage the players to reflect on the whole of their experience during the activity, and to consider the impact the war may have had on people living at the time.

Moving on to game discourse—which was mutually exclusive from historical discourse—I identified the emergent themes of engagement (with two different levels, high and low engagement, within that theme), and blending of player/character. These themes, in a general sense, reflect how engaged players were with the game and the nature of their relationship to the characters they inhabited during play. Table 4 summarizes each theme.

Of the game discourse themes, the most frequently-appearing were high engagement and blending of player/character. These themes tended to appear unprompted during game play. Table 5 shows the number of times each theme appeared, as well as the way each theme was distributed across the three prompting categories.

Table 4. Description of Emergent Game Discourse Themes

Theme	Description
Engagement	Evidence of the participants' level of engagement with the game, divided into mutually-exclusive sub-themes (high/low)
High	Indicating a sense of enjoyment, immersion, and/or interest in completing game objectives
Low	Indicating boredom, lack of enjoyment, and/or lack of interest in completing game objectives
Blending of player/character	Indicating that the player is "inhabiting" the character; a sense that player and character are one

Table 5. Number of Times Each Game Discourse Theme Appeared (by Prompting Category)

Game Discourse Themes	Unprompted	Prompted During Game	Prompted in Post-Game Interview
Blending of player/character	44	0	0
Engagement			
High	92	4	6
Low	5	0	2

To illustrate these game discourse themes briefly with some exemplars: Julian and Miles showed unprompted evidence of high engagement during the game when a new character, Anna, suddenly appeared driving a car. Visibly excited, Julian exclaimed, "What is that?? Oh!" while Miles shouted, "Oh! Car. DANG. Get hit by the car," before Julian chimed in with "Whoa!" Beverly, in contrast, indicated low engagement when I asked her whether she enjoyed playing *Valiant Hearts*. She answered, "I didn't like when we were under the bridge thing. I was like, it's getting boring!" An example of the blending of player/character occurred when Deanna, playing as the character of Emile, needed to obtain a bottle of wine from a French soldier. While doing so, she spoke to the non-player character in the first person (as if she were Emile), asking: "Okay sir, I'd like your wine?" She then thanked him afterwards: "Okay. Thank you! Now, goodbye."

In summary, the themes I identified under the main category of historical discourse included the existing themes rooted in Endacott and Brooks' (2013) framework as well as several emergent themes. Of these, historical contextualization, perspective taking, accurate knowledge application, and engagement with historical content appeared most frequently. I also noted patterns with respect to the role of prompting for historical discourse themes. Additionally, I identified game discourse themes, which mainly arose unprompted during game play. High engagement and blending of player/character appeared much more frequently than low engagement.

Research Question 2: Do Some Components of the Game Appear to Elicit Evidence of Historical Empathy More Frequently Than Others?

Some components of the game did appear to promote historical empathy more than others. Overall, the largest number of codes (72) for historical empathy were applied during, or shortly following, encounters with historical facts. Encounters with artifacts accounted for 33 of historical empathy codes during game play, cut scenes for 21, action scenes for 16, and puzzles for a mere 2.

Codes for historical contextualization were most often applied in relation to historical facts (46) or artifacts (21). Codes for perspective taking occurred most frequently in connection with historical facts (21) or artifacts (9). Notably, perspective-taking codes were more likely to be associated with cut scenes (7) compared to historical contextualization codes (4). Codes for affective connection tended to be associated with cut scenes (10), action scenes (7), or historical facts (5).

In sum, several findings helped to illuminate my second research question: Historical facts tended to be effective for historical empathy in a general sense, while puzzles and diary entries were not particularly effective at all. Through the lens of Endacott & Brooks' (2013) framework, several components of the game stood out in eliciting the different dimensions of historical empathy. Historical facts and artifacts tended to be associated with evidence of historical contextualization and perspective taking, and cut scenes and action scenes tended to be associated with affective connection.

DISCUSSION

Endacott and Brooks' (2013) cognitive-affective model proved to be a helpful lens for analyzing the ways historical empathy can manifest through videogame play. I found that evidence of historical contextualization and perspective taking occurred more often than affective connection. Additionally, I noted differences with respect to prompted vs. unprompted utterances. Most of the utterances coded as historical contextualization were prompted during the game, most of the perspective taking utterances were prompted in the post-game interview, and most of those coded as affective connection arose unprompted during game play. Utterances relating to historical contextualization and affective connection were more likely than perspective taking to arise unprompted during game play. Game discourse themes tended to emerge unprompted during game play (which was not surprising, since engagement tends to align with an activity). These findings have implications for research. Some dimensions of historical empathy may be elicited more directly by videogames; in fact, affective connection seemed to resist prompting. On the other hand, perspective taking—which was less likely to manifest spontaneously—may need to be encouraged and explored through discussion during or after the learning activity.

Playing the game from more than one perspective provided opportunities for participants to consider the motivations and backgrounds of different characters. At the same time, the participants in this study recognized several problematic stereotypes and oversimplifications in *Valiant Hearts*, such as the villainous, drunken caricatures of some German soldiers. However, these need not disqualify a videogame from being a valuable learning activity. Videogames, like most media, present players with certain models of the world; educators can help students learn to examine and critique those models (Bogost, 2008). Caricatures, oversimplifications, and stereotypes can be used as opportunities to discuss historical interpretation, and bias. For Julian and Miles in particular, oversimplifications tended to spark conversations about the importance of multiperspectivity in history education.

Another consideration illuminated by this study is that, to foster historical empathy through videogame play, it helps if players are engaged with the game itself. Players need to be comfortable with a game's mechanics, so that it provides an appropriate balance of challenge and fun (Squire, 2011). The first participant pair, Deanna and

Beverly, took much longer to complete game objectives, discovered fewer artifacts, and did not progress as far in the game as Julian and Miles. For example, Deanna and Beverly took approximately 11 minutes to successfully complete Emile's first battle sequence, while Julian and Miles took less than 2 minutes to complete the same sequence. The first participant pair also appeared to be less engaged in the activity in general (based on researcher observation and as indicated by the application of game engagement codes). It seems likely that these differences were related to varying levels of experience—some of which were captured by the self-reported data in the background survey, with more variation possible in terms participants' preferred videogame genres and platforms. Casual mobile games, for example (like *Candy Crush*) may not prepare players for a side-scrolling adventure as well as other types of games.

These findings relating to engagement have practical implications: Players who are uncomfortable or unfamiliar with videogames in general, or specifically with certain genres or platforms of games, may tend to focus on getting through the game rather than its historical content. In other words, if players struggle with the mechanics of a game, they are likely to have lower levels of engagement with both the game itself and with its educational content. Therefore, educators would be well advised to consider this when implementing a videogame as a learning activity— perhaps by surveying students about their game experience and preferences, and also by providing initial opportunities for students to become comfortable with a game's mechanics to mitigate the impact of any differences.

In terms of game components, cut scenes and action scenes appeared to be more effective in promoting affective connection within the context of this study. Unprompted evidence of affective connection arose following an action sequence in which Walt, the mercy dog who assists the main characters in the game, becomes entangled in barbed wire and starts yelping:

Julian: What?? What's wrong??
Miles: Oh shoot!
Julian: Oooohhhh… *(tapping furiously at keys trying to rescue the dog)*
Game fades out to cut scene
Julian: Well…but what happened to the dog??

Both players became visible and audibly concerned at this point in the game, and continued to focus on the question of Walt's fate (until, thankfully, he was rescued in a later sequence). Although Walt is not a human character, participants' utterances, behavior, and facial expressions showed clear evidence that they cared about him, how he was treated, and what became of him (Schrier et al., 2010). Other instances of affective connection that emerged during game play suggested that players might be imagining what it felt like to experience particular historical situations, and making connections with similar experiences they may have had themselves (see Boltz, 2017).

Historical facts and artifacts, on the other hand, tended to elicit evidence of historical contextualization and perspective taking. For example, after Julian and Miles read a historical fact about the 10 billion letters and postcards exchanged during the war, I asked the participants to consider how the experience of a soldier communicating with family and friends might have been different during that time period:

Julian: What would happen is like, you could like, send a letter, but it doesn't get to your family for the next week.
Miles: Yeah it could take longer.
Julian: And by then you could actually be…be dead. And they think you're still alive.
Miles: Yeah.
Researcher: And what about from your perspective if you're waiting on letters from home?
Julian: It would be kind of nerve-wracking because you don't really know what's going on there. So for all you know they've been…taken.
Miles: Yeah it would be seeing, like, hearing from them in the past. Rather than emails, which are like, pretty instant.

In this exchange, Miles and Julian began by engaging in historical contextualization, noting the constraints of the primary means of communication available at the time, and how this would have shaped the experiences of soldiers and their loved ones—an example that typifies historical contextualization as described by Lévesque: "contextualized, historical imagination grounded in evidence" (2008, p.149). That exchange led into perspective-taking as the participants reflected on what this experience might have been like for people waiting for letters, as they attempted to put themselves in that position. Their statements suggested that the participants were considering the perspectives of people in the past as different from their own, but also valid and worthy of consideration. They also indicated an awareness of the social and familiar networks of which historical characters would have been a part, their attitudes and positions (including how these would have been strained by war and the slower pace of communication), and the ways these factors could influence what people may have thought about their situation. For example, Miles' interesting statement that it would have been like "hearing from them in the past" reflects a contrast to the near instantaneous methods of communication often available today. The exchange also briefly touched on affective connection when Julian explained how "nerve-wracking" it would have felt, emotionally, not knowing whether loved ones were still alive.

This preliminary evidence lends support to the argument made by Kapell & Elliott (2013) that videogames which incorporate "historical artifacts, characters, settings, or events, either as a mode of storytelling or as a function of play, create a unique opportunity to affect historical understanding and improve its conventional interpretation" (p. 34). Indeed, it was interesting that historical facts were so effective in promoting historical contextualization and perspective taking, while puzzles and diary entries were not. To extend conclusions made by Diamond in his 2012 work with *Mission US,* it may be that providing players with background knowledge—in the case of *Valiant Hearts*, even in the form of in-game components—better prepares them to engage in particular dimensions of historical empathy. Taken as a whole, these findings may be instructive for those interested in selecting or designing videogames for historical empathy; it may be that each dimension of historical empathy is best promoted by a particular combination of game components.

LIMITATIONS

This was an exploratory study designed to illuminate a complex construct; as such, there were several important limitations. A small sample size was necessary to maintain feasibility in light of the large amount of data to be collected and analyzed. Findings therefore have limited generalizability due to the small number and limited diversity of the study's participants, since culture, country of origin, age, and other factors are likely to influence the ways in which players may engage in historical empathy. Additionally, although it shares common elements and features with other videogames, *Valiant Hearts* is just one example of a game about history—one that has its own unique qualities and structure. Therefore, the results of this study are not necessarily generalizable to all videogames with historical content.

Another limitation relates to technical issues that occurred during the first game play session. The screen capture software used in Deanna and Beverly's session slowed down the pace and responsiveness of the game. These participants seemed to be focused on when the activity would end, asking several times how much time was remaining, and demonstrated lower levels of engagement overall. Although there is insufficient evidence to confirm whether the underlying reasons were related to game play experience, the technical issues, or other factors, the result was that Julian and Miles progressed much further into the story than the other participants; being exposed to more content provided more opportunities to engage in discourse.

CONCLUSION

In their book *Playing with the Past*, Kapell & Elliot (2013) ask, "Do different kinds of games engage with history in different ways?" (p. 4). The results of this qualitative study put forward modest answers to that question. Certain game components appear to be more effective in promoting particular dimensions of historical empathy; players tend to be more likely to engage in historical discourse when they are engaged with the game itself; and some aspects of historical empathy tend to arise spontaneously while others may require prompting. Educators may therefore wish to select games that feature the most effective game components, to monitor how engaged students are with the game, and to provide opportunities for discussion in order to address all aspects of historical empathy. Similarly, developers may wish to design games that combine the most effective types of game components and, when possible, to provide players with in-game opportunities for reflection.

This study's findings also raise interesting questions about intersections between the blending of player/character and affective connection themes. Given that the affective connection dimension of historical empathy reflects a shifting focus between the self and the historical figure (Endacott & Brooks, 2013), and since emerging research suggests that highly-engaged players who identify with playable characters come may develop emotional connections to those characters (Li, Liau, & Khoo, 2013), might there be a "sweet spot" at which players form a connection with the videogame character they're inhabiting both in terms of engagement and also in a historical sense? Several examples, including my observation of Julian and Miles during the poisonous gas scene, seem to point to such an intersection as a potentially powerful conduit for developing historical empathy through videogame play. With a more robust data set, future studies might engage in a more in-depth analysis of historical empathy that incorporates a theoretical framework for player–avatar identification (Li, Liau, & Khoo, 2013).

In a more general sense, researchers could extend the utility of this study by determining whether these findings can be replicated with a larger and more diverse sample. Additionally, it would be helpful to collect more information about players' experience and preferences for videogame genres and platforms to determine how these prepare players to engage with game content. Ideally, future studies would integrate videogames into the investigative phase of an instructional model to more accurately reflect a pedagogical implementation. A game like *Valiant Hearts* could be used to supplement primary and secondary source activities, allowing learners "to explore the nuances of historical context in depth as well as the thoughts and feelings" of characters (Endacott & Brooks, 2013, p. 48). This approach would help researchers to obtain more qualitative data—perhaps through writing activities, debates, or other assignments—so that a deeper analysis of confounding elements could be conducted. Ensuring that learners are sufficiently introduced to the historical period before playing the game should also provide a stronger foundation for them to engage in evidence-based empathic engagement.

REFERENCES

Ashby, R., & Lee, P. (1987). Children's Concepts of Empathy and Understanding in History. In *The History Curriculum for Teachers* (pp. 62–88). London: Falmer Press.

Barton, K. C., & Levstik, L. S. (2004). *Teaching history for the common good*. Mahwah, NJ: Lawrence Erlbaum Associates.

Bogost, I. (2008). The Rhetoric of Video Games. In K. Salen (Ed.), *The Ecology of Games: Connecting Youth, Games, and Learning* (pp. 117–140). Cambridge, MA: The MIT Press. doi:10.1162/dmal.9780262693646.117

Boltz, L. O. (2017). "Like Hearing From Them in the Past": The Cognitive-Affective Model of Historical Empathy in Videogame Play. *International Journal of Gaming and Computer-Mediated Simulations*, *9*(4), 1–18. doi:10.4018/IJGCMS.2017100101

Brooks, S. (2009). Historical empathy in the social studies classroom: A review of the literature. *Journal of Social Studies Research*, *33*, 213–234.

Brooks, S. (2011). Historical Empathy as Perspective Recognition and Care in One Secondary Social Studies Classroom. *Theory and Research in Social Education*, *39*(2), 166–202. doi:10.1080/00933104.2011.10473452

Charsky, D., & Mims, C. (2008). Integrating commercial off-the-shelf video games into school curriculums. *TechTrends*, *52*(5), 38–44. doi:10.100711528-008-0195-0

Corbin, J. M., & Strauss, A. L. (2008). *Basics of qualitative research: Techniques and procedures for developing grounded theory* (3rd ed.). Los Angeles, CA: Sage Publications, Inc. doi:10.4135/9781452230153

Creswell, J. W. (2008). *Educational research: Planning, conducting, and evaluating quantitative and qualitative research*. Upper Saddle River, NJ: Pearson/Merrill Prentice Hall.

Diamond, J. (2012). *"You Weren't Doing What You Would Actually Do, You Were Doing What People Wanted You to Do": A Study of Historical Empathy in a Digital History Game* (Doctoral dissertation). Retrieved from Dissertation Abstracts International. (Order No. AAI3511399)

Endacott, J., & Brooks, S. (2013). An Updated Theoretical and Practical Model for Promoting Historical Empathy. *Social Studies Research & Practice*, *8*, 41–58.

Endacott, J. L. (2010). Reconsidering Affective Engagement in Historical Empathy. *Theory and Research in Social Education*, *38*(1), 6–47. doi:10.1080/00933104.20 10.10473415

Endacott, J. L. (2014). Negotiating the Process of Historical Empathy. *Theory and Research in Social Education*, *42*(1), 4–34. doi:10.1080/00933104.2013.826158

Endacott, J. L., & Brooks, S. (2018). Historical Empathy: Perspectives and Responding to the Past. The Wiley International Handbook of History Teaching and Learning, 203.

Jensen, J. (2008). Developing historical empathy through debate: An action research study. *Social Studies Research & Practice*, *3*, 55–66.

Kapell, M., & Elliott, A. B. R. (2013). *Playing with the past: Digital games and the simulation of history*. New York: Bloomsbury.

Lee, P. J., & Ashby, R. (2001). Empathy, perspective taking, and rational understanding. In O. L. Davis Jr, S. Foster, & E. Yeager (Eds.), *Historical Empathy and Perspective Taking in the Social Studies* (pp. 21–50). Boulder, CO: Rowman and Littlefield.

Lévesque, S. (2008). *Thinking Historically: Educating Students for the Twenty-first Century*. Toronto: University of Toronto Press.

Levstik, L. S., & Barton, K. C. (2011). *Doing history: Investigating with children in elementary and middle school*. New York: Routledge.

Li, D., Liau, A., & Khoo, A. (2013). Player-avatar identification in video gaming: Concept and measurement. *Computers in Human Behavior*, *29*(1), 257–263. doi:10.1016/j.chb.2012.09.002

López, J. M., & Cáceres, M. J. (2010). Virtual games in social science education. *Computers & Education*, *55*(3), 1336–1345. doi:10.1016/j.compedu.2010.05.028

Russell, W. B. (2011). *Contemporary Social Studies: An Essential Reader*. Charlotte, NC: Information Age Pub.

Schiffrin, D. (1994). *Approaches to discourse*. Oxford, UK: B. Blackwell.

Schrier, K., Diamond, J., & Langendoen, D. (2010). Using mission US: For crown or colony? To develop historical empathy and nurture ethical thinking. In *Ethics and Game Design: Teaching Values through Play* (pp. 255–273). Hershey, PA: Information Science Reference. doi:10.4018/978-1-61520-845-6.ch016

Squire, K. (2006). From content to context: Videogames as designed experience. *Educational Researcher, 35*(8), 19–29. doi:10.3102/0013189X035008019

Squire, K. (2011). *Video games and learning: teaching and participatory culture in the digital age.* New York: Teachers College Press.

Tekinbas, K. S., & Zimmerman, E. (2003). *Rules of Play: game design fundamentals.* Cambridge, MA: MIT Press.

Thirteen. (2010). *Mission US: For Crown or Colony?* [Videogame]. New York: WNET Thirteen.

Ubisoft. (2014). *Valiant Hearts: The Great War* [Videogame]. Montpellier: Ubisoft Group.

Ward, G. C., & Burns, K. (1994). *Baseball: An illustrated history.* New York: A.A. Knopf.

Wineburg, S. S. (1991). Historical problem solving: A study of the cognitive processes used in the evaluation of documentary and pictorial evidence. *Journal of Educational Psychology, 83*(1), 73–87. doi:10.1037/0022-0663.83.1.73

Wineburg, S. S. (2001). *Historical thinking and other unnatural acts: Charting the future of teaching the past* (6th ed.). Philadelphia: Temple University Press.

Yeager, E. A., Foster, S. J., Maley, S. D., Anderson, T., & Morris, J. W. III. (1998). Why people in the past acted as they did: An exploratory study in historical empathy. *The International Journal of Social Education, 13*(1), 8–24.

Zimet, J. (2012). *Mission Centenaire 14-18 Website.* Retrieved from http://centenaire. org/en

Chapter 9
Using Notions of "Play" Over the Life Course to Inform Game Design for Older Populations

Julie A. Brown
Ohio University, USA

Bob De Schutter
Miami University, USA

ABSTRACT

Play is a lifelong construct that is individually defined and is influenced by multiple variables that affect how play is interpreted and experienced in old age. This chapter highlights the significance of using a life course perspective to explore how play is shaped and reflected through digital gameplay and preferences as a game player ages. Using grounded theory methodology, 51 participants (age 43–77) were interviewed individually. The resulting transcripts were coded to identify emergent themes. The findings demonstrate 1) how play changes throughout the lifespan, 2) how play preferences established in childhood influence digital gameplay for aging adults, and 3) how aging adult gamers aspire to continue gaming as they grow older. Collectively, these themes provide insight into the aspects that need to be taken into account when designing games for aging gamer populations.

DOI: 10.4018/978-1-5225-7461-3.ch009

INTRODUCTION

As evidenced by multiple market reports, digital gaming among older populations has increased in popularity over the past decade (Bosmans & Maskell, 2012; ESA, 2017). Correspondingly, academic research on the topic of games and aging has slowly increased as well. However, research that has analyzed older players of digital games has mainly focused on how older adults are playing games at the time during which the study was held (e.g., De Schutter, 2011; Nap, de Kort, & IJsselsteijn, 2009; Pearce, 2008; Skalsky Brown, 2014). Nonetheless, it has been well established within both gerontology (Elder, 1994) and developmental psychology (Baltes, 1987) that the analysis of later stages of human life should be evaluated through the lens of the entire life course, as opposed to only an individual's current status. This finding has been also replicated in media studies, as media researchers have found lifespan approaches to be valuable for the study of various media, including television (van der Goot, Beentjes, & van Selm, 2006) and, to a lesser extent, digital games (e.g., De Schutter & Malliet, 2014).

The authors of this current study, therefore, argue that the pre-existing literature on the topic of actively playing older adults does not provide complete insight into the characteristics and distinctions among older age cohorts of gamers. Current recommendations for the design of games for older adults do not fully capture the nuances that are unique to older generations and have often been built on the analysis of contemporary context and the issues that older adults face when trying to play games (Gamberini et al., 2006; IJsselsteijn, Nap, de Kort, & Poels, 2007; McLaughlin, Gandy, Allaire, & Whitlock, 2012). Therefore, to capture a more holistic perspective, it is imperative to re-evaluate such recommendations through a lens that incorporates play through the older adults' entire lifespan.

This study aims to provide a broader picture by exploring individual play histories of aging gamers from a life course perspective. As such, this perspective emphasizes the need to examine the construction and maintenance of individual gaming preferences that influence current gameplay. Furthermore, because play extends into old age and contributes to quality of life (Skalsky Brown, 2014), it is critical to identify and assess variables that may influence lifelong gamers as they age. This study approaches this need by drawing attention to the significance of gaming preferences and their association to age-related factors that may either promote or hinder game playing as a gamer ages. Based on these findings, a number of design considerations for game designers who aim to develop games for older adults are provided.

RELATED LITERATURE

The research on game design for older adults dates back to Weisman (1983). This study relied on observations of the frail elderly, and recommended adaptable difficult levels, clear auditory feedback and large visual elements. While digital games have since changed dramatically, these recommendations would be repeated numerous times over the years.

More than 20 years later, Gamberini et al. (2006) published the findings of the ELDERGAMES project, which included a list of usability criteria for elderly technology users. While their framework had a broader scope than just digital games, many of its items have implications for game design, as the study's authors mention accommodations on the visual, auditory, tactile and cognitive level. A similar analysis that has a strong focus on digital games is provided by IJsselsteijn et al.'s study (2007). This much-cited study provides an overview of how age-related decline influences gameplay for older adults, and provides its own set of recommendations based on this analysis. More specifically, the authors emphasize the importance of adjustable interfaces (i.e., the font sizes, color contrasts, etc.), simplicity in interface design (i.e., that it does not require too much cognitive load or working memory), appropriate use of sound (e.g., lower frequencies), and the use of multiple communication channels (e.g., auditory, haptic and visual feedback simultaneously). Furthermore, the authors also offer a number of design recommendations that are not related to old age, but rather the specific age cohort that they were studying. In particular, they mention how games should allow older adults to experience success in order to alleviate anxieties caused by not having computer access during their formative years, and how games should look to provide content for older adults that is genuinely interesting to them. With regards to the latter, relaxation and leisure games are recommended, as well as games that offer cognitive and physical benefits.

By differentiating between usability/accessibility concerns and content preferences/health benefits, IJsselsteijn et al. (2007) provided a blueprint for papers on the design of digital games for older adults for years to come. An interesting take on this blueprint can be found in the work of McLaughlin et al. (2012). Their model for Motivated Choice View of Older Adult Gameplay relied on a cost-benefit analysis. First, the authors established that the design, the materials, their usability and any provided training is under control of the designer. Next, they argued how these are subsequently translated by older players into the benefits (e.g., fun, social interaction, achievement, etc.) and the costs (e.g., lack of control, initial frustration, time, money, etc.) of playing a game. For example, the strong social benefits of a game such as Wii Bowling arguably outweighed the relatively small costs of playing the game, which correspondingly explained the success of the game in independent and assisted living residences.

Another variation of the usability/accessibility of a game versus its content can be found in the work of Marston (2013). This study relied on both the pre-existing academic literature above, as well as a "mapping" process. This method resulted in a number of design recommendations that were labelled as either "interaction" (i.e., elements that are similar to the usability/accessibility considerations above, such as simplicity, intuitiveness, choice, clear feedback, etc.) or "content" (e.g., enable technical thinking, provide a purposes, enable mini-games, allow user-generated content, etc.).

Brown (2016) also provided insight into aging gamers by conducting a grounded theory study that assessed both older and middle-aged gamer characteristics. She identified various aspects that differ from the two age cohorts, such as digital game preferences, platforms used, and anticipated future play as they continue to age. Overall, she found that the middle-aged participants, who are a part of the next generation of older adult players, are more likely to play action-based games that are reminiscent of the digital games that they have been playing for years (and in some cases, decades). Yet, they expressed concern that game developers and designers are unaware of how to meet their age-related needs that directly influence their gameplay, e.g., declining visual acuity and reaction time, and how such forms of play are significant to their quality of life. De Schutter and Vanden Abeele (2015) and De Schutter (2017) reflected similar findings by emphasizing the need for designers to recognize the significance of gameplay in older age and to understand that older adulthood is a time of positive growth, not just decline, as is often perceived.

Finally, a number of models for game design aimed at older adults have recently been developed that exhibit integration of established, industry-based game design methods into prior academic models. First, Gerling et al.'s structural model (2012) relied on the work of Adams (2009) and Fullerton (2008) to provide recommendations at three distinct levels: the players and resources, the game's user interface, and the game's core mechanics. While their recommendations expand upon usability and accessibility criteria that are similar to the earlier literature mentioned above, their integration bridges the gap between the design vocabulary of industry-based game designers and the academic design community. Second, De Schutter et al. (2014) integrated the work of industry designers Hunicke, LeBlanc & Zubek (2001) and Salen and Zimmerman (2003) with the pre-existing literature. Their "Gerontoludic Design Framework" specifically distinguished between "geronto-aesthetics" (i.e., self-cultivation, connectedness, contribution, contemporaneity, nostalgia, and compensation) and "geronto-mechanics" (i.e., the usability and accessibility concerns that were mentioned earlier, as well as specific mechanics that are interesting for older adults).

While the literature on the design of games for older adults has had many different sources methodologically speaking (e.g., literature reviews, experiments, surveys and interviews), it has been largely the result of studying the present context of its participants. With some exceptions, the design literature typically did not review the past of older adults as an entry point towards game design. This study is specifically aimed to provide design guidelines by means of a life course perspective.

METHODS

This study employed grounded theory methodology as a means to identify themes that would lay the groundwork for theory development (Charmaz, 2006; Corbin & Strauss, 1990; Glaser & Strauss, 1967). This particular methodology is typically used in areas of inquiry that are in early stages of development and lack a theoretical framework, such as the case here. In addition, a life course perspective was used, as it takes into account the life span in full context (Watkins, 1999) and allows an understanding of how age-graded trajectories are influenced by life experiences (Elder, 1985, 1994). Thus, this perspective captures how self-perceived notions of play is shaped over time and plays a role in the integration of digital gaming within an individual's life. To assess the relationship between individual game engagement over time and its implication to game design, three questions were posed:

1.   How is play expressed and shaped over the course of a life?
2.   How are contemporary forms of play a function of past play?
3.   How might a life course perspective of play inform game design?

Initially, this study focused on persons age 60 and above. As the study developed, it was noted that gameplay trends among the younger participants within the sample differed from the older participants. To further explore these differences the age requirement was lowered (to include ages 40 to 59), thus resulting in two age cohorts – Older Gamers and Middle-Aged Gamers. (These groups are similar to the age groups that Marston (2013) refers to as second and third-age adults.) Persons within the younger aged group are not identified as "older adults", but represent, potentially, the next generation of "older gamers". As such, it was recognized that their responses could serve as a means to inform game design considerations for when they are in older adulthood.

Inclusion Criteria and Recruitment

To take part in this study, a participant had to be age 40 or above, report a health status of "fair" or better, and play digital games for at least one hour a week on average. Participants were identified via referral sampling (snowball sampling) and by an advertisement that was placed within local communities centers. Once a candidate was screened, a mutually agreed upon and private location for the interview was identified (e.g. a reserved room at a public library or university office).

This resulted in a total of 51 persons participating in the study, ranging from age 43 to age 77 (31 females, 20 males), with interviews ranging from 30 minutes in length to three hours. The older gamers ranged from age 60 to age 77 (19 females, 11 males) and averaged 11.15 hours of digital gameplay per week. The middle-aged gamers ranged from age 43 to age 59 (12 females, 9 males) and averaged 11.76 hours of digital gameplay per week. Only four of the participants identified themselves as being a member of an ethnic minority and all of the participants live in rural or suburban areas within Virginia, Kentucky, or Ohio. The majority of the participants reported that they attended college and many of these persons were either employed or are currently employed at one of the regional universities.

Interview Guide

A semi-structured interview guide was constructed for this study as a means to capture an overview of how individual play is expressed on a lifespan continuum within a life course context – from childhood to current day – and the integration of digital games as a form of play. The interview guide began with questions to establish a timeline of events such as, graduation(s), marriage, birth of children, jobs, and other points in time deemed as noteworthy by the participant. Next, the participant was asked how he or she would define "play". This was critical as it is a self-constructed notion. Questions in the guide then proceed to explore play within the participant's life by focusing on age-related stages up to current day: childhood (up to age 19), young adulthood (ages 20-39), middle adulthood (ages 40-59), and older adulthood (ages 60 and above). These stages parallel identified categories of age-related play across the life cycle with respect to developmental stages (L'Abate, 2009).

Because the interview guide was semi-structured, the general format for each participant was the same – participants shared how they engaged in various modes of self-perceived play at different stages of life – yet allowed the freedom to explore responses. For example, for the childhood segment of the interview, the participants were asked to share how they engaged in forms of play during their earlier childhood years and up through their adolescence and teenage years. Questions were also asked regarding who they engaged in play with during this stage, what particular play preferences they had, who or what encouraged them to play, and what circumstances might have hindered play during this time. If not discussed thoroughly by the participant earlier in the interview, the final segment was dedicated to exploring how they came to play digital games and the circumstances contributing to their current gameplay. This was followed by their perspective of the game industry and aspects that they believe may influence their future play.

Procedure and Analysis

Participants were individually interviewed and all interviews were recorded and transcribed. Pseudonyms were assigned to each participant to ensure anonymity and to comply with the IRB-approved protocol. Member checking was then employed to promote accuracy and to invite further clarification or insight. Transcripts were analyzed using a qualitative analysis program (NVivo9) to identify and categorize emergent themes. Analysis also included open, axial, and selective coding and the constant comparative method to distinguish characteristics (Charmaz, 2006; Corbin & Strauss, 1990; Glaser & Strauss, 1967). The findings were then used to build a theoretical framework to identify aspects related to digital gameplay in middle and older adulthood.

FINDINGS

An analysis of the transcripts resulted in the identification of three themes that relate to design considerations: childhood play, adult play and future play.

Theme I: Childhood Play

One of the first topics explored with each participant was how they engaged in play during their childhood years. All of the participants expressed having engaged in various forms of play in their childhood and their stories shared common components. Participants characterized this as a time when their play was physically active, was often outside of the home (outdoors), and was encouraged by the parents.

Paul, age 63, was asked how this aspect of play has changed from his childhood years to current day. "[It] changed a whole lot. From being very active, to [now] mostly mind games; from being outside all the time playing baseball or softball, football, basketball, to playing on the computer now. So, [I] slowed my life down a lot." The self-assessment of how play transitions from being highly active to more sedentary over time was common among the participant responses. This finding was associated with time availability. Although participants reported ample amounts of time for play when they were young, this decreased as they took on more responsibilities during their teenage years (e.g. school and chores) and then more so in adulthood.

It was found that the participant's living environment during these formative years was noteworthy in two ways: 1) If they lived in circumstances where other children were present (e.g., similar-aged siblings or a suburban neighborhood), then playtime was typically a social activity. 2) If play was a planned, structured family activity, then the participant was likely exposed to and learned games that were passed down from his/her parents. Kara (age 60), who plays socially via *Words with Friends*, shared that play was an encouraged social event within the family during her childhood years and that interaction shaped how she regarded and valued play. She commented, "That's what our parents taught us and that's what I taught my children. And she [daughter] taught her son and we hope that that carries through." With these two points in mind, participants who reported accounts of childhood play being largely social were more likely to report playing digital games in adulthood that afforded opportunities for socialization.

Conversely, participants who reported limited exposure to social settings tended to engage more often in solitary forms of play, such as playing with dolls or reading. For many of these participants, these early experiences seemed to shape their perspective of play and extended into adulthood, as evidenced by a preference for forms of play that afforded solitude, including their choice of digital games. Jane (age 70), an avid *Solitaire* player, shared how she grew up in a single-parent home in a rural area and the only person with whom she played was her much younger little brother. From this experience, she also learned to play on her own, remarking, "You learn to occupy yourself with different things."

Although both age groups shared similar stories of play activity during this time of their lives, the older gamers reported more accounts of play involving card and board games, activities which were typically learned from their parents. This was reflected in their current forms of gameplay, as the majority of older gamers (particularly the more senior members of this group) preferred digital versions of traditional card and board games, such as *Solitaire*, *Euchre*, *Free Cell*, and *Scrabble*. However, it was found that some of the younger members of the older group shared characteristics with the middle-aged gamers, such as a preference for more action-oriented games. For example, Paul (age 63), who began playing digital games when he was age 24, shared that he liked casual games (e.g. *Candy Craze*) and racing games and is planning to buy another console so he can play more battle-based games. He commented, "Oh, I'd like to play that war game, some of them war games, like the *Black Ops Special* or whatever it is, and you can't get an Xbox 360 to do them." This could be accounted for by his exposure to a variety of games and platforms over the years, as Paul frequented arcades in the era when they were popular and he played with friends who owned early versions of home consoles.

Another notable difference between the two is that most of the middle-aged gamers (and the youngest of the older gamers) reported their first exposure to digital games during their childhood years (middle-aged gamer participants reported exposure as early as age 6.) Most were introduced via an Atari console, early computer games, or public arcades. For example, Hank (age 44), who began playing at age 6, played a variety of games in his childhood years. "A lot of the things I'd do to reward myself was after I got done with my homework, I'd go play *Zork* or *Zelda* or a series called '*Might and Magic.*' I played through all the *Ultima*'s, *Bard's Tales*, *Might and Magic*, *Zork*. There was an Infocom game that came out really that were just text-only games, but you had to map it all out."

Thus, they were not only exposed to digital games at a young age, but also a variety of games that further fostered the development of genre preferences. As a natural consequence, the middle-aged gamers who integrated digital games into their lives at an early age have been exposed to them for a longer portion of their lives as compared to the majority of older gamers. In essence, this finding provides evidence that this is the first generation to incorporate digital games from childhood to older age. For many of these gamers, digital games are not merely a casual hobby but a lifelong endeavor and a necessary expression of play. This recognition led to the identification of Theme II.

Theme II: Adult Play

Participants shared that play has been and will be an important component to the quality of their lives. However, it was reported that there were periods during adulthood that time availability for play decreased dramatically. This decrease in time availability was typically associated with responsibilities related to career establishment and child rearing, which was more commonly reported by female participants. For those women who were among the first generations of mothers to work full-time outside of the home (mostly the older female gamers), there were few reports of play during their young to middle adulthood years due to family and career demands. It is noteworthy that many of older female gamers (and some of the middle-aged female gamers) indicated a preference for casual digital games that afforded the option to socially disengage, such as *Solitaire*, and have played those same games for years. Although such games are not always a primary preference for the middle-aged female gamers, these are regarded as go-to games for those who expressed high levels of stress.

Vivian (age 65), who plays *Solitaire* and *Bedazzled*, expressed, "Frankly, I don't remember a lot of play in my 30's. I really don't. I was working too hard to keep my life together, to get us moved and get my son in a good place, so I don't remember." Yet, she then went on share that she discovered the game *Bedazzled* at her job: "I'd play it on my break. That was a good thing that we could do that. On your lunch hour, you couldn't leave the building. I'd just go, 'now for the next 20 minutes I am not fooling with this [work].' It was an escape mechanism."

Although family responsibilities hindered digital gaming for some, others integrated it into family playtime. This was common among the middle-aged gamers and younger members of the older group. Participants shared stories of introducing their young children to digital games, usually via a gaming console, and used it as an opportunity to play games with them. Evan, age 43, expressed that he is raising his daughter to be a "gamer girl" and that he highly values these games as a way to spend time with her that could not be afforded otherwise. "I've done some of the online games like *Marvel Heroes*, but a lot of my play now does have to deal with my daughter. There's an online *Marvel Super Hero Squad*, which is family-friendly. It's a Flash-based game. You get characters and go run missions. She and I play that together – the Lego games, like the *Marvel Super Heroes*, *Lego DC Super Heroes*, *Lego Batman*, *Lego Harry Potter*, *Lego Indiana Jones*."

As previously mentioned and evidenced by participants like Kara, this finding is reminiscent of how some individuals learned traditional games from their parents when they were young. This suggests that there is a sense of legacy to play, as generational influences shape individual perspectives that continue into adulthood and inform the next generation. Likewise, this intergenerational component affects individual exposure to play and, by extension, digital games.

Participants were also asked if they anticipated playing digital games as they continued to age. Most of the older gamers expressed that they hoped they would still have the functional ability to do so, but overall, it was not a priority. In comparison to the middle-aged gamers, the majority of the older gamers did not begin playing digital games until middle adulthood or later. Digital games were not expressed as an integral component of their play identity, but served as a digital extension of their play preferences as they aged. For example, those who enjoyed traditional card games in their youth found the digital version more accommodating (e.g. no need for manual shuffling); this was especially true for those who are experiencing dexterity or arthritic issues with their hands. Furthermore, they expressed a desire for more suitable options with respect to platform interaction. Suzanne (age 68), who has arthritis in her fingers, remarked, "Maybe when those computers come out with the voice-activated one, that might be a little easier for me in terms of the challenges with my dexterity."

In comparison, the middle-aged gamers shared that digital games had become a regular expression and outlet for play. Thus, digital games were not a substitute for traditional games, but a continuance of a play activity that began years before. The game preferences explored and established in their youth have been nurtured over the years and are reflected in their gaming preferences today. As such, this group strongly indicated intentions to continue playing as they age. Fran (age 44) is planning to retire in seven years and intends to continue playing: "I think at that point [retirement] I will be highly motivated to continue playing. It will give me the outlet that coding gives me now... Right now, I can't commit 20 hours to sit down and play *Diablo*. Back down when I was younger I could eat ham sandwiches and play for hours and hours."

Theme III: Future Play

As an extension of Theme II, Theme III comments on factors that explore aspects related to future gaming. Toward the end of each interview, participants were asked if they were currently experiencing, or anticipate experiencing, any kind of age-related decline (physiological or cognitive) that could negatively influence their gameplay. Surprisingly, older gamers expressed few reservations with respect to any noteworthy challenges to hinder interaction with their current gameplay. This may be attributed to the preferred genre of games among the older members of this age cohort. Most reported playing casual games that are more compatible with age-related decline, such as visual acuity and reaction time. For example, these games tend not to have fast-moving components and do not require the player to react to stimuli in a time-sensitive manner.

In contrast, age-related concerns were emphasized more so by the middle-aged gamers. Most of the participants who play action-based games (e.g. first-person shooters) expressed that they are already noticing a delay in some aspects of their gameplay. For those who have been unable to find or make appropriate adjustments within the game, alternate games were sought that would be more accommodating to their self-perceived issues, such as delayed reaction time and impaired vision. Yet when this is the case, it is important to these gamers that the new game be congruent with their preferred genre. These middle-aged gamers displayed frustration with such situations and were more likely to report feelings of embarrassment for "being old."

Randy, who plays first-person shooter games, commented "Even in my game that I play online, when I tell them [younger players] I'm 55, [I hear] 'Good job, old man,' something like that. They would see things 10 times quicker than I could see it." This prompted Randy to find a game that was more accommodating to his delayed reaction time, yet still catered to his preference for first person shooters – *War 2 Victory*. With respect to this new game, he noted, "If you're being attacked, you get an alarm [that] goes off. You got so many minutes or so before they can get to your city. You have time to react to do whatever you want to do."

Other middle-aged gamers believe that in the future they will encounter age-related issues that may impede successful gameplay, such as arthritis, that will influence interaction with a multi-buttoned controller. This resulted in their questioning of whether or not game designers are aware of these needs in relation to their game preferences. The majority of the participants reported that they are either unaware of or are not confident that today's game designers are familiar with the gaming needs of the aging market.

Finally, as stated earlier in Theme I, participants reported that play activities in their youth emphasized physicality. However, all of the participants shared that play has become increasingly sedentary with age. For those who are no longer physically capable of being as active (older gamers), it was indicated that the appeal and need for digital games as a mode of play has increased with age due to the decline of available options. This aspect is related to this third theme, as digital games have become (and may continue to be) an integral form of play for the middle-aged gamers as they grow into old age. Yet this is coupled with concerns that their preferred modes of gameplay may be in jeopardy in the coming years. This is attributed to their perceptions of an incompatibility between the functional abilities that are necessary to play the game successfully and the design of the game.

DESIGN CONSIDERATIONS

Based on the three themes that emerged from the analysis, the following design considerations are proposed.

Designing Aspects for the Aging Individual

It would be too simplistic to suggest a design solution that caters to older gamers as a group without regard to individuals' respective characteristics and circumstances. Doing so has the potential to do more harm than good to this sizable segment of the current market, as there is the risk of marginalizing them based on age alone. Rather, it is imperative to recognize the importance of inclusion without highlighting age-related needs that serve as an unwarranted reminder rooted in ageist notions of being "old." Old age does not exclude one from engaging in play, yet characteristics associated with the life course and age cohorts inform how opportunities for gameplay can be emphasized.

The most common age-related concerns that participants expressed that were a decline in visual acuity, reaction time, and dexterity. With this in mind, it is important to modify or offer games that accommodate for individual needs without sacrificing elements of gameplay that are critical components to the gamer's preferred genre. In addition, it is imperative to be mindful of how individual functional abilities change, not just from one year to the next, but can fluctuate on a daily basis as an adult ages. For example, arthritic pain or stiffness for an older adult can be more pronounced during one time of the day versus another.

Incorporating the Childhood Play Experience

This consideration is possibly the one most closely related to our use of the life course perspective. Our findings demonstrated how early play experiences strongly shape the perspective of play in adulthood. Older adults who enjoyed playing solitary games (such as *Bejeweled* and *Euchre*) typically played in a solitary manner when they were children. Conversely, older adults who were social players as children still considered play to be a largely social experience. However, this was tempered by the availability of opportunities to play in a social manner. Considering such connections, it is imperative for game designers to identify the types of play that were engaged in during childhood and how those evolved in subsequent years. This includes identifying popular cultural aspects that were incorporated (and marketed) into the everyday life of select generations. For example, Evan shared that he watched Spider-Man and Superman both on TV and at the movies when he was young. Said Evan, "I remember… even the cartoons, like *Spider-Man and His Amazing Friends*, I mean, all those sorts of things. For me, personally, I have always liked that idea of the hero. There's actually a phenomenal [digital] game called *Fable*… was great because it was a succession of small choices that, over the course of the game, added up."

Preparing for the Arrival of the "Younger" Older Gamer

While most research has been focusing on (oftentimes frail) older adults who did not have access to digital games in their formative or younger adulthood years, this study highlights the characteristics of a new aging gamer that is emerging – a new generation who has grown up with digital games. They have a very different relationship with games as a lifelong component of play, and their preferences and needs differ widely from the older gamers. For them, digital games are not a leisure activity, but a continuation of meaningful form of play that was established in earlier phases of their life and nurtured throughout adulthood. This is a group of people who have expressed a need to keep playing the same genre of games, often action-oriented, as they continue to age into their later years. Correspondingly, they shared concerns for how they will likely need modifications within their preferred games to accommodate age-related decline, such as age-coded game servers or customization options that reduce the required reaction time.

Accommodating for Family Gaming as the Family Ages

While time for play tends to be ample within childhood, it decreases for working-aged adults, especially among those who have children. This time availability then increases again after retirement. Although having children influences time availability for play, it does not necessarily equate to a lack of gameplay. As evidenced earlier by Evan, gameplay is highly valued among those who have made a point of playing digital games with their children. Furthermore, many middle-aged gamers like Evan shared how they hope to continue to play with their children (and their future grandchildren) as they get older. This suggests that game design should afford opportunities for adult gamers to continue playing via a platform and games that accommodate multi-generational interests and ability levels. This takes into account not only the gaming preferences and needs of the aging adult (parent or grandparent), but also that of young family members as they age into and through adulthood.

Other Considerations

Aside from the four main recommendations outlined above, this study indicated that stress reduction and relaxation games were a popular choice among the participants of this sample. While the participants of the study did not demonstrate many age-related constraints for playing casual games, they voiced concerns about games not providing enough accessibility options. Finally, considering the trajectories by which participants arrived at their current gaming preferences, it would be worth further investigating and recreating the play experiences of their youth in digital formats.

CONCLUSION

Couched within a life course framework, the findings offered insight into how digital games are a reflection of play preferences first established in youth (Theme I). In turn, this provided a temporal perspective of how these game preferences (and the significance of play) continued into adulthood and influenced current and anticipated future gameplay for the aging adult gamer (Theme II). The findings provided evidence that a complex dynamic emerges when considering how and to what extent an adult gamer may continue to play these games, which in some cases have been played for decades, as they begin to encounter age-related physiological and cognitive decline (Theme III).

While the study was able to replicate many of the findings from prior investigations into game design for aging players (De Schutter et al., 2014; Gamberini et al., 2006; Gerling et al., 2012; IJsselsteijn et al., 2007; Marston, 2013; McLaughlin et al., 2012), it contributes to the literature by providing empirical support for the thesis that a life course perspective should be an essential part of the puzzle when designing games for older populations, including the next generation of older game players. Considering the player's past offers many insights into how a game can be meaningful in her life, or how a game can be more intuitive by mimicking design features from past play experiences. Similarly, considering the player's future can add to both the longevity and the accessibility of a game. Therefore, the authors of this study argue that designers and researchers should expand their usability/accessibility versus content models by adding a temporal dimension that can be defined as:

- **Past:** What meanings or roles does a player associate to games and other forms of play in her life?
- **Present:** How can a game accommodate to a player's current needs, content preferences, social context, and time availability?
- **Future:** How can a game accommodate to a player's future needs and content preferences, social context, and time availability?

Despite the larger than normal number of participants within this grounded theory study, there are limitations worth noting. The majority of participants had an average to above-average socioeconomic status and education history. This may not be fully representational of the larger aging gamer population. In addition, like all research that involves any level or amount of interpretation, there are biases that must be acknowledged on behalf of the interviewer. Although member checking was employed to ensure validity, there was the potential for the interviewer to misinterpret responses.

Based on the findings, it cannot be assumed that the digital game preferences of middle-aged gamers will appreciably change as they move into old age. Rather, it is suggested that the preferences nurtured over years of gameplay will continue, potentially tempered by age-related declines that affect gameplay. It is anticipated that the association between aging aspects and game design will become more pronounced to these gamers as they age. Thus, it is imperative that considerations be made with respect to designing games for this population.

This research received no specific grant from any funding agency in the public, commercial, or not-for-profit sectors.

REFERENCES

Adams, E. (2009). *Fundamentals of Game Design* (2nd ed.). Berkeley, CA: New Riders Press.

Baltes, P. B. (1987). Theoretical propositions of life-span developmental psychology: On the dynamics between growth and decline. *Developmental Psychology*, *23*(5), 611–626. doi:10.1037/0012-1649.23.5.611

Bosmans, D., & Maskell, P. (2012). *Videogames in Europe: 2012 Consumer Study*. ISFE & Ipsos MediaCT. Retrieved from http://www.isfe.eu/industry-facts/statistics

Brown, J. A. (2016). Exploring the next generation of older gamers: Middle-aged gamers. In J. Zhou & G. Salvendy (Eds.), Lecture Notes in Computer Science: Vol. 9755. *Human Aspects of IT for the Aged Population. Healthy and Active Aging. ITAP 2016*. Cham: Springer. doi:10.1007/978-3-319-39949-2_30

Charmaz, K. (2006). *Constructing Grounded Theory*. Retrieved from http://books. google.be/books?id=w2sDdv-S7PgC&printsec=frontcover&dq=0761973524&s ource=bl&ots=pZrr4YGGeu&sig=R7pxfUS9Hz43Qctzt1Z_AUPeZYs&hl=nl& ei=3MFETP2VFNW94gaHtqTPDg&sa=X&oi=book_result&ct=result&resnum =1&ved=0CBUQ6AEwAA#v=onepage&q&f=false

Corbin, J. M., & Strauss, A. L. (1990). Grounded theory research: Procedures, canons, and evaluative criteria. *Qualitative Sociology*, *13*(1), 3–21. doi:10.1007/ BF00988593

De Schutter, B. (2011). Never Too Old to Play: The Appeal of Digital Games to an Older Audience. *Games and Culture*, *6*(2), 155–170. doi:10.1177/1555412010364978

De Schutter, B. (2017). Gerontoludic design: Extending the MDA framework to facilitate meaningful play for older adults. *International Journal of Gaming and Computer-Mediated Simulations*, *9*(1), 45–60. doi:10.4018/IJGCMS.2017010103

De Schutter, B., & Malliet, S. (2014). The older player of digital games: A classification based on perceived need satisfaction. *Communications*, *39*(1), 67–88. doi:10.1515/ commun-2014-0005

De Schutter, B., Nap, H.-H., Brown, J. A., & Roberts, A. R. (2014). The Promise of Gerontoludic Design. *Gerontechnology (Valkenswaard)*, *13*(2), 277. doi:10.4017/ gt.2014.13.02.131.00

De Schutter, B., & Vanden Abeele, V. (2015). Towards a gerontoludic manifesto. *Anthropology and Aging*, *36*(2), 112–120. doi:10.5195/AA.2015.104

Elder Jr, G. H. (1985). Perspectives on the life course. *Life Course Dynamics,* 23-49.

Elder, G. H. (1994). Time, Human Agency, and Social Change: Perspectives on the Life Course. *Social Psychology Quarterly, 57*(1), 4–15. doi:10.2307/2786971

ESA. (2017). *2017 Essential Facts about the Computer and Video Game Industry.* ESA. Retrieved from http://www.theesa.com/wpcontent/uploads/2017/09/EF2017_Design_ FinalDigital.pdf

Fullerton, T. (2008). *Game Design Workshop: A Playcentric Approach to Creating Innovative Games*. Elsevier Morgan Kaufmann.

Gamberini, L., Mariano, A., Barresi, G., Fabgregat, M., Prontu, L., & Ibanez, F. (2006). Cognition, technology and games for the elderly: An introduction to ELDERGAMES Project. *PsychNology Journal, 4*(3), 285–308.

Gerling, K. M., Schulte, F. P., Smeddinck, J., & Masuch, M. (2012). *Game design for older adults: Effects of age-related changes on structural elements of digital games. In Entertainment Computing-ICEC 2012* (pp. 235–242). Springer. Retrieved from http://link.springer.com/chapter/10.1007/978-3-642-33542-6_20

Glaser, B. G., & Strauss, A. L. (1968). The Discovery of Grounded Theory: Strategies for Qualitative Research. *Aldine Transaction, 17*(4), 354-365.

Hunicke, R., LeBlanc, M., & Zubek, R. (2001). *MDA: A Formal Approach to Game Design and Game Research.* Presented at the Game Developers Conference. Retrieved from http://www.cs.northwestern.edu/~hunicke/MDA.pdf

IJsselsteijn, W. A., Nap, H. H., de Kort, Y. A. W., & Poels, K. (2007). *Digital game design for elderly users.* Toronto, Canada: ACM.

L'Abate, L. (2009). *The Praeger handbook of play across the life cycle: Fun from infancy to old age.* Santa Barbara, CA: ABC-CLIO. Retrieved from https://books.google.com/books?hl=en&lr=&id=VAOrCQAAQBAJ&oi=fnd&pg=PP1&dq=abata+the+praeger+handbook&ots=iyCJjfBz-O&sig=fVm6WndwK_AEyVRiTvjtrsOOe6k

Marston, H. R. (2013). Design Recommendations for Digital Game Design within an Ageing Society. *Educational Gerontology, 39*(2), 103–118. doi:10.1080/03601277.2012.689936

McLaughlin, A. C., Gandy, M., Allaire, J., & Whitlock, L. (2012). Putting Fun into Video Games for Older Adults. *Ergonomics in Design, 20*(2), 13–22. doi:10.1177/1064804611435654

Nap, H. H., de Kort, Y. A. W., & IJsselsteijn, W. A. (2009). Senior gamers: Preferences, motivations and needs. *Gerontechnology (Valkenswaard)*, *8*(4), 247–262. doi:10.4017/gt.2009.08.04.003.00

Pearce, C. (2008). The Truth About Baby Boomer Gamers: A study of over-forty computer game players. *Games and Culture*, *3*(2), 142–174. doi:10.1177/1555412008314132

Salen, K., & Zimmerman, E. (2003). *Rules of Play: Game Design Fundamentals*. Cambridge, MA: MIT Press.

Skalsky Brown, J. (2014, July 18). *Let's Play: Understanding the Role and Significance of Digital Gaming in Old Age*. University of Kentucky. Retrieved from http://uknowledge.uky.edu/gerontol_etds/6

Van der Goot, M., Beentjes, J. W. J., & van Selm, M. (2006). Older Adults' Television Viewing from a Life-Span Perspective: Past Research and Future Challenges. *Communication Yearbook*, *30*(1), 431–469. doi:10.120715567419cy3001_10

Watkins, J. F. (1999). Life course and spatial experience: A personal narrative approach in migration studies. In K. Pandit & S. D. Withers (Eds.), *Migration and restructuring in the United States: A geographic perspective*. Lanham, MD: Rowman & Littlefield Publishers, INC.

Weisman, S. (1983). Computer games for the frail elderly. *The Gerontologist*, *23*(4), 361–363. doi:10.1093/geront/23.4.361 PMID:6618244

Chapter 10
An Extended Study on Training and Physical Exercise in Esports

Tuomas Kari
University of Jyvaskyla, Finland

Miia Siutila
University of Turku, Finland

Veli-Matti Karhulahti
University of Turku, Finland

ABSTRACT

This chapter is an extended revision of the authors' earlier study (2016) on the training routines of professional and high-level esport players, with added focus on their physical exercise. The study is methodologically mixed with a quantitative survey sample (n=115) and a qualitative interview sample (n=7). Based on this data, high-level esport players train approximately 5.28 hours every day around the year, and professional esport players at least the same amount. Approximately 1.08 hours of that training is physical exercise. More than half (55.6%) of the professional and high-level esport players believe that integrating physical exercise into their training programs has a positive effect on esport performance; however, no less than 47.0% do the physical exercise chiefly to maintain their overall state of health. Accordingly, the study indicates that professional and high-level esport players are physically active as well: those of age 18 and older exercising more than three times the daily 21-minute physical activity recommendation given by the World Health Organization.

DOI: 10.4018/978-1-5225-7461-3.ch010

INTRODUCTION

Esports have recently become a significant part of our sports cultures. A number of journalists, policy-makers, and academics have thus ended up conceptualizing the cultural identity of the phenomenon: what are the relations between esports and sports, e-athletes and athletes, and esport play and physical exercise (see Taylor, 2012; Ferrari, 2013; von Hilvoorde, 2016; Freeman & Wohn, 2017; Karhulahti, 2017; Jenny et al., 2017; Kane & Spradley, 2017), furthermore, what are the related socio-cultural implications and what makes esport engagement rewarding to begin with? (See Lee & Schoenstedt, 2011; Witkowski, 2012a; Harper, 2013; Martončik, 2015; Nielsen & Karhulahti 2017; Hamari & Sjöblom, 2017; Hallman & Giel, 2017; Siutila & Havaste, 2018.)

This study is not explicitly concerned with the above questions but brings them into a new light. Namely, in what follows, we explore the training routines of professional and high-level esport players with added focus on their physical exercise. This paper is an extended revision of our earlier work (Kari & Karhulahti, 2016), enhanced by supplementary data and insights via qualitative interviews of five professional esport players.

The solitary earlier academic contribution that we were able to find on the topic comes from Andreas Hebbel-Seeger (2012). He quotes a study from esport organization ESL (Electronic Sports League) that apparently issued an unpublished German thesis written by Lüttmann (first name unobtainable) in 2007. According to Hebbel-Seeger (2012), the study claimed that esport players are more active in sports than the average population, with no less than 95% of them exercising traditional sports as well.

Since we have not been able to acquire the referenced study (which appears to be unpublished, non-peer-reviewed, and in German) we take its results with a grain of salt. For instance, it is not clear whether the study concerned professional players, high-level players, amateurs, or fans. Hence, for the present study, a priori hypotheses are not proposed. Training, physical exercise, and players' perceptions will be examined at a descriptive level without utilizing any prior theoretical framework.

METHODOLOGY

The quantitative part of the study leans on a data set that we gathered with an online survey between September 2015 and June 2016. The survey was created with the LimeSurvey 2.05+ software. We pre-tested it quantitatively with ten and qualitatively with four scholars from the fields of play research, videogame research, information systems research, and sports research. Based on the received feedback we made small adjustments before the launch.

The supplemental qualitative interviews were conducted in two separate occasions: June-July 2017 and April 2018. Next, we elaborate on both the quantitative and qualitative methodologies.

Reaching Respondents

The global videogame player base arguably exceeded 2B in 2016, while recent speculations talk about figures beyond 2.3B (Statista, 2018). Of those only about 9000 had ever played videogames professionally some years ago (Bräutigam, 2015), while the present number of active professional esport players, according to the website Esport Earnings, is 5950. Consequently, quantitative work on professional esport players differs significantly from that of the general player population.

We set a goal to reach a hundred professional esport players. In order to do that, we contacted 161 professional esport teams and 68 professional players directly by email and asked them to participate. As expected, only a few responded, leaving the total number of individual respondents to 31. Notwithstanding, due to our direct contact method, we have strong reasons to believe that all the above respondents are actual professional esport players (PRO) as defined by their contracts with teams or achievements in international tournaments. Of note, for us, being a professional is thereby not defined by the player's salary but status.

Due to the low response rate we started looking for more participants via popular media in early 2016. We promoted the survey through Twitter and also posted a call on six major Reddit sub forums: Counter Strike: Global Offensive (CSGO), Dota 2 (DOTA), Hearthstone (HS), Heroes of the Storm (HOTS), League of Legends (LOL), and StarCraft 2 (SC2). This time, our goal was not to reach PRO players alone but also those who were seriously striving for a PRO career. We did, however, add requirements so that each respondent should be at the topmost tiers of the ranked player base of their esport, e.g. CSGO players were demanded to have played within the top three ranks, SC2 players were demanded to have played within the top two ranks, and LOL players we demanded to have played in Diamond 3 or higher.

Altogether the Twitter and Reddit calls reached 91 self-proclaimed high-level esport players who were competing or seriously striving to compete as professionals. We went through the data manually and removed seven responses that were visibly unreliable. With reference to the widely recognized psychological factors of response bias (e.g. Nederhof, 1985; Furnham, 1986; Podsakoff, MacKenzie, Lee, & Podsakoff, 2003) and illusory superiority (e.g. Hoorens, 1995), there is a likelihood that many of these respondents have exaggerated their status. We took this into consideration by not mixing the sample with the PRO group that was reached directly, and addressing them as a distinct group of high-level players (HL) even though many of the respondents identified themselves as professionals.

In total, we thus managed to reach 115 consistent responses from PRO and HL players with various backgrounds. While the number is not high, it does derive from two relatively small target groups, which makes it unique material for analysis – quantitative studies on professional and high-level athletes being rare among sports sciences in general.

To shed light on our quantitative findings, we re-contacted some of the professional teams and individuals in order to reach them for in-depth interviews. This happened in two rounds: June-July 2017 and April 2018. During the first round, two players agreed to participate in this qualitative part of the study, followed by five more players in the second round. Hence, the total number of interviewed players is seven.

The players were all men between ages 18 and 25. At the time of the interviews, two of them were studying in a university in the US under an esports scholarship and competing and training with success in the Top 200 of North American ranked LOL players. The other five interviewees compete in Europe, four of which being signed with teams that compete nationally and internationally in HS, Tekken, and DOTA (two players). The fifth European interviewee was a Challenger ranked LOL player in EUNE server without any active contract with a team.

Survey and Interview Questions

The survey questionnaire consisted of three main sections. The total number of questionnaire items presented to each respondent was 23, some of which were conditional. The key items are presented in Appendix A. The descriptive questions concerning training, physical exercise, and players' perceptions were all closed-ended multiple-choice questions, with the exception of the two questions regarding the hours of training to which the respondents were asked to insert a numerical value. The respondents also had the response option "cannot say" with some of the questions to avoid forced responses. We grouped the respondents into two sub-samples, PRO (N = 31) and HL (N = 84), as explained earlier.

We used the IBM SPSS Statistics 22 software as our data analysis tool. The statistical significance and the strength of the dependencies between the responses and level of expertise (and others) were analyzed through contingency tables (crosstabs), the Pearson's χ^2 tests of independence, and the Cramér's V coefficients. These methods enabled us to examine not only linear but also non-linear dependencies, which suited the explorative nature of the study well.

In some cases, the common condition for the validity of $\chi2$ test – "No more than 20% of the expected counts are less than 5 and all individual expected counts are 1 or greater" (Yates, Moore, & McCabe, 1999, p. 734) – was not met. Hence, as suggested by the widely used guidelines by Agresti (2002) and Cochran (1954), the results of Pearson's $\chi2$ tests of independence were advanced by using exact tests; in this case, Monte Carlo. The Monte Carlo test was based on 10 000 sampled tables and 99% confidence level. This procedure is considered reliable and independent of the dimension, allocation, distribution, and the balance of the analyzed data (Mehta & Patel, 2012). The level of significance was set to $p < 0.05$.

The interview questions were designed to yield further insights on how the players train their skills in respective esport games. These questions primarily centered around the details of the players' training routines, their reasons for preferring some types of practice over others, and the role of physical exercise in the daily program. That said, many new questions beyond that list emerged during the sessions. Accordingly, the interviews were conducted in a semi-structured manner so that we could move flexibly from a topic to another, simultaneously allowing the interviewees to elaborate on the questions that they considered personally interesting to discuss.

RESULTS

The descriptive statistics of the quantitative sample of 115 respondents are presented in Tables 1a and 1b. The responses to the questions regarding training, physical exercise, and perceptions regarding their influence are summarized in Table 2. Table 3 summarizes the results of the Pearson's χ^2 tests of independence and Monte Carlo exact tests, which were used to examine the statistical significance and strength of dependencies between levels of expertise (those who stated "Cannot say" were excluded).

There were no statistically significant dependencies within levels of expertise, i.e. the differences between PRO and HL regarding the responses concerning training, physical exercise, or perceptions regarding their influence were not statistically significant. Also, when classifying the respondents based on their annual esports income (those who earn less than 5000 USD and those who earn 5000 USD or more) no statistically significant dependencies between the groups arose.

Table 1a. Descriptive statistics of the whole survey sample and the sub-samples

	Whole Sample (N =115)		Professional (N = 31)		High-Level (N = 84)	
	N	%	N	%	N	%
Gender						
Men	112	97.4	29	93.5	83	98.8
Women	3	2.6	2	6.5	1	1.2
Age						
−19 yrs.	50	43.5	12	38.7	38	45.2
20–24 yrs.	49	42.6	16	51.6	33	39.3
25–29 yrs.	12	10.4	3	9.7	9	10.7
30– yrs.	4	3.5	0	0.0	4	4.8
Yearly esports income						
−4999 USD	58	50.4	13	41.9	45	53.6
5,000–14,999 USD	16	13.9	8	25.8	8	9.5
15,000–24,999 USD	8	7.0	3	9.7	5	6.0
25,000– USD	8	7.0	1	3.2	7	8.3
No answer	25	21.7	6	19.4	19	22.6
Highest education						
Primary education	17	14.8	5	16.1	12	14.3
Upper secondary	45	39.1	10	32.3	35	41.7
Uni of applied sciences	26	22.6	9	29.0	17	20.2
University (BS or MS)	21	18.3	6	19.4	15	17.9
Doctoral level	1	0.9	0	0.0	1	1.2
Other	5	4.3	1	3.2	4	4.8
Nationality						
European	63	54.8	21	67.7	42	50.0
North-American	35	30.4	4	12.9	31	36.9
Other	11	9.6	4	12.9	7	8.3
No Answer	6	5.2	2	6.5	4	4.8

Sample Analysis

As to gender distribution, the quantitative sample is very unbalanced with only three respondents identifying as women and 112 as men. This is likely because the already-small group of professional esport players is very male-dominant (see Taylor, 2009; Maric, 2011; Chee, 2012; Zolides, 2015; Adams, 2016). We tried to

Table 1b. Descriptive statistics of the whole survey sample and the sub-samples

	Whole Sample (N =115)		Professionals (N = 31)		High-Level (N = 84)	
	N	%	N	%	N	%
Individual vs. team						
Individual (P vs. P)	31	27.0	10	32.3	21	25.0
Team (team vs. team)	78	67.8	20	64.5	58	69.0
N/A	6	5.2	1	3.2	5	6.0
Main esport						
Counter Strike	51	44.3	8	25.8	43	51.2
StarCraft II	15	13.0	7	22.6	8	9.5
DOTA 2	14	12.2	1	3.2	13	15.5
League of Legends	12	10.4	7	22.6	5	6.0
Other	23	20.0	8	25.8	15	17.9
Continent of team/self						
Europe	64	55.7	21	67.7	43	51.2
North America	40	34.8	8	25.8	32	38.1
Australia	4	3.5	1	3.2	3	3.6
Asia	2	1.8	0	0.0	2	2.4
Other	5	4.3	1	3.2	4	4.8
Main reason for physical training						
Physical health	54	47.0	14	45.2	40	47.6
Physical capacity	8	7.0	1	3.2	7	8.3
Physical appearance	20	17.4	7	22.6	13	15.5
Fun or enjoyment	6	5.2	1	3.2	5	6.0
To be more successful in esports	10	8.7	2	6.5	8	9.5
Other	4	3.5	2	6.5	2	2.4
Does not do any physical training	13	11.3	4	12.9	9	10.7
Who plans physical training program						
Myself	81	70.4	19	61.3	62	73.8
Personal coach	6	5.2	2	6.5	4	4.8
Team coach etc.	5	4.4	1	3.2	4	4.8
No training plan	21	18.3	7	22.6	14	16.7
Other	2	1.7	2	6.5	0	0.0

Table 2. Training, physical training, and the perceptions regarding its influence (survey)

	Whole Sample (N =115)		Professionals (N = 31)		High-Level (N = 84)	
	N	%	N	%	N	%
Overall training /day						
1-2.49 hours	10	8.7	1	3.2	9	10.7
2.5-4.99 hours	42	36.5	11	35.5	31	36.9
5-7.49 hours	43	37.4	13	41.9	30	35.7
7.5- hours	20	17.4	6	19.4	14	16.7
Physical training /day						
0	18	15.7	7	22.6	11	13.1
0<>1 hours	23	20.0	7	22.6	16	19.0
1-1,5 hours	46	40.0	11	35.5	35	41.7
1.51-2 hours	23	20.0	6	19.4	17	20.2
2- hours	5	4.2	0	0.0	5	6.0
Influence of physical training on esports						
Significantly negatively	1	0.9	0	0.0	1	1.2
Somewhat negatively	4	3.5	1	3.2	3	3.6
No significant effect	21	18.3	3	9.7	18	21.4
Somewhat positively	45	39.1	10	32.3	35	41.7
Significantly positively	19	16.5	6	19.4	13	15.5
Cannot say	25	21.7	11	35.5	14	16.7
Physical appearance can influence the performance of others						
Yes	34	29.6	11	35.5	23	27.4
To me	21 / 34	18.3/29.6	7	22.6/35.5	14	16.7/27.4
To my opponent(s)	27 / 34	23.5/29.6	10	32.3/35.5	17	20.2/27.4
No influence at all	81	70.4	20	64.5	61	72.6
Physical training compared to teammates						
Significantly less	4	3.5	2	6.5	2	2.5
Somewhat less	7	6.1	1	3.2	6	7.1
About the same	34	29.6	9	29.0	25	29.8
Somewhat more	29	25.2	4	12.9	25	29.8
Significantly more	11	9.6	4	12.9	7	8.3
N/A or cannot say	30	26.1	11	35.5	19	22.6

Table 3. Level of professionalism dependencies on training, physical training, and the perceptions regarding its influence (survey)

	N	χ^2	df	p	$p_{(Monte\ Carlo)}$	V
Overall training hours /day	115	1.801	3	0.615	0.621	0.125
Physical training hours /day	115	3.513	4	0.476	0.490	0.175
Influence of physical training on esports performance	90	2.031	4	0.730	0.765	0.150
Physical appearance can influence the performance of others	115	0.714	1	0.398	0.490 $_{(exact)}$	0.079

fix this sample unbalance first by contacting three more institutions with striving woman esport players and later by contacting ten known successful women esport players directly. We received one reply. Therefore, the distribution did not allow any gender comparisons.

Next to the well-known male-bias, another common premise or assumption concerning esport players is age. Esport players are generally believed to be teenagers or young adults (McTee, 2014), perhaps due to the physiological changes that come along with age (see Thompson et al. 2013; 2014). Our data supports these assumptions, the mean age of our respondents being 20.8 years (SD = 4.4 years) in the full quantitative sample. We should remark, however, that this age average is by no means an anomaly in sports. For instance, the average age of women swimmers in the previous Olympic finals was exactly 20.8 years (combined men and women average 21.7), whereas gymnasts are generally believed to reach their optimal level of competence at 16 or 17 with an average age of 19 in the London Olympics. Esport players are young, but so are many other athletes. We found no statistically significant differences concerning training, physical exercise, or perceptions regarding their influence between younger and older age groups.

Based on their nationalities, the respondents were distributed among three regional categories: Europe, North America, and the rest of the world. Since it is reasonable to believe that Asia covers a significant part of the professional player population (Lee, 2005; Chee & Jin, 2008; Dongsheng Xiaohang, & Daofeng, 2011; Szablewicz, 2011; Guorui, 2012) and only a few of the respondents identified as Asian, our data cannot be considered fully representative in this regard. As the groups of distinct nationalities were expectedly small, there is no reason to compare the practices between the represented nationalities per se. Instead, we compared the two distinguishable groups by region, North America and Europe, but found no statistically significant differences concerning training, physical exercise, or perceptions regarding their influence.

Many professional esport players do not play in their home country, but in teams and institutions around the world. These locations have their own cultural traditions and practices, which we believed to affect the players' training routines. Therefore, we additionally asked about the continent in which the respondents or their team was located. Again, the dominant continents were Europe (64) and North America (40). When comparing the responses between these two groups, the only part with a statistically significant dependency was the question whether "Physical appearance can influence the performance of others" ($\chi2$ (1) = 4.199, p < 0.04, V = 0.201). Of Europe-based respondents 23.4% stated yes, while within North America-based players the agreement rate was 42.5%. This implies that in North American esport scenes appearance – perhaps related to external play dynamics like trash-talk (see Conmy, 2008) – may hold a more significant role than in those of Europe.

We also inquired about players' specific esport, but the response distribution did not allow us to draw any reasonable conclusions game-wise (44.3% of the respondents coming from CSGO). A reasonable distinction could be made, nonetheless, between those playing team esports and those playing solo esports, the former group consisting of 78 respondents and the latter of 31 respondents. We found no statistically significant differences between these two groups concerning training, physical exercise, or perceptions regarding their influence.

Lastly, we inquired about the respondents' education level and financial income from esport sources, both questions being optional. The majority of our respondents came from primary and upper secondary schools (53.9%), while some of them had already reached an applied sciences (22.6%) or a university (18.3%) degree. This makes sense with reference to their average age. Also, more than half (50.4%) of them (including those in the PRO group respectively) declared that they earn less than 5 000 USD from esport play per year, which coheres with the fact that noteworthy prize pools and salaries concern only a small number of the presently striving esport players, also among those who are signed with teams. We found no significant response variance in terms of education levels or financial compensation (cf. Parshakov & Zavertiaeva, 2015).

Quantitative Training Analysis

The main reason for esport players to do physical exercise is to maintain or improve overall physical health (47.0%). This applies to both levels of expertise in our study (PRO 45.2%, HL 47.6%). Only 8.7% of the respondents considered the main purpose of their physical exercise to be more successful in esport. Likewise, only 11.3% stated that they do not do any physical exercise, meaning that 88.7% of PRO and HL players do. Additionally, 81.7% claimed to have a physical exercise program. Most of the respondents (70.4%) planned their physical exercise themselves. Only

5.2% had a personal coach to plan the program and for 4.4% the team coach or equivalent was the planner.

The respondents did an average of 5.28 hours (SD = 2.57 hours) of overall training per day including 1.08 daily hours (SD = 0.83 hours) of physical exercise. Among the sub-samples, the averages were 5.90 hours and 0.89 hours for the PROs (SD = 3.07 hours, SD = 0.70 hours) and 5.05 hours and 1.15 hours for the HLs (2.33 hours, SD = 0.86 hours).

Less than a third of the respondents (29.6%) believed that the amount of their physical exercise was about the same as that of their teammates. A quarter of the respondents (25.2%) believed it was somewhat more, and a tithe (9.6%) believed it was significantly more. Lastly, another tithe (9.6%) believed that the amount of their physical exercise was somewhat or significantly less than what their teammates did, while 26,1% could not state their belief. If these self-estimations are correct, the reached team esport players represent somewhat well the teams in which they play (with regard to questions concerning physical exercise).

As for the perceived influence of physical exercise on one's own esport performance level, most perceived it positively: either somewhat positively (39.1%) or significantly positively (16.5%). Only 18.3% stated not to have perceived significant effects, and 4.4% perceived the influence negatively.

We also asked the respondents whether they believed that the physical appearance of a player could influence the competitive performance of others. Less than a third (29.6%) stated "Yes" and 70.4% stated "No." Of all respondents, 23.5% believed that their opponent had been intimidated by their (or their teammate's) physical appearance, and 18.3% stated to have been personally intimidated by the physical appearance of their opponent.

To satisfy our special interest in the respondents' overall training hours, we ran an additional t-test over PRO and HL groups. As pointed out earlier, the t-test provided no statistically significant differences between PRO and HL groups on either overall training hours (t=1.596, df=113, p=0.424) or physical exercise hours (t=-1.518, df=113, p=0.498).

Interview Analysis

Our interviewees' training habits seem to fit relatively well with the quantitative data. Each of the interviewees were male, aged in their late teens or early 20s, and reported doing physical exercise roughly an hour per day. There were some slight differences in the players' overall training amounts: while the first four respondents trained at least 8 daily hours, the fifth one stated to train an average of 6 hours per day, and the remaining two reported four or five-hour daily minimums. As a caveat, each player noted that they typically took one day off every week. Again, the average amount of daily training in these statements lines well with our quantitative results.

Next to playing the game, the interviewees stated that a significant amount of their training time is spent on other activities related to the game such as watching their own replays and other professional play. They also stressed that discussing and theorizing the games with the team and other peers was a daily routine; moreover, they also sought game-related information on a regular basis. The players had difficulties in estimating how much time they spent on these non-play activities, yet the standard guess (excluding the HS player) was half of the training time being spent on playing and the rest on everything else.

The most deviant answers regarding play and training came from the one HS player who reported only two hours of actual daily play. He considered Hearthstone to be very different compared to other esport games: "mechanics are not really important in Hearthstone like in other games." It is possible that being successful in HS requires less play time and more theorycrafting as well as strategic planning. When these activities are taken into account, his daily averages reach the same numbers (6) as the other players.

In response to a question whether the 12-14 hours per day that professional esports athletes are often reported to train (e.g. DiChristopher, 2014; Jacobs, 2015; Stanton, 2015) were truthful or exaggerated, the interviewees unanimously considered them truthful. One of the DOTA players, for instance, pointed out that his team had recently been advised to increase their amount of daily training significantly, as others simply "train more than you and do a better job at it."

In coherence with the quantitative finding that players exercise physically largely in order to maintain their overall health, all of the interviewees considered physical exercise to be helpful in esports through generally better health and more active lifestyle. Good physical health was said to increase concentration, mood, and energy levels, thus helping to focus through daily training and tournaments.

Despite the players themselves believing in the benefits of physical exercise, their coaches and teams put relatively little emphasis on it: for those with a team contract, the minimum amount of physical exercise that the players were encouraged to do weekly was only one or two hours. In other words, the players did significantly more physical exercise contra what their coaches and teams entailed. Our interviewees did not have a physical exercise plan; instead, they engaged in various different activities. While one reported trying to "take a 20-30-minute jog twice a day," another had weights and a power wheel at home that he would use "four to five times a week about 20 minutes at a time" in addition to going for daily walks. A third one played soccer (in a team) a few times a week, and a fourth reported "working out about four times a week" next to the mandatory physical training with the esport team once per week (involving "varying activities for an hour or two"). The interviewee with the least physically intensive exercise routine reported that he most often just went for about 30-minute walks daily and sometimes did other activities like going to the gym.

We also asked about exercise as a form of preventing typical esport injuries such as those related to wrists or neck and shoulder pain. Only one of the respondents reported actively trying to remember to stretch his wrists and "move around" between games, while the others only expressed having knowledge of these things being helpful. They were more concerned about passive preventative measures like having proper gaming chairs and setup in general. The little rehabilitative or preventive exercise that was done was occasional and mostly related to already feeling some pain or stiffness ("if my neck or shoulders hurt I'll get up and move" and "stretching is good if there are problems with wrists").

There is an interesting discrepancy in the players' attitudes towards physical exercise and the amount of exercise they (are required to) do. For instance, one player described physical exercise to be possibly the most overlooked aspect of training in esports ("real physical exercise is underrated and not understood well enough how significant it is"), but at the same time admitted his own physical exercise to be somewhat random. While players clearly believe in the potential benefits of physical exercise in terms of esport performance, the physical exercise they factually do seems to be largely unstructured and unsystematic.

CONCLUSION

We conclude by summarizing three points that we consider most significant.

First, the study implies that the overall time that professional and high-level esport players spend on training might be heavily exaggerated by the popular press. While journalists and other media contributors frequently present these numbers around 12 or 14 daily hours, the average of our survey respondents was "only" 5.28 hours. There are multiple potential explanations for this. Initially, it is possible that players who take their esport seriously are engaged with the activity all around the clock, but only part of that time gets spent on actual play. In other words, the players might well spend 12–14 daily hours on related activities such as team meetings, video analysis, strategic discussions, sponsored events, interviews, and so on; however, what they count as training is solely the time they play or physically exercise. This was partially supported by the interviews, as the players explicitly stressed that their daily amounts of training (as stated) were only hard minimums and that they probably trained a lot more in reality (not excluding days that were supposed to be dedicated to rest). Another possible explanation is that the high numbers presented in various media concern merely the very top of esport players, a large part of which reside in Asia and were thus not represented manifestly in our samples.

Second, the study implies that professional and high-level esport players are relatively active also when it comes to physical exercise. On average, such players appear to exercise physically 1.08 hours every day. This is more than the World Health Organization's (2018) physical activity recommendation for both children of 5–17 years (60 minutes daily) and adults of 18–64 years (21 minutes daily). Keeping in mind that the average age of our respondents is 20.8, it appears that adult esport players do physical exercise more than three times the recommended amount. When it then comes to the balance between the physical activity recommendations of children and the training requirements of high-level play, we thus submit that, from the present viewpoint, the age restrictions set by many esport tournaments and leagues (usually at the minimum of 17) are accurate. We also entertain the possibility that the non-trivial amounts of physical exercise in top-ranked players' training regimes might have positive effects on the physical activity behaviors of amateurs and new players who see them as idols or role models (e.g. Dix, Phau & Pougnet, 2010).

Third, the study implies that the reasons behind professional and high-level esport players' relatively high physical exercise amounts are not so much due to their desire to improve competitive performance, but rather in their awareness concerning the benefits of healthy lifestyles. Almost half of the respondents (47.0%) considered the upkeep of their overall health as the main reason for their daily physical exercise, whilst more than half (55.6%) believed it to have a positive side effect on their competitive careers as well. As we disagree with scholars who decline all parallels "in the physical efforts of competitive athletes and e-athletes" (Wimmer, 2012, p. 533) and agree with those who consider the physical involvement of esport to be "identifiable not just in quick hands or self-control [but also in] managing and engaging with multiple bodily senses and actions" (Witkowski, 2012b, p. 362), it seems that the greatest potential of esport as a physical cultural practice lies in its tendency to inform those involved about the benefits of bodily routines.

While regular physical exercise may or may not have direct positive effects on esport performance, those who play esport on higher levels seem to have grasped the likely advantages that regular physical exercise generates for their overall health mentally and physically (see Warburton, Nicol, & Bredin, 2006). However, despite understanding the importance and possible positive effects of regular exercise, there seems to be a lack of knowledge concerning what kinds of exercise, how much of it, and how often it should be engaged in. Furthermore, the value of exercise as a means to prevent injuries may not have reached an optimal level yet. As for the ongoing and future debates concerning the "physicality" of esport and its suitability for children in particular, we would be less concerned about the time that aspiring young players spend training inside, and more concerned about the building of social structures that help those players recognize the advantages of training outside too as early as possible.

LIMITATIONS AND FUTURE RESEARCH

Our study has evident limitations that should be noted. The first one relates to the quantitative operationalization of the surveyed concepts (e.g. "physicality") in a relatively simplistic manner, measured by single item measures. Future research could use more rigorous operationalization by measuring concepts with multiple questions that would enable evaluating their reliability and validity. Likewise, a limitation derives also from the fact that the measures were based on the respondents' subjective perceptions. Future studies could benefit from actually following esport players and teams, thus using more objective measures to track their general training and the role of physical exercise in it.

Our study did not include any exergame players (see Kari, 2014; Kari & Makkonen, 2014). This deficiency can also be seen as a strength, as the physical activity patterns of exergame players presumably differ significantly from those studied above. It would probably be best to study them as a distinct player group. That said, the respondent numbers and variance could have been greater in general. With greater numbers and variance, potential gender differences would be a substantial subject of study. Likewise, a parallel study on Asian esport players in particular should provide an interesting point of comparison.

We also entertain the possibility that dedicated videogame play (and other forms of active play) might be related to physical activity more generally. For instance, it is possible that individuals who establish long-term ludic relationships with any kind of gaming are inclined to do regular physical exercise in the same way as professional and high-level esport players do. The hypothesis is intriguing, and a highly promising subject for follow-up studies.

Regardless of these limitations, our results should stand as a decent basis for future research. We specifically look forward to work with other methodologies and more advanced analysis tools. It would also be interesting to find out how much the training routines of the herein studied players differ from those of amateur and casual esport players. Comparative studies concerning the training of esports, motorsports, shooting sports, chess, and other activity groups with alike competitive requirements would likely yield fascinating results.

ACKNOWLEDGMENT

The study was partially supported by the Foundation for Economic Education. The authors would like to thank all esport players who participated in the study. Thanks go also to the people who provided public critical feedback after the publication of the first version of this study.

REFERENCES

Adams, J. L. (2016). Female Fighters: Perceptions of Femininity in the Super Smash Bros. Community. *Press Start*, *3*(1), 99–114.

Agresti, A. (2002). *Categorical data analysis*. New York, NY: Wiley. doi:10.1002/0471249688

Bräutigam, T. (2015, September 15). Esports Statistics: The Growth of Our Industry in Five Charts. *The Esports Observer*. Retrieved from: http://esportsobserver.com/esports-statisticsthe-growth-of-our-industry-in-five-charts/

Chee, F. (2012). *Online Games as a Medium of Cultural Communication: An Ethnographic Study of Socio-Technical Transformation* (Doctoral Dissertation). Fraser University.

Cochran, W. G. (1954). Some methods for strengthening the common χ 2 tests. *Biometrics*, *10*(4), 417–451. doi:10.2307/3001616

Conmy, O. (2008) *Trash Talk in a Competitive Setting: Impact on Self-Efficacy, Affect, and Performance* (Doctoral Dissertation). Florida State University.

DiChristopher, T. (2014, February 3). *Pro gamers story: Get big, burn out, retire young*. CNBC. Retrieved from http://www.cnbc.com/2014/02/01/pro-gamers-story-get-big-burn-out-retireyoung.html

Dix, S., Phau, I., & Pougnet, S. (2010). "Bend it like Beckham": The influence of sports celebrities on young adult consumers. *Young Consumers*, *11*(1), 36–46. doi:10.1108/17473611011025993

Dongsheng, Y., Xiaohang, Y., & Daofeng, K. (2011). The Present Situation and Development Trend of E-sports Games in China. In *2011 International Conference on Future Computer Science and Education (ICFCSE)* (pp. 384-386). IEEE. 10.1109/ICFCSE.2011.98

Ferrari, S. (2013). eSport and the Human Body: Foundations for a Popular Aesthetics. In *Proceedings of DiGRA 2013: DeFragging Game Studies*. Atlanta, GA: DiGRA.

Freeman, G., & Wohn, D. (2017). eSports as an Emerging Research Context at CHI: Diverse Perspectives on Definitions. In *Proceedings of the 2017 CHI Conference Extended Abstracts on Human Factors in Computing Systems* (pp. 1601-1608). ACM. 10.1145/3027063.3053158

Furnham, A. (1986). Response bias, social desirability and dissimulation. *Personality and Individual Differences*, *7*(3), 385–400. doi:10.1016/0191-8869(86)90014-0

Guorui, Z. (2012). Bibliometric Analysis on E-Sports in China. In *Advances in Computer Science and Engineering* (pp. 111–118). Springer. doi:10.1007/978-3-642-27948-5_16

Hallman, K. & Giel, T. (2017). eSports–Competitive Sports or Recreational Activity? *Sport Management Review*.

Hamari, J., & Sjöblom, M. (2017). What is eSports and why do people watch it? *Internet Research*, *27*(2), 211–232. doi:10.1108/IntR-04-2016-0085

Harper, T. (2013). *The Culture of Digital Fighting Games: Performance and Practice*. New York, NY: Routledge.

Hebbel-Seeger, A. (2012). The relationship between real sports and digital adaptation in e-sport gaming. *International Journal of Sports Marketing & Sponsorship*, *13*(2), 43–54. doi:10.1108/IJSMS-13-02-2012-B005

Hoorens, V. (1995). Self-favoring biases, self-presentation, and the self-other asymmetry in social comparison. *Journal of Personality*, *63*(4), 793–817. doi:10.1111/j.1467-6494.1995.tb00317.x

Jacobs, H. (2015, May 11). Here's the insane training schedule of a 20-something professional gamer. *Business Insider*. Retrieved from: http://www.businessinsider.com/pro-gamersexplain-the-insane-training-regimen-they-use-to-stay-on-top-2015-5?r=US&IR=T&IR=T

Jenny, S., Manning, R., Keiper, M., & Olrich, T. (2017). Virtual(ly) Athletes: Where eSports Fit within the Definition of "Sport". *Quest*, *69*(1), 1–18. doi:10.1080/00336297.2016.1144517

Kane, D., & Spradley, B. (2017). *Recognizing Esports as a Sport. Sport Journal.*

Karhulahti, V. (2016). Prank, Troll, Gross and Gore: Performance Issues in Esport Livestreaming. In *Proceedings of the 1st International Joint Conference of DiGRA and FDG*. Digital Games Research Association and Society for the Advancement of the Science of Digital Games.

Karhulahti, V. (2017). Reconsidering Esport: Economics and Executive Ownership. *Physical Culture and Sport Studies and Research*, *74*(1), 43–53. doi:10.1515/pcssr-2017-0010

Kari, T. (2014). Can Exergaming Promote Physical Fitness and Physical Activity?: A Systematic Review of Systematic Reviews. *International Journal of Gaming and Computer-Mediated Simulations*, *6*(4), 59–77. doi:10.4018/ijgcms.2014100105

Kari, T. & Karhulahti, V. (2016). Do E-Athletes Move? A Study on Training and Physical Exercise in Elite E-Sports. *International Journal of Gaming and Computer-Mediated Simulations*, *8*.

Kari, T., & Makkonen, M. (2014). Explaining the Usage Intentions of Exergames. In *Proceedings of the 35th International Conference on Information Systems (ICIS)*. AIS.

Lee, A. (2005). *E-Sports as a Growing Industry (Research Report)*. Samsung Economic Research Institute.

Lee, D., & Schoenstedt, L. J. (2011). Comparison of eSports and traditional sports consumption motives. *The ICHPER-SD Journal of Research in Health, Physical Education, Recreation, Sport & Dance*, *6*(2), 39.

Maric, J. (2011). Electronic Sport: How Pro-gaming Negotiates Territorial Belonging and Gender. *Platform: Journal of Media and Communication*, *3*(2), 6–23.

Martončik, M. (2015). E-Sports: Playing Just for Fun or Playing to Satisfy Life Goals? *Computers in Human Behavior*, *48*, 208–211. doi:10.1016/j.chb.2015.01.056

McTee, M. (2014). E-Sports: More Than Just a Fad. *Oklahoma Journal of Law & Technology*, *10*, 1–27.

Mehta, C. R., & Patel, N. R. (2012). *IBM SPSS Exact Tests*. Cambridge, MA: IBM Corporation.

Nederhof, A. J. (1985). Methods of coping with social desirability bias: A review. *European Journal of Social Psychology*, *15*(3), 263–280. doi:10.1002/ejsp.2420150303

Nielsen, R., & Karhulahti, V. (2017). The Problematic Coexistence of Internet Gaming Disorder and Esports. In *Proceedings of the 12th International Conference on the Foundations of Digital Games*. ACM. 10.1145/3102071.3106359

Parshakov, P., & Zavertiaeva, M. A. (2015). Success in eSports: Does Country Matter? *SSRN Scholarly Paper 2662343*. Retrieved from: http://papers.ssrn.com/abstract=2662343

Podsakoff, P. M., MacKenzie, S. B., Lee, J. Y., & Podsakoff, N. P. (2003). Common method biases in behavioral research: A critical review of the literature and recommended remedies. *The Journal of Applied Psychology*, *88*(5), 879–903. doi:10.1037/0021-9010.88.5.879 PMID:14516251

Siutila, M., & Havaste, E. (2018). "A pure meritocracy blind to identity": Exploring the Online Responses to All-Female Teams in Reddit. *Proceedings of the 2018 DiGRA International Conference.*

Stanton, R. (2015, June 22). *The secret to eSports athletes' success? Lots – and lots – of practice*. ESPN. Retrieved from: http://www.espn.com/espn/story/_/id/13053116/esports-athletes-puthours-training-reach-pinnacle

Statista. (2018). *The Statistics Portal*. Statista.com.

Szablewicz, M. (2011). From Addicts to Athletes: Participation in the Discursive Construction of Digital Games in Urban China. In Selected Papers of Internet Research 12.0 (pp. 1-21). Association of Internet Researchers.

Taylor, N., Jenson, J., & de Castell, S. (2009). Cheerleaders, Booth Babes, Halo Hoes: Pro-gaming, Gender and Jobs for the Boys. *Digital Creativity*, *20*(4), 239–252. doi:10.1080/14626260903290323

Taylor, T. L. (2012). *Raising the Stakes: E-Sports and the Professionalization of Computer Gaming*. Cambridge, MA: The MIT Press.

Thompson, J. J., Blair, M. R., Chen, L., & Henrey, A. J. (2013). Video Game Telemetry as a Critical Tool in the Study of Complex Skill Learning. *PLoS One*, *8*(9), e75129. doi:10.1371/journal.pone.0075129 PMID:24058656

Thompson, J. J., Blair, M. R., & Henrey, A. J. (2014). Over the Hill at 24: Persistent Age-Related Cognitive-Motor Decline in Reaction Times in an Ecologically Valid Video Game Task Begins in Early Adulthood. *PLoS One*, *9*(4), e94215. doi:10.1371/journal.pone.0094215 PMID:24718593

von Hilvoorde, I. (2016). *Sport and Play in a Digital World*. Sport, Ethics and Philosophy.

Warburton, D., Nicol, C., & Bredin, S. (2006). Health benefits of physical activity: The evidence. *Canadian Medical Association Journal, 174*(6), 801–809. doi:10.1503/cmaj.051351 PMID:16534088

Wimmer, J. (2012). Digital Game Culture(s) as Prototype(s) of Mediatization and Commercialization of Society. In J. Fromme & A. Unger (Eds.), *Computer Games and New Media Cultures: A Handbook of Digital Game Studies* (pp. 525–540). Heidelberg, Germany: Springer. doi:10.1007/978-94-007-2777-9_33

Witkowski, E. (2012a). *Inside the Huddle: The Phenomenology and Sociology of Team Play in Networked Computer Games* (Doctoral Dissertation). IT University of Copenhagen.

Witkowski, E. (2012b). On the Digital playing Field: How we "Do Sport" With Networked Computer Games. *Games and Culture, 7*(5), 349–374. doi:10.1177/1555412012454222

World Health Organization (WHO). (2018). *Global recommendations on physical activity for health (Report)*. WHO.

Yates, D., Moore, D., & McCabe, G. (1999). *The Practice of Statistics*. New York, NY: W.H. Freeman.

Zolides, A. (2015). Lipstick Bullets: Labour and Gender in Professional Gamer Self-Branding. *Persona Studies, 1*(2), 42–53. doi:10.21153/ps2015vol1no2art467

KEY TERMS AND DEFINITIONS

Esports: Cultural practices of exercise and contest on commercial play products that are governed by executive owners.

High-Level Esport Player: Seriously striving to become a professional player and performing similar activities as professional players, but having not yet reached international competence or team contracts.

Physical Exercise: Activity requiring physical effort, carried out to sustain or improve health and fitness.

Practice: Performing certain activities in order to become better at them, sometimes synonymous with training.

Professional Esport Player: Individual competing in sanctioned international leagues or tournaments, or playing in an officially registered team with a contract.

Training: The process of learning or becoming better at specific skill or skills, sometimes synonymous with practice.

ENDNOTE

[1]   Detailed descriptions of all the other questions are available from the authors by request.

APPENDIX: KEY SURVEY QUESTIONS REGARDING TRAINING AND ESPORTS[1]

1. **How many hours of training do you do daily**? (Hours per day on average)

Total amount of all training related to being a better or more successful player. You can also report uneven hours by using a dot. For example: 1hours 30minutes = 1.5 (hours) and 30 minutes = 0.5 (hours).

2. **How many hours of PHYSICAL training do you do daily?** (Hours per day on average) For example: running, cycling, strength, gym-training, yoga, etc.

You can also report uneven hours by using a dot. For example: 1hours 30minutes = 1.5 (hours) and 30 minutes = 0.5 (hours).

3. **Who plans your physical training** program?
   a. I do it myself o My personal coach
   b. Team's head coach o Team's physical coach/physiotherapist
   c. My team buys this as a service from outside
   d. I have no physical training plan. I just do whatever and whenever I feel like it
   e. Other: [specify your choice in the accompanying text field]
4. What is your MAIN reason for doing physical training?
   a. To maintain or improve my overall physical health
   b. To maintain or improve my physical capacity
   c. To lose weight, gain muscles, or tone my body (physical appearance)
   d. For fun or enjoyment of exercising
   e. To be more successful in esports
   f. I don't do any physical training
   g. Cannot say
   h. Other: [specify your choice in the accompanying text field]
5. How do you perceive that doing PHYSICAL training has affected your performance level in esports?
   a. Significantly negatively
   b. Somewhat negatively
   c. No significant effect
   d. Somewhat positively
   e. Significantly positively
   f. Cannot say

6. Compared to your teammates, do you believe you are doing more or less physical training than they do?
    a. Significantly less
    b. Somewhat less
    c. About the same amount
    d. Somewhat more
    e. Significantly more
    f. Cannot say
7. Do you believe that the physical appearance of a player can influence the competitive performance of others?

Please choose all that apply:

a. Yes, I believe my opponent has been intimidated by my (or my teammate's) physical appearance
b. Yes, I have been intimidated by the physical appearance of my opponent
c. No, I don't believe that there is any influence

Choose all 'Yes' -options that apply OR 'No' -option.

Compilation of References

Aalbers, T., Baars, M. A. E., Rikkert, M. G. M. O., & Kessels, R. P. C. (2013). Puzzling with online games (BAM-COG): Reliability, validity, and feasibility of an online self-monitor for cognitive performance in aging adults. *Journal of Medical Internet Research*, *15*(12), e270. doi:10.2196/jmir.2860 PMID:24300212

Aarseth, E. (2007). I fought the law: Transgressive play and the implied player. *Situated Play. Proc. DiGRA*, 24-28.

Adamo, G. (2003). Simulated and Standardized Patients in OSCEs: Achievements and Challenges 1992-2003. *Medical Teacher*, *25*(3), 262–270. doi:10.1080/0142159031000100300 PMID:12881047

Adams, E. (2009). *Fundamentals of Game Design* (2nd ed.). Berkeley, CA: New Riders Press.

Adams, J. L. (2016). Female Fighters: Perceptions of Femininity in the Super Smash Bros. Community. *Press Start*, *3*(1), 99–114.

Agarwal, R., & Karahanna, E. (2000). Time flies when you're having fun: Cognitive absorption and beliefs about information technology usage. *Management Information Systems Quarterly*, *24*(4), 665–694. doi:10.2307/3250951

Agresti, A. (2002). *Categorical data analysis*. New York, NY: Wiley. doi:10.1002/0471249688

Al-Awar, J., Chapanis, A., & Ford, W. R. (1981). Tutorials for the first-time computer user. *IEEE Trans. Profess. Commun*, *24*(1), 30–37.

Amazon.com. (n.d.). *The Lean Startup: How Today's Entrepreneurs Use Continuous Innovation to Create Radically Successful Businesses*. Retrieved June 17, 2018, from https://www.amazon.com/Lean-Startup-Entrepreneurs-Continuous-Innovation/dp/0307887898

Anderson, J. R., Greeno, J. G., Reder, L. M., & Simon, H. A. (2000). Perspectives on learning, thinking, and activity. *Educational Researcher*, *29*(4), 11–13. doi:10.3102/0013189X029004011

Andreatta, P. (2016). *An Independent Analysis of a Virtual Standardized Patient System*. Unpublished Government Report, directly communicated from author.

Anguera, J. A., Boccanfuso, J., Rintoul, J. L., Al-Hashimi, O., Faraji, F., Janowich, J., ... Gazzaley, A. (2013). Video game training enhances cognitive control in older adults. *Nature, 501*(7465), 97–101. doi:10.1038/nature12486 PMID:24005416

Annetta, L. A. (2010). The "I's" have it: A framework for serious educational game design. *Review of General Psychology, 14*(2), 105–112. doi:10.1037/a0018985

Annetta, L. A., Minogue, J., Holmes, S. Y., & Cheng, M.-T. (2009). Investigating the impact of video games on high school students' engagement and learning about genetics. *Computers & Education, 53*(1), 74–85. doi:10.1016/j.compedu.2008.12.020

Ashby, R., & Lee, P. (1987). Children's Concepts of Empathy and Understanding in History. In *The History Curriculum for Teachers* (pp. 62–88). London: Falmer Press.

Attali, Y., & Arieli-Attali, M. (2015). Gamification in assessment: Do points affect test performance? *Computers & Education, 83*, 57–63. doi:10.1016/j.compedu.2014.12.012

Baig, L. A., Beran, T. N., Vallevand, A., Baig, Z. A., & Monroy-Cuadros, M. (2014). Accuracy of Portrayal by Standardized Patients: Results from four OSCE stations conducted for high stakes examinations. *BMC Medical Education, 14*(1), 97. doi:10.1186/1472-6920-14-97 PMID:24884744

Baker, R. S., & Clarke-Midura, J. (2013). Predicting successful inquiry learning in a virtual performance assessment for science. In S. Carberry, S. Weibelzahl, A. Micarelli, & G. Semeraro (Eds.), *User Modeling, Adaptation, and Personalization* (pp. 203–214). Berlin: Springer. doi:10.1007/978-3-642-38844-6_17

Bales, R. F. (1950). *Interaction Process Analysis*. Cambridge, MA: Addison-Wesley.

Baltes, P. B. (1987). Theoretical propositions of life-span developmental psychology: On the dynamics between growth and decline. *Developmental Psychology, 23*(5), 611–626. doi:10.1037/0012-1649.23.5.611

Barrows, H. S., & Abrahamson, S. (1964). The Programmed Patient: A Technique for Appraising Student Performance in Clinical Neurology. *Academic Medicine, 39*(8), 802–805. PMID:14180699

Barton, K. C., & Levstik, L. S. (2004). *Teaching history for the common good*. Mahwah, NJ: Lawrence Erlbaum Associates.

Basak, C., Boot, W. R., Voss, M. W., & Kramer, A. F. (2008). Can training in a real--time strategy video game attenuate cognitive decline in older adults? *Psychology and Aging, 23*(4), 765–777. doi:10.1037/a0013494 PMID:19140648

Bautista, M., Leeds, A., Tokel, T., & Talbot, T. B. (2016). Spoken vs typed questioning in a conversational medical interview with virtual standardized patients. *International Meeting on Simulation in Healthcare*.

Bavelier, D., Green, C. S., Han, D. H., Renshaw, P. F., Merzenich, M. M., & Gentile, D. A. (2011). Brains on video games. *Nature Reviews. Neuroscience, 12*(12), 763–768. doi:10.1038/nrn3135 PMID:22095065

Bergin, R. A., & Fors, U. G. (2003). Interactive Simulated Patient—an Advanced Tool for Student-Activated Learning in Medicine and Healthcare. *Computers & Education*, *40*(4), 361–376. doi:10.1016/S0360-1315(02)00167-7

Berkhof, M., Rijssen, H. J., Schellart, A. J., Anema, J. R., & Beek, A. J. (2011). Effective training strategies for teaching communication skills to physicians: An overview of systematic reviews. *Patient Education and Counseling*, *84*(2), 152–162. doi:10.1016/j.pec.2010.06.010 PMID:20673620

Berland, M., Baker, R. S., & Blikstein, P. (2014). Educational data mining and learning analytics: Applications to constructionist research. *Technology, Knowledge, and Learning*, *19*(1-2), 205–220. doi:10.100710758-014-9223-7

Betz, J. A. (1995). Computer games: Increase learning in an interactive multidisciplinary environment. *Journal of Educational Technology Systems*, *24*(2), 195–205. doi:10.2190/119M-BRMU-J8HC-XM6F

Billings, R. S., Milburn, T. W., & Schaalman, M. L. (1980). A Model of Crisis Perception: A Theoretical and Empirical Analysis. *Administrative Science Quarterly*, *25*(2), 300–306. doi:10.2307/2392456

Black, J. B., Segal, A., Vitale, J., & Fadjo, C. L. (2012). Embodied cognition and enhancing learning and motivation. In D. Jonassen & S. Land (Eds.), *Theoretical foundations of learning environments*. New York: Routledge.

Black, P., & Wiliam, D. (2009). Developing the theory of formative assessment. *Educational Assessment, Evaluation and Accountability*, *21*(1), 5–31. doi:10.100711092-008-9068-5

Bloom, B. S. (1976). *Human Characteristics and School Learning*. New York: McGraw-Hill.

Bogolub, E. B. (1986). Tape Recorders in Clinical Sessions: Deliberate and Fortuitous Effects. *Clinical Social Work Journal*, *14*(4), 349–360. doi:10.1007/BF01892595

Bogost, I. (2007). *Persuasive games: The expressive power of videogames*. MIT Press. Retrieved from https://books.google.ca/books?hl=en&lr=&id=vjbOnZw1wfUC&oi=fnd&pg=PP6&dq=ian+bo gost&ots=xkkxhHzOC2&sig=kFr1ICwyE-moUXdfqsN5uywhsM8

Bogost, I. (2008). The Rhetoric of Video Games. In K. Salen (Ed.), *The Ecology of Games: Connecting Youth, Games, and Learning* (pp. 117–140). Cambridge, MA: The MIT Press. doi:10.1162/dmal.9780262693646.117

Boin, A., 't Hart, P., Stern, E., & Sundelius, B. (2005). *The Politics of Crisis Management: Public Leadership under Pressure*. Cambridge, UK: Cambridge University Press. doi:10.1017/CBO9780511490880

Boltz, L. O. (2017). "Like Hearing From Them in the Past": The Cognitive-Affective Model of Historical Empathy in Videogame Play. *International Journal of Gaming and Computer-Mediated Simulations*, *9*(4), 1–18. doi:10.4018/IJGCMS.2017100101

Bornstein, M. H. (1990). Attention in infancy and the prediction of cognitive capacities in childhood. In J. Enns (Ed.), *Development of Attention: Research and Theory*. Elsevier. doi:10.1016/S0166-4115(08)60448-3

Borodzicz, E. P. (2005). *Risk, Crisis and Security Management*. West Sussex, UK: John Wiley & Sons Ltd.

Bosmans, D., & Maskell, P. (2012). *Videogames in Europe: 2012 Consumer Study*. ISFE & Ipsos MediaCT. Retrieved from http://www.isfe.eu/industry-facts/statistics

Bostrom, R. P., & Anson, R. G. (1992). *A Case for Collaborative Work Support Systems in a Meeting Environment* (Unpublished working paper). Department of Management, University of Georgia.

Boyle, E. A., Connolly, T. M., & Hainey, T. (2011). The role of psychology in understanding the impact of computer games. *Entertainment Computing*, *2*(2), 69–74. doi:10.1016/j.entcom.2010.12.002

Bransford, J. D., Brown, A. L., & Cocking, R. R. (1999). *How people learn: Brain, mind, experience, and school*. National Academy Press.

Bräutigam, T. (2015, September 15). Esports Statistics: The Growth of Our Industry in Five Charts. *The Esports Observer*. Retrieved from: http://esportsobserver.com/esports-statisticsthe-growth-of-our-industry-in-five-charts/

Braver, M. W., & Braver, S. L. (1988). Statistical treatment of the Solomon four-group design: A meta-analytic approach. *Psychological Bulletin*, *104*(1), 150–154. doi:10.1037/0033-2909.104.1.150

Brooke, J. (1996). SUS: a "quick and dirty" usability scale. In *Usability Evaluation in Industry*. London: Taylor and Francis.

Brooks, S. (2009). Historical empathy in the social studies classroom: A review of the literature. *Journal of Social Studies Research*, *33*, 213–234.

Brooks, S. (2011). Historical Empathy as Perspective Recognition and Care in One Secondary Social Studies Classroom. *Theory and Research in Social Education*, *39*(2), 166–202. doi:10.1080/00933104.2011.10473452

Brown, J. A. (2016). Exploring the next generation of older gamers: Middle-aged gamers. In J. Zhou & G. Salvendy (Eds.), Lecture Notes in Computer Science: Vol. 9755. *Human Aspects of IT for the Aged Population. Healthy and Active Aging. ITAP 2016*. Cham: Springer. doi:10.1007/978-3-319-39949-2_30

Buchanan, R. (1992). Wicked problems in design thinking. *Design Issues*, *8*(2), 5–21. doi:10.2307/1511637

Buckley, B. C., Gobert, J. D., Kindfield, A. C. H., Horwitz, P., Tinker, R. F., Gerlits, B., ... Willett, J. (2004). Model-based teaching and learning with Biologica™: What do they learn? How do they learn? How do we know? *Journal of Science Education and Technology*, *13*(1), 23–41. doi:10.1023/B:JOST.0000019636.06814.e3

Campbell, J. C., Hays, M. J., Core, M., Birch, M., Bosack, M., & Clark, R. E. (2011). Interpersonal and Leadership Skills: Using Virtual Humans to Teach New Officers. *Proceedings of the 33rd Interservice/Industry Training, Simulation, and Education Conference (I/ITSEC)*.

Carroll, J. B. (1963). A model of School Learning. *Teachers College Record*, *64*, 723–733.

Charmaz, K. (2006). *Constructing Grounded Theory*. Retrieved from http://books.google.be/ books?id=w2sDdv-S7PgC&printsec=frontcover&dq=0761973524&source=bl&ots=pZrr4YG Geu&sig=R7pxfUS9Hz43Qctzt1Z_AUPeZYs&hl=nl&ei=3MFETP2VFNW94gaHtqTPDg&s a=X&oi=book_result&ct=result&resnum=1&ved=0CBUQ6AEwAA#v=onepage&q&f=false

Charsky, D. (2010). From edutainment to serious games: A change in the use of game characteristics. *Games and Culture*, *5*(2), 177–198. doi:10.1177/1555412009354727

Charsky, D., & Mims, C. (2008). Integrating commercial off-the-shelf video games into school curriculums. *TechTrends*, *52*(5), 38–44. doi:10.100711528-008-0195-0

Chee, F. (2012). *Online Games as a Medium of Cultural Communication: An Ethnographic Study of Socio-Technical Transformation* (Doctoral Dissertation). Fraser University.

Chesler, N. C., Ruis, A. R., Collier, W., Swiecki, Z., Arastoopour, G., & Shaffer, D. W. (2015). A novel paradigm for engineering education: Virtual internships with individualized mentoring and assessment of engineering thinking. *Journal of Biomechanical Engineering*, *137*(2), 024701. doi:10.1115/1.4029235 PMID:25425046

Choudhury, N., & Gorman, K. (2000). The relationship between attention and problem solving in 17–24 month old children. *Infant and Child Development*, *9*, 127–146. doi:10.1002/1522-7219(200009)9:3<127::AID-ICD225>3.0.CO;2-5

Clark, D. B. (2012). *Designing Games to Help Players Articulate Productive Mental Models* [Video file]. Keynote commissioned for the Cyberlearning Research Summit 2012 hosted by SRI International, the National Geographic Society, and the Lawrence Hall of Science with funding from the National Science Foundation and the Bill and Melinda Gates Foundation, Washington, DC. Retrieved from https://www.youtube.com/watch?v=xlMfk5rP9yI

Clark, D. B., Sengupta, P., Brady, C., Martinez-Garza, M., & Killingsworth, S. (2015). Disciplinary Integration in Digital Games for Science Learning. *International STEM Education Journal*, *2*(2), 1-21. Retrieved from http://www.stemeducationjournal.com/content/pdf/s40594-014-0014-4.pdf

Clark, D. B., & Martinez-Garza, M. (2012). Prediction and explanation as design mechanics in conceptually-integrated digital games to help players articulate the tacit understandings they build through gameplay. In C. Steinkuehler, K. Squire, & S. Barab (Eds.), *Games, learning, and society: Learning and meaning in the digital age*. Cambridge, MA: Cambridge University Press. doi:10.1017/CBO9781139031127.023

Clark, D. B., Nelson, B. C., Chang, H.-Y., Martinez-Garza, M. M., Slack, K., & D'Angelo, C. M. (2011). Exploring Newtonian mechanics in a conceptually-integrated digital game: Comparison of learning and affective outcomes for students in Taiwan and the United States. *Computers & Education, 57*(3), 2178–2195. doi:10.1016/j.compedu.2011.05.007

Clark, D., Tanner-Smith, E., Killingsworth, S., & Bellamy, S. (2013). *Digital Games for Learning: A Systematic Review and Meta-Analysis (Executive Summary)*. Menlo Park, CA: SRI International.

Clarke-Midura, J., & Dede, C. (2010). Assessment, technology, and change. *Journal of Research on Technology in Education, 42*(3), 309–328. doi:10.1080/15391523.2010.10782553

Cline, R. J. W. (1994). Groupthink and the Watergate cover up. The illusion of unanimity. In L. R. Frey (Ed.), *Group Communication in Context: Studies of Natural Groups*. Lawrence Erlbaum Associates.

Cochran, W. G. (1954). Some methods for strengthening the common χ 2 tests. *Biometrics, 10*(4), 417–451. doi:10.2307/3001616

Coller, B., & Scott, A. A. (2009). Effectiveness of using a video game to teach a course in mechanical engineering. *Computers & Education, 53*(3), 900–912. doi:10.1016/j.compedu.2009.05.012

Colombo, J., & Cheatham, C. L. (2006). The emergence and basis of endogenous attention in infancy and early childhood. In R. Kail (Ed.), *Advances in Child Development and Behavior* (Vol. 34, pp. 283–310). Oxford, UK: Academic Press. doi:10.1016/S0065-2407(06)80010-8

Conmy, O. (2008) *Trash Talk in a Competitive Setting: Impact on Self-Efficacy, Affect, and Performance* (Doctoral Dissertation). Florida State University.

Connolly, T. M., Boyle, E. A., MacArthur, E., Hainey, T., & Boyle, J. M. (2012). A systematic literature review of empirical evidence on computer games and serious games. *Computers & Education, 59*(2), 661–686. doi:10.1016/j.compedu.2012.03.004

Cook, S., & Goldin-Meadow, S. (2006). The Role of Gesture in Learning: Do Children Use Their Hands to Change Their Minds. *Journal of Cognition and Development, 7*(2), 211–232. doi:10.120715327647jcd0702_4

Coombs, T. (2007). *Ongoing crisis communication: Planning, managing and responding*. Thousand Oaks, CA: Sage Publications.

Cooper, H., Robinson, J. C., & Patall, E. A. (2006). Does homework improve academic achievement? A synthesis of research, 1987–2003. *Review of Educational Research, 76*(1), 1–62. doi:10.3102/00346543076001001

Corbett, A. T., & Anderson, J. R. (1994). Knowledge tracing: Modeling the acquisition of procedural knowledge. *User Modeling and User-Adapted Interaction, 4*(4), 253–278. doi:10.1007/BF01099821

Corbin, J. M., & Strauss, A. L. (1990). Grounded theory research: Procedures, canons, and evaluative criteria. *Qualitative Sociology, 13*(1), 3–21. doi:10.1007/BF00988593

Corbin, J. M., & Strauss, A. L. (2008). *Basics of qualitative research: Techniques and procedures for developing grounded theory* (3rd ed.). Los Angeles, CA: Sage Publications, Inc. doi:10.4135/9781452230153

Cordova, D. I., & Lepper, M. R. (1996). Intrinsic motivation and the process of learning: Beneficial effects of contextualization, personalization, and choice. *Journal of Educational Psychology, 88*(4), 715–730. doi:10.1037/0022-0663.88.4.715

Cornelius, S., Gordon, C., & Harris, M. (2011). Role engagement and anonymity in synchronous online role play. *International Review of Research in Open and Distance Learning, 12*(5), 57–73. doi:10.19173/irrodl.v12i5.923

Creswell, J. W. (2008). *Educational research: Planning, conducting, and evaluating quantitative and qualitative research*. Upper Saddle River, NJ: Pearson/Merrill Prentice Hall.

Cronbach, L., & Snow, R. (1977). *Aptitudes and Instructional Methods: A Handbook for Research on Interactions*. New York: Irvington.

Csikszentmihalyi, M. (1991). *Flow: The Psychology of Optimal Experience* (1st ed.). Harper Perennial.

de Freitas, S. (2018). Are games effective learning tools? A review of educational games. *Journal of Educational Technology & Society, 21*(2), 74–84.

De Schutter, B. (2011). Never Too Old to Play: The Appeal of Digital Games to an Older Audience. *Games and Culture, 6*(2), 155–170. doi:10.1177/1555412010364978

De Schutter, B. (2017). Gerontoludic design: Extending the MDA framework to facilitate meaningful play for older adults. *International Journal of Gaming and Computer-Mediated Simulations, 9*(1), 45–60. doi:10.4018/IJGCMS.2017010103

De Schutter, B., & Malliet, S. (2014). The older player of digital games: A classification based on perceived need satisfaction. *Communications, 39*(1), 67–88. doi:10.1515/commun-2014-0005

De Schutter, B., Nap, H.-H., Brown, J. A., & Roberts, A. R. (2014). The Promise of Gerontoludic Design. *Gerontechnology (Valkenswaard), 13*(2), 277. doi:10.4017/gt.2014.13.02.131.00

De Schutter, B., & Vanden Abeele, V. (2015). Towards a gerontoludic manifesto. *Anthropology and Aging, 36*(2), 112–120. doi:10.5195/AA.2015.104

Dede, C. (2011). Developing a research agenda for educational games and simulations. In S. Tobias & J. D. Fletcher (Eds.), *Computer Games and Instruction* (pp. 233–247). Charlotte, NC: Information Age Publishing.

Delacruz, G. C. (2012). Impact of incentives on the use of feedback in educational videogames: CRESST report 813. National Center for Research on Evaluation, Standards, and Student Testing, 1-18.

Deleeuw, K. E., & Mayer, R. E. (2011). Cognitive consequences of making computer-based learning activities more game-like. *Computers in Human Behavior, 27*(5), 2011–2016. doi:10.1016/j.chb.2011.05.008

DeMarie-Dreblow, D., & Miler, P. H. (1988). The development of children's strategies for selective attention: Evidence for a transitional period. *Child Development, 59*(6), 1504–1513. doi:10.2307/1130665 PMID:3208562

DeNavas-Walt, C., & Proctor, B. D. (2015). Income and poverty in the United States: 2014. *US Census Bureau, Current Population Reports*. Retrieved from: https://www.census.gov/content/dam/Census/library/publications/2015/demo/p60-252.pdf

Deterding, S., Dixon, D., Khaled, R., & Nacke, L. (2011, September). From game design elements to gamefulness: defining gamification. In *Proceedings of the 15th international academic MindTrek conference: Envisioning future media environments* (pp. 9-15). ACM. 10.1145/2181037.2181040

Diamond, A. (2006). The early development of executive functions. In E. Bialystok & F. Craik (Eds.), Lifespan Cognition: Mechanisms of Change (pp. 7-95). Oxford University Press. doi:10.1093/acprof:oso/9780195169539.003.0006

Diamond, J. (2012). *"You Weren't Doing What You Would Actually Do, You Were Doing What People Wanted You to Do": A Study of Historical Empathy in a Digital History Game* (Doctoral dissertation). Retrieved from Dissertation Abstracts International. (Order No. AAI3511399)

Diamond, A. (2002). Normal development of prefrontal cortex from birth to young adulthood: Cognitive functions, anatomy, and biochemistry. In D. T. Stuss & R. T. Knight (Eds.), *Principles of frontal lobe function* (pp. 466–503). London, UK: Oxford University Press. doi:10.1093/acprof:oso/9780195134971.003.0029

Diamond, A. (2012). Activities and programs that improve children's executive functions. *Current Directions in Psychological Science, 21*(5), 335–341. doi:10.1177/0963721412453722 PMID:25328287

Diamond, A. (2013). Executive functions. *Annual Review of Psychology, 64*(1), 135–168. doi:10.1146/annurev-psych-113011-143750 PMID:23020641

DiChristopher, T. (2014, February 3). *Pro gamers story: Get big, burn out, retire young.* CNBC. Retrieved from http://www.cnbc.com/2014/02/01/pro-gamers-story-get-big-burn-out-retireyoung.html

Dickens, P. (2003). Don't Be Brainwashed by Groupthink. The Scotsman, p. 9.

DiDonato, M. D., Martin, C. L., Hessler, E. E., Amazeen, P. E., Hanish, L. D., & Fabes, R. A. (2012). Gender consistency and flexibility: Using dynamics to understand the relation between gender and adjustment. *Nonlinear Dynamics Psychology and Life Sciences, 16*(2), 159–184. PMID:22452931

DiLalla, L. F., & Watson, M. W. (1988). Differentiation of fantasy and reality: Preschoolers' reactions to interruptions in their play. *Developmental Psychology, 24*(2), 286–291. doi:10.1037/0012-1649.24.2.286

diSessa, A. (1988). Knowledge in pieces. In G. Forman & P. B. Pufall (Eds.), *Constructivism in the Computer Age*. Hillsdale, NJ: Lawrence Erlbaum Associates.

Disessa, A. A., & Sherin, B. L. (2000). Meta-representation: An introduction. *The Journal of Mathematical Behavior, 19*(4), 385–398. doi:10.1016/S0732-3123(01)00051-7

Dixon, J. A., & Dohn, M. C. (2003). Redescription disembeds relations: Evidence from relational transfer and use in problem solving. *Memory & Cognition, 31*(7), 1082–1093. doi:10.3758/BF03196129 PMID:14704023

Dix, S., Phau, I., & Pougnet, S. (2010). "Bend it like Beckham": The influence of sports celebrities on young adult consumers. *Young Consumers, 11*(1), 36–46. doi:10.1108/17473611011025993

Doerr, J. (2018). *Measure what Matters: How Google, Bono, and the Gates Foundation Rock the World with OKRs*. Penguin.

Dondlinger, M. J. (2007). Educational video game design: A review of the literature. *Journal of Applied Educational Technology, 4*(1), 21-31.

Dongsheng, Y., Xiaohang, Y., & Daofeng, K. (2011). The Present Situation and Development Trend of E-sports Games in China. In *2011 International Conference on Future Computer Science and Education (ICFCSE)* (pp. 384-386). IEEE. 10.1109/ICFCSE.2011.98

Dubbels, B. (2014). Cognitive Ethnography as a Mixed-Method for Game User Research. *CHI 2014*.

Dubbels, B. (2016). Pedagogy & Play: Creating Playful Curriculum for Academic Achievement and Engaged Learning. In Learning, Education, and Games. (Vol. 2). Etc. Press.

Dubbels, B. R. (2017). Gamification Transformed: Gamification Should Deliver the Best Parts of Game Experiences, Not Just Experiences of Game Parts. *Transforming Gaming and Computer Simulation Technologies across Industries*, 17–47. doi:10.4018/978-1-5225-1817-4.ch002

Dubbels, B. (2011). Cognitive Ethnography. *International Journal of Gaming and Computer-Mediated Simulations, 3*(1), 68–78. doi:10.4018/jgcms.2011010105

Dubbels, B. R. (2012). *The Brain Is For Action: Embodiment, Causality, and Conceptual Learning with Video Games to Improve Reading Comprehension and Scientific Problem Solving*. University of Minnesota.

Duncan, G. J., Dowsett, C. J., Claessens, A., Magnuson, K., Huston, A. C., Klebanov, P., ... Japel, C. (2007). School readiness and later achievement. *Developmental Psychology, 43*(6), 1428–1446. doi:10.1037/0012-1649.43.6.1428 PMID:18020822

Eccles, J. S., & Wigfield, A. (2002). Motivational beliefs, values, and goals. *Annual Review of Psychology, 53*(1), 109–132. doi:10.1146/annurev.psych.53.100901.135153 PMID:11752481

Eisenmann, T. R., Ries, E., & Dillard, S. (2012). *Hypothesis-driven entrepreneurship: The lean startup.* Academic Press.

Elder Jr, G. H. (1985). Perspectives on the life course. *Life Course Dynamics,* 23-49.

Elder, G. H. (1994). Time, Human Agency, and Social Change: Perspectives on the Life Course. *Social Psychology Quarterly, 57*(1), 4–15. doi:10.2307/2786971

Emerson, J. W., Green, W. A., Schloerke, B., Crowley, J., Cook, D., Hofmann, H., & Wickham, H. (2012). The Generalized Pairs Plot. *Journal of Computational and Graphical Statistics, 22*(1), 79–91. doi:10.1080/10618600.2012.694762

Emmitt, G. E., & Gorse, C. A. (2006). *Communication in construction teams.* London: Spon, Taylor & Francis.

Endacott, J. L., & Brooks, S. (2018). Historical Empathy: Perspectives and Responding to the Past. The Wiley International Handbook of History Teaching and Learning, 203.

Endacott, J. L. (2010). Reconsidering Affective Engagement in Historical Empathy. *Theory and Research in Social Education, 38*(1), 6–47. doi:10.1080/00933104.2010.10473415

Endacott, J. L. (2014). Negotiating the Process of Historical Empathy. *Theory and Research in Social Education, 42*(1), 4–34. doi:10.1080/00933104.2013.826158

Endacott, J., & Brooks, S. (2013). An Updated Theoretical and Practical Model for Promoting Historical Empathy. *Social Studies Research & Practice, 8,* 41–58.

Erickson, L. C., Thiessen, E. D., Godwin, K. E., Dickerson, J. P., & Fisher, A. V. (2014). Endogenously- but not Exogenously-driven Selective Sustained Attention is Related to Learning in a Classroom-like Setting in Kindergarten Children. In P. Bello, M. Guarini, M. McShane, & B. Scassellati (Eds.), *Proceedings of the 36th Annual Conference of the Cognitive Science Society* (pp. 457-462). Austin, TX: Cognitive Science Society.

ESA. (2017). *2017 Essential Facts about the Computer and Video Game Industry.* ESA. Retrieved from http://www.theesa.com/wpcontent/uploads/2017/09/EF2017_Design_ FinalDigital.pdf

Evans, J. S. B. T. (2008). Dual-Processing Accounts of Reasoning, Judgment, and Social Cognition. *Annual Review of Psychology, 59*(1), 255–278. doi:10.1146/annurev.psych.59.103006.093629 PMID:18154502

Ferrari, S. (2013). eSport and the Human Body: Foundations for a Popular Aesthetics. In *Proceedings of DiGRA 2013: DeFragging Game Studies.* Atlanta, GA: DiGRA.

Fischer, S. C., Morrin, K. A., & Joslyn, S. (2003). *Measuring Multi-tasking Ability.* Report prepared for the Office of Naval research by Anacapa Sciences, Inc.

Fisher, A. V., Godwin, K. E., & Seltman, H. (2014). Visual environment, attention allocation, and learning: When too much of a good thing may be bad. *Psychological Science, 25*(7), 1362–1370. doi:10.1177/0956797614533801 PMID:24855019

Fisher, A. V., & Kloos, H. (2016). Development of selective sustained attention: The Role of executive functions. In L. Freund, P. McCardle, & J. Griffin (Eds.), *Executive function in preschool age children: Integrating measurement, neurodevelopment and translational research.* APA Press. doi:10.1037/14797-010

Fisher, A. V., Thiessen, E., Godwin, K., Kloos, H., & Dickerson, J. P. (2013). Mechanisms of focused attention in 3- to 5-year-old children: Evidence from a new object tracking task. *Journal of Experimental Child Psychology, 114*(2), 275–294. doi:10.1016/j.jecp.2012.07.006 PMID:23022318

Flin, R. (1996). *Sitting in the Hot Seat: Leaders and Teams for Critical Incidents.* Chichester, UK: Wiley.

Forster, M. (2009). *Informative Assessment—understanding and guiding learning.* Retrieved from http://research.acer.edu.au/research_conference/RC2009/17august/11/

Foster, A., & Mishra, P. (2008). Games, Claims, Genres and Learning. In R. E. Ferdig (Ed.), *Handbook of research on effective electronic gaming in education* (pp. 33–50). Hershey, PA: Information Science Reference. doi:10.4018/978-1-59904-808-6.ch002

Frederiksen, D. L., & Brem, A. (2017). How do entrepreneurs think they create value? A scientific reflection of Eric Ries' Lean Startup approach. *The International Entrepreneurship and Management Journal, 13*(1), 169–189. doi:10.100711365-016-0411-x

Freeman, G., & Wohn, D. (2017). eSports as an Emerging Research Context at CHI: Diverse Perspectives on Definitions. In *Proceedings of the 2017 CHI Conference Extended Abstracts on Human Factors in Computing Systems* (pp. 1601-1608). ACM. 10.1145/3027063.3053158

Freeman, M., & Capper, J. M. (1999). Exploiting the web for education: An anonymous asynchronous role simulation. *Australian Journal of Educational Technology, 15*(1), 95–116.

Frey, B. J., & Dueck, D. (2007). Clustering by passing messages between data points. *Science, 315*(5814), 972–976. doi:10.1126cience.1136800 PMID:17218491

FTC. (2016, January 5). *Lumosity to pay $2 million to settle FTC deceptive advertising charges for its "Brain Training" program* [Press release]. Retrieved from https://www.ftc.gov/news-events/press-releases/2016/01/lumosity-pay-2-million-settle-ftc-deceptive-advertising-charges

Fullerton, T. (2008). *Game Design Workshop: A Playcentric Approach to Creating Innovative Games.* Elsevier Morgan Kaufmann.

Furnham, A. (1986). Response bias, social desirability and dissimulation. *Personality and Individual Differences, 7*(3), 385–400. doi:10.1016/0191-8869(86)90014-0

Gabadinho, A., Ritschard, G., Müller, N. S., & Studer, M. (2011). Analyzing and Visualizing State Sequences in R with TraMineR. *Journal of Statistical Software, 40*(4), 1–37. doi:10.18637/jss.v040.i04

Gamberini, L., Mariano, A., Barresi, G., Fabgregat, M., Prontu, L., & Ibanez, F. (2006). Cognition, technology and games for the elderly: An introduction to ELDERGAMES Project. *PsychNology Journal, 4*(3), 285–308.

Garris, R., Ahlers, R., & Driskell, J. E. (2002). Games, motivation, and learning: A research and practice model. *Simulation & Gaming, 33*(4), 441–467. doi:10.1177/1046878102238607

Geary, K. E. (2011). *The impact of choice on child sustained attention in the preschool classroom* (Unpublished Thesis). Louisiana State University, Baton Rouge, LA.

Gee, J. P. (2007). What Video Games Have to Teach Us About Learning and Literacy (2nd ed.). New York, NY: Palgrave Macmillan.

Gee, J. P. (2007). *Good Video Games + Good Learning: Collected essays on video games, learning and literacy* (Vol. 27). Peter Lang. doi:10.3726/978-1-4539-1162-4

Gee, J. P., & Shaffer, D. W. (2010). Looking where the light is bad: Video games and the future of assessment. *EDge, 6*(1), 2–19.

Geertz, C. (1973). Thick Description: Towards an Interpretive Theory of Culture. In *The Interpretation of Cultures* (pp. 3–30). New York, NY: Basic Books.

Gerling, K. M., Schulte, F. P., Smeddinck, J., & Masuch, M. (2012). *Game design for older adults: Effects of age-related changes on structural elements of digital games. In Entertainment Computing-ICEC 2012* (pp. 235–242). Springer. Retrieved from http://link.springer.com/chapter/10.1007/978-3-642-33542-6_20

Gijlers, H., & de Jong, T. (2013). Using Concept Maps to Facilitate Collaborative Simulation-Based Inquiry Learning. *Journal of the Learning Sciences, 22*(3), 340–374. doi:10.1080/10508406.2012.748664

Gilad, I. (2018, February 1). *Why you should stop using product roadmaps and try GIST Planning.* Retrieved July 1, 2018, from https://hackernoon.com/why-i-stopped-using- product-roadmaps-and-switched-to-gist-planning-3b7f54e271d1?ref=http%3A%2F%2Fproduct-frameworks.com

Gitelman, D. R. (2003). Attention and its disorders: Imaging in clinical neuroscience. *British Medical Bulletin, 65*(1), 21–34. doi:10.1093/bmb/65.1.21 PMID:12697614

Glaser, B. G., & Strauss, A. L. (1968). The Discovery of Grounded Theory: Strategies for Qualitative Research. *Aldine Transaction, 17*(4), 354-365.

Glaser, R. O. (1993). *Groupthink index: can we manage our agreements? Facilitator guide.* Organization Design and Development.

Glasslab. (2014). *Pyschometric Considerations in Game-Based Assessments.* White Paper Released by Glasslab, 160.

Glenberg, A. M., Witt, J. K., & Metcalfe, J. (2013). From the revolution to embodiment: 25 years of cognitive psychology. *Perspectives on Psychological Science, 8*(5), 573–585. doi:10.1177/1745691613498098 PMID:26173215

Gobert, J. D., Sao Pedro, M. A., & Baker, R. S., Toto, E., & Montalvo, O. (2012). Leveraging educational data mining for real-time performance assessment of scientific inquiry skills within microworlds. *Journal of Educational Data Mining, 4*(1), 111–143.

Gobet, F. (2005). Chunking Models of Expertise: Implications for Education. *Applied Cognitive Psychology, 19*(2), 183–204. doi:10.1002/acp.1110

Godwin, K. E., & Fisher, A. V. (in press). Wiggleometer: Measuring selective sustained attention in children. *Proceedings of the 40th Annual Meeting of the Cognitive Science Society.*

Godwin, K.E., Lomas, D., Koedinger, K. R., Fisher, A. V., (2015). Monster Mischief: Designing a video game to assess selective sustained attention. *International Journal of Gaming and Computer-Mediated Simulations: Assessing human Capabilities in Video Games and Stimulations, 7*(4), 18-39.

Godwin, K. E., Almeda, M. V., Seltman, H., Kai, S., Skerbetz, M. D., Baker, R. S., & Fisher, A. V. (2016). Off-task behavior in elementary school children. *Learning and Instruction, 44*, 128–143. doi:10.1016/j.learninstruc.2016.04.003

Goldin-Meadow, S. (2014). Widening the lens: What the manual modality reveals about learning, language and cognition. *Philosophical Transactions of the Royal Society, Biological Sciences., 369*(20130295).

Goldin-Meadow, S. (2011). Learning through gesture. *Wiley Interdisciplinary Reviews: Cognitive Science, 2*(6), 595–607. doi:10.1002/wcs.132 PMID:24187604

Goodman, L. (1990). *Time and learning in the special education classroom.* SUNY Press.

Gredler, M. E. (1992). *Designing and evaluating games and simulations.* London: Kogan Page.

Green, C. S., & Bavelier, D. (2008). Exercising Your Brain: A Review of Human Brain Plasticity and Training-Induced Learning. *Psychology and Aging, 23*(4), 692–701. doi:10.1037/a0014345 PMID:19140641

Green, C. S., Benson, C., Kersten, D., & Schrater, P. (2010). Alterations in choice behavior by manipulations of world model. *Proceedings of the National Academy of Sciences of the United States of America, 107*(37), 16401–16406. doi:10.1073/pnas.1001709107 PMID:20805507

Green, C., & Bavelier, D. (2003). Action video game modifies visual selective attention. *Nature, 423*(6939), 534–537. doi:10.1038/nature01647 PMID:12774121

Guorui, Z. (2012). Bibliometric Analysis on E-Sports in China. In *Advances in Computer Science and Engineering* (pp. 111–118). Springer. doi:10.1007/978-3-642-27948-5_16

Hallman, K. & Giel, T. (2017). eSports–Competitive Sports or Recreational Activity? *Sport Management Review*.

Halverson, R., & Owen, V. E. (2014). Game-based assessment: an integrated model for capturing evidence of learning in play. *International Journal of Learning Technology*. Retrieved from http://www.inderscienceonline.com/doi/abs/10.1504/IJLT.2014.064489

Hamari, J., & Sjöblom, M. (2017). What is eSports and why do people watch it? *Internet Research*, *27*(2), 211–232. doi:10.1108/IntR-04-2016-0085

Hammer, D., & Elby, A. (2003). Tapping Epistemological Resources for Learning Physics. *Journal of the Learning Sciences*, *12*(1), 53–90. doi:10.1207/S15327809JLS1201_3

Hanus, M., & Fox, J. (2015). Assessing the effects of gamification in the classroom: A longitudinal study on intrinsic motivation, social comparison, satisfaction, effort, and academic performance. *Computers & Education*, *80*, 152–161. doi:10.1016/j.compedu.2014.08.019

Harper, T. (2013). *The Culture of Digital Fighting Games: Performance and Practice*. New York, NY: Routledge.

Harpstead, E., Myers, B. A., & Aleven, V. (2013). In search of learning: facilitating data analysis in educational games. In *Proceedings of the SIGCHI Conference on Human Factors in Computing Systems* (pp. 79–88). New York, NY: ACM. 10.1145/2470654.2470667

Hauk, O., Johnsrude, I., & Pulvermüller, F. (2004). Somatotopic representation of action words in human motor and premotor cortex. *Neuron*, *41*(2), 301–307. doi:10.1016/S0896-6273(03)00838-9 PMID:14741110

Hays, M. J., Campbell, J. C., Poore, J. C., Webb, A. K., King, T. K., & Trimmer, M. A. (2012). Can Role-Play with Virtual Humans Teach Interpersonal Skills? *Proceedings of the 34th Interservice/Industry Training, Simulation, and Education Conference (I/ITSEC)*.

Hays, R. T. (2006). *The Science of Learning: A Systems Theory Perspective*. Universal-Publishers.

Heathcote, A., Eidels, A., Colman, J., Watson, J., & Strayer, D. (2014). Multi-tasking in working memory. *Proceedings of the Annual Meeting of the Cognitive Science Society*, 601–606.

Hebbel-Seeger, A. (2012). The relationship between real sports and digital adaptation in e-sport gaming. *International Journal of Sports Marketing & Sponsorship*, *13*(2), 43–54. doi:10.1108/IJSMS-13-02-2012-B005

Heeter, C., Lee, Y.-H., Medler, B., & Magerko, B. (2013). *Conceptually meaningful metrics: Inferring optimal challenge and mindset from gameplay. In Game Analytics* (pp. 731–762). Springer.

Hermann, C. (1963). Some consequences of crisis which limit the viability of organizations. *Administrative Science Quarterly*, *8*(1), 61–82. doi:10.2307/2390887

Hiltz, S. R. (1978). The impact of a new communications medium upon scientific research communities. *Journal of Research-Communication Studies*, *1*, 111–124.

Holmgård, C., Togelius, J., & Henriksen, L. (2016). *Computational Intelligence and Cognitive Performance Assessment Games. Computational Intelligence and Games.* CIG.

Hoorens, V. (1995). Self-favoring biases, self-presentation, and the self-other asymmetry in social comparison. *Journal of Personality*, *63*(4), 793–817. doi:10.1111/j.1467-6494.1995.tb00317.x

Hooshyar, D., Yousefi, M., & Lim, H. (2018). Data-Driven Approaches to Game Player Modeling: A Systematic Literature Review. *ACM Computing Surveys*, *50*(6), 90. doi:10.1145/3145814

Hou, H. T. (2012). Exploring the behavioral patterns of learners in an educational massively multiple online role-playing game (MMORPG). *Computers & Education*, *58*(4), 1225–1233. doi:10.1016/j.compedu.2011.11.015

Howley, L., Szauter, K., Perkowski, L., Clifton, M., & Mcnaughton, N. (2008). Quality of Standardised Patient Research Reports in the Medical Education Literature: Review and Recommendations. *Medical Education*, *42*(4), 350–358. doi:10.1111/j.1365-2923.2007.02999.x PMID:18298448

Hunicke, R., LeBlanc, M., & Zubek, R. (2001). *MDA: A Formal Approach to Game Design and Game Research.* Presented at the Game Developers Conference. Retrieved from http://www.cs.northwestern.edu/~hunicke/MDA.pdf

Hunicke, R., LeBlanc, M., & Zubek, R. (2004). MDA: A formal approach to game design and game research. In *Proceedings of the Workshop on Challenges in Game AI, 19th National Conference on Artificial Intelligence.* AAAI Press.

Husson, F., Josse, J., Le, S., & Mazet, J. (2015). *FactoMineR: Multivariate Exploratory Data Analysis and Data Mining.* Retrieved from http://CRAN.R-project.org/package=FactoMineR

Hutchins, E. L. (2011, December 15). *Cognitive Ethnography.* Retrieved from http://hci.ucsd.edu/102b/

IJsselsteijn, W. A., Nap, H. H., de Kort, Y. A. W., & Poels, K. (2007). *Digital game design for elderly users.* Toronto, Canada: ACM.

Jack, B., Chetty, V., Anthony, D., Greenwald, J., Sanchez, G., Johnson, A., ... Culpepper, L. (2009). A Reengineered Hospital Discharge Program to Decrease Rehospitalization: A Randomized Trial. *Annals of Internal Medicine*, *150*(3), 178–187. doi:10.7326/0003-4819-150-3-200902030-00007 PMID:19189907

Jacobs, H. (2015, May 11). Here's the insane training schedule of a 20-something professional gamer. *Business Insider.* Retrieved from: http://www.businessinsider.com/pro-gamersexplain-the-insane-training-regimen-they-use-to-stay-on-top-2015-5?r=US&IR=T&IR=T

Jaeggi, S. M., Buschkuehl, M., Jonides, J., & Perrig, W. J. (2008). Improving fluid intelligence with training on working memory. *Proceedings of the National Academy of Sciences of the United States of America*, *105*(19), 6829–6833. doi:10.1073/pnas.0801268105 PMID:18443283

Jang, S., Vitale, J., Jyung, R., & Black, J. (2016). *Direct manipulation is better than passive viewing for learning anatomy in a three-dimensional virtual reality environment* (Vol. 106). Academic Press.

Janis, I. L. (1972). *Victims of Groupthink: A Psychological Study of Foreign Policy Decisions*. Boston: Houghton Mifflin.

Janis, I. L. (1982). *Groupthink* (2nd ed.). Boston: Houghton Mifflin.

Jenny, S., Manning, R., Keiper, M., & Olrich, T. (2017). Virtual(ly) Athletes: Where eSports Fit within the Definition of "Sport". *Quest*, *69*(1), 1–18. doi:10.1080/00336297.2016.1144517

Jensen, J. (2008). Developing historical empathy through debate: An action research study. *Social Studies Research & Practice*, *3*, 55–66.

Johnson-Glenberg, M. C. (2012). *Pilot study with SMALLab summer camp attendees*. Unpublished.

Johnson-Glenberg, M. C. (submitted). *Immersive VR and education: Embodied design principles that include gesture and hand controls*. Academic Press.

Johnson-Glenberg, M. C. (2017). Embodied education in mixed and mediated realities: Principles for content design. In D. Liu, C. Dede, & J. Richards (Eds.), *Virtual, Augmented, and Mixed Realities in Education* (pp. 193–218). Springer Verlag. doi:10.1007/978-981-10-5490-7_11

Johnson-Glenberg, M. C., Birchfield, D., Koziupa, T., & Tolentino, L. (2014). Collaborative embodied learning in mixed reality motion-capture environments: Two science studies. *Journal of Educational Psychology*, *106*(1), 86–104. doi:10.1037/a0034008

Johnson-Glenberg, M. C., Birchfield, D., Megowan-Romanowicz, M. C., Tolentino, L., & Martinez, C. (2009). Embodied Games, Next Gen Interfaces, and Assessment of High School Physics. *International Journal of Learning and Media*, *1*(2). doi:10.1162/ijlm.2009.0017

Johnson-Glenberg, M. C., Birchfield, D., Megowan-Romanowicz, M. C., & Uysal, S. (2009). SMALLab: Virtual geology studies using embodied learning with motion, sound, and graphics. *Educational Media International*, *46*(4), 267–280. doi:10.1080/09523980903387555

Johnson-Glenberg, M. C., & Hekler, E. B. (2013). Alien Health game: An embodied, motion-capture exer-game teaching nutrition and *MyPlate*. *Games for Health Journal*, *6*(2). doi:10.1089/g4h.2013.0057

Johnson-Glenberg, M. C., & Megowan-Romanowicz, M. C. (2017). Embodied science and mixed reality: How gesture and motion capture affect physics education. *Cognitive Research: Principles and Implications*, *2*(24). doi:10.118641235-017-0060-9 PMID:28603770

Johnson-Glenberg, M. C., Savio-Ramos, C., & Henry, H. (2014). "Alien Health": A nutrition instruction exergame using the *Kinect* sensor. *Games for Health Journal: Research, Development, and Clinical Applications*, *3*(4), 241–251. doi:10.1089/g4h.2013.0094 PMID:25083315

Johnson, S. B., Riis, J. L., & Noble, K. G. (2016). State of the art review: Poverty and the developing brain. *Pediatrics*, *137*(4), 1–16. doi:10.1542/peds.2015-3075 PMID:26952506

Jonides, J. (1981). Voluntary vs. Automatic control over the mind's eye's movement. In J. B. Long & A. D. Baddeley (Eds.), *Attention and Performance IX*. Hillsdale, NJ: Lawrence Erlbaum Associates.

Kahneman, D. (2003). Maps of Bounded Rationality: Psychology for Behavioral Economics. *The American Economic Review*, *93*(5), 1449–1475. doi:10.1257/000282803322655392

Kane, D. (2003). Finding a place for discount usability engineering in agile development: throwing down the gauntlet. In *Agile Development Conference, 2003. ADC 2003. Proceedings of the* (pp. 40–46). IEEE. Retrieved from http://ieeexplore.ieee.org/xpls/abs_all.jsp?arnumber=1231451

Kane, D., & Spradley, B. (2017). *Recognizing Esports as a Sport. Sport Journal*.

Kapell, M., & Elliott, A. B. R. (2013). *Playing with the past: Digital games and the simulation of history*. New York: Bloomsbury.

Kaput, J. J. (1994). The representational roles of technology in connecting mathematics with authentic experience. *Didactics of mathematics as a scientific discipline*, 379-397.

Karhulahti, V. (2016). Prank, Troll, Gross and Gore: Performance Issues in Esport Livestreaming. In *Proceedings of the 1st International Joint Conference of DiGRA and FDG*. Digital Games Research Association and Society for the Advancement of the Science of Digital Games.

Karhulahti, V. (2017). Reconsidering Esport: Economics and Executive Ownership. *Physical Culture and Sport Studies and Research*, *74*(1), 43–53. doi:10.1515/pcssr-2017-0010

Kari, T. & Karhulahti, V. (2016). Do E-Athletes Move? A Study on Training and Physical Exercise in Elite E-Sports. *International Journal of Gaming and Computer-Mediated Simulations*, 8.

Kari, T. (2014). Can Exergaming Promote Physical Fitness and Physical Activity?: A Systematic Review of Systematic Reviews. *International Journal of Gaming and Computer-Mediated Simulations*, *6*(4), 59–77. doi:10.4018/ijgcms.2014100105

Kari, T., & Makkonen, M. (2014). Explaining the Usage Intentions of Exergames. In *Proceedings of the 35th International Conference on Information Systems (ICIS)*. AIS.

Kebritchi, M., Hirumi, A., & Bai, H. (2010). The effects of modern mathematics computer games on mathematics achievement and class motivation. *Computers & Education*, *55*(2), 427–443. doi:10.1016/j.compedu.2010.02.007

Ke, F. (2008a). A case study of computer gaming for math: Engaged learning from gameplay? *Computers & Education*, *51*(4), 1609–1620. doi:10.1016/j.compedu.2008.03.003

Ke, F. (2008b). Computer games application within alternative classroom goal structures: Cognitive, metacognitive, and affective evaluation. *Educational Technology Research and Development, 56*(5-6), 539–556. doi:10.100711423-008-9086-5

Kerr, D., & Chung, G. K. W. K. (2012). Identifying key features of student performance in educational video games and simulations through cluster analysis. *Journal of Educational Data Mining, 4*(1), 144–182.

Kidron, I., & Zehavi, N. (2002). The Role of Animation in Teaching the Limit Concept. *International Journal of Computer Algebra in Mathematics Education, 9*(3), 205–227.

Kim, J., Vande Velde, A., Thiessen, E., & Fisher, A. V. (2017). Variables Involved in Selective Sustained Attention Development: Advances in Measurement. *Proceedings of the 39th Annual Meeting of the Cognitive Science Society*, 670-675.

Kim, S., & Chang, M. (2010). Computer Games for the Math Achievement of Diverse Students. *Journal of Educational Technology & Society, 13*(3), 224–232.

Kinnebrew, J. S., Killingsworth, S. S., Clark, D. B., Biswas, G., Sengupta, P., Minstrell, J., ... Krinks, K. (2017). Contextual Markup and Mining in Digital Games for Science Learning: Connecting Player Behaviors to Learning Goals. *IEEE Transactions on Learning Technologies, 10*(1), 93–103. doi:10.1109/TLT.2016.2521372

Kolb, A. Y., & Kolb, D. A. (2005). Learning styles and learning spaces: Enhancing experiential learning in higher education. *Academy of Management Learning & Education, 4*(2), 193–212. doi:10.5465/amle.2005.17268566

Kwong, A. W., Healton, B., & Lancaster, R. (1998). *State of siege: new thinking for the next decade of design. IEEE Aerospace Conference, 4*, pp. 85–93. doi:10.1109/AERO.1998.682158

L'Abate, L. (2009). *The Praeger handbook of play across the life cycle: Fun from infancy to old age*. Santa Barbara, CA: ABC-CLIO. Retrieved from https://books.google.com/books?hl=en& lr=&id=VAOrCQAAQBAJ&oi=fnd&pg=PP1&dq=abata+the+praeger+handbook&ots=iyCJ jfBz-O&sig=fVm6WndwK_AEyVRiTvjtrsOOe6k

Lamb, R. L., Annetta, L., Vallett, D. B., & Sadler, T. D. (2014). Cognitive diagnostic like approaches using neural-network analysis of serious educational videogames. *Computers & Education, 70*, 92–104. doi:10.1016/j.compedu.2013.08.008

Lee, A. (2005). *E-Sports as a Growing Industry (Research Report)*. Samsung Economic Research Institute.

Lee, C.-Y., & Chen, M.-P. (2009). A computer game as a context for non-routine mathematical problem solving: The effects of type of question prompt and level of prior knowledge. *Computers & Education, 52*(3), 530–542. doi:10.1016/j.compedu.2008.10.008

Lee, D., & Schoenstedt, L. J. (2011). Comparison of eSports and traditional sports consumption motives. *The ICHPER-SD Journal of Research in Health, Physical Education, Recreation, Sport & Dance, 6*(2), 39.

Lee, P. J., & Ashby, R. (2001). Empathy, perspective taking, and rational understanding. In O. L. Davis Jr, S. Foster, & E. Yeager (Eds.), *Historical Empathy and Perspective Taking in the Social Studies* (pp. 21–50). Boulder, CO: Rowman and Littlefield.

Lee, Y.-H., Heeter, C., Magerko, B., & Medler, B. (2012). Gaming mindsets: Implicit theories in serious game learning. *Cyberpsychology, Behavior, and Social Networking*, *15*(4), 190–194. doi:10.1089/cyber.2011.0328 PMID:22165916

Leighton, J. P., & Gierl, M. J. (2007). Defining and evaluating models of cognition used in educational measurement to make inferences about examinees' thinking processes. *Educational Measurement: Issues and Practice*, *26*(2), 3–16. doi:10.1111/j.1745-3992.2007.00090.x

Lesh, R., & Zawojewski, J. (2007). Problem solving and modeling. Second handbook of research on mathematics teaching and learning, 2, 763-804.

Lévesque, S. (2008). *Thinking Historically: Educating Students for the Twenty-first Century*. Toronto: University of Toronto Press.

Levstik, L. S., & Barton, K. C. (2011). *Doing history: Investigating with children in elementary and middle school*. New York: Routledge.

Liang, X., & Zhou, Q. (2009). Students' experiences of mathematics learning in technology integrated classrooms. *Teaching and Learning*, *5*(1), 62–74.

Li, D., Liau, A., & Khoo, A. (2013). Player-avatar identification in video gaming: Concept and measurement. *Computers in Human Behavior*, *29*(1), 257–263. doi:10.1016/j.chb.2012.09.002

Lindgren, R., & Johnson-Glenberg, M. C. (2013). Emboldened by embodiment: Six precepts regarding the future of embodied learning and mixed reality technologies. *Educational Researcher*, *42*(8), 445–452. doi:10.3102/0013189X13511661

Linehan, C., Kirman, B., Lawson, S., & Chan, G. (2011). Practical, Appropriate, Empirically-validated Guidelines for Designing Educational Games. In *Proceedings of the SIGCHI Conference on Human Factors in Computing Systems* (pp. 1979–1988). New York: ACM. 10.1145/1978942.1979229

Lithner, J. (2004). Mathematical reasoning in calculus textbook exercises. *The Journal of Mathematical Behavior*, *23*(4), 405–427. doi:10.1016/j.jmathb.2004.09.003

Loewenstein, G. (1994). The Psychology of curiosity: A review and reinterpretation. *Psychological Bulletin*, *116*(1), 75–98. doi:10.1037/0033-2909.116.1.75

Loftus, G., & Loftus, E. R. (1983). *Mind at Play: The Psychology of Video Games*. Basic Books.

Logie, R. H., Trawley, S., & Law, A. (2011). Multitasking: Multiple, domain-specific cognitive functions in a virtual environment. *Memory & Cognition*, *39*(8), 1561–1574. doi:10.375813421-011-0120-1 PMID:21691876

Lok, B., Ferdig, R. E., Raij, A., Johnsen, K., Dickerson, R., Coutts, J., & Lind, D. S. (2006). Applying Virtual Reality in Medical Communication Education: Current Findings and potential Teaching and Learning Benefits of immersive Virtual Patients. *Virtual Reality (Waltham Cross)*, *10*(3-4), 185–195. doi:10.100710055-006-0037-3

Lomas, D., Patel, K., Forlizzi, J. L., & Koedinger, K. R. (2013). Optimizing challenge in an educational game using large-scale design experiments. In *Proceedings of the SIGCHI Conference on Human Factors in Computing Systems* (pp. 89-98). ACM. 10.1145/2470654.2470668

López, J. M., & Cáceres, M. J. (2010). Virtual games in social science education. *Computers & Education*, *55*(3), 1336–1345. doi:10.1016/j.compedu.2010.05.028

Lopez-Morteo, G., & López, G. (2007). Computer support for learning mathematics: A learning environment based on recreational learning objects. *Computers & Education*, *48*(4), 618–641. doi:10.1016/j.compedu.2005.04.014

Lui, M., Kuhn, A., Acosta, A., Niño-Soto, M. I., Quintana, C., & Slotta, J. D. (2014). Using mobile tools in immersive environments to support science inquiry. *CHI '14 Extended Abstracts on Human Factors in Computing Systems, 978*, 403-406. doi:10.1145/2559206.2574796

Lumsden, J., Edwards, E. A., Lawrence, N. S., Coyle, D., & Munafò, M. R. (2016). Gamification of Cognitive Assessment and Cognitive Training: A Systematic Review of Applications and Efficacy. *JMIR Serious Games*, *4*(2), e11. doi:10.2196/games.5888 PMID:27421244

Luna, B. (2009). Developmental changes in cognitive control through adolescence. *Advances in Child Development and Behavior*, *37*, 233–278. doi:10.1016/S0065-2407(09)03706-9 PMID:19673164

Malone, T. (1981). Toward a theory of intrinsically motivating instruction. *Cognitive Science*, *5*(4), 333–369. doi:10.120715516709cog0504_2

Maric, J. (2011). Electronic Sport: How Pro-gaming Negotiates Territorial Belonging and Gender. *Platform: Journal of Media and Communication*, *3*(2), 6–23.

Marston, H. R. (2013). Design Recommendations for Digital Game Design within an Ageing Society. *Educational Gerontology*, *39*(2), 103–118. doi:10.1080/03601277.2012.689936

Martinez-Garza, M. M., & Clark, D. B. (2017). Two systems, two stances: a novel theoretical framework for model-based learning in digital games. In P. Wouters & H. van Oostendorp (Eds.), *Instructional Techniques to Facilitate Learning and Motivation of Serious Games* (pp. 37–58). Cham, Switzerland: Springer; doi:10.1007/978-3-319-39298-1_3

Martinez-Garza, M. M., Clark, D., & Nelson, B. (2013). Advances in Assessment of Students' Intuitive Understanding of Physics through Gameplay Data. *International Journal of Gaming and Computer-Mediated Simulations*, *5*(4), 1–16. doi:10.4018/ijgcms.2013100101

Martinez-Garza, M., Clark, D. B., & Nelson, B. C. (2013). Digital games and the US National Research Council's science proficiency goals. *Studies in Science Education*, *49*(2), 170–208. doi:10.1080/03057267.2013.839372

Martončik, M. (2015). E-Sports: Playing Just for Fun or Playing to Satisfy Life Goals? *Computers in Human Behavior, 48*, 208–211. doi:10.1016/j.chb.2015.01.056

Mayer, R. E., Griffith, E., Jurkowitz, I. T. N., & Rothman, D. (2008). Increased Interestingness of Extraneous Details in a Multimedia Science Presentation Leads to Decreased Learning. *Journal of Experimental Psychology. Applied, 14*(4), 329–339. doi:10.1037/a0013835 PMID:19102616

Mayer, R. E., & Moreno, R. (2003). Nine ways to reduce cognitive load in multimedia learning. *Educational Psychologist, 38*(1), 43–52. doi:10.1207/S15326985EP3801_6

Mayo, M. J. (2009). Video games: A route to large-scale STEM education? *Science, 323*(5910), 79–82. doi:10.1126cience.1166900 PMID:19119223

McGrath, J. E. (1984). Groups: Interaction and Performance. Englewood Cliffs, NJ: Prentice-Hall, Inc.

Mclaughlan, R. G., & Kirkpatrick, D. (2005). *Online text-based role play-simulation: The challenges ahead.* Simulation Industry Association of Australia.

McLaughlin, A. C., Gandy, M., Allaire, J., & Whitlock, L. (2012). Putting Fun into Video Games for Older Adults. *Ergonomics in Design, 20*(2), 13–22. doi:10.1177/1064804611435654

McPherson, J., & Burns, N. R. (2008). Assessing the validity of computer-game-like tests of processing speed and working memory. *Behavior Research Methods, 40*(4), 969–981. doi:10.3758/BRM.40.4.969 PMID:19001388

McTee, M. (2014). E-Sports: More Than Just a Fad. *Oklahoma Journal of Law & Technology, 10*, 1–27.

Medlock, M. (2014, March). *History of Video Games User Research.* Keynote presented at the Games User Research Summit, San Francisco, CA. Retrieved from http://www.gamesuserresearchsig.org/gur-sig---library.html

Medlock, M. C., Wixon, D., Terrano, M., Romero, R., & Fulton, B. (2002). Using the RITE method to improve products: A definition and a case study. *Usability Professionals Association, 51.* Retrieved from http://www.computingscience.nl/docs/vakken/musy/RITE.pdf

Mehta, C. R., & Patel, N. R. (2012). *IBM SPSS Exact Tests.* Cambridge, MA: IBM Corporation.

Méndez, A., Martín, A., Pires, A. C., Vásquez, A., Maiche, A., González, F., & Carboni, A. (2015). Temporal perception and delay aversion: A videogame screening tool for the early detection of ADHD. *Revista Argentina de Ciencias del Comportamiento, 7*(3).

Merchant, Z., Goetz, E. T., Cifuentes, L., Keeney-Kennicutt, W., & Davis, T. J. (2014). Effectiveness of virtual reality-based instruction on students' learning outcomes in K-12 and higher education: A meta-analysis. *Computers & Education, 70*, 29–40. doi:10.1016/j.compedu.2013.07.033

Merzenich, M. M., Jenkins, W. M., Johnston, P., Schreiner, C., Miller, S. L., & Tallal, P. (1996). Temporal processing deficits of language-learning impaired children ameliorated by training. *Science*, *271*(5245), 77–81. doi:10.1126cience.271.5245.77 PMID:8539603

Metz, K. (1985). The development of children's problem solving in a gears task: A problem space perspective. *Cognitive Science*, *9*(4), 431–471. doi:10.120715516709cog0904_4

Milgram, P., & Kishino, A. F. (1994). Taxonomy of mixed reality visual displays. *IEICE Transactions on Information and Systems*, *E77-D*(12), 1321–1329.

Miller, E. K., & Cohen, J. D. (2001). An integrative theory of prefrontal cortex function. *Annual Review of Neuroscience*, *24*(1), 167–202. doi:10.1146/annurev.neuro.24.1.167 PMID:11283309

Miranda, S. M. (1994, February). A voidance of groupthink: Meeting management using group support systems. *Small Group Research*, *25*(1), 105–136. doi:10.1177/1046496494251007

Mishra, J., Anguera, J. A., & Gazzaley, A. (2016). Video Games for Neuro-Cognitive Optimization. *Neuron*, *90*(2), 214–218. doi:10.1016/j.neuron.2016.04.010 PMID:27100194

Mislevy, R. J., Almond, R. G., & Lukas, J. F. (2003). A brief introduction to evidence-centered design. *ETS Research Report Series, 2003*(1), i–29. doi:10.1002/j.2333-8504.2003.tb01908.x

Mislevy, R. J., Corrigan, S., Oranje, A., DiCerbo, K., Bauer, M. I., von Davier, A., & John, M. (2016). Psychometrics and game-based assessment. *Technology and Testing: Improving Educational and Psychological Measurement*, 23-48.

Mislevy, R. J., Oranje, A., Bauer, M. I., von Davier, A., Hao, J., Corrigan, S., … John, M. (2014). *Psychometric considerations in game-based assessment* (white paper). Retrieved from http://www.instituteofplay.org/work/projects/glasslab-research/

Mislevy, R. J., Behrens, J. T., DiCerbo, K. E., & Levy, R. (2012). Design and discovery in educational assessment: Evidence-centered design, psychometrics, and educational data mining. *JEDM-Journal of Educational Data Mining*, *4*(1), 11–48.

Miyake, A., Friedman, N. P., Emerson, M. J., Witzki, A. H., Howerter, A., & Wager, T. D. (2000). The unit and diversity of executive functions and their contributions to complex "frontal lobe" tasks: A latent variable analysis. *Cognitive Psychology*, *41*(1), 49–100. doi:10.1006/cogp.1999.0734 PMID:10945922

Morbini, F., Devault, D., Sagae, K., Gerten, J., Nazarian, A., & Traum, D. (2013). FLoReS: A Forward Looking, Reward Seeking, Dialogue Manager. *Natural Interaction with Robots, Knowbots and Smartphones*, 313-325. doi:10.1007/978-1-4614-8280-2_28

Morgan, P., & Ritter, S. (2002). *An experimental study of the effects of Cognitive Tutor® Algebra I on student knowledge and attitude*. Pittsburgh, PA: Carnegie Learning, Inc.

Mori, M. (1970). The Uncanny Valley. *Energy*, *7*(4), 33–35.

Nap, H. H., de Kort, Y. A. W., & IJsselsteijn, W. A. (2009). Senior gamers: Preferences, motivations and needs. *Gerontechnology (Valkenswaard)*, *8*(4), 247–262. doi:10.4017/gt.2009.08.04.003.00

Nathan, M. J., Walkington, C., Boncoddo, R., Pier, E. L., Williams, C. C., & Alibali, M. W. (2014). Actions speak louder with words: The roles of action and pedagogical language for grounding mathematical reasoning. *Learning and Instruction, 33*, 182-193.

Nederhof, A. J. (1985). Methods of coping with social desirability bias: A review. *European Journal of Social Psychology*, *15*(3), 263–280. doi:10.1002/ejsp.2420150303

Nielsen, J. (1994). Guerrilla HCI: Using discount usability engineering to penetrate the intimidation barrier. *Cost-Justifying Usability*, 245–272.

Nielsen, J. (2009). Discount usability: 20 years. *Jakob Nielsen's Alertbox*. Available at http://www. useit. com/alertbox/discount-usability. html

Nielsen, R., & Karhulahti, V. (2017). The Problematic Coexistence of Internet Gaming Disorder and Esports. In *Proceedings of the 12th International Conference on the Foundations of Digital Games*. ACM. 10.1145/3102071.3106359

Oakes, L., Kannass, K. N., & Shaddy, D. J. (2002). Developmental changes in endogenous control of attention: The role of target familiarity on infants' distraction latency. *Child Development*, *73*(6), 1644–1655. doi:10.1111/1467-8624.00496 PMID:12487484

Oehrtman, M. (2009). Collapsing dimensions, physical limitation, and other student metaphors for limit concepts. *Journal for Research in Mathematics Education*, 396–426.

Orasanu, J., & Fischer, U. (1997). Finding decisions in natural environments: the view from the cockpit. In C. E. Zsambok & G. Klein (Eds.), *Naturalistic Decision Making*. Mahwah, NJ: Lawrence Erlbaum.

Ota, K. R., & DuPaul, G. J. (2002). Task engagement and mathematics performance in children with attention-deficit hyperactivity disorder: Effects of supplemental computer instruction. *School Psychology Quarterly*, *17*(3), 242–257. doi:10.1521cpq.17.3.242.20881

Pagulayan, R. J., Steury, K. R., Fulton, B., & Romero, R. L. (2005). Designing for fun: User-testing case studies. In *Funology* (pp. 137–150). Springer. Retrieved from http://link.springer.com/content/pdf/10.1007/1-4020-2967-5_14.pdf

Pangaro, L. N., Worth-Dickstein, H., Macmillan, M. K., Klass, D. J., & Shatzer, J. H. (1997). Performance of "Standardized Examinees" in a Standardized-Patient Examination of Clinical Skills. *Academic Medicine*, *72*(11), 1008–1011. doi:10.1097/00001888-199711000-00021 PMID:9387827

Papastergiou, M. (2009). Digital Game-Based Learning in high school Computer Science education: Impact on educational effectiveness and student motivation. *Computers & Education*, *52*(1), 1–12. doi:10.1016/j.compedu.2008.06.004

Parker, L., & Lepper, M. (1992). Effects of fantasy contexts on children's learning and motivation: Making learning more fun. *Journal of Personality and Social Psychology, 62*(4), 625–633. doi:10.1037/0022-3514.62.4.625 PMID:1583588

Parnafes, O., & diSessa, A. (2004). Relations between Types of Reasoning and Computational Representations. *International Journal of Computers for Mathematical Learning, 9*(3), 251–280. doi:10.100710758-004-3794-7

Parshakov, P., & Zavertiaeva, M. A. (2015). Success in eSports: Does Country Matter? *SSRN Scholarly Paper 2662343*. Retrieved from: http://papers.ssrn.com/abstract=2662343

Parsons, T. D., Kenny, P., Ntuen, C. A., Pataki, C. S., Pato, M. T., Rizzo, A., & Sugar, J. (2008). Objective Structured Clinical Interview Training Using a Virtual Human Patient. *Studies in Health Technology and Informatics, 132*, 357–362. PMID:18391321

Pashler, H., Johnston, J. C., & Ruthruff, E. (2001). Attention and performance. *Annual Review of Psychology, 52*(1), 629–651. doi:10.1146/annurev.psych.52.1.629 PMID:11148320

Patton, J. (2002). Designing requirements: incorporating usage-centered design into an agile SW development process. In *Conference on Extreme Programming and Agile Methods* (pp. 1–12). Springer. 10.1007/3-540-45672-4_1

Patton, J., & Economy, P. (2014). *User story mapping: discover the whole story, build the right product.* O'Reilly Media, Inc.

Pearce, C. (2008). The Truth About Baby Boomer Gamers: A study of over-forty computer game players. *Games and Culture, 3*(2), 142–174. doi:10.1177/1555412008314132

Perkins, D. N., & Salomon, G. (1988). Teaching for transfer. *Educational Leadership, 46*(1), 22–32.

Pintrich, P. R. (2000). Multiple goals, multiple pathways: The role of goal orientation in learning and achievement. *Journal of Educational Psychology, 92*(3), 544–555. doi:10.1037/0022-0663.92.3.544

Plass, J., Homer, B., & Kinzer, C. (2014). *Playful Learning: An Integrated Design Framework* (White paper #02/2014). Games for Learning Institute. doi:10.13140/2.1.4175.6969

Podsakoff, P. M., MacKenzie, S. B., Lee, J. Y., & Podsakoff, N. P. (2003). Common method biases in behavioral research: A critical review of the literature and recommended remedies. *The Journal of Applied Psychology, 88*(5), 879–903. doi:10.1037/0021-9010.88.5.879 PMID:14516251

Poole, M. S., & DeSanctis, G. (1992). Micro level Structuration in Computer- Supported Group Decision Making. *Human Communication Research, 19*(1), 5–49. doi:10.1111/j.1468-2958.1992.tb00294.x

Poore, J., Webb, A., Hays, M. J., Campbell, J., Trimmer, M., & Major, L. M. (2012). *Emulating Sociality: A Comparison Study of Physiological Signals from Human and Virtual Social Interactions.* Poster presented at Social & Affective Neuroscience Society Annual Meeting.

Portney, K. E., & Cohen, S. (2006). Practical contexts and theoretical frameworks for teaching complexity with digital role-play simulations. In S. Cohen, K. E. Portney, D. Rehberger, & C. Thorsen (Eds.), *Virtual Decisions*. Mahwah, NJ: Lawrence Erlbaum.

Posner, M. I. (1980). Orienting of attention. *The Quarterly Journal of Experimental Psychology*, *32*(1), 3–25. doi:10.1080/00335558008248231 PMID:7367577

Posner, M. I., & Petersen, S. E. (1990). The attention system of the human brain. *Annual Review of Neuroscience*, *13*(1), 25–42. doi:10.1146/annurev.ne.13.030190.000325 PMID:2183676

Posner, M. I., & Rothbart, K. R. (2007). Research on attention networks as a model for the integration of psychological science. *Annual Review of Psychology*, *58*(1), 1–23. doi:10.1146/annurev.psych.58.110405.085516 PMID:17029565

Prensky, M. (2006). *Don't bother me Mom - I'm learning!: how computer and video games are preparing your kids for twenty-first century success - and how you can help!* Paragon House. Retrieved from http://www.worldcat.org/isbn/1557788588

Prins, P. J., Dovis, S., Ponsioen, A., ten Brink, E., & van der Oord, S. (2011). Does computerized working memory training with game elements enhance motivation and training efficacy in children with ADHD? *Cyberpsychology, Behavior, and Social Networking*, *14*(3), 115–122. doi:10.1089/cyber.2009.0206 PMID:20649448

Pylyshyn, Z. W., & Storm, R. W. (1988). Tracking multiple independent targets: Evidence for a parallel tracking mechanism. *Spatial Vision*, *3*(3), 179–197. doi:10.1163/156856888X00122 PMID:3153671

Read, J. C., & MacFarlane, S. (2006) Using the fun toolkit and other survey methods to gather opinions in child computer interaction. *Proceeding of the 2006 conference on Interaction design and children - IDC '06*, 81. 10.1145/1139073.1139096

Redick, T. S., Shipstead, Z., Wiemers, E. A., Melby-Lervag, M., & Hulme, C. (2015). What's working in working memory training? An educational perspective. *Educational Psychology Review*, *27*(4), 617–633. doi:10.100710648-015-9314-6 PMID:26640352

Reyna, V. F., & Ellis, S. C. (1994). Fuzzy-trace theory and framing effects in children's risky decision making. *Psychological Science*, *5*(5), 275–279. doi:10.1111/j.1467-9280.1994.tb00625.x

Richards, J. E. (2003). The development of visual attention and the brain. In The cognitive neuroscience of development. East Sussex, UK: Psychology Press.

Rieber, L. P. (1996). Seriously considering play: Designing interactive learning environments based on the blending of microworlds, simulations, and games. *Educational Technology Research and Development*, *44*(2), 43–58. doi:10.1007/BF02300540

Ries, E. (2013, May 22). *The Lean Start Up Methodology*. Retrieved May 22, 2013, from http://theleanstartup.com/principles

Ries, E. (2011). *The lean startup: How today's entrepreneurs use continuous innovation to create radically successful businesses*. Crown Books.

Ries, E. (2012). *The lean startup methodology*. The Lean Startup.

Ritter, F., & Schooler, L. (2001) The learning curve. International Encyclopedia of the Social and Behavioral Sciences, 8602–8605.

Rizzo, A., Kenny, P., & Parsons, T. (2011). Intelligent Virtual Humans for Clinical Training. *International Journal of Virtual Reality and Broadcasting*, *8*(3).

Rizzo, A., Lange, B., Buckwalter, J. G., Forbell, E., Kim, J., Sagae, K., & Kenny, P. (2011). SimCoach: An Intelligent Virtual Human System for Providing Healthcare Information and Support. *International Journal on Disability and Human Development*, *10*(4), 213. doi:10.1515/IJDHD.2011.046

Rosander, M., Stiwne, D., & Granström, K. (1998). "Bipolar groupthink": Assessing groupthink tendencies in authentic work groups. *Scandinavian Journal of Psychology*, *39*(2), 81–92. doi:10.1111/1467-9450.00060 PMID:9676161

Rose, H., & Betts, J. R. (2004). The effect of high school courses on earnings. *The Review of Economics and Statistics*, *86*(2), 497–513. doi:10.1162/003465304323031076

Rosetti, M. F., Gómez-Tello, M. F., Victoria, G., & Apiquian, R. (2017). A video game for the neuropsychological screening of children. *Entertainment Computing*, *20*, 1–9. doi:10.1016/j.entcom.2017.02.002

Rosvold, H. E., Mirsky, A. F., Sarason, I., Bransome, E. D., & Beck, L. H. (1956). A Continuous performance test of brain damage. *Journal of Consulting Psychology*, *20*(5), 343–350. doi:10.1037/h0043220 PMID:13367264

Rowe, E., Asbell-Clarke, J., & Baker, R. S. (2015). Serious games analytics to measure implicit science learning. In C. S. Loh, Y. Sheng, & D. Ifenthaler (Eds.), *Serious Games Analytics* (pp. 343–360). Springer International Publishing. doi:10.1007/978-3-319-05834-4_15

Rowe, E., Asbell-Clarke, J., Baker, R. S., Eagle, M., Hicks, A. G., Barnes, T. M., ... Edwards, T. (2017). Assessing implicit science learning in digital games. *Computers in Human Behavior*, *76*, 617–630. doi:10.1016/j.chb.2017.03.043

Ruff, A. H., & Lawson, K. R. (1990). Development of sustained, focused attention in young children during free play. *Developmental Psychology*, *26*(1), 85–93. doi:10.1037/0012-1649.26.1.85

Ruff, H. A., & Rothbart, M. K. (1996). *Attention in early development: Themes and variations*. New York, NY: Oxford University Press.

Ruff, H., & Capozzoli, M. (2003). Development of attention and distractibility in the first 4 years of life. *Developmental Psychology*, *39*(5), 877–890. doi:10.1037/0012-1649.39.5.877 PMID:12952400

Russell, W. B. (2011). *Contemporary Social Studies: An Essential Reader.* Charlotte, NC: Information Age Pub.

Ryan, R. M., Rigby, C. S., & Przybylski, A. (2006). The motivational pull of video games: A self-determination theory approach. *Motivation and Emotion, 30*(4), 347–365. doi:10.100711031-006-9051-8

Salas, E., Bowers, C., & Rhodenizer, L. (1998). It Is Not How Much You Have but How You Use It: Toward a Rational Use of Simulation to Support Aviation Training. *The International Journal of Aviation Psychology, 8*(3), 197–208. doi:10.120715327108ijap0803_2 PMID:11541532

Salen, K., & Zimmerman, E. (2003). *Rules of Play: Game Design Fundamentals.* Cambridge, MA: MIT Press.

Sarid, M., & Breznitz, Z. (1997). Developmental aspects of sustained attention among 2- to 6-year-old children. *International Journal of Behavioral Development, 21*(2), 303–312. doi:10.1080/016502597384884

Schiffrin, D. (1994). *Approaches to discourse.* Oxford, UK: B. Blackwell.

Schneider, W., & Shiffrin, R. M. (1977). Controlled and automatic human information processing: I. Detection, search, and attention. *Psychological Review, 84*(1), 1–66. doi:10.1037/0033-295X.84.1.1

Schneid, T. D., & Collins, L. (2001). *Disaster Management and Preparedness.* New York: Lewis.

Schrier, K., Diamond, J., & Langendoen, D. (2010). Using mission US: For crown or colony? To develop historical empathy and nurture ethical thinking. In *Ethics and Game Design: Teaching Values through Play* (pp. 255–273). Hershey, PA: Information Science Reference. doi:10.4018/978-1-61520-845-6.ch016

Segal, A., Black, J., & Tversky, B. (2010). *Do Gestural Interfaces Promotoe Learning? Congruent Gestures Promote Performance in Math.* Paper presented at the 51st Meeting of the Psychonomic Society Conference, St. Louis, MO.

Sengupta, P., Krinks, K. D., & Clark, D. B. (2015). Learning to Deflect: Conceptual Change in Physics during Digital Game Play. *Journal of the Learning Sciences, 24*(4), 638–674. doi:10.1080/10508406.2015.1082912

Setliff, A. E., & Courage, M. L. (2011). Background television and infants allocation of their attention during toy play. *Infancy, 16*(6), 611–639. doi:10.1111/j.1532-7078.2011.00070.x

Shaffer, D. W. (2006). *How computer games help children learn.* Macmillan. doi:10.1057/9780230601994

Shaffer, D. W., Squire, K. D., Halverson, R., & Gee, J. P. (2005). Video games and the future of learning. *Phi Delta Kappan, 87*(2), 104–111. doi:10.1177/003172170508700205

Shaffer, D., Hatfield, D., Svarovsky, G., Nach, P., Nulty, A., Bagley, E., ... Mislevy, R. (2009). Epistemic Network Analysis: A Prototype for 21st Century Assessment of Learning. *International Journal of Learning and Media, 1*(1).

Shrivastav, H., & Hiltz, S. R. (2013). Information Overload in Technology-Based Education: A Meta-Analysis. *Proceedings of the 19th Americas Conference on Information Systems. Overload in Technology-Based education,* 1–10.

Shute, V. J. (2011). Stealth Assessment in Computer-Based Games To Support Learning. *Computer Games and Instruction,* 503–524.

Shute, V. J. (2011). Stealth assessment in computer-based games to support learning. In S. Tobias & J. D. Fletcher (Eds.), *Computer Games and Instruction* (Vol. 55, pp. 503–524). Charlotte, NC: Information Age Publishing. Retrieved from http://pdf.thepdfportal.net/PDFFiles/6536.pdf

Shute, V., & Ventura, M. (2013). *Stealth assessment: Measuring and supporting learning in video games.* Cambridge, MA: MIT Press.

Siegler, R. (2009). *Implications of cognitive science research for mathematics education.* Academic Press.

Siklos, S., & Kerns, K. A. (2004). Assessing multitasking in children with ADHD using a modified Six Elements Test. *Archives of Clinical Neuropsychology, 19*(3), 347–361. doi:10.1016/S0887-6177(03)00071-4 PMID:15033221

Simpson, R. L., Lacava, P. G., & Graner, P. S. (2004). The No Child Left Behind Act Challenges and Implications for Educators. *Intervention in School and Clinic, 40*(2), 67–75. doi:10.1177/10534512040400020101

Siutila, M., & Havaste, E. (2018). "A pure meritocracy blind to identity": Exploring the Online Responses to All-Female Teams in Reddit. *Proceedings of the 2018 DiGRA International Conference.*

Skalsky Brown, J. (2014, July 18). *Let's Play: Understanding the Role and Significance of Digital Gaming in Old Age.* University of Kentucky. Retrieved from http://uknowledge.uky.edu/gerontol_etds/6

Skulmowski, A., & Rey, G. D. (2018). Embodied learning: Introducing a taxonomy based on bodily engagement and task integration. *Cognitive Research, 3*(1), 6. doi:10.118641235-018-0092-9 PMID:29541685

Slater, M., & Sanchez-Vives, M. V. (2016). Enhancing our lives with immersive virtual reality. *Frontiers in Robotics and AI, 3*(74). doi:10.3389/frobt.2016.00074

Slater, S., Joksimović, S., Kovanovic, V., Baker, R. S., & Gasevic, D. (2017). Tools for educational data mining: A review. *Journal of Educational and Behavioral Statistics, 42*(1), 85–106. doi:10.3102/1076998616666808

Sloman, S. A. (1996). The empirical case for two systems of reasoning. *Psychological Bulletin, 119*(1), 3–22. doi:10.1037/0033-2909.119.1.3 PMID:8711015

Smith, G. E., Housen, P., Yaffe, K., Ruff, R., Kennison, R. F., Mahncke, H. W., & Zelinski, E. M. (2009). A Cognitive Training Program Based on Principles of Brain Plasticity: Results from the Improvement in Memory with Plasticity-based Adaptive Cognitive Training (IMPACT) Study. *Journal of the American Geriatrics Society, 57*(4), 594–603. doi:10.1111/j.1532-5415.2008.02167.x PMID:19220558

Sniezek, J., Wilkins, D., & Wadlington, P. (2001). Advanced Training for Crisis Decision Making: Simulation, Critiquing, and Immersive Interfaces. *HICSS, 3*, 3042.

Snow, E. L., Allen, L. K., Jacovina, M. E., & McNamara, D. S. (2015). Does agency matter?: Exploring the impact of controlled behaviors within a game-based environment. *Computers & Education, 26*, 378–392. doi:10.1016/j.compedu.2014.12.011

Solomon, R. L. (1949). An extension of control group design. *Psychological Bulletin, 46*(2), 137–150. doi:10.1037/h0062958 PMID:18116724

Spotnitz, S. (2001). *Intrinsic motivation in students with learning disabilities as examined through computer based instruction in mathematics* (Unpublished thesis). Columbia University.

Squire, K. (2005). *Game-based learning: Present and future state of the field*. Masie Center e-Learning Consortium. Retrieved from https://pantherfile.uwm.edu/tjoosten/LTC/Gaming/Game-Based_Learning.pdf

Squire, K. (2003). Video games in education. *International Journal of Intelligent Games & Simulation, 2*(1), 49–62.

Squire, K. (2006). From content to context: Videogames as designed experience. *Educational Researcher, 35*(8), 19–29. doi:10.3102/0013189X035008019

Squire, K. (2011). *Video games and learning: teaching and participatory culture in the digital age*. New York: Teachers College Press.

Squire, K. D., DeVane, B., & Durga, S. (2008). Designing centers of expertise for academic learning through video games. *Theory into Practice, 47*(3), 240–251. doi:10.1080/00405840802153973

Squire, K., Jenkins, H., Holland, W., Miller, H., O'Driscoll, A., Tan, K. P., & Todd, K. (2003). Design Principles of Next-Generation Digital Gaming for Education. *Educational Technology, 43*(5), 17–23.

Squire, K., & Klopfer, E. (2007). Augmented Reality Simulations on Handheld Computers. *Journal of the Learning Sciences, 16*(3), 371–413. doi:10.1080/10508400701413435

Stafford, T., & Dewar, M. (2013). Tracing the trajectory of skill learning with a very large sample of online game players. *Psychological Science*. doi:10.1177/095679761351146

Stanley, S. S. (2002). Revitalizing precalculus with problem-based learning. *The Journal of General Education, 51*(4), 306–315. doi:10.1353/jge.2003.0016

Stanovich, K. E. (1999). *Who is rational? Studies of individual differences in reasoning.* Mahwah, NJ: Lawrence Erlbaum Associates.

Stanton, R. (2015, June 22). *The secret to eSports athletes' success? Lots – and lots – of practice.* ESPN. Retrieved from: http://www.espn.com/espn/story/_/id/13053116/esports-athletes-puthours-training-reach-pinnacle

Statista. (2018). *The Statistics Portal.* Statista.com.

Steinkuehler, C., & Duncan, S. (2008). Scientific habits of mind in virtual worlds. *Journal of Science Education and Technology, 17*(6), 530–543. doi:10.100710956-008-9120-8

Szablewicz, M. (2011). From Addicts to Athletes: Participation in the Discursive Construction of Digital Games in Urban China. In Selected Papers of Internet Research 12.0 (pp. 1-21). Association of Internet Researchers.

Talbot, T. B., Sagae, K., John, B., & Rizzo, A. (2012b). Designing Useful Virtual Standardized Patient Encounters. *Interservice/Industry Training, Simulation and Education Conference Proceedings (I/ITSEC).*

Talbot, T.B., Kalisch, N., Christoffersen, K., Lucas, G., Forbell, E. (2016a). Natural Language Understanding Performance & Use Considerations in Virtual Medical Encounters. *Studies in Health Technology and Informatics, 220,* 407-413. doi:10.3233/978-1-61499-625-5-407

Talbot, T. B., Lyon, T. D., Rizzo, A., & John, B. (2016b). *Virtual Child Witness: Effects of Single and Multiple Use on Performance with Novice and Expert Cohorts in a Structured Virtual Human Interview.* Interservice/Industry Training, Simulation, and Education Conference. I/ITSEC.

Talbot, T. B., Sagae, K., John, B., & Rizzo, A. (2012a). Sorting Out the Virtual Patient: How to Exploit Artificial Intelligence, Game Technology and Sound Educational Practices to Create Engaging Role-Playing Simulations. *International Journal of Gaming and Computer-Mediated Simulations, 4*(3), 1–19. doi:10.4018/jgcms.2012070101

Tall, D. (1991). *Advanced mathematical thinking* (Vol. 11). Springer. doi:10.1007/0-306-47203-1

Tamblyn, R. M., Klass, D. J., Schnabl, G. K., & Kopelow, M. L. (1991). Sources of Unreliability and Bias in Standardized-Patient Rating. *Teaching and Learning in Medicine, 3*(2), 74–85. doi:10.1080/10401339109539486

Tamblyn, R. M., Klass, D. J., Schnabl, G. K., & Kopelow, M. L. (1991). The Accuracy of Standardized Patient Presentation. *Medical Education, 25*(2), 100–109. doi:10.1111/j.1365-2923.1991.tb00035.x PMID:2023551

Taylor, N., Jenson, J., & de Castell, S. (2009). Cheerleaders, Booth Babes, Halo Hoes: Pro-gaming, Gender and Jobs for the Boys. *Digital Creativity, 20*(4), 239–252. doi:10.1080/14626260903290323

Taylor, T. L. (2012). *Raising the Stakes: E-Sports and the Professionalization of Computer Gaming*. Cambridge, MA: The MIT Press.

Tekinbas, K. S., & Zimmerman, E. (2003). *Rules of Play: game design fundamentals*. Cambridge, MA: MIT Press.

Tellinghuisen, D. J., Oakes, L. M., & Tjebkes, T. L. (1999). The influence of attentional state and stimulus characteristics on infant distractibility. *Cognitive Development*, *14*(2), 199–213. doi:10.1016/S0885-2014(99)00002-7

Tenorio Delgado, M., Arango Uribe, P., Aparicio Alonso, A., & Rosas Díaz, R. (2014). TENI: A comprehensive battery for cognitive assessment based on games and technology. *Child Neuropsychology*, 1–16. PMID:25396766

Thirteen. (2010). *Mission US: For Crown or Colony?* [Videogame]. New York: WNET Thirteen.

Thompson, J. J., Blair, M. R., Chen, L., & Henrey, A. J. (2013). Video Game Telemetry as a Critical Tool in the Study of Complex Skill Learning. *PLoS One*, *8*(9), e75129. doi:10.1371/journal.pone.0075129 PMID:24058656

Thompson, J. J., Blair, M. R., & Henrey, A. J. (2014). Over the Hill at 24: Persistent Age-Related Cognitive-Motor Decline in Reaction Times in an Ecologically Valid Video Game Task Begins in Early Adulthood. *PLoS One*, *9*(4), e94215. doi:10.1371/journal.pone.0094215 PMID:24718593

Timeline of psychology. (2015, February 17). In *Wikipedia, the free encyclopedia*. Retrieved from http://en.wikipedia.org/w/index.php?title=Timeline_of_psychology&oldid=647514853

Tobias, S., & Fletcher, J. D. (2007). What Research Has to Say about Designing Computer Games for Learning. *Educational Technology*, *47*(5), 20–29.

Triola, M., Feldman, H., Kalet, A. L., Zabar, S., Kachur, E. K., Gillespie, C., & Lipkin, M. (2006). A Randomized Trial of Teaching Clinical Skills Using Virtual and Live Standardized Patients. *Journal of General Internal Medicine*, *21*(5), 424–429. doi:10.1111/j.1525-1497.2006.00421.x PMID:16704382

Ubisoft. (2014). *Valiant Hearts: The Great War* [Videogame]. Montpellier: Ubisoft Group.

Van der Goot, M., Beentjes, J. W. J., & van Selm, M. (2006). Older Adults' Television Viewing from a Life-Span Perspective: Past Research and Future Challenges. *Communication Yearbook*, *30*(1), 431–469. doi:10.120715567419cy3001_10

Van Eck, R. (2006). Digital game-based learning: It's not just the digital natives who are restless. *EDUCAUSE Review*, *41*(2), 16.

Vellido, A., Martin-Guerroro, J. D., & Lisboa, P. (2012). Making machine learning models interpretable. *Proceedings of the 20th European Symposium on Artificial Neural Networks, Computational Intelligence and Machine Learning (ESANN)*, 163–172.

Ventura, M., Shute, V., & Small, M. (2014). Assessing persistence in educational games. *Design Recommendations for Intelligent Tutoring Systems*, 93-101.

Ventura, M., Shute, V., & Zhao, W. (2013). The relationship between video game use and a performance-based measure of persistence. *Computers & Education, 60*(1), 52–58. doi:10.1016/j.compedu.2012.07.003

von Hilvoorde, I. (2016). *Sport and Play in a Digital World.* Sport, Ethics and Philosophy.

Vygotsky, L. S. (1978). *Mind in Society: The Development of Higher Psychological Processes.* Cambridge, MA: The Harvard University Press.

Warburton, D., Nicol, C., & Bredin, S. (2006). Health benefits of physical activity: The evidence. *Canadian Medical Association Journal, 174*(6), 801–809. doi:10.1503/cmaj.051351 PMID:16534088

Ward, G. C., & Burns, K. (1994). *Baseball: An illustrated history.* New York: A.A. Knopf.

Waterfall model. (2018, June 3). In *Wikipedia.* Retrieved from https://en.wikipedia.org/w/index.php?title=Waterfall_model&oldid=844245639

Watkins, J. F. (1999). Life course and spatial experience: A personal narrative approach in migration studies. In K. Pandit & S. D. Withers (Eds.), *Migration and restructuring in the United States: A geographic perspective.* Lanham, MD: Rowman & Littlefield Publishers, INC.

Weber, R., & Popova, L. (2012). Testing equivalence in communication research: Theory and application. *Communication Methods and Measures, 6*(3), 190–213. doi:10.1080/19312458.2012.703834

Weisman, S. (1983). Computer games for the frail elderly. *The Gerontologist, 23*(4), 361–363. doi:10.1093/geront/23.4.361 PMID:6618244

Wendling, A., Halan, S., Tighe, P., Le, L., Euliano, T., & Lok, B. (2011). Virtual Humans Versus Standardized Patients: Which Lead Residents to More Correct Diagnoses? *Academic Medicine, 86*(3), 384–388. doi:10.1097/ACM.0b013e318208803f PMID:21248598

Wickham, H. (2014). Tidy data. *Journal of Statistical Software, 59*(10), 1–23. doi:10.18637/jss.v059.i10 PMID:26917999

Wiliam, D., & Thompson, M. (2007). *Integrating assessment with learning: what will it take to make it work?* Retrieved July 4, 2012, from http://eprints.ioe.ac.uk/1162/

Wiliam, D. (2007). Changing classroom practice. *Educational Leadership, 65*(4), 36.

Wills, S., Leigh, E., & Ip, A. (2011). *The power of role-based e-learning: Designing and moderating online role play.* New York: Routledge.

Wills, S., & McDougall, A. (2008). Reusability of online role-play as learning objects or Learning designs. In L. Lockyer, S. Bennett, S. Agostinho, & B. Harper (Eds.), *Handbook of Research on Learning Design and Learning Objects, Issues, Applications and Technologies*. IGI Group. doi:10.4018/978-1-59904-861-1.ch037

Wills, S., Rosser, E., Devonshire, E., Leigh, E., Russell, C., & Shepherd, J. (2009). *Encouraging role based online learning environments by Building, Linking, Understanding, Extending: The BLUE Report*. Australian Learning and Teaching Council.

Wilson, M. (2002). Six views of embodied cognition. *Psychonomic Bulletin & Review*, *9*(4), 625–636. doi:10.3758/BF03196322 PMID:12613670

Wimmer, J. (2012). Digital Game Culture(s) as Prototype(s) of Mediatization and Commercialization of Society. In J. Fromme & A. Unger (Eds.), *Computer Games and New Media Cultures: A Handbook of Digital Game Studies* (pp. 525–540). Heidelberg, Germany: Springer. doi:10.1007/978-94-007-2777-9_33

Wineburg, S. S. (1991). Historical problem solving: A study of the cognitive processes used in the evaluation of documentary and pictorial evidence. *Journal of Educational Psychology*, *83*(1), 73–87. doi:10.1037/0022-0663.83.1.73

Wineburg, S. S. (2001). *Historical thinking and other unnatural acts: Charting the future of teaching the past* (6th ed.). Philadelphia: Temple University Press.

Winn, W. (1997, January). Advantages of a theory-based curriculum in instructional technology. *Educational Technology*, 34–41.

Witkowski, E. (2012a). *Inside the Huddle: The Phenomenology and Sociology of Team Play in Networked Computer Games* (Doctoral Dissertation). IT University of Copenhagen.

Witkowski, E. (2012b). On the Digital playing Field: How we "Do Sport" With Networked Computer Games. *Games and Culture*, *7*(5), 349–374. doi:10.1177/1555412012454222

Womack, J. P., & Jones, D. T. (1997). Lean thinking—banish waste and create wealth in your corporation. *The Journal of the Operational Research Society*, *48*(11), 1148–1148. doi:10.1057/palgrave.jors.2600967

World Health Organization (WHO). (2018). *Global recommendations on physical activity for health (Report)*. WHO.

Wouters, P., Nimwegen, C., Oostendorp, H., & van der Spek, E. (2013). A meta-analysis of the cognitive and motivational effects of serious games. *Journal of Educational Psychology*, *105*(2), 249–265. doi:10.1037/a0031311

Yantis, S. (1992). Multielement visual tracking: Attention and perceptual organization. *Cognitive Psychology*, *24*(3), 295–340. doi:10.1016/0010-0285(92)90010-Y PMID:1516359

Yates, D., Moore, D., & McCabe, G. (1999). *The Practice of Statistics*. New York, NY: W.H. Freeman.

Yeager, E. A., Foster, S. J., Maley, S. D., Anderson, T., & Morris, J. W. III. (1998). Why people in the past acted as they did: An exploratory study in historical empathy. *The International Journal of Social Education, 13*(1), 8–24.

Young, M. F., Slota, S., Cutter, A. B., Jalette, G., Mullin, G., Lai, B., ... Yukhymenko, M. (2012). Our Princess Is in Another Castle: A Review of Trends in Serious Gaming for Education. *Review of Educational Research, 82*(1), 61–89. doi:10.3102/0034654312436980

Yu, C., & Smith, L. B. (2012). Embodied attention and word learning by toddlers. *Cognition, 125*(2), 244–262. doi:10.1016/j.cognition.2012.06.016 PMID:22878116

Zimet, J. (2012). *Mission Centenaire 14-18 Website*. Retrieved from http://centenaire.org/en

Zolides, A. (2015). Lipstick Bullets: Labour and Gender in Professional Gamer Self-Branding. *Persona Studies, 1*(2), 42–53. doi:10.21153/ps2015vol1no2art467

About the Contributors

Brock Dubbels specializes in user experience, user research, and assessment. He helped create the GScale Game Development and Testing Laboratory at Mc-Master University, and is currently in the Department of Psychology Neuroscience & Behaviour. He has worked as a Fulbright Scholar at the Norwegian Institute of Science and Technology; at Xerox PARC and Oracle, and as a research associate at the Center for Cognitive Science at the University of Minnesota. His specialties include user research, user experience, and software project management. He teaches course work on user experience research. games and cognition, and how learning research can improve game design for return on investment (ROI). He is the founder and principal learning architect at www.vgalt.com for design, production, usability assessment and evaluation of learning systems and games.He is also the founder of the HammerTownCoderDojo.org, an organization providing free programming instruction to children, and is the Editor in Chief of the International Journal of Games and Computer Mediated Simulations. He currently on the UXPA-MN board and facilitates the UXPA Mentorship program.

* * *

Liz Boltz is a doctoral student in Michigan State University's Educational Psychology & Educational Technology program, where she researches videogames for learning. Specifically, her research interests focus on the ways in which videogames can promote disciplinary reasoning and habits of mind. She is also a program coordinator and instructor for MSU's Master of Arts in Educational Technology program. In addition to teaching and research, she makes music, websites, art, and games.

Julie A. Brown, Ph.D., is an Assistant Professor of Gerontology within the Department of Social and Public Health at Ohio University (Athens, Ohio). With a specialization in gerontechnology, her research focuses upon technology use among older populations, and specifically, digital gamer characteristics. This includes the assessment of preferences, motivation, benefits and barriers to digital technologies.

Currently, Dr. Brown is continuing life course research on middle-aged and older adult digital gamers and potential VR applications.

Doug Clark is the Werklund Research Chair of Design-Based Learning at the University of Calgary's Werklund School of Education. His research focuses on students' conceptual change processes, computational thinking, modeling, and use of representations in digital and non-digital inquiry and game environments. Doug has been awarded multiple funded grants from the US National Science Foundation, Department of Education, and the US National Academy of Education/Spencer Foundation.

Bob De Schutter is a Belgian video game designer and researcher, who is the C. Michael Armstrong professor of Applied Game Design at Miami University (Oxford, Ohio). He is best known for his work on the design of video games for players in middle through late adulthood. He has advocated the importance of play in later life and has spoken out against the stereotyping of older video game players in marketing and game design. He has also published on the design of experimental classrooms for gameful instruction.

Javier Elizondo is the Digital Game-Based Learning producer at the K20 Center for Educational and Community Renewal in the University of Oklahoma. He received his M.A in Broadcasting and Production from the University of Western Illinois. His work focuses on the research-based implementation of game mechanics to pursue instructional goals. Research papers based on his work have been published by the International Journal of Gaming and Computer-Mediated Simulations, International Journal of Game-Based Learning, Computers in Human Behavior. He has presented his work in leading conferences in the game development field such as International Communication Association, the Serious Games Summit at the Game Developers Conference, National Education Computer Conference and GLS (Games+Learning+Society).

Karrie Godwin is an Assistant Professor in Educational Psychology at Kent State University. She earned her Ph.D. in Developmental Psychology from Carnegie Mellon University where she was also an IES fellow in the Program for Interdisciplinary Education Research. Karrie also holds a M.Ed. in Human Development and Psychology from Harvard University. Her research examines how cognitive and environmental factors shape children's development and learning in the laboratory and in the classroom. Her research interests include the development of attention, executive function, language acquisition, and categorization.

Veli-Matti Karhulahti is a researcher of play, games, and other exciting cultural things with a great variety of evolving interests. Recently, his work has centered around esports. He has published quite a bit, and his upcoming book Esport Phenomenology: Passion, Obsession, and Psycholudic Development is currently in review. At the time of writing, Karhulahti works as an Adjunct Professor on Play and Games in University of Turku.

Tuomas Kari is a Postdoctoral Researcher (Information Systems Science) at the University of Jyväskylä, Finland. His dissertation is about the usage of exergames. His research interest is the use of technology in everyday life, especially in the context of health and wellness. His topics of research include exergaming, sports-, health-, and wellness technology, self-tracking, information systems usage, user behaviour, adoption and diffusion, gamification, and eSports among others. He has published, for example, in International Conference on Information Systems (ICIS), International Journal of Networking and Virtual Organizations, and International Journal of Gaming and Computer-Mediated Simulations.

Nancy Law is a Professor in the Faculty of Education, University of Hong Kong. She was the Founding Director of the Centre for Information Technology in Education (CITE), Faculty of Education (1998-2013) and is currently one of the Deputy Directors. She also serves as a Co-convener for the Sciences of Learning Strategic Research Theme of the University of Hong Kong. Professor Law is internationally known for her work in the area of applying information technology (IT) to enhance learning and teaching, particularly in the area of international comparative studies of pedagogical innovations using IT, models of ICT integration in schools and change leadership, and IT supported knowledge building for students, teachers and professional communities.

Yu-Hao Lee's research focuses on how people process information in interactive media, including social media and video games.

Lawrence Leung is Principal Technical Officer of the Hong Kong Police College. His duties include R&D in learning technologies and e-Learning for police training. His research interests include e-Learning, computer simulation, game-based learning and computer-mediated communication. Dr. Lawrence Leung holds BA (Computer Science) from the University of California at San Diego, MSc (Computer Science) from City University of Hong Kong, Master of Technology Management from Hong Kong University of Science and Technology, MSc (IT in Education) and Doctor of Education from The University of Hong Kong.

Mario Martinez-Garza completed his PhD at Vanderbilt University. A life-long gamer and student of games, his main area of interest is the application of good design principles to support learning from, and through, games of all kinds. He has alternated careers between technology and education, serving as a quantitative user researcher at Microsoft, a middle-school math and science teacher, a competition math coach, and also co-founder and lead game designer of an educational games start-up.

Colleen Megowan-Romanowicz is Senior Fellow of the American Modeling Teachers Association. Her expertise is in physics education research, and her research focus is on understanding how the construction, representation and use of the fundamental conceptual models of physics affects students' thinking and learning.

Albert "Skip" Rizzo received his Ph.D. in Clinical Psychology from the State University of New York at Binghamton. Dr. Rizzo conducts research on the design, development and evaluation of Virtual Reality systems targeting the areas of clinical assessment, treatment and rehabilitation. This work spans the domains of psychological, cognitive and motor functioning in both healthy and clinical populations.

Miia Siutila is a Doctoral Student in University of Turku. She is working on a dissertation about the future of esports with a general interest toward gaming culture as a whole. She will soon publish in the leading scientific journals of the field.

Thomas Talbot is the Principal Medical Expert at the USC Institute for Creative Technologies and adjunct associate research professor at Keck School of Medicine of USC. Dr. Talbot was the founder of the Armed Forces Simulation Institute for Medicine at the Telemedicine and Advanced Technology Research Center and established, at the Department of Defense, the nation's largest medical education focused research and development program, encompassing more than $275 million and 150 projects under his leadership. He has been at the center of many of the nation's major medical simulation R&D efforts. At the ICT Medical Virtual Reality Laboratory (MedVR), he is designing the next generation of virtual standardized patients and exploring virtual reality interactive science for medical and educational applications. Dr. Talbot is a veteran of the US Army with war deployment experience and has more than 18 years' experience as a medical education developer. As a pediatrician and scientist, Dr. Talbot endeavors to create meaningful improvements that will advance the state of the art in medical education and patient care. Work interests include serious games, natural user interfaces, virtual and augmented reality, virtual interactive humans and microcontrollers.

Scott Wilson is the Director of Innovative Learning at the University of Oklahoma's K20 Center. While this educational research center is dedicated to the research of effective teaching and learning in Kindergarten to graduate educational environments, Scott leads a team of researchers, designers, and developers in the application of digital game-based learning to engage learners in authentic learning experiences. He holds a PhD in Instructional Leadership and Academic Curriculum and has served as a designer, producer, and researcher of novel learning experiences and their impact on learning. A focus for Scott and the K20 Center's game team is to develop, validate through randomized controlled trials, and release serious games for use that will engage students in meaningful learning.

Index

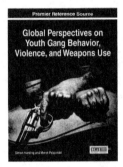

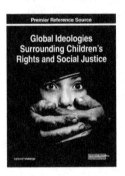
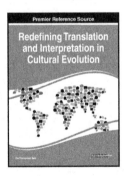

Ensure Quality Research is Introduced to the Academic Community

Become an IGI Global Reviewer for Authored Book Projects

Premier Reference Source

Emerging GIS Applications for Emergency and Disaster Management

Premier Reference Source

Managerial Strategies and Green Solutions for Project Sustainability

Premier Reference Source

Comparative Approaches to Using R and Python for Statistical Data Analysis

Premier Reference Source

Solutions for High-Touch Communications in a High-Tech World

The overall success of an authored book project is dependent on quality and timely reviews.

In this competitive age of scholarly publishing, constructive and timely feedback significantly expedites the turnaround time of manuscripts from submission to acceptance, allowing the publication and discovery of forward-thinking research at a much more expeditious rate. Several IGI Global authored book projects are currently seeking highly qualified experts in the field to fill vacancies on their respective editorial review boards:

Applications may be sent to:
development@igi-global.com

Applicants must have a doctorate (or an equivalent degree) as well as publishing and reviewing experience. Reviewers are asked to write reviews in a timely, collegial, and constructive manner. All reviewers will begin their role on an ad-hoc basis for a period of one year, and upon successful completion of this term can be considered for full editorial review board status, with the potential for a subsequent promotion to Associate Editor.

If you have a colleague that may be interested in this opportunity, we encourage you to share this information with them.

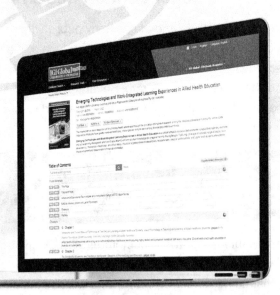